DATE DUE

OC 1 7 '06			
NO 0 '06			
NO 2 7 05			

DEMCO 38-296

DEMOCRACY IN ASIA AND AFRICA

SEYMOUR MARTIN LIPSET

Editor in Chief

 CONGRESSIONAL QUARTERLY INC.
Washington, D.C.

Book design and production by Kachergis Book Design,
Pittsboro, North Carolina

Printed and bound in the United States of America

The paper used in this publication meets the minimum requirements of the American National Standard for Information Sciences—Permanence of Paper for Printed Library Materials, ANSI Z39.48-1984.

COVER IMAGE: Athena, the patron goddess of Athens, appears on a silver coin from the fifth century B.C.—the high point of Athenian democracy. The publisher appreciates the assistance of Elvira Clain-Stefanelli of the Smithsonian Institution for locating the coin and wishes to thank Numismatic Fine Arts for graciously providing a photograph.

African Charter on Human and Peoples' Rights copyright © Amnesty International Publications. Reprinted by permission.

LIBRARY OF CONGRESS CATALOGING-IN-PUBLICATION DATA

Democracy in Asia and Africa / Seymour Martin Lipset, editor in chief.

    p. cm.

    Includes bibliographical references and index.

    ISBN 1-56802-123-2 (hc. : alk. paper)

    1. Democracy—Asia.   2. Democracy—Africa.   I. Lipset, Seymour Martin. II. Congressional Quarterly, Inc.

JC421.D4633   1997

321.8'095—dc21   97-42289

ABOUT THE EDITOR IN CHIEF

SEYMOUR MARTIN LIPSET is the Virginia E. Hazel and John T. Hazel Jr. Professor of Public Policy and Professor of Sociology at the Institute of Public Policy at George Mason University. He is also the Caroline S. G. Munro Professor in the Departments of Political Science and Sociology emeritus, and Senior Fellow at the Hoover Institution on War, Revolution, and Peace, Stanford University. He received his Ph.D. from Columbia University.

Professor Lipset is a past president of the American Political Science Association and the American Sociological Association. He served as editor in chief of the *Encyclopedia of Democracy*. He is coeditor of the *International Journal of Public Opinion Research* and is the author of many books, articles, and monographs, including *Political Man: The Social Bases of Politics; Revolutions and Counterrevolution; Continental Divide: Values and Institutions of the United States and Canada;* and most recently *American Exceptionalism: A Double-Edged Sword.*

CONTENTS

List of Articles by Region   ix

Contributors   xi

Preface   xiii

Africa, Horn of   3

Africa, Lusophone   7

Africa, Subsaharan   11

African independence movements   22

Algeria   27

Armenia   30

Asia, Central   34

Asia, Southeast   37

Australia and New Zealand   42

Botswana   48

Burma   51

Caucasus, The   55

China   58

Congo, Democratic Republic of the   66

Dominant party democracies in Asia   69

Egypt   73

Ghana   77

India   80

Indonesia   85

Iran   89

Iraq   92

Israel   95

Japan   100

Jordan   107

Kenya   110

Kuwait   113

Kyrgyzstan   116

Lebanon   119

Malaysia   123

Middle East   125

Morocco   130

Namibia   133

Nigeria   136

Pakistan   143

Philippines   148

Senegal   152

Singapore   155

South Africa   157

South Korea   163

Sri Lanka   166

Sudan   170

Taiwan   175

Thailand   179

Theory, African   183

Tunisia   189

Turkey   192

Uganda   198

Zambia   202

Zimbabwe   205

REFERENCE MATERIAL

Constitution of Japan (1947)   211

Israeli Declaration of
    Independence (1948)   218

African National Congress Freedom
    Charter (1955)   220

African Charter on Human and
    Peoples' Rights (1981)   223

Index   231

LIST OF ARTICLES BY REGION

Asia
Dominant party democracies in Asia

CENTRAL ASIA AND THE SUBCONTINENT
Armenia
Asia, Central
Caucasus, The
India
Kyrgyzstan
Pakistan
Sri Lanka
Turkey

EAST ASIA
China
Japan
Philippines
South Korea
Taiwan

SOUTHEAST ASIA
Asia, Southeast
Australia and New Zealand
Burma
Indonesia
Malaysia
Singapore
Thailand

MIDDLE EAST
Egypt
Iran
Iraq
Israel
Jordan
Kuwait
Lebanon
Middle East

Africa
African independence movements
Theory, African

NORTH AFRICA
Algeria
Morocco
Tunisia

SUBSAHARAN AFRICA
Africa, Horn of
Africa, Lusophone
Africa, Subsaharan
Botswana
Congo, Democratic Republic of the
Ghana
Kenya
Namibia
Nigeria
Senegal
South Africa
Sudan
Uganda
Zambia
Zimbabwe

CONTRIBUTORS

Arutiunov, Sergei A.
Russian Academy of Sciences

Bratton, Michael
Michigan State University

Cruise O'Brien, D. B.
University of London

Dawisha, Adeed
George Mason University

Deegan, Heather
Middlesex University

Diamond, Larry
Hoover Institution

Dudwick, Nora
George Washington University

Ekeh, Peter P.
State University of New York at Buffalo

Emmerson, Donald K.
University of Wisconsin—Madison

Fewsmith, Joseph
Boston University

Forrest, Joshua Bernard
University of Vermont

Friedman, Steven
Centre for Policy Studies, Johannesburg

Herbst, Jeffrey
Princeton University

Holm, John D.
Cleveland State University

Hudson, Michael C.
Georgetown University

Hunter, Shireen T.
Center for Strategic and International Studies, Washington, D.C.

Jung, Courtney
Yale University

Kassimir, Ronald
Columbia University

Keller, Edmond J.
University of California, Los Angeles

Kim, Ilpyong J.
University of Connecticut

Krauss, Ellis S.
University of Pittsburgh

Lyons, Terrence
Brookings Institution, Washington, D.C.

McAllister, Ian
University of New South Wales

Myers, Ramon H.
Hoover Institution

Neher, Clark D.
Northern Illinois University

Olcott, Martha Brill
Colgate University

Orvedahl, Jerry A.
Congressional Quarterly

Purkitt, Helen E.
U.S. Naval Academy

Pye, Lucian W.
Massachusetts Institute of Technology

Rothchild, Donald
University of California, Davis

Rustow, Dankwart A.
City University of New York

Schatzberg, Michael G.
University of Wisconsin—Madison

Sklar, Richard L.
University of California, Los Angeles

Sprinzak, Ehud
Hebrew University

Steinberg, David I.
Georgetown University

Varshney, Ashutosh
Harvard University

Weinbaum, Marvin G.
University of Illinois at Urbana—Champaign

Widner, Jennifer A.
University of Michigan

Wriggins, W. Howard
Columbia University

PREFACE

DEMOCRACY—defined minimally as a political system in which free and fair elections inclusive of all social groups are held regularly and basic civil and political liberties are respected—arose first in northern Europe and spread to North America. The development of democracy in those societies was gradual, and its consolidation achieved piecemeal over the course of several centuries. This evolutionary process, characterized by occasional setbacks, was nurtured by favorable circumstances: Political rights expanded in these societies in a simpler, preindustrial era, when the state was less a source of power and advantage and people's expectations of government were much lower than they are today. As economic development progressed and these societies became more affluent, an independent middle class arose gradually. The middle class, buoyed by its economic power, created a civil society of powerful institutions—associations, parties, labor unions, and interest groups of various types—that weakened state power. Over time, the elites of society and the middle class came to share a common political culture, characterized by respect for the rule of law and belief in free, fair, and regular elections.

Such a gradual evolution toward a democratic political culture was not the norm in most countries of Asia and Africa, where democracy was transplanted into societies radically different from those of the Old World. Democracy is firmly rooted today in only a handful of African states—Benin, Botswana, South Africa, Mauritius, to name a few of the more long-standing. At the other extreme, democracy does not exist in such states as Burundi, Libya, Rwanda, the Democratic Republic of the Congo, and Somalia. Elsewhere on the continent, the principles of democratic rule remain threatened by gross inequality; entrenched civil and military elites; animosity among ethnic groups and social classes; and tension between church and state and agriculture and industry. Superficially, democracy on the continent is gaining ground: only a few outright military dictatorships and two kingdoms—Morocco and Swaziland—remain. But even in the African countries where elections are regularly held, the victors are often military leaders in civilian dress or traditional autocrats in democratic garb, and the electoral outcomes often suspect.

Asian democracy is more variegated in development and practice than its African counterpart. Asia comprises the former Soviet republics of the Caucasus and Central

Asia; the religious-based states of the Middle East, including some of the world's last absolute monarchies; the British-influenced Indian subcontinent; and the widely diverse states of Southeast and East Asia. Where democracy is growing roots in Asia, it is molding itself to the local circumstances, as seen in the phenomenon of one-party-dominant states.

Democracy in Asia and Africa traces its lineage to Congressional Quarterly's *Encyclopedia of Democracy* (1995), a four-volume guide to the topic compiled under the general editorial supervision of Seymour Martin Lipset. The factual, analytical, and summary elements of each *Encyclopedia* article have been researched and reevaluated in light of the significant developments that have occurred since publication of the *Encyclopedia.*

Major changes have transpired in Asia and Africa, not only in the chronically unstable countries of these continents but in the democratically well developed states as well. In these pages, the contributors and editors bring you up to date on innumerable developments, including:

• The return of the Liberal Democratic Party to power in Japan in 1996 after three years out of government

• The electoral reforms introduced in Japan while the Liberal Democratic Party was out of power

• The enhanced political competition in South Korea, where the Democratic Liberal Party lost control of the lower house of the National Assembly in April 1996 elections

• The slow decline of the Nationalist Party on Taiwan, where the once invincible party managed only to hold a bare majority of seats in December 1995 Legislative Yuan elections

• The first-ever popular election of a Chinese leader, Lee Teng-hui of Taiwan, in March 1996 presidential balloting

• The bribery scandals that rocked South Korea in 1996 and 1997

• The appointment in June 1996 and ouster one year later of Turkey's first pro-Islamic head of government since 1923 over issues related to the secular nature of the state

• The use for the first time of a new, fully proportional electoral system in New Zealand in 1996

• The first-ever direct election of an Israeli prime minister, Binyamin Netanyahu, whose Likud Party failed to win a majority of seats in the Knesset

• The creation by constitutional amendment of a new lower house in Morocco, to be directly elected beginning in 1998

• The adoption in late 1996 of a new South African constitution, which took effect in February 1997

• The overthrow of Mobutu Sese Seko in the former Zaire

• The rising level of politically and religiously inspired violence in Algeria

But *Democracy in Asia and Africa* is more than reportage. Political, electoral, and constitutional developments on the continents are analyzed and interpreted in the broader contexts of democratic theory and practice. The implications of these developments for practical governance are addressed, as are the many factors that underpin democratic politics: economic conditions, class and race relations, ethnic and religious factors, and cultural differences.

Democracy in Asia and Africa is further set apart by its multifaceted approach to the topic. Herein are narrowly focused articles on specific countries; broader pieces that analyze democratic development by region (for example, the Middle East), by continent (African independence movements), and by colonizer (Lusophone Africa); and theoretical treatises on democracy as an idea as opposed to a practical system of rule. This volume addresses democracy in Asia and Africa from a historical as well as contemporary perspective and delves into its setbacks as well as its triumphs.

The editors of *Democracy in Asia and Africa* also provide the text of four documents fundamental to the development of democracy on the two continents. Each is preceded by an introductory note that puts the document in historical context and explains its significance.

Acknowledgments

The parent volume could not have been created but for the contributions of many people. First and foremost, the publisher is indebted to Seymour Martin Lipset, professor of public policy at George Mason University and emeritus professor of political science and sociology at Stanford University. Members of the *Encyclopedia*'s editorial board, who contributed immeasurably to the shape and content, are Larry Diamond, the Hoover Institution; Ada W. Finifter, Michigan State University; Gail W. Lapidus, Stanford University; Arend Lijphart, the University of California, San Diego; Juan J. Linz, Yale University; Thomas L. Pangle, the University of Toronto; Lucian W. Pye, Massachusetts Institute of Technology; George H. Quester, the University of Maryland; and Philippe C. Schmitter, Stanford University. The publisher also wishes to thank consulting editors Samuel P. Huntington, Harvard University; Michael Saward, the University of London; and the many authors, named in the list of contributors, whose expertise, eloquence, and cooperation made the project a success. At Congressional Quarterly, Megan Campion, Ann Davies, Jeanne Ferris, Jamie Holland, Nancy Lammers, and Jerry Orvedahl were instrumental in bringing this volume to fruition.

DEMOCRACY IN ASIA AND AFRICA

Africa, Horn of

The northeast African countries of Djibouti, Eritrea, Ethiopia, Somalia, and sometimes Sudan (which is treated separately in this volume). Although there have been historic political openings that might have led to democratic consolidation, the countries of the Horn of Africa have actually had little experience with democracy.

Somalia, which was nominally democratic at independence in 1960, succumbed to authoritarian military regimes in the first decade. In Djibouti the party in power at independence in 1977 became increasingly authoritarian in the first decade. In Eritrea multiparty democracy flourished in the years leading to federation with Ethiopia in 1952, but it was almost immediately eliminated on federation. And in Ethiopia pluralist democracy was untried until a halting experiment in the 1990s.

Underlying the political authoritarianism and turmoil of this region of Africa have been common problems: profound underdevelopment; limited or no preparation for democratic politics during the colonial period; deep ethnic and clan rivalries that often have exploded into violence; protracted civil wars generating humanitarian as well as political crises; and a bitter legacy of superpower proxy involvement in the Horn region during the cold war.

Ethiopia

Ethiopia is one of the few African countries that was never colonized by Europeans. The modern imperial state was consolidated between 1855 and 1908. Emperor Haile Selassie I introduced its first written constitution in 1931. Patterned after the Japanese constitution of 1889, it established Ethiopia as a constitutional monarchy, guided by an emperor who traced his ancestry back to King Solomon of Jerusalem and the Queen of Sheba.

The constitution also provided for the secularization and centralization of the bureaucracy. Rules were drawn to professionalize the bureaucracy, judiciary, and budgetary institutions. Perhaps the most remarkable innovation was the inauguration of legislative institutions, the Chamber of Deputies and the Senate. Although these bodies were meant to recommend democratic reforms to the Crown, they were not empowered to make laws autonomously. Neither house was popularly elected. The Chamber of Deputies, it was envisioned, would eventually be elected by the people when they were prepared to accept this weighty responsibility.

The 1931 constitution left little doubt that the authority of the Crown was absolute. Almost half of the fifty-five articles related to the power and prerogatives of the emperor. What few rights were accorded the citizenry could be suspended at will by the emperor or any of his agents.

A new and different constitution, reflecting the influence of American advisers, came into effect in 1955. Like the American Constitution, it provided for a separation of power among the three branches of government. Furthermore, it gave new power to the legislative branch, and fully twenty-eight of its articles addressed the rights and duties of citizens. This constitution, like the previous one, however, imposed no formal restraints on the powers of the emperor, who continued to rule in an authoritarian fashion. Although deputies but not senators were now popularly elected, political parties were still forbidden, and candidates had to meet property qualifications to stand for office.

Between 1955 and 1974 popular pressures for democracy grew rapidly, in part inspired by the winds of change sweeping across the colonized world. Emperor Haile Selassie responded to the times by convening yet another constitutional reform commission, but a new constitution never went into effect. A military coup toppled his regime in September 1974. In the immediate aftermath of the

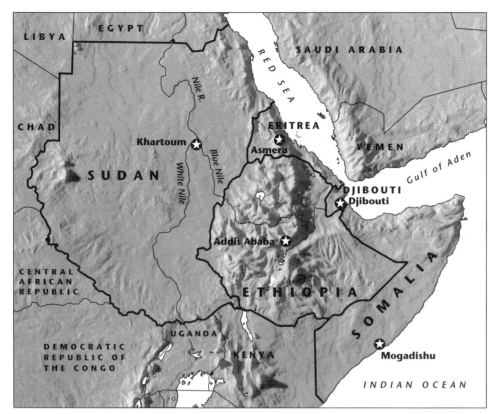

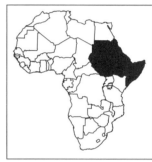

coup, the political climate opened as never before. Exiled intellectuals returned home to contribute to the debate over the character of the "new Ethiopia." This openness was short lived, however. Over the next two years the new regime either neutralized, co-opted, or liquidated voices that questioned its own vanguard role in the revolution. In response to urban terror campaigns by various leftist opposition groups, the government responded with its own "Red Terror Campaign." Its aim was to wipe out all voices of opposition and to lay the groundwork for an authoritarian, statist development strategy. Between 1977 and 1978 roughly 5,000 people were killed in the Red Terror Campaign. This massacre was followed by a fifteen-year attempt to organize society according to the principles of Marxism-Leninism.

Under the regime of Mengistu Haile-Mariam, all rural and urban property was decreed to be state owned. The state attempted to gain complete control of the means of production, distribution, and exchange and to engage in central planning. In an effort to promote collectivization in the agricultural sector, it set up state farms and forced the rural population into village communities and resettlement schemes. These coercive policies were pursued at great cost to human life. Government repression, arbitrary

military conscription and arrest, and strict surveillance of the general population became the order of the day. The government used the Workers' Party of Ethiopia to carry out its brutal mission.

Introduced in 1984, the vanguard Workers' Party proclaimed a commitment to the principles of democratic centralism. In practice, however, the party favored centralized, bureaucratic control of all aspects of civil life. By 1990 it was clear that the socialist experiment had failed. Ethiopia's leaders disbanded the Workers' Party and declared themselves amenable to multiparty democracy. This gesture proved to be too little, too late. Ethiopia's second revolutionary government assumed power in April 1991 after a bloody civil war of almost a decade.

The new regime, headed by the Ethiopian People's Revolutionary Democratic Front, convened a reconciliation conference in July 1991 involving thirty-one political organizations. The Revolutionary Democratic Front sought to form a broad-based pact that included most of the substantial political groups, except for those that seriously opposed its leadership, such as former members of the Workers' Party and the deposed Mengistu regime. Consequently, radical leftist groups, along with several conservative Ethiopian nationalist groups, were excluded from the conference. By mid-1992 the number of registered political parties had grown to almost 200, but only a few had significant popular support.

Conference participants signed a charter calling for a transitional period of no more than two years and the creation of a Representative Council to facilitate the drafting of a new constitution and to prepare for democratic national elections. The council promulgated two controversial resolutions: one agreeing to Eritrean self-determination and the other administratively reorganizing Ethiopia into regions based on ethnicity. Both of these resolutions heightened tensions and forced the Ethiopian People's Revolutionary Democratic Front (EPRDF) to act in undemocratic ways, although it did implement some new liberal policies. By mid-1993 the ruling coalition, led by Meles Zenawe, had become very narrow. The transitional government forged ahead, however, and drafted a new constitution, which was adopted December 8, 1994. National elections were finally held in May 1995, but they were boycotted by several of the major ethnically based parties, and the EPRDF won 493 of 550 seats in the lower house. Democracy is still in doubt.

Eritrea

Italy colonized Eritrea in the 1880s and remained there until the British captured it in 1941. The British tried to enlist the support of the Eritreans in World War II, promising them self-determination. After the war, however, it became apparent that Eritrean self-determination was not guaranteed.

At the Paris Peace Conference between 1946 and 1947, a formula was negotiated for the disposal of former Italian colonies in Africa. The matter of Eritrea was turned over to the General Assembly of the United Nations (UN), which established a special study commission. In response to the commission's recommendations, which were submitted in June 1949, the United Nations finally agreed to federate Eritrea with Ethiopia, an arrangement not favored by all Eritreans. Nevertheless, the federal constitution was implemented.

Eritrean political organizations emerged as early as 1944. By 1952 the various factions had coalesced into three political parties: the Unionist Bloc, which favored union with Ethiopia, and the Democratic Party and the Muslim League of the Western Province, both of which favored independence. In the March 1952 elections for the legislative assembly, the Unionists won thirty-two of the sixty-eight seats, the Democratic Party won eighteen seats, and the Muslim League won fifteen seats.

On the assumption that Eritrean autonomy was protected, the new assembly ratified the federal constitution. Throughout the deliberations, Haile Selassie had lobbied to ensure that the Unionists could influence who would secure the most important positions in the new government. Those efforts continued throughout the period of federation and facilitated the undermining of Eritrean autonomy.

The year 1952 was a watershed. It marked the beginning of federation, and it was the year the Eritrean constitution was suspended. A year later all trade unions were banned. In 1956 political parties were banned, and the national assembly was "temporarily" suspended. Eritrea was completely annexed by Ethiopia in 1962.

Political groups went underground, formed movements of national liberation, and waged a thirty-year war against Ethiopia. The most successful group was the Eritrean People's Liberation Front, which in 1991 defeated the Ethiopian army, setting the stage for a UN-sanctioned referendum on Eritrean self-determination. In the April 1993 referendum more than 98 percent voted for independence. A month later the Republic of Eritrea was declared. The new government of Eritrea came to power proclaiming a commitment to multiparty democracy. The draft constitution tabled in July 1996 by the interim Assembly provided for just such a system, but opponents of the government complained that the drafting process was anything but democratic.

Somalia

Immediately upon securing their separate independence from the British and Italians, respectively, in July 1960, the national assemblies of northern and southern Somaliland voted to merge the two polities into the Republic of Somalia. Because all citizens were ethnic Somalis, many felt that this would be a lasting union. However, the different colonial experiences of the two regions and endemic clan rivalries among the Somalis caused immediate tensions. The political system left to Somalia was a liberal democracy based on the principles of multiparty competition. Rather than contributing to a smoothly functioning political system, this legacy proved disastrous.

Democratic politics compounded the problems of nation building and state building. By March 1969 there were sixty-four political parties, most of them organized along clan lines. The election for the national assembly held that month resulted in unimaginable chaos. Corruption, intimidation, and political assassination abounded. In the confusion Gen. Mohamed Siad Barre launched a military coup, promising to eliminate corruption and unify the country.

Siad Barre ruled repressively for more than twenty years until he was overthrown in a civil war in January 1991. Toward the end of his rule, he abandoned his scientific socialist program and claimed to be open to multiparty democracy. His regime was overthrown before reforms could be implemented, however. In Somalia, unlike in Ethiopia, opposition groups had not formed a united front before they overthrew the dictator. A viable pact for a transitional government was not formed. Civil war, based upon clan and subclan rivalries, escalated until Somalia virtually ceased to be a viable state. Even a large-scale intervention by the United States and United Nations from late 1992 to November 1994, ostensibly to protect relief workers distributing food aid, could not quell the chaos. At the end of 1997 there was still no functioning government in the country nor any prospects for one.

Djibouti

During the European "scramble for Africa" in the late 1800s, France laid claim to a small enclave on the coast of the Red Sea, calling it the Territory of the Afars and the Issas. The colony was valued mainly for its strategic location. France granted the territory, or Djibouti, independence in June 1977. The new government was headed by an Issa, Hassan Gouled Aptidon, and his party, the African People's League for Independence. The Issa and their Somali relatives make up about 80 percent of the population; the remainder are mostly from the Afar ethnic group. The Afar collaborated with the French during the waning days of colonial rule; this collaboration enhanced Hassan's reputation among the Issas as a liberator.

In 1979 Hassan formed a new party, the Popular Rally for Progress, and created a de jure one-party state. In response, the Afar formed an opposition party in exile, the Democratic Front for the Liberation of Djibouti. By the mid-1980s overt opposition to the hegemony of the Popular Rally for Progress had surfaced. In 1986 a former minister in the Hassan government was expelled from it; he formed his own party, the Djiboutian National Movement for the Installation of Democracy, with the stated purpose of restoring multiparty democracy. In January 1990 the Democratic Front merged with this party, forming the Union of Democratic Movements.

Alleging systematic ethnic discrimination, a significant segment of the Afar population flocked to the guerrilla-based Front for the Restoration of Unity and Democracy, a new party created in 1991. From this point Afar opposition to the government became more intense, culminating in what some Afar termed a "massacre" in the Afar quarter of the capital, Djibouti, in December 1991. Some well-respected members of the Popular Rally government consequently defected, calling for a return to multiparty democracy. Finally, Hassan acceded, agreeing to a constitutional reform that would allow for up to four political parties.

The first test of this new dispensation was the parliamentary election of December 1992. Only two parties participated: the Popular Rally for Progress and the Party of Democratic Renewal. Many observers, and the party itself, felt that this arrangement favored the Party of Democratic Renewal. However, the Popular Rally for Progress won by a margin of more than three to one. Two reasons for the victory were Hassan's personal popularity and a party-list, winner-take-all system heavily weighted in favor of the urban-based Popular Rally. Most Afar boycotted the vote. There were considerable electoral irregularities, but the results stood.

In May 1993 presidential elections were held. Again most Afar boycotted the vote. Hassan faced four opponents, and he secured about 60 percent of the vote, avoiding a runoff. There was evidence of massive vote rigging, but again the results were upheld.

Outlook for the Future

Although the political upheavals of the early and mid–1990s created new possibilities for democracy in the Horn of Africa, severe obstacles to the successful functioning of democracy remain. Prominent among these obstacles are the difficulty of finding viable formulas for managing ethnic and regional conflict, the lack of tolerance and trust among competing political forces, and the extreme weakness and fragmentation of political parties and democratic institutions more generally. The prospects for democratic evolution are dim in Ethiopia, they remain clouded in Eritrea, and they appear elusive in Djibouti. In Somalia the road to democracy—or to political order of any kind—looks long and arduous.

See also *African independence movements; Sudan.*

BIBLIOGRAPHY

Africa Watch. *Somalia: A Government at War with Its People.* New York: Africa Watch, 1990.

Clapham, Christopher. *Transformation and Continuity in Revolutionary Ethiopia.* Cambridge and New York: Cambridge University Press, 1988.

Harbeson, John W. *The Ethiopian Transformation.* Boulder, Colo.: Westview Press, 1988.

Keller, Edmond J. "Drought, War, and the Politics of Famine in Ethiopia and Eritrea." *Journal of Modern African Studies* 30 (December 1992): 609–624.

———. *Revolutionary Ethiopia: From Empire to People's Republic.* Bloomington: Indiana University Press, 1988.

Laitin, David, and Said S. Samatar. *Somalia: Nation in Search of a State.* Boulder, Colo.: Westview Press; Aldershot: Gower, 1987.

Okbazghi, Yohannes. *Eritrea: A Pawn in World Politics.* Gainesville: University of Florida Press, 1991.

Pateman, Roy. *Eritrea: Even the Stones Are Burning.* Trenton, N.J.: Red Sea Press, 1991.

Saint Varan, Robert. *Djibouti: Pawn of the Horn of Africa.* Metuchen, N.J.: Scarecrow Press, 1981.

Africa, Lusophone

The five former Portuguese colonies of Angola, Cape Verde, Guinea-Bissau, Mozambique, and São Tomé and Principe (the last two are one nation). Portugal's five African colonies gained independence in 1974 and 1975, in large part because of popular opposition in Portugal to costly wars in the distant colonies. All the colonies had nationalist movements, some of which had been fighting Lisbon for more than a decade.

Colonial Rule and Beyond

The Portuguese arrived in Africa in the late fifteenth and early sixteenth centuries to establish trading outposts at ports along the coast. It was not until the early twentieth century, however, that Portugal established colonial rule over African territory. Even within the context of European colonialism, the Portuguese ruled their colonies in a highly exploitative fashion and gave them no preparation for self-rule. Thousands of Portuguese, fearful of retribution and African rule, fled after independence was granted, often destroying the property they did not take with them. Most of the former colonies could count only two or three lawyers and five or six doctors in their entire population. There also was very little administrative, technical, or professional expertise to sustain the new regimes because few Africans had served as local administrators in the Portuguese colonial governments.

All the former Portuguese colonies instituted single-party systems, incorporating varying degrees of socialist rhetoric and policies. Both Angola and Mozambique declared themselves Marxist-Leninist. They modeled their nascent political and economic structures on Eastern European blueprints and courted Soviet and Eastern bloc aid. The government of São Tomé espoused Marxist ideas but never formally embraced Marxism-Leninism as its official ideology. Cape Verde and Guinea-Bissau were strictly nonaligned; they courted Western aid but had single-party systems and centrally planned economies.

Beginning in the late 1980s, Lusophone Africa, along with many other developing and former Eastern bloc countries, began to liberalize under pressure for reform from foreign donors as well as internal democratic movements. Often reform was used, albeit unsuccessfully, as a conservative measure to mollify popular opposition to one-party rule while retaining control of the government. In Angola and Mozambique liberalization was part of a strategy for negotiating an end to civil war.

Angola

Three rival nationalist movements—the Popular Movement for the Liberation of Angola (MPLA), the National Front for the Liberation of Angola (FNLA), and the National Union for the Total Independence of Angola (UNITA)—formed a transitional government and took power from Lisbon in January 1975. The MPLA quickly seized control of the government, and within months the three groups were engaged in a bloody civil war that soon attracted outside support for all sides. Zaire assisted the FNLA, South Africa and the United States aided UNITA and the FNLA, and Cuba and the Soviet Union provided aid and troops to the MPLA.

Although the FNLA was soon marginalized, UNITA and the MPLA kept fighting, spurred on by ethnic and power rivalries and competition for superpower support. UNITA, which professed a commitment to democracy and a free market system, controlled a large section of southeastern Angola, from which it launched sabotage attacks that rendered much of the country impassable. Angola's infrastructure was destroyed and its economy paralyzed (except for the country's significant oil reserves in Cabinda). Between 1975 and 1991 Angolan society was decimated: an estimated 500,000 Angolans were killed, and the war left many more displaced and starving.

The withdrawal of South African and Cuban troops after 1988 and the gradual lessening of assistance to the warring parties from the Soviet Union and the United States forced UNITA and the MPLA to negotiate a settlement, which was reached in May 1991. The internationally monitored transition to democracy in Namibia then became a blueprint for peace in Angola.

Angola's attempt at democratic transition coincided with reconciliation between the warring parties. Prompted by increased international pressure for peace, Angolan president José Eduardo dos Santos led the MPLA Third Congress to establish a multiparty democracy in December 1990. Despite opposition from intransigent members of his politburo, dos Santos favored a multiparty system because he believed it would provide a mechanism for peaceful opposition and the integration of UNITA into national politics. The MPLA laid the foundation for political pluralism by approving a new constitution to provide for fundamental freedoms, granting the right to strike, ensuring an independent judiciary, and protecting private property. The MPLA officially abandoned Marxism-Leninism in 1991 and adopted a democratic socialist platform.

After the peace agreement was signed, the two parties—in addition to eleven other parties that emerged to vie for power—began to prepare for elections that were held in September 1992. Elections were partially funded and monitored by the United Nations. However, the money and personnel provided by the UN were insufficient to oversee the elections adequately, given the country's tremendous size, logistical obstacles, and UNITA's recalcitrance. The MPLA won the 1992 elections under terms that the United Nations called generally free and fair. UNITA leader Jonas Savimbi rejected the election outcome, however. Revealing his shallow commitment to democracy, Savimbi declared that the election was rigged and returned to war. In November 1994 the MPLA and UNITA signed another peace agreement, but Savimbi resisted implementing any of its terms until international pressure forced his grudging compliance in 1996. By mid–1997 Savimbi still was resisting the complete demobilization of UNITA's military forces, nor had UNITA filled the government positions accorded it under the 1994 peace agreement.

Mozambique

Mozambique achieved independence in June 1975 under the leadership of Samora Machel, head of the Mozambique Liberation Front (Frelimo), which had waged a campaign for independence since 1962. The new regime faced the challenge of governing an extremely poor and unevenly developed country. (The lion's share of infrastructural resources were deployed in the south.) Although Frelimo was a strictly nationalist organization at its inception, it moved into the socialist sphere after its first leader, Eduardo Mondlane, died in 1969.

At independence, Frelimo declared itself Marxist-Leninist and was formally allied with the Soviet Union and the Eastern bloc. The government tried to achieve rapid development through central direction of the economy, big heavy-industry projects, and state-run farms. By forcibly moving thousands of people to state farms, undermining the authority of traditional ethnic leaders, and confiscating church properties, Frelimo alienated a significant portion of the population, particularly in the rural areas of central Mozambique.

Adding to Frelimo's woes was a violent terrorist challenge by Renamo, the Mozambique National Resistance. Renamo was created by the Rhodesian Central Intelligence Organization to counter Mozambican support for the liberation of Rhodesia (now Zimbabwe). Renamo drew volunteers from disaffected Frelimo members, former criminals, traditional leaders, and ethnic groups, such as the Ndau, that were underrepresented in the Frelimo government. When Zimbabwe gained independence in 1980, South Africa assumed sponsorship of the rebel group, which grew in size and scope under Pretoria's tutelage. By 1985 Renamo had some 15,000 members and conducted sabotage operations throughout Mozambique.

Although Renamo had only a vague political agenda, it professed commitment to multiparty democracy and a free market system (no doubt at the insistence of South Africa and of right-wing backers in Europe and the United States). Recognizing that a military solution to the civil war was probably unattainable because of a massive reduction in Soviet support, Mozambican president Joaquim Chissano began to move toward a multiparty system in 1989 in order to preempt the rebels' political agenda and to deny them substantive leverage in negotiations. In November 1990 the government ratified a new constitution providing for universal suffrage, direct legislative and executive elections, multiple parties, private ownership, basic social and religious freedoms, and the right to strike.

Mozambique's first multiparty elections, held in October 1994, were narrowly won by Frelimo. Chissano (Frelimo's leader) won 53 percent of the vote in a separate presidential poll; Renamo's leader, Afonso Dhlakama, won 34 percent. Despite problems ironing out Renamo's precise role in government, both sides rejected a coalition arrangement, and Dhlakama appeared committed to working within the system rather than returning to war.

As in Angola, the pressures for democracy in Mozambique were primarily external: the collapse of Eastern Europe and the Soviet Union as ideological models, the end of the cold war and the withdrawal of Soviet military and advisory support, the consequent need to court the West as a source of aid, South African support for a settlement, and negotiations for peace in Angola. As in Angola, democratic transition was closely intertwined with the peace process: reform was designed to undercut the insurgents and bring them into the political system. The West had firmly set democracy as a precondition to much-needed aid, and Chissano, a pragmatic politician, recognized the value of espousing democracy.

São Tomé and Principe

São Tomé's first president, Manuel Pinto da Costa, ruled under a one-party constitution from independence in 1975 until multiparty elections in 1991. In an effort to rescue the country from economic ruin and to stem the rising tide of political discontent, his government began a process of economic and political liberalization in 1985. Although political reform was somewhat slower than economic reform, the ruling Movement for the Liberation of São Tomé and Principe (MLSTP) started to implement long-promised liberalization in 1987. It recognized factions within the ruling party and invited exiled opposition groups to return home. The movement finally agreed to multiparty democracy in 1989, when increasingly vocal internal opposition was reinforced by events in Eastern Europe. In an August 1989 referendum 72 percent of the electorate ratified the decision.

A number of exiled parties returned to São Tomé to contest elections in 1991. The ruling party tried to position itself for elections by adopting a social democratic platform, but it was no challenge to the Party of Democratic Convergence–Reflection Group (PDC). This breakaway faction of the ruling party backed the former prime minister, Miguel Anjos da Cunha Trovoada, to win 82 percent of the vote in the presidential elections and thirty-three of fifty-five parliamentary seats.

In July 1994, Trovoada, under pressure from the MLSTP, deposed the PDC-backed prime minister. The new prime minister, though nominally a PDC member, was opposed by that party, which called for a new presidential election. In response, Trovoada dissolved the National Assembly. In legislative elections held October 2, 1994, the MLSTP returned to power, capturing a near majority twenty-seven seats. But the party's lack of a decisive majority complicated its efforts to form a stable government. There ensued over the following three years near continual jockeying for position and cabinet portfolios among the parties. Although not a threat to the basic constitutional order, the constant ferment undermined the business of government by diverting attention from the more pressing issues.

Trovoada was reelected president in close second-round balloting in July 1996. His frustration with the intrigues of coalition government led him to propose constitutional amendments in November that would make the government more presidential in form.

Cape Verde

The African Party for the Independence of Guinea and Cape Verde (PAIGC) was founded in 1956. Its goal was freedom from Portugal and unification of the two countries. After independence in July 1975, it led the postcolonial governments of both countries under a one-party system. Following the 1980 coup in Guinea-Bissau, however, Cape Verde's PAIGC was dissolved and replaced by the African Party for the Independence of Cape Verde (PAICV).

The Third Party Congress in 1988 marked a turning point in Cape Verde's postcolonial history by moving decisively to liberalize the country politically and economically. The government enacted sweeping constitutional reforms and opened the economy to the private sector, allowing private health care and education. In 1990 the ruling party amended the constitution to allow multiparty elections and enacted legislation guaranteeing opposition parties freedom to organize and use the media. The transition was motivated by the eloquent pro-democracy demands of a small but strategic group of some 600 technocrats in Praia, who later formed the main opposition party, the Movement for Democracy.

Cape Verde held its first multiparty presidential elections in February 1991. The leader of the Movement for Democracy (MPD), António Monteiro, was elected by direct universal suffrage for a five-year term. The PAICV moved into the role of loyal opposition.

Although considerable ill feeling between the two leading parties slowed promised liberalization and political decentralization, the governing system remained stable and functional. In regularly scheduled legislative elections conducted in December 1995, five parties fielded candidates. The MPD gained a comfortable ruling majority of fifty seats in the seventy-two-seat legislature; the PAICV won twenty-one. Monteiro was reelected president in February 1996.

Guinea-Bissau

Guinea-Bissau's first postindependence government was formed by the African Party for the Independence of Guinea and Cape Verde (PAIGC) in 1974, and Luis Cabral became president under a one-party system. In 1980 Cabral was deposed by his prime minister, João Vieira, in a coup that enjoyed considerable popular support because of the shortage of food in the country. Legislative elections in 1989 suggest that the ruling party did not face significant internal demands for change. Vieira was reelected president, and PAIGC candidates garnered 95 percent of the vote. Nevertheless, the government faced some internal opposition to one-party rule among local elites, as well as vocal dissent and demands for democracy from opponents exiled in Portugal and Senegal.

In response to this pressure and to external pressure from donor countries, Vieira announced in 1990 that he favored a multiparty system. Over the next three years the government adopted a new constitution, legalized opposition, and provided for freedom of expression. In 1992 emerging political parties demanded the creation of a multiparty transition commission. This commission, which included the ruling party and eight legalized parties, drafted legislation to prepare for the country's first free presidential and legislative elections, which were held in July 1994.

Vieira won the presidential ballot, and the PAIGC took sixty-two of one hundred seats in the National People's Assembly. The two largest opposition parties vowed to remain a loyal opposition, and they have despite their calls for a greater voice in the government.

Prospects for Democratic Consolidation

The wave of democratic transitions in Lusophone Africa in the 1990s was driven in large part by economic failure (which undermined the ruling parties' domestic support) and external pressure. The ideological hegemony of democracy in the world today is likely to produce formally democratic and procedurally accountable governments in most, and maybe all, of these countries. It is unlikely, however, that these governments will extend full rights and liberties to most of their poorly organized and ill-informed citizens. The institutions of power will almost certainly remain concentrated in the hands of a small elite. Although the governments may be responsive to the demands of a visible urban segment, remote, uneducated, and poor rural populations are not likely to be much affected by a multiparty system. Absent a strong civil society that will hold the leadership accountable beyond the transition period, few elites will retain a commitment to a democratic system that could undermine their power base.

Lusophone Africa's attempt to democratize will also be troubled by poverty and other socioeconomic and development problems. Most years Mozambique (with a per capita income of less than $90) vies with Bangladesh for the status of the poorest country in the world. Angola's per capita income is deceptively high because of its substantial oil reserves; roads, schools, and medical facilities have been destroyed, and thousands of Angolans have been displaced by the civil war. The other three countries are slightly better off but well below even the middling levels of economic development conducive to democracy.

Nevertheless, these five countries, which were extremely disadvantaged by colonial rule, have made significant strides toward better governance since independence. All five have held generally free and fair, multiparty elections; Cape Verde and São Tomé and Principe have each held two national elections. And Mozambique and Angola—with the end of civil war and the apparent end of civil war, respectively—have better conditions and prospects for economic development, human rights and liberties, and democracy than at any point since 1960.

See also *African independence movements.*

BIBLIOGRAPHY

Alden, Chris, and Mark Simpson. "Mozambique: A Delicate Peace." *Journal of Modern African Studies* 31 (March 1993): 109–130.

Hamilton, Kimberley A. *Lusophone Africa, Portugal, and the United States: Possibilities for More Effective Cooperation.* Washington, D.C.: Center for Strategic and International Studies, 1992.

Hanlon, Joseph. *Apartheid's Second Front: South Africa's War Against Its Neighbours.* Harmondsworth and New York: Penguin Books, 1986.

Hodges, Tony. *Angola to the 1990s: The Potential for Recovery.* London: Economist Publications, 1987.

Isaacman, Allen F., and Barbara Isaacman. *Mozambique: From Colonialism to Revolution, 1900–1982.* Boulder, Colo.: Westview Press, 1983; Aldershot: Gower, 1984.

Isaacman, Allen F., and David Wiley, eds. *Southern Africa: Society, Economy, and Liberation.* East Lansing, Mich.: African Studies Center at Michigan State University and the Department of African American and African Studies at the University of Minnesota, 1981.

McCulloch, Jack. *In the Twilight of Revolution: The Political Theory of Amilcar Cabral.* Boston: Routledge and Kegan Paul, 1983.

Pereira, Anthony W. "The Neglected Tragedy: The Return to War in Angola, 1992–93." *Journal of Modern African Studies* 32 (March 1994): 1–28.

Silva, Josue da. *Era uma vez: Tres guerras em Africa.* Cacem, Portugal: Edicoes Ro, 1981.

Soremukun, Fola. *Angola: The Road to Independence.* Ile-Ife, Nigeria: University of Ife Press, 1983.

Africa, Subsaharan

The forty-eight independent countries of the African continent (and islands in the region as far away as Mauritius) that lie in and to the south of the Sahara desert. Subsaharan Africa encompasses all the African countries except the five North African countries that border the Mediterranean Sea: Egypt, Libya, Tunisia, Algeria, and Morocco. The region has had a turbulent and largely unsuccessful experience with democracy since Sudan and Ghana led the way to independence in 1956 and 1957, respectively.

In a relatively short period of time, virtually all the formally democratic systems left behind by the departing colonial rulers gave way to authoritarian regimes of one kind or another. In most cases the demise of constitutional democracy began with the movement to one-party, and typically one-man, rule. In some countries, such as Senegal and the Côte d'Ivoire, this development followed from the electoral supremacy of the ruling party and the cohesiveness of the country's elites before independence, although authoritarian rule was not consolidated without repression. In other countries, primarily former British colonies such as Kenya, Zambia, Ghana, and Uganda, one-party regimes (officially or effectively) were established only a few years after independence, but with extensive coercion and concentration of power in one person.

In Nigeria's First Republic (1960–1966), turbulent mul-

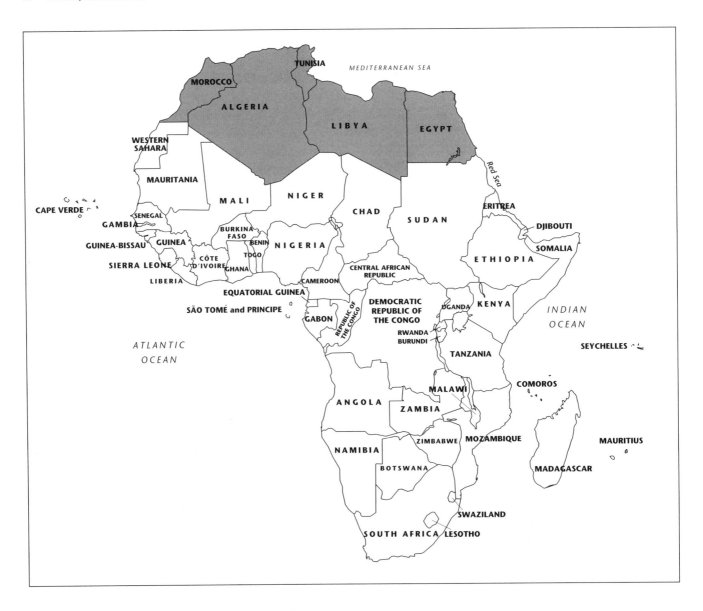

tiparty competition was diminished by the consolidation of single-party rule in each of the three regions; there followed increasingly severe constraints on liberty and electoral competition. In Nigeria and elsewhere (as in Sierra Leone and the Democratic Republic of the Congo), growing instability surrounding electoral competition paved the way for military intervention, which also swept away the more fragile one-party regimes.

By the early 1970s virtually all the independent regimes in Subsaharan Africa were either military or one-party. When Portugal's African colonies finally broke free in 1974–1975, after years of armed challenge to some of the most exploitative and authoritarian of all African colonial regimes, those new countries (principally Angola and Mozambique) also became one-party states, with Marxist-Leninist orientations.

Success and Near Success

Multiparty democracy endured for several decades in three African countries: Botswana, Gambia, and Mauritius (all of them small in population and former British colonies). In Botswana, where the bureaucracy dominates, democracy, although paternalistic, has nevertheless become more vigorous and pluralistic over time. The island nation of Mauritius has consistently maintained the most liberal and competitive political system in Africa since it won independence in 1968; the nation is multiethnic (predominantly Indian) and prosperous. By contrast, after thirty years of continuous rule by the same party and president (Dawda Jawara), and rising discontent over corruption, Gambia's democracy fell to a military coup in 1994.

Yet by the end of the twentieth century, numerous other African countries had legalized party competition and established democratic constitutional forms. Most of these had no previous experience with multiparty democracy or had seen it expire quickly after independence. These included several former French colonies (Benin, Mali, Niger, Madagascar, the Republic of Congo, and the Central African Republic); two former British colonies (Zambia and Malawi); two former Portuguese colonies (the tiny island states of Cape Verde and São Tomé and Principe); and two former apartheid states (Namibia and, most significantly for the drama of its transition and the implications for the entire continent, South Africa).

A number of African countries that experienced political transitions during the early 1990s fell short of the mark of fully democratic rule. These included Niger, the Central African Republic, Comoros, the Republic of Congo, Ghana, Seychelles, and Mozambique (which held a successful transition election in 1994). In these countries, multiparty constitutional regimes were installed. But significant abridgments of democracy remained, such as lingering military influence over government, limitations on rights of opposition and dissent, compromise of judicial independence, and electoral biases and irregularities. Despite the great promise of its pathbreaking electoral transition in 1991, Zambia witnessed a significant narrowing of competition and liberty because of states of emergency, crackdowns on the opposition, corruption, and political intolerance.

Some African countries (such as Uganda, Tanzania, and Ethiopia) had yet to clearly establish their constitutional form and political identity. Several promised transitions fizzled out or were quashed by authoritarian rulers, as in Togo and the Democratic Republic of the Congo. In Nigeria a continually delayed and almost completed democratic transition was aborted by the military in June 1993, when it annulled the results of the freest and fairest presidential elections in that country's history; for the first time Nigeria appeared to have elected a southerner from the Yoruba ethnic group to the country's highest office.

Such regime ambiguity, or dissonance between form and substance, has been a familiar story in postindependence Africa. Since the restoration of multiparty competition in 1976, Senegal has lived uncomfortably with some genuine pluralism and liberty, matched with the state manipulation, electoral fraud and pervasive clientelism, patronage, and corruption necessary to maintain the dominance of the ruling Socialist Party. Zimbabwe has perpetuated a similar type of semidemocracy since it came into being as an independent country in 1980, though with rather less liberty and greater use of violence and intimidation by the ruling party.

Ghana, Kenya, Cameroon, and Gabon adopted ambiguous regime forms in the early 1990s. In each case, the authoritarian rulers—Jerry Rawlings, Daniel arap Moi, Paul Biya, and Omar Bongo, respectively—were forced by domestic and international pressures to concede to multiparty elections. In each case the incumbent dictators won dubious and disputed election or reelection as president in 1992 or 1993 through force, fraud, intimidation, and heavy manipulation of state power and electoral rules (though Ghana's election was somewhat cleaner than the others). In each case, subsequent abridgments of opposition and individual rights put the regimes on the margin between semidemocracy and authoritarianism. There was an improvement in tolerance for political opposition and the operation of civil society, but Kenya and Cameroon soon reverted to harsh repression of opposition.

Postcolonial Failures

Two types of developments, distinct but not mutually exclusive, signaled the failure of democratic systems in Subsaharan Africa following independence. In a great many countries, especially the former French colonies, the new rulers and ruling parties eliminated political competition, more or less quickly, and established one-party regimes. Where political support was too divided or political leadership insufficiently willful and authoritarian to permit the construction of single-party dominance, political competition typically tore the polity apart in spasms of political deadlock and crisis, ethnic polarization, partisan violence, state repression, and electoral fraud, paving the way for military intervention.

In Ghana, Senegal, Kenya, Uganda, and elsewhere the first postindependence elected leaders eliminated democracy through various measures that amounted to executive coups. After three years of political insecurity, authoritarian overreaction, and abuse of power, Ghana's coup was carried out by Prime Minister Kwame Nkrumah through a national referendum in 1960, which established a centralized presidential system under Nkrumah's leadership. A highly personalized, one-party dictatorship followed; it decimated the country's economy and brought on a military coup in 1966. Significantly, the transition from political pluralism to authoritarianism was also marked and consolidated in Senegal, Uganda, and Kenya by constitutional change from a parliamentary to a presidential system, with extreme concentration of power in the presidency and marked diminution of legislative authority. These were among a number of African countries that descended into authoritarianism not by military coup (at least not initially) but through various political measures constraining and ultimately proscribing opposition parties.

Colonial Background

Several factors account for the failure of democracy in the new states of postcolonial Africa. Many of these had their origin in European colonial rule. To be sure, colonial rule left behind some of the infrastructure and institutions of a modern economy and society—transportation and communication grids, monetary systems, public education, and a state bureaucracy. Under French and especially under British colonial rule, there also emerged for the first time modern elements of political pluralism and civil society: political parties, trade unions, churches, organized interest groups, newspapers, universities, and intellectuals. Even during long periods of subsequent authoritarian rule, this societal pluralism would endure and evolve in many English-speaking and French-speaking countries, exerting crucial pressure for democratization.

The British saw preparation of the colonies for self-rule as part of their mission. In contrast to India and the Caribbean, however, that preparation came quite late in the British colonies of Africa, even later in the French ones (save for Senegal, especially Dakar), and not at all in the Belgian and Portuguese colonies. Thus, while the former British colonies had some limited success with competitive party politics, at least for a time, and some intellectual and social pluralism survived in countries like Nigeria, Ghana, and Kenya (and among the former French colonies, most notably Senegal), what democratic processes there were quickly collapsed in most of the rest of Africa.

A number of underlying features of colonial rule throughout Africa left a highly unfavorable legacy for democracy. It was in the nature of colonial rule everywhere to be authoritarian and paternalistic. Even the more liberal systems, like the British colonies in West Africa, allowed only limited participation in government, confined mainly to a small elite and to the local levels of governance until a few years before independence. For most of the sixty or so years of formal colonial rule, colonial officials enjoyed extraordinary powers with exalted status and few checks. In contrast to India, which had gradually built up a strong, indigenous "steel frame" of public administration under its much longer British colonial rule, African countries had few of their own in the upper reaches of the state bureaucracy when independence came. Most newly independent states thus quickly embarked on sweeping programs of "Africanization" as a means of asserting political control and, symbolically, of national identity as well. These programs opened wide opportunities but diminished governmental capacity and integrity. (Perhaps not coincidentally, Botswana, the one country to have maintained democracy continuously since independence, also took a much more gradual and cautious approach to Africanization of the state bureaucracy.)

The paternalism of colonial rule was particularly damaging in its transmission of institutional frameworks borrowed almost wholly from the colonizer, with little concern for incorporation of indigenous practices and symbols. As a result, African peoples and politicians alike felt little sense of ownership of, or identification with, the new, postcolonial constitutional structures. Aspiring autocrats, civilian and military, thus encountered little resistance in sabotaging or overthrowing them.

The colonial state was not simply authoritarian and paternalistic, it was often brutal as well. Resistance and protest were readily, and if need be, bloodily repressed. Dissidents and nationalist "agitators" were jailed. It was this model, and not the model of British or French democracy, that was to be emulated by the postcolonial elite and that helped to breed from the start a political culture of intolerance.

The Statist Legacy

The colonial legacy was not only authoritarian but also statist. The colonial bureaucracy (like the military) was surprisingly small, and in the case of the British, often ruled indirectly through traditional systems of authority. Nevertheless, the state imposed extensive controls over internal and external trade; established monopoly control over the marketing of agricultural cash crops, the largest source of cash income; and awarded itself exclusive control over the mining of minerals and the development of infrastructure. This incipient statism, along with favoritism toward capital and imported goods from the colonizing power, preempted the emergence of an independent, indigenous capitalist class in the colonies. Even more significantly, the bureaucracy provided a welcome means for the new African political elite to accumulate personal wealth and consolidate its grip on power after independence. At the same time, African economies were left dependent on international trade and capital and vulnerable to abrupt swings in commodity prices.

Colonial rule, and the carving of Africa into colonial territories (formally initiated with the Berlin Conference of 1884–1885), produced the seeds of modern ethnic conflict as well. The colonial demarcation of African boundaries followed European rather than African political logic, splitting up some cultural and historical groups while throwing together others with little in common—except perhaps a history of warfare and enmity. This initial cultural complexity was aggravated by the uneven spread of education, economic development, military recruitment, and other Western influences; thus some regions and peoples were distinctly advantaged over others. Colonial policies and institutions emphasized ethnic differences as part of a strategy of "divide and rule." British imperial policy deliberately encouraged ethnic and regional consciousness, as opposed to an incipient national consciousness, and strengthened institutions of traditional rule. In Nigeria, Sudan, and Uganda, British colonial rule crystallized and tenaciously preserved regional structures and cleavages that ultimately led to civil war.

In at least a few countries where decolonization occurred without mass mobilization and violence, such as Nigeria, Ghana, Senegal, Gambia, and Botswana, some currents of pluralism and democratic culture were felt. Where decolonization occurred through armed struggle, a militant, ideological, or at least rhetorically revolutionary authoritarian regime was typically the result, as in the Portuguese colonies of Angola, Mozambique, and Guinea-Bissau and, to a lesser extent, Zimbabwe. There the black majority government of Robert Mugabe rigorously respected the protections for white minority rights codified in the 1979 constitution but gradually assumed much of the repressive character of the African one-party state. Given this legacy, it is all the more remarkable that South Africa has found its way to democracy after apartheid, despite the considerable violence, mass mobilization, and state repression that attended the decades-long struggle for a society that would not be based on race.

Postcolonial Politics and Society

The problems and contradictions of colonial rule were greatly exacerbated by the African political leaders who came to power with independence. Some historians maintain that failures of democracy, and more broadly of governance, in this period were virtually predestined by the structural patterns, conflicts, and weaknesses inherited from colonial rule. Others maintain that the problems were produced by self-serving elites who did little to forge a different style of politics and governance. Where similar historical outcomes occur in several dozen countries, one cannot dispute the powerful role of common structural

and historical factors. In the context of extreme poverty and economic dependence, deep ethnic divisions, little democratic experience, weak and artificial governmental structures, shallow constitutional legitimacy, meager civil societies, and sweeping state controls over the formal economy, the maintenance of a relatively liberal and democratic regime would probably have required political leadership exceptional in its self-discipline, democratic commitment, and skill at coalition building.

In virtually every country—save for a few with small populations, like Mauritius and Botswana, where the challenges were less daunting—such leadership was missing. Yet leadership was not irrelevant. During the 1960s and 1970s Senegal and Kenya managed to preserve some elements of pluralism and constitutionalism and to avoid the more grotesque degrees of repression and state failure, partly because of the leadership of Léopold Senghor and Jomo Kenyatta, respectively. For five years the accommodating style and personal restraint of Nigeria's prime minister, Abubakar Tafawa Balewa, helped to hold disaster at bay and a multiparty regime in place. Botswana's democratic development was heavily shaped from the beginning by the strong convictions and political vision and skill of Seretse Khama, who governed with more self-restraint and success (despite a paternalistic style) than perhaps any other African ruler of his time. And South Africa's largely peaceful transition to democracy, and its subsequent embrace of racial and political reconciliation and power sharing, owed much to the leadership, vision, direction, and charisma of Nelson Mandela.

For the most part, however, newly independent African states succumbed more or less quickly to centralizing and authoritarian political temptations. In some cases (particularly in French-speaking countries) this process was facilitated by the relative paucity of organized opposition and the more centralized political character of French colonial regimes and of France's own political system. Elsewhere, ethnic fragmentation and rising opposition led political leaders like Kwame Nkrumah in Ghana and Milton Obote in Uganda to abandon democracy in order to maintain control. In Zambia, President Kenneth Kaunda tolerated multiparty competition for almost a decade after independence in 1964. But when his ruling party was threatened with defeat in parliamentary elections, he clamped down the lid of repression in 1973, having amended the constitution to ban opposition parties.

A common feature behind all these movements to authoritarian rule was the weakness of democratic norms and values. In some cases—as with Sékou Touré in Guinea and Julius Nyerere in Tanzania (and Nkrumah in Ghana as he moved to the socialist left)—one-party rule was declared out of ideological commitment to a communitarian socialist ideology and to African cultural traditions emphasizing consensus.

Through the 1960s and 1970s ideas of developmentalism and dependency gained favor. Leaders stressed the necessity for centralized authoritarian rule to preempt class divisions, manage relations with exploitative economic forces in the world economy, and organize the society for rapid development. Marxist revolutionary doctrines—which took hold in Angola, Mozambique, Ethiopia, Guinea-Bissau, and a few other African countries—went further, justifying terrible repression in the battle against imperialism, class privilege, and ethnic consciousness. Increasingly, democrats in Africa were on the defensive intellectually as well as politically. By the 1970s most African states that were not under military rule had a one-party system, a form of government they proclaimed to be distinctively appropriate for Africa.

A number of postindependence African political leaders had intellectual (and, in effect, political) training in Britain and France; Senghor had even served in the French National Assembly. The Nigerian nationalist leaders Nnamdi Azikiwe and Obafemi Awolowo manifested in their speeches and extensive writings a broad, passionate, and sophisticated appreciation of the value and character of liberal democracy. However, even where these expressions of principle were sincere, as with Awolowo and Azikiwe, they were often undermined by abrasive or autocratic political styles, or by the pressures of political conflict in structural circumstances that were not conducive to the mutual security, trust, and tolerance among competing political forces that make democracy possible.

Seeds of Corruption

These structural factors were probably more important than ideas or ideology alone in explaining the almost universal absence or failure of democracy in Africa during the first three decades of independence. Mostly rooted in colonial rule, the failures took on more crippling dimensions after independence. At the hub of all these structural factors was the swollen African state—too large and interventionist to allow market forces to generate growth, yet too weak to undertake the quest for the kind of state-led development that took place at the same time in East Asia. The typical African state owned or controlled by far the greatest share of wealth outside the subsistence economy—in min-

ing, agriculture, and even industry and services. It became the leading purchaser of goods and services; the provider of schools, roads, clinics, and markets for communities; the principal source of wage employment, contracts, careers, commissions, and scholarships.

Because of the pervasive poverty and the extreme underdevelopment of indigenous entrepreneurship, the African state became the primary arena of class formation after independence, the chief means (through political corruption and patronage) for the accumulation of personal wealth and the opening of economic opportunities to family, friends, clients, and ethnic kin. State power became extremely valuable. Those who held it became rich and had resources available to them; those who did not were virtually without opportunity.

Politics became a zero-sum game, in which winning was everything and no one could afford to lose. What democratic ideals and inclinations there were could not survive these structural pressures and insecurities. The idea of "anything goes" prevailed in the struggle for power: violence, vituperation, demagoguery, intimidation, assassination, rigging of elections, census manipulation, arrests, repression.

Where civilian politicians did not put an end to multiparty competition, it became so chaotic and corrupt that the military was easily able to seize control, initially with enthusiastic popular support. Invariably, however, military rulers fell victim to the same temptations as had civilian politicians. But the military rulers displayed even less respect for law and opposition, even weaker capacity to build multiethnic coalitions, and even greater disposition to use violence and repression as substitutes for legitimacy. Political decay and popular alienation and disengagement thus intensified.

Statism and corruption had other devastating consequences for democracy. Pervasive state controls stifled incentives for investment to raise agricultural productivity and launch new business ventures. Unchecked by any restraints from independent institutions, such as the judiciary or the mass media, nepotism and corruption turned into gross mismanagement and brazen plunder of public resources. Economies were driven into effective bankruptcy, with massive foreign debt, staggering inequality, and explosive public anger. Subsequent attempts at democracy in Ghana, Nigeria, and Sudan failed even more dramatically than the initial attempts; public patience evaporated more quickly, and the military, fattened from the previous spoils of office, proved hungrier to intervene again. No country fell further than Nigeria, which squandered billions of dollars in oil revenue during the four-year Second Republic while generating massive shortages of basic consumer goods and $20 billion of foreign debt.

Institutional arrangements did little to soften the competition for power throughout Africa. In most countries, power was highly centralized and was monopolized by a single ethnic group or narrow coalition. Groups that did not find their way into the ruling coalition could expect short shrift in the distribution of resources. The most far-reaching and imaginative experiment in federalism on the continent, in Nigeria, did generate a significantly more complex and fluid political pattern. The splitting up of the three major regions of the First Republic into first twelve and then nineteen states, many of them dominated by ethnic minorities, activated divisions within ethnic groups and facilitated cross-cutting alignments. However, the premium on control of the central government remained intense, since that was the locus of most state resources. Although polarized ethnic and regional conflict did not figure prominently in the breakdown of the Second Republic in 1983, corruption and mismanagement did. Constitution makers had failed to create effective mechanisms to monitor the conduct of public officials and check the abuse of power.

The need for federalism, decentralization, and power sharing constitutes one of the principal lessons of Africa's postindependence political experience. Only by giving different ethnic groups some sense of political security and autonomy—and some control over their own resources—can ethnic and regional conflict be effectively managed. Only by inducing or requiring political parties to forge broad ethnic coalitions can stability be achieved.

Such mechanisms would probably have prevented the destructive civil wars that occurred in Nigeria, Uganda, and Sudan. For a time during the 1970s the granting of substantial political autonomy to the southern region did bring a halt to the civil war in Sudan, until President Jaafar Muhammed al-Numeiri effectively abrogated the agreement in 1983 in an effort to consolidate his waning support in the north.

Fortunately, South Africa seems to have learned something from previous African experience. Despite the strong historical disposition of the African National Congress toward a unitary system, it agreed to a new political system of nine regions, with independently elected assemblies and premiers and some significant autonomous powers. Power sharing has also been facilitated in South Africa and Namibia by the use of proportional representation in legislative elections and the formation of coalition governments.

A final factor that must be weighed in assessing the causes of democratic failure in Africa is international politics. Throughout the period of decolonization and postindependence politics—from the 1950s through the late 1980s—the principal powers in the cold war viewed Africa primarily as an arena of competition for geopolitical and occasionally military advantage. The Soviet bloc provided crucial support to Marxist and quasi-Marxist regimes like those in Ethiopia, Angola, and Mozambique. Without Soviet support these regimes might have fallen (though probably not to any democratic alternative). Soviet bloc nations also supported liberation movements in Zimbabwe, South Africa, and Namibia.

The United States, Great Britain, and France backed their own allies and surrogates in the struggle, especially the authoritarian regime of Mobutu Sese Seko in Zaire (now the Democratic Republic of the Congo). This regime became pivotal in the United States's strategy to stem and undermine the spread of Soviet influence in Africa. The United States also offered close support to al-Numeiri in Sudan; to Samuel Doe's dictatorship in Liberia; to Moi's increasingly repressive one-party state in Kenya; and to the dictatorship of Mohamed Siad Barre in Somalia after it bolted from its pro-Soviet alliance. France turned a blind eye to pervasive corruption and repression while maintaining intimate and even heavily controlling ties with the governments of its former African colonies. Despite rhetorical and diplomatic objections, Western countries, including the United States, also supported and did business with the apartheid regime in South Africa into the 1970s (and, more discreetly, the 1980s). If there was one thing that did not seem to matter much to the major world powers in their aid, trade, and military assistance relationships with Africa, it was democracy.

The Second Liberation

In February 1990 two historic political events took place that were to transform the character of politics in Africa. In Benin, the National Conference of Active Forces of the Nation, called by the one-party state to consider constitutional reforms that might revive its depleted legitimacy, instead seized sovereign power and effective authority from President Mathieu Kerekou, established a transitional government, and prepared the way for multiparty elections under a new constitution. And in South Africa, recently installed President Frederik W. de Klerk lifted the ban on the African National Congress (as well as the Pan-Africanist Congress and the South African Communist Party) and released Mandela from prison, effectively initiating a transition to democracy.

Over the next three years a wave of democratic transitions swept across Africa. Inspired by Benin's experience, several French-speaking African countries—Togo, Niger, Madagascar, the Democratic Republic of the Congo, the Republic of Congo, and Mali (following a military coup to depose the stand-pat dictator)—organized national conferences. In four of the six (Mali, Niger, Madagascar, and the Republic of Congo), constitutional change and multiparty elections followed. Under rising domestic and international pressure and criticism, one African dictator after another legalized the opposition and agreed to hold multiparty elections: Kaunda in Zambia, Moi in Kenya, Rawlings in Ghana, Bongo in Gabon, Biya in Cameroon. Malawi joined the list when 63 percent of the voters in a June 1993 referendum endorsed the multiparty option in a stunning rejection of Hastings Kamuzu Banda's twenty-nine-year dictatorship.

In two years the political map of Subsaharan Africa was transformed. At the end of 1989 thirty-three of the then forty-seven Subsaharan African states were rated "not free" by Freedom House (an organization headquartered in New York City); in 1991 only twenty were so rated, and the number of "free" states had risen from three to eight. Three years later the number of free states held at eight, and another dozen or so countries had multiparty systems that approached democracy to varying degrees. But some of the countries with democratic openings had slipped back into authoritarianism and state breakdown, and twenty-six of the Subsaharan countries were classified as not free.

The early 1990s was a time of democratic mobilization and experimentation in Africa. Between 1990 and 1994 more than two dozen African countries held multiparty elections. Only about two-thirds of these were judged free and fair by independent observers. Yet in eleven countries—including South Africa, Zambia, Madagascar, and Malawi—incumbent parties and rulers were voted out. And those dictatorships that survived through fraud at the polls, as in Kenya, Cameroon, and Gabon, had to contend with more vigorous civil societies and more energetic political oppositions.

International and domestic factors converged powerfully to generate this wave of African democratic movements, which has been called Africa's second liberation. It was no coincidence that the two igniting events in Benin

and South Africa came on the heels of the collapse of the Berlin Wall in 1989. The downfall of communism in Europe transformed the international environment, discrediting the main ideological rival to political and economic liberalism on the African scene. And the end of the cold war freed the United States from its absorption with countering Soviet influence on the continent, enabling it to give democracy and human rights a much higher priority in diplomacy and foreign aid allocations.

International Pressures

Beginning in 1990 the United States moved increasingly to integrate the promotion of democracy and human rights into its foreign aid programs worldwide and to impose democratic conditions for assistance. Britain and France moved in the same direction.

A turning point came in June 1990, at the Franco-African summit at La Baule, when French President François Mitterrand announced a dramatic turn in France's traditionally dominating and commercially driven relations with its former African colonies. Henceforth, Mitterrand warned, France would link its aid to institutional progress toward democracy, as evidenced by free and fair elections between competing parties, press freedom, and judicial independence. In fact, France's determination to pull the plug on Kerekou's political life-support system, by suspending aid, had been a prime factor in the Beninois president's decision to call the National Conference four months previously. Now other former colonies were put on notice that badly needed French aid would be directly linked to democratic and human rights reforms. Political openings soon swept through French-speaking Africa, some leading to genuine transitions to democracy and others to more cosmetic reforms that nevertheless created more space for opposition and dissent.

In English-speaking Africa, external pressure had its most visible effects in Kenya and Malawi. For years, both the foreign policy aid agencies of individual states and international agencies had become increasingly offended by the growing scale and brazenness of corruption and repression under the Moi regime in Kenya. Finally, in November 1991, after months of warnings of an aid cutoff by the United States and Scandinavian countries, Kenya's aid donors suspended new aid for six months and established explicit political conditions for its resumption. One week later Kenya's ruling party repealed the ban on opposition parties, paving the way for multiparty elections—a change that Moi bitterly attributed to Western pressure. A similar decision by international donors in May 1992 to freeze $74 million in aid to Malawi (following the first mass protests in twenty-eight years) was similarly critical in prompting the Banda regime to release political prisoners, legalize opposition movements, and conduct the 1993 referendum on the existence of multiple parties, which proved its undoing.

Western pressure was pivotal in prying open the heavy lid of authoritarianism in Africa. Private foundations and groups in the West, as well as publicly funded democracy initiatives like the U.S. National Endowment for Democracy, also played an important role in giving assistance to African democratic movements and civil society organizations. External pressure and support could not have succeeded, however, were it not for the emergence of indigenous democratic movements of unprecedented scope and vigor, demanding a new political order.

The rise of civil society from the cynicism, repression, and chaos of authoritarianism in Africa provided the driving wedge for Africa's democratic resurgence in the 1990s. In the face of economic and political decline during the 1970s and 1980s there emerged a host of independent associations, movements, networks, and media to advance popular interests and challenge or displace the predatory power of the African state. In addition to more traditional professional associations—of lawyers, doctors, journalists, teachers, university staff, and students—human rights and pro-democracy groups formed specifically around issues of democratic reform. Groups included the Civil Liberties Organization, the Constitutional Rights Project, and the Campaign for Democracy in Nigeria; the Law Society of Kenya and the Federation of Women Lawyers in Kenya; and the Zimbabwe Human Rights Association and the Forum for Democratic Reform in Zimbabwe. These were on the forefront of campaigns for democracy in their countries.

Intellectuals—disillusioned with socialism and what they increasingly came to see as the inevitable corruption and abuse of one-party rule—eloquently argued that Africa could not advance without the pluralism and accountability of multiparty democracy. Successful movements require broad coalitions across civil society, however. In Zambia the powerful trade union movement, led by the Zambian Congress of Trade Unions and its chairman, Frederick Chiluba, spearheaded a coalition of labor, students, businesspeople, and dissident politicians; it eventually took shape in (and won power as) the Movement for Multiparty Democracy.

In many African countries, religious figures and organizations took the lead in denouncing authoritarian rule and providing both legitimacy and sanctuary to vulnerable opponents. Powerful moral impetus for the anti-apartheid movement in South Africa came from outspoken black clergy like Anglican Archbishop Desmond Tutu and iconoclastic white clergy like the Reverend Beyers Naude. Clerics like Bishop Henry Okullu, chairman of the National Council of Churches of Kenya, and the Reverend Timothy Njoya rallied popular sentiment for multiparty democracy in Kenya. In several countries, well-publicized sermons and pastoral letters gave moral support and political momentum to the democratic cause. Such a letter by seven Catholic bishops helped to inspire the popular movement for democracy in Malawi. In both Benin and the Republic of Congo, Roman Catholic prelates presided over the national conferences.

Popular movements for democracy arose out of long-time frustration with the mounting failures and injustices of every type of authoritarian rule. During the 1980s Subsaharan Africa's per capita gross national product shrank at a rate of 1.1 percent annually. By 1989 its total external debt stood at $147 billion, 99 percent of gross domestic product and four times the annual export earnings. On virtually every dimension of economic and human development, African countries ranked among the poorest and most miserable in the world, despite an annual aid inflow of $15 billion. Decades of decay in education, infrastructure, health, and other public services were capped by fiscal crises that left states like Benin unable even to pay civil servants' salaries (a critical factor in stimulating protest).

In the midst of such intense poverty and economic decline, the gross venality and arrogance of ruling elites, their arbitrary use of power and abuse of human rights, and their reliance on increasingly narrow and exclusive ethnic bases of support ruptured the remaining bonds of political legitimacy. Alternative, informal channels of production and exchange proliferated as people sought to escape the predation of the state, and political opposition grew in breadth, boldness, organization, and moral fervor. Where such movements could not congeal, the alternative in several states, such as Liberia, Somalia, Sudan, Angola, and Rwanda, was civil war and state disintegration.

Toward Democratic Development?

Africa gained a new chance at democratic development in the 1990s, but with no assurances of success. Although one-party, socialist, and military regimes have been utterly discredited, democracy has yet to garner positive and broad legitimacy as an alternative. The movements that brought down authoritarianism were largely critical and oppositional in nature. Africa has yet to develop a healthy symbiosis between state and civil society. Civil society organizations and mass media generally have yet to find the balance between democratic vigilance and oversight, on the one hand, and positive engagement with the state and respect for its authority, on the other. And, for the most part, rival political factions and ethnic groups have yet to work out enduring modes of accommodation and coexistence among themselves. As Africa's past political travails have poignantly shown, democracy encompasses more than competition and participation. It requires tolerance, trust, moderation, accommodation, and accountability.

To be successful, democracy in Africa thus will demand broad changes in political culture, beginning with the political elite. No challenge is more important for the future of democracy in Africa than structuring institutions wisely. Strong autonomous institutions are needed to build a rule of law, regulate electoral contestation, and monitor conduct in public office. Layers of insulation are needed so that the judiciary and electoral administration will not be politicized again but can gain the confidence of all factions and groups through high standards of professional recruitment and operation.

To control corruption, two types of institutions are essential: an audit agency to monitor all government accounts and transactions and a commission to scrutinize the assets and conduct of all public officials. These institutions as well need rigorous professional standards and powerful insulation from partisan politics; top officers must be appointed from outside the political process (perhaps by the judiciary) and enjoy tenure of office that can be removed only by special procedures for demonstrated cause. They also need the resources to exercise effective oversight and to deter and punish corruption: sizable staffs of trained investigators, lawyers, and accountants; substantial computer technology; sufficiently competitive salaries to attract qualified professionals and deter temptation; and tough, savvy, truly independent administrators.

These structures of oversight will not come cheaply, but they will more than pay for themselves by deterring waste and theft or recovering monies wasted or stolen. Unless the virulent malignancy of corruption is contained and diminished, and a new ethic of public service and developmental purpose is generated, competitive, multiparty politics in Africa cannot possibly develop the mutual restraint and popular legitimacy necessary to survive.

Institutional innovations are also needed for managing Africa's ethnic diversity democratically. One institutional imperative for ethnically divided societies is federalism—or some functional equivalent that devolves meaningful power, autonomy, and resources to regional and local governments. Only through such devolution can the stakes of controlling political power at the center be reduced and governmental responsiveness to grassroots concerns and initiatives increased. Devolution of power will improve accountability as well as the sense of responsibility on the part of citizens for their own development and for monitoring the political process.

In this way, citizenship—the most basic building block of democracy—will be actively nurtured in Africa for the first time, as Africans learn that democratic participation means more than electing an ethnic "son of the soil" and waiting for him to bring back from the capital their "share of the national cake," in the form of contracts, jobs, money, and other patronage. In addition, by raising through taxation even modest funds for community development, local governance might teach the important lesson that the state is no longer some alien colonial entity but that it belongs to all citizens and requires vigilant scrutiny and responsible participation from all.

Innovative provisions for ethnic power sharing and accommodation must also be crafted. Presidentialism offers the advantage of a single, unifying symbol of national political authority. Nigeria has led the way in showing how a presidential party system can generate incentives for transethnic politics. Nigeria's system requires a broad ethnic and regional distribution of support for election to the presidency, mandates broad ethnic representation in government appointments, ensures ethnic and regional balance in the "zoning" of party offices and nominations to different ethnic regions, and bans avowedly ethnic or regional parties.

Yet presidential power is also easily aggrandized and abused. An alternative strategy for encouraging ethnically broad electoral alliances or coalition governments would involve a parliamentary system coupled with proportional representation in districts small enough to provide effective linkages between voters and representatives.

Whatever the electoral system, political parties must develop greater institutional depth, reach, and capacity if they are to be effective instruments for representing and aggregating interests. An effective system requires not only appropriate institutional incentives but also creative political entrepreneurship to develop party structures that are independent of particular personalities and ethnic groups—to make parties into cross-cutting, issue-based political associations. The same is necessary with respect to independent organizations and interest groups in civil society. Yet institutionalization also requires patience and time; it will occur in Africa only if competitive, constitutional politics can, for the first time there, gain a long run without interruption by a military or presidential coup or by civil war.

Economic and International Prerequisites

Market-oriented reforms are indispensable to the future of democracy in Africa for two reasons: first, to reduce the scope for politicians to manipulate state economic regulations and controls for their own corrupt profit; and second, to unleash the entrepreneurial energy and investment that have been evident in the African informal sector and that must be mobilized formally, and on a large scale, if Africa is to develop. Yet the transitional costs of reform are enormous: socially, in terms of lost jobs and consumer subsidies; financially, in terms of the needs for government restructuring and social safety nets to ease adjustment; and politically, in terms of the instability that can result if the other costs of adjustment are not somehow met. One of the most pressing dilemmas facing the new and emerging democracies of Africa is thus financial: how to obtain the resources to manage adjustment and rekindle economic development.

Except for a few mineral-rich countries like Botswana, Nigeria, and Angola (and the last two have bankrupted themselves), most African countries have little prospect of economic recovery without renewed international assistance. Properly conditioned on open, liberal, accountable governance and responsible macroeconomic policies, international assistance could do much to ease the costs of structural adjustment, reduce crippling burdens of external debt, attract new business investment, and raise productivity through well-managed public investments in infrastructure, education, health, and capital funds for small businesses.

Yet the end of the cold war has been a mixed blessing for Africa. Although it has largely ended the proclivity of the major world powers to manipulate Africa's internal conflicts and embrace its authoritarian regimes, it has also greatly diminished their interest in Africa altogether. With Africa accounting for a virtually invisible 1 percent of world trade, internationalist forces in the West find it difficult to summon other than humanitarian and idealistic justifications for continued engagement in Africa. Africans have thus found themselves in the paradoxical position of being urged to reform and democratize—and making progress in doing so—while receiving less interest and support from the established democracies, especially the United States, than they did before reform and democratization.

To be successful, democracy in Africa will also require more support from within the community of African nations. Although the Organization of African Unity has increasingly committed its member nations to human rights and democracy in recent years, it has barely ventured beyond rhetoric. Two efforts in 1994 were auspicious. In August the presidents of South Africa, Zimbabwe, and Botswana successfully pressured the monarch of Lesotho to reverse his decision to disband the parliament. And in October the leaders of the former Front-Line states in the anti-apartheid struggle, joined by those of South Africa, Lesotho, Swaziland, and Malawi, met with the leaders of the two major competing parties in Mozambique on the eve of its United Nations–supervised elections. These outsiders obtained the parties' pledges to respect the results—thus enhancing mutual trust and helping to pave the way for a peaceful electoral transition.

Even in the face of a hopeful "second beginning," the future of democracy in Africa faces troubling questions. How long can the new democracies (and quasi-democracies) of Africa survive without renewing economic development and improving their peoples' material lives? How long will elected governments in Africa stick with painful economic reforms if those reforms fail to rekindle economic growth? In the face of so much economic scarcity and uncertainty, what ruling elite will summon the courage and self-discipline to institute the hard measures necessary to ensure public accountability? Will South Africa find the political stability and economic dynamism to become the democratic model and developmental engine that many Africans have been looking for on the continent? Will the Western democracies realize that the cost of investing in democracy and economic reform in Africa is far cheaper than the likely alternative of responding to an endless stream of humanitarian emergencies, civil wars, and collapsed states?

Increasingly, Africans recognize that democracy is not a luxury or a mere ideal but a necessity for development, justice, and conflict management in their countries.

See also *Africa, Horn of; Africa, Lusophone; African independence movements; Botswana; Democratic Republic of the Congo; Ghana; Kenya; Namibia; Nigeria; Senegal; South Africa; Sudan; Uganda; Zambia; Zimbabwe.*

BIBLIOGRAPHY

Ake, Claude. "Rethinking African Democracy." *Journal of Democracy* 2 (January 1991): 32–44.

Diamond, Larry. "Promoting Democracy in Africa." In *Africa in World Politics,* edited by John W. Harbeson and Donald Rothchild. 2d ed. Boulder, Colo.: Westview Press, 1995.

Diamond, Larry, Juan J. Linz, and Seymour Martin Lipset, eds. *Democracy in Developing Countries: Africa.* Boulder, Colo.: Lynne Rienner; London: Adamantine Press, 1988.

Harbeson, John W., Donald Rothchild, and Naomi Chazan, eds. *Civil Society and the State in Africa.* Boulder, Colo.: Lynne Rienner, 1994.

Hyden, Goran, and Michael Bratton, eds. *Governance and Politics in Africa.* Boulder, Colo.: Lynne Rienner, 1992.

Joseph, Richard. "Africa: The Rebirth of Political Freedom." *Journal of Democracy* 2 (October 1991): 11–24.

Luckham, Robin. "The Military, Militarization and Democratization in Africa: A Survey of Literature and Issues." *African Studies Review* 37 (September 1994): 13–75.

Nyong'o, Peter Anyang'. "Africa: The Failure of One-Party Rule." *Journal of Democracy* 3 (January 1992): 90–96.

Oyugi, Walter O., E. D. Atieno Odhiambo, Michael Chege, and Afrika K. Gitonga, eds. *Democratic Theory and Practice in Africa.* Portsmouth, N.H.: Heinemann; London: James Currey, 1988.

Robinson, Pearl T. "The National Conference Phenomenon in Francophone Africa." *Comparative Studies in Society and History* 36 (July 1994): 575–610.

Rothchild, Donald, and Naomi Chazan, eds. *The Precarious Balance: State and Society in Africa.* Boulder, Colo.: Westview Press, 1988.

Sklar, Richard L. "Democracy in Africa." *African Studies Review* 26 (September–December 1983): 11–24.

———. "Developmental Democracy." *Comparative Studies in Society and History* 29 (October 1987): 686–714.

———. "The Nature of Class Domination in Africa." *Journal of Modern African Studies* 17 (1979): 531–552.

Tordoff, William. *Government and Politics in Africa.* 2d ed. London: Macmillan; Bloomington: Indiana University Press, 1993.

Widner, Jennifer A., ed. *Economic Change and Political Liberalization in Sub-Saharan Africa.* Baltimore: Johns Hopkins University Press, 1994.

Wiseman, John A., *Democracy in Black Africa: Survival and Revival.* New York: Paragon House, 1990.

African independence movements

African independence movements were the democratic responses to European rule and decolonization in Africa. Nationalism in colonial Africa signified redemption from servitude enforced by means of racial oppression and alien rule. Accordingly, racial emancipation and national self-determination were core values for the African nationalist intelligentsia.

The related value of political freedom emerged from more complex intellectual origins. During the colonial era, African thinkers freely subscribed to the progressive ideals of Western liberalism and socialism. Many of them opted for principled cooperation with the colonial powers. For example, Edward Wilmot Blyden (1832–1912), a renowned father of African nationalism, expressly welcomed the advent of colonial rule. A patriotic citizen of the independent Republic of Liberia, Blyden supported, in word and deed, African cooperation with European colonial administrations if they demonstrated respect for African cultural values and provided opportunities for the advancement of African interests. Similar attitudes motivated pioneer nationalists everywhere in Africa. Hence both cooperation with colonial governments and resistance to colonial rule left their imprint on African democratic thought.

Although African nationalist thought incorporates precolonial precepts, its principles were formulated mainly in response to the partition and occupation of Africa by Europeans. Taking into account all forms of European rule in colonial Africa, one can distinguish three basic patterns of power: autochthony, diffusion, and despotism. Autochthonous forms of colonial rule relied on the adaptation of indigenous African political institutions. Rule by diffusion transferred European institutions to the colony. Despotic rulers did not recognize subordinate African authorities and acknowledged little, if any, legal restraint on their exercise of power over Africans. In practice, these three forms were mixed, but one type of rule was always predominant. Furthermore, each type regularly produced its characteristic nationalist response.

Democratic Responses to Colonial Rule

In colonial Africa the principle of autochthony underpinned a widely practiced policy known as "indirect rule," the exercise of political power through the medium of indigenous authorities. Indirect rule was the method of choice in British colonies, particularly those where the white settler element was relatively small and insignificant. In such countries African democrats confronted two kinds of rulers who were not accountable to their subjects: colonial officials and African "chiefs," who were recognized as traditional rulers by the colonial governments. For example, in the theocratic Muslim emirates of northern Nigeria, radical democrats attacked the biracial alliance between ruling African dynasties and their British imperial overlords.

The method of diffusion, or re-creating European institutions in African societies, was pursued more systematically in the French colonies than elsewhere. African democrats challenged the architects of the French Fourth Republic (1946–1958) to honor their promise of emancipation to the people of France overseas. In 1946 the interterritorial, federated African Democratic Rally of French West Africa called for equal social and political rights within a freely accepted union of the peoples of Africa and the people of France. Not until 1957, by which time France had set arbitrary and inequitable limits to African representation in the metropolitan National Assembly, did the African Democratic Rally proclaim the goal of independence as an inalienable right.

Far removed from the dialogue on African rights in most of British and French colonial Africa were the despotic systems of rule in the Belgian, Portuguese, and Spanish colonies, as well as in the white settler states of Kenya, Rhodesia, and South Africa. In these places a latent tendency toward messianic or revolutionary violence was never far beneath the surface of manifestly dependent behavior. In the Belgian Congo a rigidly paternalistic regime granted few political rights or opportunities for postprimary education to Africans. Consequently, national leaders were ill prepared to cope with independence when it was granted precipitously by a demoralized Belgian government in 1960. Congolese nationalists were also deeply divided among themselves. One faction favored a unitary state; its opponents preferred a federal union with a high degree of regional autonomy. These rivals united for a bold experiment in democracy that was aborted, tragically, by an army mutiny only four days after independence.

In the European settler states of British East and Central Africa, and in Portuguese Africa, nationalists of the post–World War II era spurned reformist substitutes for the goal of sovereign independence based on majority rule. For example, in 1953 the Federation of Rhodesia and Nyasaland was created by British settlers who proposed to maintain a relatively liberal form of white minority rule compared with apartheid in South Africa and the authoritarian Portuguese regimes in Angola and Mozambique. The federation was bitterly opposed by African nationalists in Northern Rhodesia and Nyasaland. They perceived it to be an attempt to perpetuate white rule by extending the range of white power in Southern Rhodesia to the northern protectorates, where the white settler communities were smaller and still subject to salutary supervision by the British imperial government. In Southern Rhodesia, Africans were more inclined to believe that an interterritorial federation based on multiracial principles might actu-

ally mitigate the severity of racial repression in their own country. The federation, however, eventually was destroyed by resolutely antifederal African nationalism in the northern protectorates.

In 1962 African nationalists in Southern Rhodesia faced a difficult choice. Relatively moderate whites sought their support for a new constitution that offered some African representation in the parliament in return for a promise by white leaders to reduce, and gradually eliminate, white supremacy. But no mainstream African nationalist movement of the post–World War II era had ever accepted a constitution designed to perpetuate African political subordination. Following a debate on the merits of incremental reform, the Rhodesian (now Zimbabwean) nationalists rejected the white moderates' proposed constitution. As a result, the white electorate lost confidence in the ability of moderate leaders to resolve racial questions and entrusted its fate to a party of extreme racialists who favored a Rhodesian variation of the South African system of apartheid. The Africans then resolved to win their freedom and independence by means of armed struggle, which culminated in the replacement of Rhodesia by Zimbabwe in 1980.

The Pan-African Movement

The question of armed struggle, as an alternative to nonviolent methods of agitation for racial equality and national self-determination, was debated by delegates to the All-African People's Conference of December 1958. Prime Minister Kwame Nkrumah of Ghana convened the conference in fulfillment of a commitment made by leaders of the pan-African movement in 1945 to hold their next general meeting in a liberated country on African soil. Representing nongovernmental organizations from all parts of Africa, including liberation movements, political parties, trade unions, and women's groups, the conferees shared their hopes, fears, and proposals to liberate and democratize African societies.

The merits of nonviolent political action were strongly defended by Tom Mboya, conference chairman and general secretary of the Kenya Federation of Labor, and by Jordan Ngubane, delegation leader of the South African Liberal Party. Algerian delegates, reflecting the circumstance of guerrilla warfare against French rule in their country, were foremost among proponents of armed struggle. At length, a compromise resolution pledged support to all fighters for freedom in Africa—those using peaceful means of nonviolence and civil disobedience as well as those compelled to retaliate against violence. This measured endorsement of liberating violence in response to repressive violence was widely understood to express a preference for nonviolent political strategies, reserving violence as a method of last resort.

Scarcely two months earlier, in September 1958, Julius Nyerere, leader of the Tanganyikan African nationalist movement, had invited delegates from seven countries to a conference at Mwanza, Tanganyika. This conference inaugurated the Pan-African Freedom Movement of East and Central Africa (PAFMECA). Its constitution contained a declaration of intent to champion nonviolence in nationalist struggles. Eventually, in 1962, membership in this organization was offered to the freedom movements of southern Africa, entailing a name change to Pan-African Freedom Movement of Eastern, Central, and Southern Africa (PAFMECSA). In 1963 Nelson Mandela, leader of the underground military wing of the African National Congress of South Africa, addressed a PAFMECSA conference in Addis Ababa, Ethiopia. He explained that, regrettably, violence in his country could not be avoided. PAFMECSA then repealed its constitutional commitment to nonviolence.

At its inaugural (1958) conference, PAFMECA had adopted a freedom charter that pledged to oppose white racialism and black chauvinism and to uphold the Universal Declaration of Human Rights. Comparable resolutions relating to the protection of individual rights and minority racial rights, however, had divisive effects at the subsequent inaugural meeting of the All-African People's Conference. Three delegations—the Action Group of Nigeria (one of three leading parties in that country), the United Party (an opposition party) of Ghana, and the ruling party of Liberia—sponsored a resolution calling on African states to give legislative effect to the Universal Declaration of Human Rights. This proposal was rejected.

Soon thereafter the United Party succumbed to Nkrumah's intolerance of opposition. Paradoxically, the Action Group, under pressure to restrict its activities in Nigeria after independence, obtained paramilitary assistance in 1960 from Nkrumah. Given its notorious record of repression at home, Liberia's gesture of support for political rights was dubious. Concerning racial minority rights (particularly the rights of Europeans and Indians in African countries), there were memorable statements by delegates from Kenya and South Africa. Ezekiel Mphalele, chief delegate of the African National Congress of South Africa, declared that an African was a person of any color who was born in Africa and considered it home. Although the conference resolutions skirted the question of African identity, they did condemn racial discrimination as such and called for the formation of a committee to examine alleged abuses of human rights anywhere in Africa.

These early debates about universal standards of human rights, minority racial rights, and armed struggle for freedom culminated with the establishment of the Organization of African Unity at Addis Ababa in 1963. The charter and related resolutions, adopted by that summit conference of independent African states, followed the example of PAFMECSA by both endorsing the Universal Declaration of Human Rights and establishing a permanent committee to coordinate all forms of assistance to national liberation movements.

Democracy and the Party System

At midcentury there were only four independent countries in Africa—Ethiopia, Liberia, Egypt, and South Africa (in order of their attainment of sovereignty in modern times). During the 1950s six more African states became independent—Libya, Sudan, Morocco, Tunisia, Ghana, and Guinea. In the watershed year 1960 no fewer than seventeen African states attained independence. Fifteen more followed between 1961 and 1970. With few exceptions—notably Algeria and the former Belgian colonies—decolonization involved the creation of democratic political institutions for these newly independent states. In all but a few cases, the postcolonial democracies perished during the first decade of national independence. The causes of democratic decline in postcolonial Africa are complex and variable, but one cause is clearly attributable to the impact of revolutionary ideology on the anticolonial freedom movement.

During the late 1950s and the 1960s many intellectuals in Africa, as elsewhere, became convinced that some form of political dictatorship would be required to facilitate rapid economic development and social reconstruction. Although this viewpoint was expressed more frequently, clearly, and precisely after independence than before, antidemocratic tendencies were evident in the pre-independence thought and practice of various leaders, particularly those who fostered the creation of personality cults and the organization of political parties designed to dominate the state. Eventually some of those leaders embraced Leninist and Maoist concepts of party organization and rule, although no African party in power ever tried to restrict its membership as rigorously as was required by the tenets of orthodox Leninism. The Marxist-Leninist leaders of Angola, Mozambique, and Rhodesia during the 1970s, however, did emulate the doctrinaire political thought of Nkrumah in his later years.

The effect of communitarian socialist thought on democracy in Africa is more difficult to assess. Many African socialists were inclined to believe that traditional communalism had minimized divisive class conflicts. Hence, they concluded, socialist societies could be consolidated in Africa without class struggles by returning, ideologically, "to the source," that is, to Africa's own cultural tradition. Such revolutionary thinkers as Nkrumah and Ahmed Sékou Touré (who defied Charles de Gaulle and persuaded the voters of Guinea to choose independence in 1958 rather than association with the French community) subscribed to that belief.

No one questions the democratic pedigree of communitarian socialism, but problems for democracy emerged when communitarians disputed the desirability of more than one political party once the "correct" political party had taken over. In Africa, communitarian socialists frequently resorted to the Marxist idea that political parties represent the conflicting interests of social classes. Absent class conflict, they argued, a genuine people's party would be morally legitimate, while other parties would be dysfunctional at best, agents of imperialism at worst. When populist myths of political unity and social harmony no longer sufficed, communitarian socialists shifted easily to other justifications of one-party rule: the inexorable growth of class conflict in Africa, solidarity against capitalist imperialism, the threat of ethnic political separatism.

Renowned for his intellectual integrity and consistency, Julius Nyerere is Africa's preeminent communitarian socialist. Unlike contemporaries who forgot their communitarian roots and lost touch with the people, Nyerere, as president of Tanzania, remained faithful to his nationalist ideals. He advocated a one-party state on the ground that it would actually enhance freedom of choice and democratic participation because one national party would be universally identified with general interests rather than sectional or class interests. He also continued to apply egalitarian standards of judgment in criticizing the oligarchic tendencies besetting his one-party government. Yet the basic contradiction between his egalitarian precepts and the enforcement of a one-party state by high officials would never be resolved in his theory or practice of government.

The multiparty persuasion in African nationalist thought was silenced unceremoniously by advocates of one-party rule in most of the newly independent African states. A few nationalist leaders, however, were able to create durable multiparty systems at the dawn of independence. They include Seretse Khama in Botswana, Dawda K. Jawara in Gambia, Seewoosagur Ramgoolam in Mauritius, and the Nigerian democratic nationalists, principally Obafemi Awolowo and Nnamdi Azikiwe.

Awolowo believed that cultural-linguistic groups were entitled to self-determination within multicultural federations. In addition to reasonable autonomy as compared with other groups, they should have the right to restore positive elements of traditional government that had been suppressed or distorted by colonial rulers. In societies that were constitutional as well as monarchical before colonial rule (for example, Awolowo's own Yoruba people), federal systems of government would protect regional reformers who wished to restore the constitutional balance between kings, chiefs, and people. Thus did Awolowo's party, the Action Group, turn the colonial principle of autochthony into a rampart of constitutional democracy. Largely because of its efforts, the federal principle was firmly established as the essential bedrock of Nigerian national unity. In practice, however, Awolowo and his followers compromised this ideal of cultural federalism by supporting the creation of large, multicultural constituent regions (subsequently states) of the Nigerian federation.

Meanwhile, during the final decade of colonial rule in Francophone Africa, the diffusionist vision of African emancipation within a unitary French empire was discarded by nationalists in favor of political autonomy. Léopold Sédar Senghor, poet, philosopher, and Senegalese statesman, cherished the idea of a Franco-African federation. At the very least, he hoped to preserve the multiterritorial federation of French West Africa as a sovereign, postcolonial entity. But federalism in Francophone West Africa succumbed to the balkanizing drive for territorial separatism, fostered principally by Senghor's rival, Félix Houphouët-Boigny, of the Côte d'Ivoire. Had Senghor's federal concept prevailed, the defense of democratic principles in Francophone Africa might have fared at least as well as it has in federal Nigeria, despite the travails there of persistent political instability.

Democratic Response to Decolonization

The concept of decolonization has provoked controversy because it implies the primacy of European rather than African initiatives in the movement for colonial freedom. In reality, complex patterns of shared agency were unmistakable: Britain and France employed various democratic measures, consistent with African nationalist values, to protect their interests and control the pace of political change.

Among British colonial thinkers, there was broad agreement on the desirability of three distinct phases of transition from the empire to a commonwealth of independent nations. These were identified as good government, responsible government, and self-government, in that order. Good government implied effective administration by local officials who had accepted full responsibility for development. Responsible government meant that high officials had become accountable for their actions to a territorial parliament, consisting of elected representatives of the people. Self-government signified the transfer of state power to indigenous officeholders. The architects of decolonization were deeply convinced that a premature transfer of power to politicians and administrators who did not believe in good government would be disastrous: responsible government could not then be maintained, and self-government would soon degenerate into bad government.

Nationalist thinkers, in British and French colonies alike, reversed the order of sequence. They were inclined to put self-government, based on democratic representation, first. They expected that responsible governments would then be chosen freely, resulting in good government for the independent countries. Hence they made every effort to mobilize the people to demand immediate democratic representation. By 1955 their demands had become virtually irresistible in British West Africa; by 1958 independence was on the agenda in most of Francophone Africa. Eventually, the democratic revolution prevailed against paternalistic caution and reluctance everywhere.

As a colonial creed, "good government" captured few hearts among passionate nationalists in Africa. Moreover, the leaders of independence movements readily identified public finance as a resource that could be used to fund their political machines as well as their ambitious programs for national development. Thirty years later a more cautious generation of African intellectuals, having experienced the failures of economic statism and the damage caused by rulers who were scarcely accountable to anyone for their performance in office, has revived the colonial idea of good government. Now it is widely espoused as the principle of "governance," which is understood to mean public accountability for officials, honesty in fiscal management, and respect for the rule of law.

To be sure, the African independence movements made their own crucial contributions to the ideal of good government. Nationalists, in general, assigned the highest priority to educational opportunity in their plans for a renascent Africa. In the eyes of most of the early beneficiaries of that commitment, the nationalist political leaders were authentic heroes; but the role models for upwardly mobile graduates were their professional predecessors who pioneered pathways to success in the public services, legal systems, and comparable institutions of modern society. A few of these pioneers are widely renowned; for example, Simeon Adebo, the quintessential Nigerian civil servant whose distinguished career was capped by an appointment as assistant secretary general at the UN Institute for Training and Research, and William Ndala Wamalwa, a Kenyan civil servant who is esteemed for his many contributions to public administration in Africa and who has been elected to successive terms as president of the African Association of Public Administration and Management. Thousands of their kind, bred for public service during the advance to independence, are unsung heroes of the movement for democracy and good government.

See also *Theory, African.* In Reference Materials section, see *African National Congress Freedom Charter (1955); African Charter on Human and Peoples' Rights (1981).*

BIBLIOGRAPHY

Awolowo, Obafemi. *Path to Nigerian Freedom.* London: Faber, 1947.

Cox, Richard. *Pan-Africanism in Practice.* London: Oxford University Press, 1964.

Hodgkin, Thomas. *Nationalism in Colonial Africa.* London: Frederick Muller, 1956.

July, Robert W. *The Origins of Modern African Thought.* New York: Praeger, 1967.

Lee, J. M. *Colonial Development and Good Government.* Oxford: Clarendon Press, 1967.

Legum, Colin. *Pan-Africanism: A Short Political Guide.* Rev. ed. New York: Praeger, 1965.

Morgenthau, Ruth Schachter. *Political Parties in French-Speaking West Africa.* Oxford: Clarendon Press, 1964.

Munger, Edwin S. "All-African People's Conference." American Universities Field Staff Reports, Africa, 1959.

Nyerere, Julius K. *Freedom and Unity.* Dar es Salaam: Oxford University Press, 1966.

Sklar, Richard L. "The Colonial Imprint on African Political Thought." In *African Independence,* edited by Gwendolen M. Carter and Patrick O'Meara. Bloomington: Indiana University Press, 1985.

Algeria

A predominantly Islamic republic situated in northwest Africa and bordered on the west by Morocco, on the south by Mauritania, Mali, and Niger, and on the east by Libya and Tunisia. The Algerian military intervened on January 11, 1992, to stop a runoff legislative election when early returns indicated that the Islamic Salvation Front (Front Islamique du Salut, or FIS), a diverse group of Islamic fundamentalists, would win the national election.

The coup interrupted a political reform process that had begun in the late 1980s and reforms that had promised to transform Algeria from a socialist, one-party state into a multiparty democracy. Military leaders who participated in the 1992 palace coup pressured Chadli Benjedid, who was then president, to dissolve the National People's Assembly and step down as president. After the coup the struggle with Islamic militants intensified. By the end of 1993 nearly 2,000 Algerians had been killed; by 1994 the number had risen to more than 4,000 Algerians and nearly 60 foreigners. The death toll increased dramatically during 1994, as militants increasingly targeted civilians, including foreigners. Although official figures stated that 6,388 civilians died from political violence in 1994, many unofficial observers estimated that the total number killed by the end of 1994 was 30,000. By 1995 many feared that the country was sliding toward an all-out civil war. The key question was whether Algeria would be able to restore peace and develop a governmental system able to blend Islamic fundamentalism and democracy.

The political crisis engulfing Algeria as it approaches the twenty-first century reflects longstanding tensions between the influences of Islamic culture (which began to dominate in the seventh century) and Western culture (which arrived in the thirteenth century), the loss of legitimacy of the postindependence political system, and the growing economic problems heightened by a marked drop in oil and natural gas revenues, which account for most foreign revenue.

Early Cultural Tensions

Throughout history a succession of outsiders challenged the political status of the Berbers, the earliest inhabitants and the largest ethnic group in the region today. The northern portions of Algeria, known as Numidia, were ruled as Berber kingdoms until the second century B.C., when the area became a Roman province. Rome again

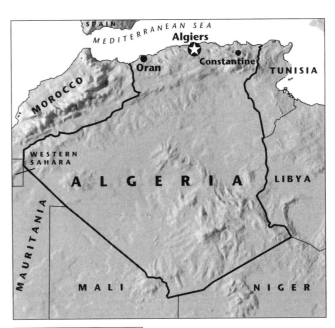

ruled the region after a brief reign by the Vandals, a Germanic tribe who crossed from Spain in A.D. 429, but during this early period much of the interior remained independent and was organized into a loose confederation of tribes.

Arab raids during the seventh century culminated in the incorporation of the region into the great medieval Moorish empires that eventually extended across North Africa to Spain. Most Berbers converted to Islam while continuing to resist Arab political rule. Throughout the next three hundred years the area experienced conflicts among various Arab dynasties and Berber tribal lines. The Berber tribes of the Almoravids, from Morocco, restored order in the twelfth century. The Almohads, who succeeded the Almoravids, unified the entire North African area and ruled this region and Muslim Spain as a unified and highly prosperous entity. But the region had become politically unstable and was in a period of decline by the mid-thirteenth century.

The rise of the Christian kingdoms in Spain led to a series of Spanish crusades against Muslim power in North Africa at the end of the fifteenth century. Spain met little local resistance and gained control of a number of enclaves. In the early sixteenth century the capital city of Algiers and several other towns were formally placed under the protection of the Ottoman sultan. Portions of the country were ruled as a nominal province of the Ottoman Empire for three hundred years, but effective political power remained in the hands of local rulers.

In coastal areas, local rulers (deys) retained power as long as they sent tribute to the Ottoman sultan, were able to satisfy the demands of local merchants and military forces, and permitted the pirate trade to flourish. European maritime countries, and the United States after independence, routinely paid local deys huge sums to protect national vessels from pirates. The United States ceased payments only in the early nineteenth century after a U.S. naval force and a combined English and Dutch naval force forced the dey of Algiers to end piracy off the coast of North Africa.

France, which had replaced Spain as the principal Western power in the region by the eighteenth century, sent military expeditions to Algeria in 1827 and in 1830 and formally annexed the territory in 1834. But France confronted fierce local opposition, the most formidable organized by Abd al-Kadir, who claimed to be a direct descendant of the prophet Muhammad. Abd al-Kadir unified the Berbers and Arabs against the French in a war that lasted from 1839 until 1847. But even after his defeat, sporadic rebellions against French rule continued. Much of this opposition was organized by the *moudjahidines,* early Islamic religious militants, who fought the French during a period when nationalism was defined largely by Muslim heritage and religious leaders.

France countered local opposition by encouraging large-scale European emigration to Algeria and by confiscating large tracts of land from rebellious Muslims. By the twentieth century European settlers dominated economic and political life. Modern nationalism surfaced among Algerian Muslims after World War I, but France refused to compromise until after World War II, when a new constitution promising French citizenship was formulated. But the 1947 constitution was never fully implemented. Instead, the nationalistic National Liberation Front (Front de Libération Nationale, FLN) led an open revolt against the French in 1954. As a result, one million Algerians died and more than two million were interned in camps before France granted independence in 1962.

Postindependence Problems

After independence, the Republic of Algeria operated as a secular state controlled by the army and secular factions of the FLN. A civilian government led by a hero of the war for independence, Ahmed Ben Bella, was established in 1963, and the FLN became the sole political party. Ben Bel-

la consolidated power by suppressing political opponents and assuming the positions of secretary general of the party, head of state and government, and commander in chief of the armed forces. A split in leadership and a near collapse of the economy, however, presented serious problems for the new FLN-led state. An emergency austerity plan carried out in the name of Algerian socialism failed to lessen concerns about the economy or about Ben Bella's dictatorial tendencies.

In 1965 a bloodless military coup led by the minister of defense, Col. Houari Boumedienne (another hero of the war for independence), deposed Ben Bella, and the National Council of the Algerian Revolution became the supreme political authority, presiding over a major reorientation of the country's international and domestic policies. In 1967 Algeria joined other Arab states in declaring war against Israel. Diplomatic ties between Algeria and the United States suffered as Algeria established closer political and military ties with the Soviet Union and the Eastern bloc countries, while maintaining an active role as a leader of the nonaligned movement. Domestic policies also were reoriented to stimulate rapid economic growth, based on industrialization and funded by oil and natural gas exports. A new class of technocrats ran nationalized industries and government agencies.

In 1976 Boumedienne, who had called for major reforms in Algerian society, was elected president. A new constitution, drafted the same year and approved by referendum, reaffirmed Algeria's commitment to socialism under FLN guidance and recognized Islam as the state religion. The national legislature consisted of members selected by the FLN.

When Boumedienne died suddenly in 1978, the military supervised the political transition by decreeing that the National Council of the Algerian Revolution, which had no official status in the 1976 constitution, would maintain continuity. Col. Chadli Benjedid, a compromise candidate of the military, technical, and party cadres, was selected as leader of the council. In 1979 Benjedid was elected president in a national referendum.

Growing Political and Economic Problems

The army remained Benjedid's main supporter throughout his tenure. But he acknowledged the country's serious problems: dependence on hydrocarbons, reduced agricultural output, shortages of food and consumer goods, bureaucratic corruption, and extreme inequality in the distribution of wealth and growing unemployment, especially among the 70 percent of the population under thirty. A new national charter, adopted by the FLN in 1985, encouraged private enterprise and proposed a balance between socialism and Islam as the state ideology.

Despite these steps, the declining price of oil, government-imposed austerity programs in the face of widespread corruption, and growing foreign debts led to political unrest, increased support for Islamic fundamentalists, and a surge in migration to France. Widespread riots in 1988 in response to rising bread prices indicated the extent of discontent with the political status quo.

In the aftermath of the riots the FLN's thirty years of one-party rule came to an end. Beginning in July 1989 the government sponsored a series of constitutional amendments and laws that represented a break with the past. Among other things, Benjedid ended the identification of the state with the FLN, relinquished his post as secretary general of the party, and supported a move to make the prime minister responsible to the National People's Assembly. In a referendum more than 73 percent of the voters supported the proposals. Benjedid was reelected president for a third term, and the National People's Assembly passed a bill permitting opposition political parties to contest future elections.

In the 1990 elections the Islamic Salvation Front, an amalgam of several groups ranging from political moderates willing to work within the existing framework to militants calling for a holy war, gained control of about 80 percent of the country's municipal and departmental councils by winning almost 65 percent of the votes cast. The FIS victory, in the first competitive elections held since 1962, underscored just how out of touch the ruling elite had become.

In 1991 national elections were postponed after an FLN effort at gerrymandering triggered large-scale protests. The military intervened by arresting the top leaders of the FIS. In September 1991 the state of siege was lifted, and the Islamic Salvation Front again functioned as a political party. In December 1991 the FIS won the first round of voting for a new National People's Assembly. Candidates representing nearly fifty political parties, including the first green party in the Arab world, participated. The FIS won the majority of the ballots cast (but won the votes of only 25 percent of all registered voters, due to low voter turnout), and its victory in the second round of elections was virtually assured. The military then pressured Benjedid to suspend the National People's Assembly and resign as president.

After the coup, Muhammad Boudiaf, a veteran politician and leader during the war for independence, was brought back from self-imposed exile to serve as the figurehead of a newly formed High State Council, which was to act as an interim government. The council curtailed a nascent free press, abolished the FIS as a political party, suspended all local assemblies, and removed local FIS elected officials. A state security system detained FIS leaders and sent thousands of sympathizers to Sahara detention camps.

Promises of jobs, housing, and food subsidies failed to stem Islamic fundamentalism. So too did a campaign against violence, a crackdown on corruption, and efforts by Boudiaf to encourage talks among all parties about an alternative to an Islamic republic or a militarized secular state. Boudiaf was assassinated in June 1992 by a member of his own security guard. The murder, as well as the government's claim that the assassin was an FIS sympathizer, increased polarization.

The military appointed a series of individuals to the figurehead position of head of state after Boudiaf's assassination. Ali Kafi, a lesser known independence war veteran who was named head of state in mid-1992, resigned by 1993. Former prime minister Redha Malek, who was appointed president at the end of 1993 after the High State Council dissolved itself, was replaced as president by retired major general Liamine Zeroual in January 1994. Zeroual, who retained his post as minister of national defense, presided over national talks with five of the eight recognized political parties about proposed reforms but refused to negotiate with the FIS.

The talks came to nothing, and the military-backed regime proceeded to implement its own program. In May, five months after Zeroual was appointed, a new, appointive National Transitional Council was established to act as an interim legislature pending adoption of a new constitution. Meanwhile, the level of violence practiced by both the government and militant Islamic groups escalated dramatically. By mid–1995 the death toll since 1992 may have reached as high as 50,000.

The regime's next step toward a return to responsible government was the presidential election of November 16, 1995. The FIS remained banned from participation, and most opposition parties called for a boycott. To the contrary, however, heavy voter turnout undercut the FIS contention that it, not the regime, commanded majority support among the people. Zeroual was elected president with 61 percent of the vote.

Buoyed by the presidential outcome, the regime put to referendum on November 28, 1996, constitutional amendments that banned political parties founded on a religious basis. The FIS and other fundamentalist parties would remain illegal indefinitely. The regime proclaimed the referendum to have passed and set elections to the new, 380-member National People's Assembly for June 1997.

The June elections gave the progovernment National Democratic Rally 156 seats and the National Liberation Front 62; seven other parties also won seats, including the Islamic-oriented Movement for a Peaceful Society, with 69 seats. But the return to nominal constitutional government and multiparty politics has done nothing to resolve the fundamental polarization between the secular and Islamic visions of Algerian society. To the contrary, the violence escalated further in the latter half of 1997.

Future Outlook

In the future, higher oil and gas revenues and a lowering of the national debt may improve the economy and reduce the fervor of many Algerians for a political change that would transform the country into an Islamic state. So far, however, increased repression and efforts toward a national dialogue between the government and selected political parties and individuals have only contributed to instability. Several radical militant Islamic groups continue to operate underground, independent of FIS. They are financed by Algerian shopkeepers and farmers as well as—according to government allegations—by Iran. Terrorist acts continue despite expanded security crackdowns.

BIBLIOGRAPHY

"Algeria." In *The Middle East and North Africa 1993*. 39th ed. London: Europa Publications, 1993.

Entelis, John P. *Algeria: The Revolution Institutionalized*. Boulder, Colo.: Westview Press, 1986.

———, and Phillip C. Naylor, eds. *State and Society in Algeria*. Boulder, Colo.: Westview Press, 1992.

Zartman, I. William, and William Mark Habeeb, eds. *Polity and Society in Contemporary North Africa*. Boulder, Colo.: Westview Press, 1993.

Armenia

A republic in the Transcaucasian region, formerly part of the Soviet Union. Armenia is a small, densely populated country, about the size of Belgium, with 3.7 million people (a figure that does not take into account the large emigration from the country in recent years). Mountainous, poor in natural resources, and landlocked, Armenia is bordered by Georgia, Azerbaijan, Iran, and Turkey.

During the Soviet period, Armenia's trade-dependent economy was based on light industry, agriculture, food processing, machine building, and metalworking. A well-educated, Western-oriented Christian people in a largely Muslim region, Armenians now look toward Europe and America for models by which to structure their fledgling democracy.

Historical Background

Armenians first appeared as a distinct ethnic entity about 600 B.C. in Anatolia. Adoption of Christianity as the state religion at the beginning of the fourth century A.D. and the creation of an Armenian alphabet a century later under church sponsorship played major roles in establishing and preserving a distinctive ethnic identity. Early Armenia consisted of feuding dynastic principalities under a succession of Roman, Byzantine, and Ottoman empires in the West and Iranian empires in the East. Beginning in the eleventh century, Turkic and Mongol invasions stimulated extensive Armenian migration throughout Europe, Russia, and the Middle East, creating a far-flung diaspora.

In the Ottoman Empire, Armenians were ruled as an ethnoreligious community through their religious leaders. In the eighteenth and nineteenth centuries a nationalist awakening began in the Armenian diaspora, traditionally a conduit for European Renaissance and Enlightenment learning. In Constantinople the new middle class of Armenian doctors, lawyers, writers, teachers, and small manufacturers challenged the elite control of church leaders, forcing them to adopt democratic reforms.

For Armenians, as for other ethnic communities living in multiethnic empires or states, issues of democratization (self-rule) have always been tied up with nationalism (freedom from domination by different and more powerful ethnic groups). The second half of the nineteenth century saw the founding of several parties that combined a program of enlightenment and democratization with nationalism. The parties articulated a program of autonomy, even independence, for Armenians in the Ottoman Empire, the majority of whom lived in eastern Anatolia as an impoverished, semiliterate peasantry subject to persecution and government-organized massacres.

The nationalist movement ended during World War I, however, when the Ottoman authorities organized the destruction of the Armenian community because of its perceived pro-Russian sympathies and desire for independence. Between 1915 and 1917, an estimated 1 million Armenians were executed outright or died during forced marches across the Anatolian interior. Survivors poured across the border into Russia, into neighboring Middle Eastern countries, and eventually to Europe and the Americas. Today Armenians living outside Armenia (approximately 7 million) outnumber residents of the republic two to one.

As a prosperous commercial bourgeoisie, Armenians in the Russian empire had consistently fared better than those under Ottoman rule. After the genocide, hundreds of thousands of Armenian refugees entered Russian Armenia (annexed from Persia in the first decades of the nineteenth century). After the collapse of czarist power and the retreat of Russian forces in 1918, Armenians founded an independent republic and attempted to construct a functioning democratic government while coping with Turkish Armenian refugees, famine, and epidemics. In 1920, again threatened by Turkish forces, the defeated and discouraged Armenian government signed away its powers to the Bolsheviks.

As a result of the genocide, most Armenians accepted Soviet rule as the price of protection against Turkey. The small dissident movement in the 1960s, which called for independence from the Soviet Union, received little attention or support from the Armenian population. During the Soviet period, Armenians channeled political and economic grievances into protests about suppression of ethnic and cultural rights. It was only in 1991, with the dissolution of the Soviet Union imminent, that Armenians voted for independence in a national referendum.

Path to Independence

Since 1988 democratization of state and society in Armenia has been closely linked to a nationalist agenda. Indeed, the popular movement that launched the democratization process in 1988 developed in response to the ethnic activism of Armenians living in Nagorno-Karabakh, an autonomous region in Azerbaijan where Armenians made up about 75 percent of the population. Their demands to join Armenia mobilized the Armenian National Movement (ANM) in Armenia. The ANM's agenda rapidly broadened to address Armenia's serious ecological problems, widespread political corruption, and endemic violation of political rights.

Between 1988 and the formal achievement of national independence in 1991, the Karabakh conflict gradually escalated into violence and war between Armenians and Azerbaijanis (a conflict that was in part provoked by Com-

munist Party authorities to divert attention from demands for democratization). An Azerbaijani blockade of fuel and other vital supplies was put in place. The December 7, 1988, earthquake in northeast Armenia—which leveled cities and towns, directly killed 25,000 to 30,000 people, made 530,000 homeless, and destroyed a significant portion of Armenia's manufacturing capacity—was a further blow to this beleaguered nation.

The war, blockade, and earthquake destruction all shaped political debate and policy. In 1990 the Armenian National Movement, running on a platform of democratic reform, attention to ecological issues, privatization, and support for the unification of Nagorno-Karabakh with Armenia, emerged as the strongest political force in multiparty elections to the Armenian parliament. Despite widespread anticommunist sentiment, independence was not part of the platform.

Building a democratic polity in Armenia has involved

the daunting task of restructuring a unified party-state system in which legislative, executive, and judicial functions were combined in the Communist Party, and government functioned merely as the party's administrative arm. In August 1991 the Armenian parliament established the post of president to address the leadership struggle between the executive and legislative bodies that emerged after the Communist Party's collapse. Levon Ter-Petrossian, a leading activist in the Armenian National Movement and chairman of the parliament since 1990, was elected president in a national election. Ter-Petrossian vowed to establish a democratic state and introduce a free market economy.

Although the government initiated consultations with Western experts in constitutional law, it resisted the early implementation of a constitution. Instead, Ter-Petrossian advocated a more gradual approach, constructing a workable governmental framework through incremental legislation. A strong presidential system developed, in which the president had the power to rule through decree, declare martial law, and appoint or dismiss ministers. The parliament retained the power to impeach ministers and override presidential vetoes.

The final draft of the constitution, adopted by referendum July 5, 1995, with a 68 percent approval vote, closely mirrored the strong presidential system Ter-Petrossian and the ANM had advocated. The opposition had preferred a parliamentary form of government. In the legislative elections held simultaneously with the referendum, the ANM and several allied parties, campaigning as the Republic Bloc, won a combined 120 seats in the 190-seat body. But these elections and the presidential election of September 22, 1996, in which Ter-Petrossian was reelected, were marred by internationally observed voting irregularities. Most important, the principal opposition party, the Armenian Revolutionary Federation, was banned from participating in the legislative elections.

Constructing a Government

Formally, the Armenian government functions as a multiparty, pluralistic system. Despite the presence of more than a dozen parties and several groupings in parliament, and the relative freedom with which most opposition parties operate, political parties remain weakly developed. Rather than representing articulated interests within society, they tend to appeal to the Armenian nation as a whole in the name of a single overriding vision of state and society. Politics remains focused on individuals rather than their parties.

Although the Armenian National Movement continues to be the strongest force in government, its popular standing has fallen sharply as a result of governmental failures and the flagrant corruption of some ANM representatives. The concentration of power in the Ministry of Internal Affairs, assassinations of several public figures, attacks on opposition newspaper offices, and the 1994 trial and sentencing of a security expert, allegedly due to his links with the opposition, raised fears about eroding civil liberties. The war with Azerbaijan also slowed development of an active opposition by encouraging opposition parties to restrain criticism of government in the interest of preserving a united front.

Processes and structures for negotiating and building coalitions to pass legislation barely exist, given that the unicameral parliament is dominated by the ANM. The parties' difficulty in formulating and pursuing clearly articulated programs has also slowed the pace of legislative action. Voters increasingly view the parliament as ineffective. As a result, cynicism and alienation are widespread among the electorate.

Armenia has taken steps to provide a legal basis for protecting the political and civil liberties of its citizens. The Armenian parliament has adopted the International Covenant on Civil and Political Rights as a bill of rights. All inhabitants of Armenian territory, regardless of ethnicity, have the right to become citizens of the republic. Armenian citizens now enjoy more freedom of speech, assembly, and press than they did before 1988. Although the government controls both television and radio, hundreds of journals and newspapers (some financed by parties based abroad) exist, some highly critical of the government.

Antigovernment demonstrations organized by opposition parties have taken place, usually without overt interference or arrests, although violent clashes did take place between demonstrators and security forces over several days in Yerevan following the September 1996 presidential election. Armenia's relatively positive human rights record was tarnished in December 1994, when the government suspended activities of the Armenian Revolutionary Federation and closed down affiliated organizations and publications on the grounds that the party harbored a clandestine terrorist group engaged in racketeering, drug trafficking, and espionage. Many Armenians ascribed the ban to the government's fear of losing control of parliament. The government was slow to lift travel restrictions. Armenian citizens were unable to obtain passports or exit visas for travel outside the former Soviet Union without obtaining permission from the Ministry of Internal Affairs. By 1995, an estimated 700,000 Armenians, including businesspeople, scientists, and scholars, had left the republic in search of employment and stable living conditions.

Challenges to Armenian Democracy

Democratic governance cannot occur apart from a functioning economy. Serious shortages of energy and supplies have sharply curtailed industrial production and forced Armenians to endure successive winters virtually without gas or electricity. The government has tried to balance conflicting demands from international financial organizations and Armenian citizens regarding decentralization and privatization, but it is constrained by the need to coordinate limited resources. Shortly after independence, most collective and state farms were privatized, although absence of laws regulating conveyance of land, deeding, and titling impeded development of a land market. Housing and commercial enterprises have since been privatized as well, and privatization of industry began in 1995.

Armenia still lacks an effective banking system and a legal infrastructure to protect local and foreign investments. This lack, in combination with the energy crisis and problems of transportation, has forced many local entrepreneurs to leave for other republics or the West. In addition, traditional links between the old Communist Party apparatus and the criminal underworld have penetrated new government structures and continue to dominate the economy, hindering development of an autonomous sphere of production and commerce.

Developed democratic polities are characterized by civic engagement on the part of an informed citizenry. In Armenia, however, several factors discourage civic engagement. During the Soviet period, civil society and a public sphere of free and informed debate and discussion were drastically reduced. The network of voluntary, religious, professional, and trade organizations; businesses; neighborhood groups; and clubs that links individuals to society and society to the state is still rudimentary. Armenians' primary ties traditionally have been to the extended family; society has remained an abstraction without practical implications. Moreover, the enormous hardships created by shortages and hyperinflation have meant that most citizens are too busy trying to survive to participate actively in public life.

Perhaps the most serious obstacle to developing a stable democracy is the weakness of the state. Old Soviet state structures have been seriously weakened, but new structures are not yet functioning effectively. The population lacks confidence in a government that cannot enforce the law, stop the disastrous fall in living standards, or control endemic corruption, rising crime, and war profiteering. This distrust also represents the pervasive antistate mood and fear of parties and ideologies that are a legacy of the Soviet era.

The Armenian government has yet to institute a civil service based on a merit system of recruitment, selection, and promotion. Loyalty and connections remain more important than ability, and old ways of getting things done tend to subvert change. Moreover, when a ministry does change leadership, a complete shake-up often results, and experienced personnel have to leave.

Prospects for Democratization

The state's weakness and the ongoing conflict with Azerbaijan remain grave obstacles to democratization. The war and economic dislocation have led to continuing drops in industrial production and to dramatic emigration, providing the government with a ready excuse for failures and mistakes.

Despite its many disadvantages, Armenia nevertheless has a literate, well-educated population and a far-flung international diaspora that can provide technical assistance and contacts with other societies and states. In addition, since the 1988 deportation of 160,000 Azerbaijanis, Armenia is practically monoethnic. Its homogeneity will reduce opportunities for the kinds of manipulation of ethnic, religious, or linguistic differences for political ends that have disrupted other postcommunist states. When the war with Azerbaijan ends (an internationally observed ceasefire has been in place since late 1994) and Armenia normalizes relations with its neighbors, its citizens will be able to concentrate their energy and skills on building a civil society and functioning economy, both important prerequisites to a stable democracy.

See also *Caucasus, The.*

BIBLIOGRAPHY

Dudwick, Nora. "Armenia: The Nation Awakens." In *Nations and Politics in the Soviet Successor States,* edited by Ian Bremmer and Ray Taras. Cambridge and New York: Cambridge University Press, 1993.

Libaridian, Gerard. *Armenia at the Crossroads: Democracy and Nationhood in the Post-Soviet Era: Essays, Interviews and Speeches by the Leaders of the National Democratic Movement in Armenia.* Watertown, Mass.: Blue Crane, 1991.

———, ed. *The Karabagh File.* Watertown, Mass.: Zoryan Institute, 1988.

Rutland, Peter. "Democracy and Nationalism in Armenia." *Europe-Asia Studies* (formerly *Soviet Studies*) 46 (1994): 839–861.

Smith, Hedrick. *The New Russians.* New York: Avon Books, 1990; New ed. London: Arrow Books, 1991.

Suny, Ronald Grigor. *Looking toward Ararat: Armenia in Modern History.* Bloomington: Indiana University Press, 1993.

Walker, Christopher J. *Armenia: The Survival of a Nation.* 2d ed. New York: St. Martin's, 1990.

Asia, Central

The collective name for the nations of Turkmenistan, Uzbekistan, Tajikistan, Kyrgyzstan, and Kazakhstan, which declared independence from the Soviet Union in 1991. The region is bounded on the north by Russia, on the west by the Caspian Sea, on the east by China, and on the south by Afghanistan and Iran.

Kazakhstan is by far the largest state, with 1,049,155 square miles. Its population is estimated to be 17 million, of whom about 41 percent are Kazakh and 38 percent are Russian. Uzbekistan, with about 20 million people (of whom 70 percent are Uzbek and 10 percent are Russian), is the most populous state. It has a territory of 186,400 square miles. Turkmenistan is about the same size, but with a population of only 3.8 million (of whom 70 percent are Turkmen, 10 percent are Uzbek, and 9 percent are Russian), it is the least populous state in the region. Kyrgyzstan is much smaller in area, with 76,640 square miles, and has a population of about 4.3 million, of whom about 54 percent are Kyrgyz, 20 percent are Russian, and 13 percent are Uzbek. Tajikistan—the smallest state, with 57,250 square miles—has a population of about 5.3 million, of whom 62 percent are Tajik, 23 percent are Uzbek, and 7 percent are Russian.

Historical Background

The peoples for whom the states are named have been established in the region for centuries. But the present states result from Soviet-era administrative divisions, which were designed both to create homelands and to make the states' independent existence impossible. As a consequence, these new nations, and the region as a whole, face formidable impediments in the transition from dependency.

Central Asian peoples have been under Russian control for periods of approximately 100 years (Tajikistan, Turkmenistan, and parts of Uzbekistan) to 200 years (Kazakhstan), but they are very distinct from the Russians linguistically, culturally, and historically. All are of Sunni Muslim heritage, although they were converted to Islam at various times from the tenth to the eighteenth centuries. The Tajiks are Persian speakers, inheritors of cultures that have been in the region for millennia. The other four peoples are descendants of Turkic nomads who came to the area later; some, like the Kyrgyz, also have considerable infusions of Mongol culture.

In Soviet times (about 1920–1989) Central Asia was the most economically depressed and politically conservative area of the USSR. Most industry was administered from Moscow and staffed by Russians and other Europeans, whom the Soviet authorities imported in large numbers. These "stranded Russians" are now a significant problem in all the new Central Asian states.

Soviet policies encouraged the growth of large native administrations, which to a great extent were staffed by members of the old traditional elites. Thus large parts of traditional Central Asian society were virtually unaffected by Soviet power. As Soviet power has receded, these traditional elites have been content to part with communism but have shown no readiness to give up political power. One reason for Central Asia's political fealty to Moscow was that the region was tightly bound to Russia economically. Once the ties to Russia were severed or strained, the economies even of the areas richest in resources became depressed to the point of collapse.

The Struggle for Sovereignty

In the transition to nationhood (1989–1991), there was a groundswell of spontaneous or quasi-spontaneous mass political participation, usually stimulated by cultural issues. (The groundswell was much smaller in Central Asia than elsewhere in the Soviet Union, however.) Perhaps the two most common demands were to increase the role and status of the native languages and to rewrite the histories, so that conquest by Russian imperialists was no longer presented as a historically progressive act. Political activists, who early on began to call themselves democrats, were able to mobilize considerable support on these sorts of issues, some of which gelled into movements and political parties.

In Uzbekistan, language-rights demonstrations in 1989 spawned Birlik (Unity), which adopted a nationalist, prodemocratic platform that demanded sovereignty but stopped short of calling for secession. This group, and its women's auxiliary, participated widely in the republic's 1990 parliamentary elections. Ten of the candidates whom the Unity Party endorsed were elected, although all ten lat-

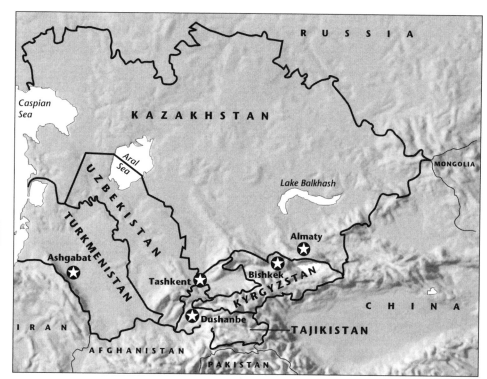

er disavowed the connection. In 1991, at the time of independence, the Unity Party claimed about 400,000 members. The other large Uzbek democratic party, Erk (Will), began when Unity cofounders Abdurakhim Pulatov and Muhammad Solikh disagreed and Solikh left to found his own pro-democratic party. Solikh ran for president in 1991. Although soundly defeated by Islam Karimov, whom Moscow had appointed as party and republic leader in 1989, Solikh and his campaign gave Uzbekistan one of only two contested presidential elections in the region.

The other contested election took place in Tajikistan, where two candidates, Davla Koudonazarov and Rakhman Nabiyev, contested the seat of Moscow appointee Khakhor Makhkamov, whom popular demonstrations had pushed from power in September 1991. The years 1989–1991 were also a period of mass political participation in Tajikistan, but the focus was regional and ethnic from the beginning. Because the republic was made up of disparate groups of peoples who had different histories, cultures, and even languages, and because it had a long history of rule by clans from one region, it was unstable well before the Soviet Union broke up. The three major parties that began to coalesce had different orientations, but they also had regional and clan underpinnings. The Democratic Party and Rastokhez (Renaissance) were secular parties, while the Islamic

Renaissance Party was more religiously oriented. Nabiyev, a political boss from the era of Leonid Brezhnev whom Mikhail Gorbachev had dismissed, put together a coalition of democrats and the religious parties to come back to power, staving off a strong showing by Koudonazarov, who had the backing of democrats in Moscow.

In Kazakhstan the first political movement was ecological rather than national. Prominent Kazakh poet Olzhas Suleimenov organized the Nevada-Semipalatinsk movement to press for the end of the testing of Soviet nuclear weapons in the republic, a practice that had been devastating to the population and the environment. That movement was multiethnic, mobilizing large numbers of Russians and Kazakhs. So far it is the only group that has been able to appeal to both nationalities. Because its population is about equally Kazakh and Russian, Kazakhstan has attempted to inhibit the growth of nationalist parties. Nevertheless, the period 1989–1991 saw the emergence of several Kazakh movements. These include Azat (Freedom), the Republican Party, the Civil Movement, and Zheltoksan (December). The most nationalist of the groups is Alash, named for the legendary founder of the Kazakh people, which also calls for a greater role for Islam. The Russians also spawned nationalist movements—Harmony, Unity, and Democratic Progress—as did the Cossacks, the descendants of imperial border guards, who see themselves as a separate nationality, although the Kazakhs regard them as Russians.

In Kyrgyzstan democratic parties appeared in society and within the Communist Party. The former were motivated by language issues and economic problems, while the latter were more concerned with issues of power. Ashar (Help) grew out of groups who were spontaneously seizing land. Ethnic riots in the republic's south in 1990 led to political crisis, during which a breakaway faction of the party formed Erkin (Freedom), which later became the parent party of the Kyrgyzstan Democratic Movement. In October 1990 the Democratic Movement succeeded in blocking the presidential aspirations of Moscow appointee Absamat Masaliyev and elected instead Askar Akayev, thus making Kyrgyzstan the first Soviet republic to select its own leader.

Independent but Not Democratic

Turkmenistan was the only exception to the general rising tide of pre-independence political participation. Appointed as republic leader by Gorbachev in 1985, Sapamurad Niyazov successfully controlled political participation in his republic. The first organizational meeting for the nationalist group Azy-birlik (Unity) was not held until March 1991, and it was attended by no more than twenty people. Since independence, even that degree of democracy has disappeared. Niyazov, who has begun calling himself Turkmenbashi, or "head of the Turkmen," has been elected president for life and has installed his own personality cult. There is little evidence, however, of any real opposition to Niyazov in this sparsely populated, oil-rich state. International human rights activists have learned of only four Turkmen "democrats," all of whom have disappeared.

Democracy has fared no better in Uzbekistan since independence. The Karimov government has suppressed the Unity and Will Parties with ruthless efficiency. Many of the leaders of the democratic groups were beaten or jailed, and all have been forced into exile. There is some effort to sustain a pro-democracy movement from abroad but without visible success.

The general hostility to broader political participation in Central Asia stems in part from the example of Tajikistan, which has essentially collapsed as a state. The Nabiyev coalition proved short lived. It was replaced in April 1992 by the government of Akbarsho Iskandarov, which included members of the Islamic Renaissance Party. Fears of "Islamification" led Russia and Uzbekistan in October 1992 to support the attempt by Speaker of the Parliament Imamali Rakhmanov to take power. This intervention precipitated a civil war that spread to neighboring Afghanistan. The Rakhmanov government, with Uzbek and Russian support, has jailed or killed the political opposition within the territory it controls, but large portions of this mountainous, extremely poor nation remain beyond Rakhmanov's reach.

Relative Successes of Democracy

The only two Central Asian nations in which democracy may be said to be making some headway are Kazakhstan and Kyrgyzstan. All the Central Asian states have adopted post-Soviet constitutions, but only in these two countries is some serious effort being made to observe the rule of constitutional law.

After independence there was strong support for Akayev in Kyrgyzstan, but the rapidly deteriorating economy and growing evidence of favoritism and nepotism have soured relations between the democrats and the government. Akayev conducted a costly plebiscite on his presidency in January 1994, from which he secured a Soviet-style approval rating of 99 percent. Since then the democrats have complained of increasing harassment. Antidemocratic steps included the dissolution of the parliament and the closing of opposition newspapers in September 1994. Later in 1994, in violation of the constitution, a referendum was called on modifications to the constitution proposed by the president. The changes were ratified. Further amendments, adopted by referendum in February 1996, granted the president the power to appoint and dismiss the prime minister (with parliamentary approval).

Demography and democracy work against each other in Kazakhstan. Consequently, the government maintains strict controls on the media and on the growth of political parties. Unlike the other Central Asian republics, though, Kazakhstan allows parties to function so long as they are not monoethnic and can demonstrate support across most of the state's huge territory. In practice, most postindependence parties have been government sponsored, due to President Nursultan Nazarbayev's search for a functional (not ideological) replacement for the old Communist Party.

Because the country's constitution does not allow the president to hold office in other civic organizations, including parties, Nazarbayev has sponsored but not led these parties. The first was the Socialist Party, which initially inherited much of the Communist Party membership. The Congress Party was founded in 1992 by poets Suleimenov and Mukhtar Shakhanov, who at the time were pro-Nazarbayev. When that party remained small and unpopular, a Union of National Unity for Kazakhstan was formed but this too has been a disappointment. Nazarbayev's desire to make the Union of National Unity the dominant political force in the republic led to considerable manipulation of the March 1994 parliamentary elections. Stringent registration requirements, and the rigid, sometimes fraudulent, elimination of some independent candidates, combined to deny seats in the new parliament to strong nationalists from both ethnic groups.

What may spell trouble for the future is that Kazakhs are heavily overrepresented in the new parliament, while Russians are badly underrepresented. The Russians of Kazakhstan see the Kazakhs as an obvious threat, which will make the further democratization of Kazakhstan hazardous—and therefore unlikely. At the same time, though, the Russians see themselves as excluded from the political process, with nowhere except Russia to address their grievances.

Russia has tried to promote a policy of dual citizenship for Russians throughout Central Asia, but only Turkmenistan has agreed. Russian populations in Uzbekistan and Kyrgyzstan are small enough that emigration may solve the problem. In Kazakhstan, however, Russians constitute far too large a percentage of the republic's population to be ignored politically and are far too numerous to be absorbed into Russia proper. For that reason Russia will remain actively interested in Kazakhstan's politics, and intervention will be a constant possibility.

The biggest obstacle to the development of democracy in the region, though, is the general economic decline following independence. Although the elites of the Soviet era have managed to retain and even enlarge their privileges, life for the bulk of the population has worsened dramatically everywhere. The gap has sharpened antagonisms, so the compromises that are necessary for successful democratization have become much more difficult to design. The specter of Tajikistan's failure has led even the most democratically inclined of the present rulers, Nazarbayev in Kazakhstan and Akayev in Kyrgyzstan, to see the preservation of stability as more important than democratization.

See also *Kyrgyzstan.*

BIBLIOGRAPHY

Allworth, Edward A. *The Modern Uzbeks.* Stanford, Calif.: Hoover Institution Press, 1990.

Central Asia. Special issue of *Current History* (April 1994).

Fierman, William, ed. *Soviet Central Asia: The Failed Transformation.* Boulder, Colo.: Westview Press, 1991.

Mandelbaum, Michael, ed. *Central Asia and the World.* New York: Council on Foreign Relations Press, 1994.

Olcott, Martha Brill. "Central Asia's Catapult to Independence." *Foreign Affairs* (summer 1992): 108–130.

———. *The Kazakhs.* Stanford, Calif.: Hoover Institution Press, 1987.

Poliakov, Sergei P. *Everyday Islam: Religion and Tradition in Rural Central Asia.* Armonk, N.Y.: M. E. Sharpe, 1992.

Asia, Southeast

The region that encompasses the mainland or island nations of Brunei, Burma (Myanmar), Cambodia, Indonesia, Laos, Malaysia, the Philippines, Singapore, Thailand, and Vietnam. The number and variety of countries in Southeast Asia make it the most diverse region in Asia.

Culturally, the region is a kaleidoscope. In eight of Southeast Asia's ten states the most numerous ethnic community is different racially or linguistically from its counterpart in every other country in the region. (The exceptions are Brunei and Malaysia, both of which have Malay majorities.) In nine of the ten states the main religion—Islam, Theravada Buddhism, Mahayana Buddhism, Roman Catholicism, or Confucianism—is different from the main religion in at least one of its neighboring Southeast Asian states. (The exception is Burma, which shares Theravada Buddhism with its neighbors Laos and Thailand.)

Historically, different parts of the region have been influenced in different ways by a variety of outside cultures and powers. In religion, language, and the arts, legacies of Indian civilization can be found throughout Southeast Asia. Late in the second century B.C., the people of what is now Vietnam fell under Chinese suzerainty for about a thousand years. In the sixteenth century Spain Catholicized and colonized the Philippines. In the nineteenth century Britain acquired the territories that are now Brunei, Burma, Malaysia, and Singapore, while Vietnam, Cambodia, and Laos fell to the French. The Portuguese, the first Westerners to seize land in Southeast Asia, were the last to leave, abandoning East Timor, the sole remaining colony in the region, in 1975. Thailand, which was useful to the British and the French as a buffer between their Southeast Asian possessions, avoided colonization altogether.

Economically, as well, the Southeast Asian nations differ

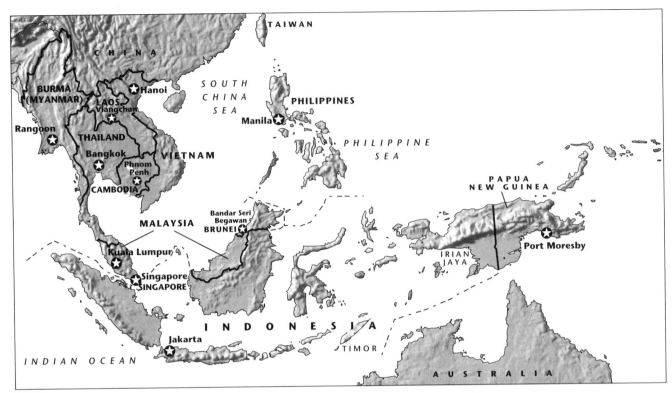

greatly. They include a tiny city-state specializing in services and manufacturing (Singapore); an even less populous enclave almost wholly dependent on oil and gas revenues (Brunei); small and still overwhelmingly agricultural countries (Cambodia, Laos); larger agricultural and manufacturing economies (the Philippines, Thailand); and the diverse and fourth most populous country in the world, Indonesia. Ranked by their per capita incomes in 1991, the nations of Southeast Asia ranged from very wealthy (Singapore, $13,900; Brunei, $8,800) to extremely poor (Laos, $220; Cambodia, $130). Economic performances also varied greatly; estimated rates of real growth in gross domestic product in 1992 ran from 8.0 percent (Malaysia) and 7.4 percent (Thailand) to 0.0 percent (the Philippines) and -1.0 percent (Burma). In the early 1990s these economies also differed in the extent to which their domestic markets were free from government intervention and protected from foreign competition, though all were more or less open to foreign investment.

Politically, nine different types of regimes were represented in Southeast Asia in the mid-1990s. These were an unconstitutional military junta (Burma); an absolute monarchy without parties or elections (Brunei); a nascent constitutional monarchy with two prime ministers (Cambodia); a military-influenced, multiparty, parliamentary-democratic constitutional monarchy (Thailand); a one-party-dominant parliamentary democracy under a rotating monarchy (Malaysia); a one-party-dominant parliamentary democracy with a directly elected president (Singapore); a military-dominant presidential autocracy with sponsored parties and elections (Indonesia); an American-style presidential-legislative democracy (Philippines); and two formally communist single-party states (Laos, Vietnam).

Levels of Growth and Freedom

According to the quantitative rankings released annually by Freedom House, a New York–based organization that monitors changing levels of freedom around the world, Southeast Asia was the least free region in Asia in the early 1990s. If Freedom House's country ratings for 1993 (drawn from *Freedom in the World*, 1994) are grouped and averaged for each of the four main parts of Asia, the results are these: with a perfect score of 1.0, Australasia (Australia, New Zealand) was Asia's only "free" region. "Partly free" were North Asia (China, Japan, Mongolia, North Korea, Russia, South Korea, Taiwan) with a score of 3.9 and South

Asia (Bangladesh, Bhutan, India, Maldives, Nepal, Pakistan, Sri Lanka) with a score of 4.6. Southeast Asia, at 5.5, was "not free" by Freedom House's standards.

The location of Australia and New Zealand at the "freest" end of this ranking suggests an explanation: the higher the per capita income of a country, the "freer" that country is likely to be. Applied to three of the four Asian regions (Australasia, North Asia, and South Asia), this hypothesis works well. Ranked in order from freest to least free in 1993, Australasia, North Asia, and South Asia had levels of average real GDP per capita purchasing power parities of $14,766, $6,401, and $1,304, respectively, in 1991. Yet Southeast Asia, distinctly the "least free" region, registered a mean income level ($4,845) much higher than South Asia and not far below that of North Asia. The idea that freedom is a function of relative income levels also does not fare well in a comparison among Southeast Asian countries. Across the ten nations, the two variables are unrelated.

Faced with this negative result, one may question the dependent variable, freedom. But although freedom and democracy are not the same thing, the definition of "freedom" used by Freedom House has advantages in the present context. The definition incorporates twenty-two rights and liberties that are comprehensive and explicitly political, or have clear political implications, and that refer not to a country's constitution or formal regime but to actually prevailing conditions. The Philippines, for example, is a democracy in the legal-institutional meaning of the term. But the Freedom House rating of the Philippines as only "partly free" takes into account the actual operation of a full range of politically relevant rights and liberties. The Freedom House definition of "freedom," however, is imbued with the idea of a liberal democracy centered on the individual rather than on the group or community.

One could use economic growth rather than income level as the independent variable, arguing that even if wealthier polities are not consistently more democratic than poorer ones, rapidly growing ones ought to be more democratic than slowly growing ones. But there is no correlation across the ten Southeast Asian states between the rate of growth in GDP in 1992 and the level of freedom in 1993.

This independent variable may cover too short a time. Perhaps only the accumulated effects of economic growth over a period of years could be expected to differentiate the economy, enlarge the middle class, and open the political

system to rising social pluralism. Applied to Southeast Asia, an independent variable showing economic growth over time does indicate that prolonged economic development encourages democracy, but mainly for places that have neither: Burma and Indochina (Cambodia, Laos, Vietnam). In these countries one may at least believe that future development will lead to democratization.

Poor and missing data make comparisons of Burma, Cambodia, Laos, and Vietnam difficult. But clearly they did regress, stagnate, or grow very little in the decades before 1993. In that year three of the four were "not free" by Freedom House's definition, and the one exception, "partly free" Cambodia, had only just been upgraded to reflect the multiparty elections held there in May. Indochina had been under Leninist dictatorships since 1975, while the military autocracy in Burma had lasted even longer, since 1962. In all of Southeast Asia, for 1993, Vietnam and Burma (both 7.0), and Laos, Indonesia, and Brunei (all 6.5) were rated "not free." Singapore (5.0), Malaysia and Cambodia (both 4.5), Thailand (4.0), and the Philippines (3.5) were labeled "partly free."

If the cases of Burma and Indochina support the idea that persisting economic stagnation inhibits democracy, however, Singapore, Indonesia, Thailand, Malaysia, and the Philippines do not show any correlation between sustained economic growth and democratization. Despite a stunning 6.5 percent average annual gain in gross national product per person from 1965 to 1990, Singapore had the second worst freedom score in the group for 1993. Indonesia, Thailand, and Malaysia also did well economically—their respective rates of growth were 4.5, 4.4, and 4.0 percent—but in 1993 Indonesia was "not free," while Malaysia and Thailand were only "partly free." Almost a mirror image of Singapore was the Philippines, which had by far the worst economic performance in 1965–1990—a mere 1.3 percent growth per capita per year—yet achieved the highest freedom rating of any state in Southeast Asia in 1993.

Roughly speaking, for these five countries, the greater their economic growth, the less freedom their citizens enjoyed. If comparable data were available for Brunei, they might reinforce this finding. Brunei's oil-based economy surely grew rapidly during the petroleum industry boom of the 1970s, and the country still lacks political freedom. Brunei did suffer from falling oil prices in the 1980s, however, and it did not become independent from Great Britain until 1984.

Histories of Growth and Freedom

Considered historically, the proposition that a high or rising national income enlarges freedom and democracy does not even work very satisfactorily for that part of Southeast Asia where poverty has long coexisted with autocracy: Burma and Indochina. The authoritarian pasts of these four countries illustrate less the power of economics to determine politics than the autonomous influence of political variables, including violence, organization, and ideology.

Burma's civil wars have been more numerous and longer lasting than those of any other Southeast Asian state. The country gained its independence from Britain in January 1948. Three months later local communists revolted; two army battalions joined them. Despite constitutional safeguards for Burma's many ethnoregional minorities—in the early 1990s only 68 percent of all Burmese were ethnically Burman—the new government discriminated in favor of the Burman majority. In 1949 a revolt among the Christianized Karen ethnic group—Burmans are largely Buddhist—was strengthened by the defection of three battalions of Karen troops. Other ethnic groups also took up arms against the central government, which managed to avoid defeat in part because its many antagonists tended also to fight each other. From the late 1940s through the early 1990s, while the extent, severity, parties, and outcomes of these conflicts fluctuated, the general pattern—a debilitating welter of insurgencies—endured.

In Vietnam, in December 1946 the Viet Minh (Vietnamese Independence League) under Ho Chi Minh began fighting the effort by the French to regain control over their former colony. This First Indochina War ended in a French military defeat at Dien Bien Phu, a negotiated division of Vietnam at the seventeenth parallel in 1954, and the consolidation of a communist-ruled Democratic Republic of Vietnam north of that line. But within five years warfare resumed in the south, between the U.S.-backed state of Vietnam and its communist opponents. In 1975, following the withdrawal of U.S. forces and the deaths of well over one million Vietnamese, the communists won this Second Indochina War as well. A scant three years later Vietnam invaded and occupied Cambodia. Although Vietnam announced in 1989 that it had withdrawn its troops from Cambodia, the Cambodian core of this Third Indochina War was still in progress in the early 1990s. This summary does not cover the death toll in Cambodia and Laos from the First and Second Indochina Wars, the 1979 Sino-Vietnamese border war, or the deaths of up to one million Khmers under Pol Pot's reign of terror in Cambodia in 1975–1978.

Alongside endemic violence, centralized organization and socialist ideology further stymied whatever potential these countries may have had to become liberal democracies. Burma's military regime, for example, in power since Gen. Ne Win's coup in 1962, headed a one-party state (1964–1988) that badly mismanaged the economy in the name of a "Burmese way to socialism."

In Cambodia in the 1960s Prince Norodom Sihanouk advocated "royal Buddhist socialism." Political rivalries and a local communist revolt led Sihanouk to assume special powers in 1967, only to be ousted three years later in a military coup that plunged the country into civil war. In 1975 Pol Pot's Maoist-Leninist communists won that struggle. They erected a Leninist state with a fanatically anticapitalist agrarian ideology and set about destroying what urban educated class there was. The regime imposed on Cambodia by its Vietnamese invaders in 1979, though much less brutal and more pragmatic than Pol Pot's had been, brooked no opposition to the rule of its own Leninist party. Neither did its neighbor regimes in the Socialist Republic of Vietnam and the Lao People's Democratic Republic.

In Burma and Indochina, poverty alone cannot explain authoritarianism. Autocracy was at least as responsible for prolonging poverty as poverty was for prolonging autocracy. Only in the 1980s and early 1990s, when these began to open up and grow, was it possible to explore the positive side of the economic argument for democracy: not that deprivation and stagnation retard democracy but that development induces it.

Economic and Political Reforms

In Indochina market-oriented economic reforms were not set in motion by any renunciation of Marxism and conversion to capitalism. Rather, they arose from a pragmatic awareness that policies hostile to the private sector had failed to bring about desired growth. Along with that narrowly economic rationale came the idea that in politics the Leninist state, which had kept its rulers in power, was not broken and did not need fixing. Indeed, if economic liberalization could revive the economy, that would strengthen the authoritarian state and eliminate the need for significantly liberalizing political reforms and the instabilities they might trigger. In countries that had already demonstrated the relative autonomy of political elites and ideas, the justification of economic reform as a way of avoiding political reform did not augur well for democratization.

The Laotian case is of particular interest because its leaders preceded their counterparts in Burma, Cambodia, and Vietnam down the path of economic reform. In Laos the political consequences of economic loosening had more time to appear. In 1979 plummeting production and peasant unrest—brought on by earlier decisions to nationalize industry, control markets, and collectivize agriculture—obliged Laotian communist leaders to acknowledge a capitalist component within the national economy. Soon thereafter noncommunist technocrats were appointed to the government to help improve its efficiency. Orthodox socialist policies were modestly relaxed in the 1980s, and the economy revived just enough to embolden pragmatists within the ruling Lao People's Revolutionary Party (LPRP) to continue the reform process. By 1988 Laos had begun actively encouraging foreign investment and selectively reprivatizing nationalized firms.

At its Fifth Congress in 1991, a year in which real gross domestic product grew a respectable 5.0 percent, the LPRP reaffirmed its commitment to market principles. But the constitution finally adopted that same year, while acknowledging private ownership rights in the economy, reaffirmed the leading role of the LPRP. In 1992 three former officials accused of advocating a multiparty system were sentenced to fourteen-year prison terms. If the charges were true, they suggested that economic reform and growth were motivating some Laotians to press for political pluralism, which the regime was not ready to grant.

Short of democratization, three kinds of political reform can be observed in Laos and Vietnam: those concerning lawmaking, the electoral process, and the government. The writing and ratifying of constitutions and the specification of laws created a basis of authority other than that of the communist party. The process of lawmaking itself entailed the legitimate expression of disagreements. Vietnam's hotly debated 1992 constitution, for example, stated that the ruling Communist Party of Vietnam (CPV) was not above the law. Because Laos had had no constitution since 1975, the adoption of one in 1991 could be understood as limiting, at least in principle, the LPRP's freedom of action. But in both countries it proved difficult to implement written laws against the wishes of party conservatives.

In Laos (1988–1989) and Vietnam (1989–1992) elections were held in stages from local to national levels. For the first time in Vietnam candidates who were not CPV members were permitted to run. Market-minded leaders hoped

in this way to bypass party hard-liners and create from the bottom up a constituency for economic reform. Often, however, the victors were local bosses more interested in payoffs than in reforms. For this reason, far from becoming the natural allies of decentralization, some reformist leaders favored tighter central control. The elections did not threaten party rule. Roughly one-tenth of the 601 candidates who contested the Vietnamese National Assembly's 395 seats in 1992 did not belong to the CPV, but only two of them were truly independent, and they both lost.

Liberal Democracy?

In the early 1990s the prospects for liberal democracy in Southeast Asia were not encouraging. In Cambodia the demand for the elections that were finally held in May 1993 arose not from the Khmer people but from international negotiations to end the Third Indochina War. Although the balloting succeeded in isolating Pol Pot's followers, the Khmer Rouge, who had boycotted it, it also resulted in a divided government whose two prime ministers were still unable to defeat the Khmer Rouge. Moreover, relations between the Cambodian prime ministers had deteriorated into civil war by 1997. In Burma the military leaders tolerated a free election in 1990 that rejected them overwhelmingly; they then annulled it and remained in power. In Thailand the promise of 1992, a banner year for democratization, faded into wrangling over constitutional amendments. In Indonesia labor unrest threatened to invite a crackdown by the armed forces, already anxious over the succession to President Suharto.

In Malaysia and Singapore years of rapid economic growth, far from bringing significant political liberalization, enabled the existing democracies to become even more institutionalized. By the mid–1990s the long-awaited democratizing effect of Bruneian students returning from the West with Western ideas had not materialized.

As for the Philippines, that formally liberal democracy was in practice burdened with cronyism, venal elites, and stalemated institutions ill suited to achieving the rates of economic growth enjoyed by its more overtly authoritarian neighbors. Nevertheless, the economy improved in 1993. In 1994 a coalition of the governing party with its chief opposition in the Philippine Senate reduced the pluralism of party politics. Yet the move strengthened the hand of the government to make the difficult decisions necessary for further economic growth.

All this does not mean that democracy has no future in Southeast Asia. Rather, one may expect that diversity will probably continue to characterize the region's polities—

including effective autocracies and illiberal democracies. In the long run, economic development could well liberalize these relatively closed polities. But in the near term, one should not overestimate the prospects for liberal democracy through economic growth in Southeast Asia.

See also *Burma; Dominant party democracies in Asia; Indonesia; Malaysia; Philippines; Singapore; Thailand.*

BIBLIOGRAPHY

Chan Heng Chee. "Evolution and Implementation: An Asian Perspective." In *Democracy and Capitalism: Asian and American Perspectives,* edited by Robert Bartley, Chan Heng Chee, Samuel Huntington, and Shijuro Ogata. Singapore: Institute of Southeast Asian Studies, 1993.

Crouch, Harold A. *Economic Change, Social Structure, and the Political System in Southeast Asia.* Singapore: Institute of Southeast Asian Studies, 1985.

Diamond, Larry, Juan J. Linz, and Seymour Martin Lipset, eds. *Democracy in Developing Countries: Asia.* Boulder, Colo.: Lynne Rienner; London: Adamantine Press, 1989.

Emmerson, Donald K. "Walking on Two Legs: Polity and Economy in the ASEAN Countries." In *Asia in the 1990s: American and Soviet Perspectives,* edited by Robert A. Scalapino and Gennady I. Chufrin. Berkeley: University of California, Institute of East Asian Studies, 1991.

Hewison, Kevin, Richard Robison, and Garry Rodan, eds. *Southeast Asia in the 1990s: Authoritarianism, Democracy, and Capitalism.* St. Leonard's, Australia: Allen and Unwin, 1993.

Ljunggren, Börje, ed. *The Challenge of Reform in Indochina.* Cambridge, Mass.: Harvard Institute for International Development; London: Harvard University Press, 1993.

Neher, Clark D. "Democratization in Southeast Asia." *Asian Affairs: An American Review* 18 (fall 1991): 139–152.

Taylor, Robert, ed. *Elections in Southeast Asia.* Washington, D.C.: Woodrow Wilson International Center for Scholars, 1996.

Thayer, Carl, and David Marr, eds. *Vietnam and the Rule of Law.* Canberra: Australian National University, Research School of Pacific Studies, 1993.

Australia and New Zealand

Pacific nations and members of the British Commonwealth that have a long tradition of maintaining democratic institutions. Although Australia and New Zealand share a common British heritage, their political development has diverged in several important respects. The two countries differ considerably in size. Australia is an entire continent, nearly as large as the United States in area. New Zealand comprises only slightly more than 100,000 square miles.

Historical Background

A long-established Aborigine population inhabited Australia when white settlers began colonizing the island continent in 1788. The separate colonies founded by the settlers—New South Wales, Victoria, South Australia, Tasmania, Queensland, and Western Australia—were effectively self-governing until 1901, when they entered a federal arrangement. Two territories, the Northern Territory (formerly part of South Australia) and the Australian Capital Territory (formerly part of New South Wales), joined the federation in 1911.

New Zealand, a small island nation, lies in the Pacific Ocean about 1,200 miles southeast of Australia. New Zealand's European settlers came somewhat later than Australia's, after the formal establishment of British sovereignty in 1840. In 1852 legislation passed by the British Parliament established an institutional framework of government. National elections were first held in 1854.

The populations of the countries are quite different in origin and outlook. Australia's early white population con-

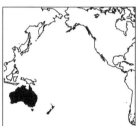

sisted mainly of convicts transported from Britain, together with their guards. Since 1947 there has been a large influx of non-British immigrants. The nineteenth-century British working-class immigrants to Australia influenced the new country's class consciousness, attitudes toward women, and accent. Australia's Irish immigrants contributed anti-British sentiment and Catholicism. By contrast, convicts were never transported to New Zealand, and until very recently that nation has relied mainly on Great Britain for immigrants. New Zealand received more middle-class English immigrants than did Australia and had a larger proportion of farm owners, making its mainstream political values more like those of the English middle class.

Although both countries have indigenous populations, the Aborigines in Australia constitute only 1 percent of the population, whereas the Maori in New Zealand make up 12 percent of the population, and Pacific islanders comprise a further 4 percent. Questions of racial equity in democratic institutions have therefore been given greater priority in New Zealand.

Australian Federalism

Of several themes that have shaped Australia's twentieth-century experience of democracy, perhaps the most important is federalism, itself a consequence of size. The Constitution makes a clear distinction between the functions of the state and federal governments: the states accept responsibility for community services such as health and transportation, and the federal government handles foreign affairs, trade, and defense. Judicial interpretation of the constitution, the antipathy of the Australian Labor Party toward the states, and the increasing complexity of modern government, however, have led to a shift in political power in favor of the federal government. The most significant event in this shift occurred in 1942, when the High Court, the nation's supreme legal body, upheld the federal government's right to deny the states income tax powers. Since then the states have been dependent on the federal government for revenue.

Australian democracy has placed the state in a central, regulatory role. The Australian state has traditionally taken on a wide range of social and economic responsibilities, including intervention in the economy, the regulation of trade, and the control of industrial relations. The role of the state originated in the political values of the early settlers, whose outlook reflected the Benthamite utilitarianism (a philosophy based on the work of Jeremy Bentham, 1748–1832) that was prevalent in early nineteenth-century Britain. The Australian state is regarded as an instrument for arbitrating disputes rather than as an agent for preserving individual liberty and freedom, as in the United States. The clearest political embodiment of these utilitarian values is the system of compulsory voting, adopted for federal elections in 1924 as a solution to the problem of declining turnout. Australia is one of the few democracies in the world to enforce compulsory voting.

A strong two-party system is another characteristic of Australian democracy. The Australian Labor Party is the nation's oldest party. Founded in 1891, it originated in the trades and labor councils of the 1870s and 1880s. Australia formed the world's first Labor government, which took office in Queensland for seven days in 1899. Between 1901 and 1997 the Australian Labor Party held federal office for thirty-three years. The Liberal Party was formed in 1944 on the instigation of Robert Menzies, who wanted to combine his United Australia Party with other non-Labor groups to form a single conservative party. A third party, the National Party of Australia, began as the Country Party during World War I and was renamed in 1982. The party has been in permanent coalition with the Liberals, with short breaks. With the exception of the 1990 election, since federation in 1901 no other party has won more than 10 percent of the vote in elections for the lower house, the House of Representatives.

This strong two-party system has conveyed great stability to Australian democracy during the course of the century. The stable two-party system reinforces the Westminster system of government, which was embodied in the constitution. The Westminster system (named for Westminster in London, where the British Parliament is located) is based on responsible party government: voters choose between competing parties that offer alternative social and economic policies. The executive, who is closely identified with one of the parties, is answerable to the legislature.

Parliament enacts legislation under a system of strong party discipline. Although Australian party discipline is a legacy of British practice, it exceeds anything found in the Westminster Parliament: voting against one's party in Australia is almost unheard of and is regarded as a cardinal political sin. Westminster conventions of collective cabinet responsibility and ministerial responsibility have also been adopted from British practice, although they are less frequently observed.

Australian society is based almost entirely on massive immigration. It has a higher percentage of foreign-born residents than any other advanced industrial society, with the exception of Israel. Despite the ethnic, cultural, and linguistic diversity of these immigrants, they have had comparatively little effect on the character or style of Australian democracy, including its institutions, political parties, or major actors.

Early in the twentieth century the policy of assimilation ensured that immigrants would conform to existing social norms. Since 1972 the policy of multiculturalism has relaxed this demand, though loyalty to Australian institutions remains a requirement. It is also clear, however, that many immigrants have been socialized into other political systems and have come to Australia for economic, not political, reasons; their interest in politics is therefore limited.

Australian Elections

Australia's electoral arrangements are complex. Since 1918 preferential voting based on single-member districts (known as electorates) has been used for the House of Representatives. Since 1949 the single transferable vote method of proportional representation has been used for the upper house, the Senate. (The states determine their own electoral arrangements for state elections, and they use a variety of systems.) The 148 members of the House of Representatives are elected for a maximum three-year term of office, although elections may be called early if the Senate twice rejects a bill from the lower house. The 76 members of the Senate are usually elected for a six-year term, with half the seats up for election every three years (in a "half Senate" election). When a "full Senate" election is held, half the members are elected for three-year terms and half for six-year terms.

In practice, the responsibility for calling an election rests with the government. The prime minister can request that the governor general (the head of state) dissolve the House of Representatives and half of the Senate or the House of Representatives and all of the Senate if the technical conditions are met. (The latter is called a double dissolution election.) In recent years, double dissolution elections have become more frequent, since governments often do not control the Senate, and they see such an election as an opportunity to extend their control to the upper house, thereby facilitating passage of their legislation.

The Senate was designed to represent the interests of the

states and territories. The six states have an equal number of senators, despite their vastly different population sizes. The Senate was also seen as a house of review, like the British House of Lords; this concept was implicit in senators' longer period of tenure. Party discipline, however, has come to dominate the Senate, like the House of Representatives, undermining its traditional function as a house of review. At the same time, the adoption of proportional representation in 1949 for Senate elections has frequently left the balance of power in the Senate in the hands of minor parties and independents. This has meant that governments have had to negotiate the passage of contentious legislation.

The federal constitution, drafted in 1900, did not guarantee universal suffrage. Those who were entitled to vote in elections to colonial parliaments were automatically given the same right in federal elections. Because women had the vote only in South Australia and Western Australia, only in those states could women vote in federal elections. This anomaly was rectified in 1908, when the last state to deny women the vote, Victoria, granted universal suffrage. In 1973 the voting age for all Australians was lowered from twenty-one years to eighteen years.

Racial discrimination in the franchise has persisted until comparatively recently. Aborigines were effectively denied the vote until 1949, when they were permitted to vote in federal elections if they were registered to vote in state elections or if they served in the military. In 1962 all Aborigines were given the right to vote, although registration remained voluntary. In 1984 enrollment for Aborigines became compulsory and they, like other Australians, were obliged to vote in federal elections.

Democratic Trends in Australia

In today's Australian federal democracy, two related themes are of increasing importance. There is greater discussion than ever before about the relevance of Australia's British heritage to an ethnically and racially heterogeneous society located on the edge of Southeast Asia. This debate has its origins in World War II, when Britain, engaged in the European war, was unable to help Australia in the fight against Japan, and Australia looked to the United States for military and economic assistance. More recently, Britain's entry into the European Community in 1972 altered Australia's traditional trading relations and forced Australia to look to Asia. The large number of non-British immigrants who do not identify with Britain or with British political traditions is an additional factor. Politically, the discussion

has focused on proposals to make Australia a republic, to replace the queen as head of state, and to remove the British Union Jack from the Australian flag.

As Australia's traditional British ties weaken, there is increasing economic involvement in the Asian-Pacific region. This involvement is a logical consequence of Britain's withdrawal from Asia, completed with the reversion of Hong Kong to China on July 1, 1997. But it also reflects the changing power relations within the Pacific Rim, including the economic dominance of Japan, the rapid economic growth of countries such as Thailand and Malaysia, the collapse of the Soviet Union, and the withdrawal of U.S. military forces from the Philippines. All these factors have forced Australia to play a greater political, economic, and military role in the Asian-Pacific region and to reconsider its European, and specifically British, identity.

New Zealand's Democratic Setting

New Zealand, small in area and population, has always suffered from a greater sense of isolation than has Australia. This isolation, coupled with the nation's greater reliance on British settlers, has made New Zealand more conscious of its British identity. New Zealand's highly centralized government provides a perfect example of British parliamentary, or Westminster, democracy.

Egalitarianism is a major theme in New Zealand democracy—as it is in Australia. New Zealand established a strong welfare state early on. The commitment of successive governments to providing individual economic security was reflected in a very low level of unemployment until the 1980s, when unemployment rapidly increased. While the state played a major role, the economy was essentially a capitalist, free enterprise system. Within New Zealand political culture, the two themes are not contradictory but complementary.

The organized settlement of New Zealand dates from 1840, when the Treaty of Waitangi was signed between the British and some Maori chiefs. Later, Maori fought the settlers in a series of wars between 1860 and 1876. After the Maori were defeated, they were granted token separate representation in Parliament.

The 1852 New Zealand Constitution Act provided for six separate provincial assemblies (which were abolished in 1876) as well as for a national parliament. The legislature was made up of a lower house popularly elected every five years (reduced to three years in 1879) and a Legislative Council, whose members were appointed for life by the queen. The role of the Legislative Council was never clearly defined, and the council was abolished in 1950. Since then the legislature has been unicameral.

After brief experiments with a second ballot system and multimember districts, elections from 1911 until 1996 were exclusively conducted using the plurality system based on single-member districts (known as electorates). This electoral system promoted stability and two-party dominance, but it engendered much criticism as well for distorting the popular will. In two consecutive elections, 1978 and 1981, the party with the most votes, Labour, secured fewer seats than its National opponent. In 1986 a Royal Commission on the Electoral System recommended that New Zealand adopt a modified version of the mixed-member proportional system used in Germany. In a 1992 referendum, voters were asked whether the existing plurality electoral system should be changed and, if so, which of four alternative systems should be run off in a second referendum against the plurality system. Of the 55 percent of the electorate who voted in the first referendum, 85 percent voted for change, with a clear preference for the mixed-member proportional system on the second question. A second referendum was held in 1993, in conjunction with the general election; voters were asked to choose between retaining the plurality system and adopting the mixed-member proportional system. Of the 83 percent of the electorate who voted, 54 percent favored the mixed-member proportional system and 46 percent favored the plurality system. The new electoral system, which is fully proportional in effect, was first implemented in the elections of October 1996.

In 1852 suffrage was restricted to men aged twenty-one years and over who could claim some property rights. The property qualification excluded almost all the Maori; the only ones who qualified were the few who owned or leased land under the European system of land titles. To permit Maori parliamentary representation, the 1867 Maori Representation Act provided for two separate electoral systems, one general and one Maori. Maori could choose to register in the Maori electoral roll and to vote in one of four Maori electorates. Although this separate system guarantees only minimal representation for the Maori, since 1975 they have been allowed to (and often do) choose instead to register in non-Maori electorates.

The property qualification was removed, and universal male suffrage was introduced in 1879. In 1893 full voting rights were extended to women, although women could not stand for election to the House of Representatives until the passage of the Women's Parliamentary Rights Act in 1919. In 1973 the voting age was lowered to eighteen years.

Registration is compulsory, although voting is voluntary. Traditionally, turnout in New Zealand has been among the highest in the established democracies; in recent years, however, turnout has declined.

Parties in New Zealand

New Zealand has a fairly complex party history. The first political party to emerge was the Liberal Party, which was organized in 1890 and was elected to form the government early the following year. The Liberals held power until 1912. From that time until 1935 the farmer-based Reform Party dominated a situation of complex three-party politics. The Labour Party was formed in 1916, first came to power in 1935, and held office until 1949. It was succeeded by the National Party, formed in 1936 from the remnants of the various anti-Labour party organizations. By 1938 the modern two-party system had been formed. A variety of other minor parties have contested elections—New Zealand could boast, for example, the world's first national environmental party, the Values Party, formed in 1972. In the pre–1996 plurality electoral system the success of minor parties was limited; minor parties fared better in 1996 under the proportional representation system, but so far they have not undermined the essentially two-party system.

Like Australia, New Zealand looked to the United States for military assistance during World War II. Defense arrangements were formalized in a mutual defense treaty among the three countries, signed in 1951. The Labour government elected in 1984, however, banned visits by ships carrying nuclear arms or powered by nuclear energy. As a result the United States cut all defense ties with New Zealand. Antinuclear popular sentiments have remained strong in New Zealand, and in 1987 the Labour government enacted its antinuclear policy into law. The 1984–1990 Labour government also undertook a thorough revision of the government's economic interventionist role, cutting state subsidies, reducing social welfare payments, and privatizing government-owned utilities—a policy called Rogernomics after the main instigator and Labour finance minister, Roger Douglas.

Although the character and style of New Zealand's democratic culture and institutions have changed little during the course of the century, recent events have suggested several directions in which New Zealand democracy may evolve in the twenty-first century. The change in the electoral system, given the long-term trend of increasing support for minor parties, may remove a substantial institutional foundation of the two-party system and perhaps lead to a period of political uncertainty. Changes to the traditionally interventionist role of the state under Labour resulted in significant shifts in the distribution of wealth, although how much this altered popular democratic values is unclear. Meanwhile, the Maori are demanding compensation for past injustices and greater recognition of their language and culture in society and government.

Divergent Trends

While Australia is becoming a multicultural society, with increasing Asian influence, in New Zealand the future appears increasingly bicultural, with a new balance between European and Pacific influences. Finally, although a free trade area encompasses Australia and New Zealand, the absence of New Zealand defense ties with the United States places a question mark over a key aspect of New Zealand's long-term role in the region.

BIBLIOGRAPHY

Aitkin, Don A. *Stability and Change in Australian Politics.* 2d ed. Canberra: Australian National University Press, 1982.

Catt, Helena, Paul Harris, and Nigel S. Roberts. *Voters' Choice: Electoral Change in New Zealand?* Palmerston North, New Zealand: Dunmore Press, 1992.

Collins, Hugh. "Political Ideology in Australia: The Distinctiveness of a Benthamite Society." *Daedalus* 114 (1985): 147–169.

Emy, Hugh V., and Owen E. Hughes. *Australian Politics: Realities in Conflict.* 2d ed. Melbourne: Macmillan, 1992.

Gold, Hyam. *New Zealand Politics in Perspective.* 2d ed. Auckland: Longman Paul, 1989.

McAllister, Ian. *Political Behaviour: Citizens, Parties and Elites in Australia.* Melbourne: Longman Cheshire, 1992.

———, Malcolm Mackerras, Alvaro Ascui, and Susan Moss. *Australian Political Facts.* Melbourne: Longman Cheshire, 1990.

Vowles, Jack, and Peter Aimer. *The Voters' Vengeance: The 1990 Election in New Zealand and the Fate of the Fourth Labour Government.* Auckland: Auckland University Press; New York: Oxford University Press, 1993.

B

Botswana

A republic located north of South Africa and the only uninterrupted liberal democracy in postcolonial Africa. Most of Botswana's 1.5 million inhabitants reside along the eastern edge of the country, where rainfall is sufficient to sustain arid farming. The Kalahari Desert is in the southwest. The economy is based primarily on mining, cattle production, and labor migration to South Africa.

Since gaining independence in 1966, Botswana has conducted competitive elections every five years, established a record unequaled on the continent with respect to civil rights, and created a military that has remained firmly under civilian control. No other country on the African continent (and only Mauritius offshore) has maintained such a democratic record since independence.

Politics of Democratic Development

The structure of Botswana's government, established in the 1966 constitution, was the result of pre-independence negotiations between Botswana's political leaders and their British rulers. The constitution creates a parliament with two houses: the National Assembly and the House of Chiefs. The latter advises the former. The Assembly now includes forty representatives (originally thirty-one) elected on the basis of single-member districts; four additional persons selected by the Assembly; and an appointed attorney general and the president of the country, both of whom serve ex officio. The elected members of the Assembly select the president of the country, who then appoints a cabinet from members of the Assembly. A no-confidence vote for the president by the Assembly mandates its dissolution.

Botswana's democracy is best characterized as develop-

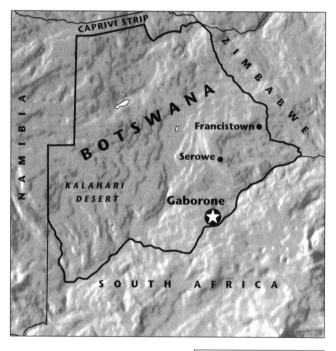

ing. The process of liberalization for almost three decades provides insight into the realities confronting the current crop of states moving toward democracy. Slowly a transition is taking place in Botswana from party competition based on ethnicity to polarization of the parties on the basis of class, policy, and candidate personality. The Botswana Democratic Party has ruled continuously since independence. It forged its winning coalition based on the allegiance of the Bamangwato and the Bakwena, the two largest of the eight main Tswana tribes, which together constitute two-thirds of Botswana's population. In addition, the ruling party mobilizes varying degrees of support from several other Tswana and non-Tswana groups. The main opposition parties—the Botswana National Front and the Botswana People's Party—rely mostly on ethnic alienation from the ruling coalition to win supporters. The supporters of the National Front come mainly from Tswana groups, while the People's Party relies on the Kalanga, who are not Tswana.

The emergence of nonethnic competition has been slow. Beginning in the 1980s the Botswana National Front used populist Marxist appeals to secure a majority of the urban working class. This constituency is not sufficient to win control of the parliament. Thus the National Front has tried to establish an electoral coalition with the People's Party and other ethnically based parties. Despite repeated attempts, the conflict between class and ethnicity has prevented realization of this goal.

Botswana's democracy is also developing in the sense that the Democratic Party's domination of the parliament and the cabinet has not allowed it to set major policies related to land reform, urban housing, transportation, and agriculture. These and other initiatives come from the civil service and its dialogue with foreign aid agencies and the World Bank. Until the end of the 1980s the primary, if not the only, role of politicians was to sell new programs to their constituents. A new generation of Democratic Party parliamentarians has begun to exercise some policy leadership, especially with regard to privatization. Top civil servants have shown some resistance, but it is tempered in the case of privatization by the fact that civil servants can invest in the new enterprises.

A major challenge to the development of democracy in Botswana is its autocratic political culture. Particularly in the rural areas, an almost automatic deference exists toward authority figures, whether they are chiefs, elders, or top civil servants. At the time of independence, the Democratic Party took advantage of this tradition by selecting Seretse Khama to be the party's leader and then president of the country. Khama was heir apparent to the Bamangwato chieftaincy, which had long ruled over the largest ethnic group (one-third of the population) in the country. Many in the rural population perceived Khama's presidency from a traditional Tswana perspective. They saw it as a new form of chieftaincy and thus as a permanent, rather than elected, position. After voting for Khama in 1965, many did not vote again until 1984, when Quett Masire was the Democratic Party's candidate for president following the death of Khama.

Interest groups have been slow to secure influence in the policy process. Only in the 1980s did organized groups begin to think in terms of influencing government policy. In the 1990s their numbers are still small, and the most effective employer and environmental groups are led by Europeans. African dominated groups lack funds and a will to exercise their influence. They are content with "advisory" councils, which make policy recommendations concerning incomes, land allocation, government purchasing, and rural development. In these councils civil servants solicit reactions to policy initiatives being developed. To retain the compliance of group leaders who participate, the government generously funds ongoing projects of their organizations. In addition, the government sometimes provides in-kind support such as free transportation to national conventions of the groups.

Most policy debate still takes place within the bureaucracy, where ministries compete with each other to shape and control programs. The Ministry of Finance plays a key role. No new initiatives are taken seriously until its permanent secretary announces that the ministry will provide major funding. Its officials preside over the ensuing debate and negotiation in interministerial committees. To enhance their power, weaker ministries solicit public opinion surveys and resolutions of support for policies from local councils and community groups.

Public opinion drives policy making only during the implementation stage, however. Ministries are obliged to gain community support before actual execution begins. This support is particularly important in the rural areas, where consultation takes place in the traditional community gathering, the *kgotla*. Prior to and during the colonial period the chiefs and headmen held *kgotlas* periodically as a means to consult and persuade their followers on a new policy. In the postindependence era civil servants have used local *kgotlas* to mobilize support, in part as a means of keeping politicians out of decision making. Although *kgotlas* are easily induced to go along with government plans, some refuse, often because of the leadership of a local chief or headman. Changes are then made; for example, a clinic is relocated, or certain roads are given priority over others for upgrading. On rare occasions the community resists proposals for a dam or a fencing scheme. The result of having this *kgotla* gauntlet to run is that ministries try to anticipate local reactions. Failure to do so is likely to embarrass the ministries and elicit inquiries by the cabinet, parliament, and press.

Another manifestation of the developmental character of Botswana's democracy relates to the role of women in politics. Traditionally, women were excluded from public affairs. They could not attend *kgotlas,* let alone speak. In the modern system they are free to speak but are hesitant to do so except on issues of manifest importance to them (for example, the upbringing of children). Although women make up 40–70 percent of most grassroots party organizations, they are rarely nominated to run in elections, and they hold almost no national offices within party structures. Women influence government policy largely through membership in organizations, which range from the conservative Red Cross and the moderate YWCA to the more radical Emang Basadi, which represents professional women. The government provides all these groups with significant funding to promote women's education related to health, family law, and employment.

The Economic Base

The steady expansion of Botswana's economy has provided a firm base for the stability of Botswana's developing democracy. The real rate of growth of the gross national product has been more than 10 percent annually for the past twenty-five years. The financial foundation of this expansion has been the government's joint development of diamond mining with Debeers, the international diamond marketing cartel. Botswana's diamond production is now larger in monetary terms than that of any other country in the world. The government, through the Ministry of Finance, has reinvested a major portion of its profits in accordance with very sophisticated five-year development programs. The ministry has also minimized corruption, especially compared with that of other African countries, and has constantly put pressure for reform on inefficient government programs and unprofitable public corporations.

This managed growth has had two critical consequences for Botswana's democracy. First, the government promotes development that expands employment at a rapid rate. The result is that social discontent arising from unemployment, particularly among the youth, has been greatly reduced. Second, to keep its rural electoral support, the Democratic Party government has provided extensive social services. These services include health clinics, clean water, free public education, numerous types of agricultural extension, and food relief in periods of drought. All are available even in the most remote villages. The net effect is to channel a significant portion of the country's economic growth to low-income groups, thus giving the regime widespread legitimacy.

The Future

The 1980s witnessed a number of developments that should put Botswana's democracy on a firmer foundation. Most significant is the emergence of private newspapers as a significant force in politics. By 1990 five weeklies were distributed in the major urban centers and large villages. Each seeks to uncover government scandals as a way of increasing readership. As a result the ruling Democratic Party leadership and its civil service allies have been forced to reform a number of programs, particularly with respect to land allocation. One newspaper, *Mmegi,* has consistently presented sophisticated policy analysis as well. Although the government continues to publish its *Botswana Daily Mail,* the literate public increasingly looks to the private newspapers for serious reporting on national political conflicts.

There are some signs that government is beginning to lose control over its corporatist interest group structure. Trade unions are engaging in strikes, although no strike has yet been sufficiently crippling to force a major readjustment of the country's low wage scales. Some professional groups, especially the main teachers organization, are finding their constituencies eroded by new and competing groups that do not sit on advisory councils or take government subsidies.

Botswana's democracy has functioned mostly for the benefit of the Tswana population. The Democratic Party and its allies in the civil service showed little inclination to recognize significant minority groups, including the Kalanga, the Bushmen, or the Bayei. The schools used only Tswana and English; the national radio station offered no programs in other languages; and government publications were likewise restricted. As nationalist groups have begun to emerge among non-Tswana populations, both the ruling party and the opposition are beginning to articulate some minority interests. In the not too distant future, government policy on language and culture is likely to recognize more cultural diversity.

In sum, recent developments in Botswana's democracy are expanding the scope of public debate, the role of interest groups, and minority group involvement in party politics.

See also *Africa, Subsaharan.*

BIBLIOGRAPHY

Harvey, Charles, and Steven R. Lewis, Jr. *Policy Choice and Development Performance in Botswana.* London: Macmillan; New York: St. Martin's, 1990.

Hitchcock, Robert K., and John D. Holm. "Bureaucratic Domination of Hunter-Gatherer Societies: A Study of the San in Botswana." *Development and Change* 24 (1993): 305–338.

Holm, John. "Botswana: A Paternalistic Democracy." In *Democracy in Developing Countries: Africa,* edited by Larry Diamond, Juan Linz, and Seymour Martin Lipset. Boulder, Colo.: Lynne Rienner; London: Adamantine Press, 1988.

Holm, John, and Patrick Molutsi, eds. *Democracy in Botswana.* Athens: Ohio University Press, 1989.

Molutsi, Patrick P., and John Holm. "Developing Democracy When Civil Society Is Weak: The Case of Botswana." *African Affairs* 89 (1990): 323–340.

Sklar, Richard L. "Developmental Democracy." *Comparative Studies in Society and History* 29 (1987): 686–714.

Stedman, Stephen John, ed. *Botswana: The Political Economy of Democratic Development.* Boulder, Colo.: Lynne Rienner, 1993.

Burma

The largest state in mainland Southeast Asia, with borders on China, Bangladesh, India, Laos, and Thailand. Burma has had limited experience with democracy since gaining independence from Great Britain in 1948. The military government that took power in 1988 changed the name of the state to Myanmar in 1989, though opposition groups did not accept the change. In this article, *Myanmar* is used only for the period since 1989, while the name *Burma* is retained for earlier periods. The adjective *Burmese* refers to the citizens of Burma/Myanmar, while *Burmans* refers to the major ethnic group.

In the precolonial era Burma traditionally was governed by an autocratic monarchy tempered only by its limited administrative capacity and the Buddhist clergy. Burma became a British colony after three Anglo-Burmese wars (1824–1826, 1852, and 1895–1896) that resulted in the partition of the Burmese state. Bent on revenue collection and law and order, the British governed Burma from India.

At the time of independence, in 1948, Burma adopted a civilian, multiparty democratic system dominated by a political coalition. This gave way to a military regime in 1958. Civilian, democratic rule was reinstituted through elections in 1960 and lasted until 1962. On March 2, 1962, the military launched a coup that kept it in power in the following decades and prevented the development of a democratic system of governance. Democratic and independence movements in Burma were linked to anticolonialism and nationalism, as well as to ethnic identity.

Traditional Decision Making

Burma traditionally has had many ethnic and linguistic groups. The Buddhist Burmans have been dominant in the heartland for most of the period since the eleventh century. In the south the Buddhist Mons established pre-Burman kingdoms, and in the Arakan Peninsula Hindu-Buddhist kingdoms existed from about the first century A.D. to the end of the eighteenth century. In the northeast the Shans evolved a traditional Buddhist set of small hereditary kingdoms. The Chins and Nagas in the west, the Kachins in the north, and the Karens in the east all had tribal societies with animist religions. Christianity has made major inroads among the animist groups since the nineteenth century. Burman Buddhists traditionally have held women in high regard. Since early times women have had high literacy rates and equal rights, including the right to inherit.

Several types of consensual decision making were found in the traditional village-level societies within the boundaries of the present country. These were not democratic in terms of the election of leaders through some sort of formal or constitutional process, and they lacked the potential for a peaceful transfer of authority from one political group or individual to another. The Burman areas of Burma in the precolonial period, however, did have informal mechanisms whereby the village headmen—often hereditary positions—were viewed as representing the village to the central court. Some minority groups, such as the Kachins and Karens, showed a clearer pattern of consensual rule by elders or authority figures of the village or clan.

With a long history in Burma, Buddhism became established in the eleventh century. Theravada Buddhism is the religion of more than three-quarters of the Burmese, including most ethnic Burmans. Some scholars of religion argue that Theravada Buddhism fosters a sense of individualism and equality, both of which may contribute to the democratic process.

Beginning in 1922 the British rulers of Burma instituted a legislative council, with 80 of the 130 members elected by a limited electorate. The issue of separation from India dominated politics at that time, and a vote held in 1932 rejected separation. In 1935 a new constitution created a bicameral legislature: a Senate, of whose members half were elected and half were appointed by the British governor, and a more powerful elected House of Representatives.

The political process was characterized by the personalization of power. Burma had a strong tradition of person-

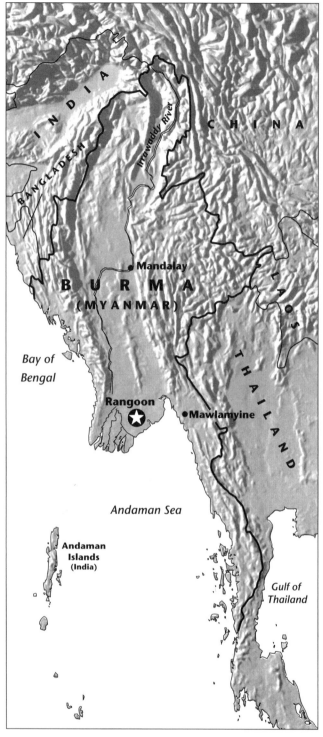

alism, dating back more than 900 years, in which loyalty was given to the individual monarch and not to the office of the throne.

Burma's experience with responsible parliamentary government proved fleeting; it lasted from 1937, when Burma gained separation from India, until 1941, when World War II began in Asia. Japanese forces occupied Burma during World War II. That period saw the rise of a pseudo-independent state run by a dictatorship, or *adipati,* which soon became discredited. Eventually, resistance to the Japanese gave rise to a loose political confederation called the Anti-Fascist People's Freedom League (AFPFL). The AFPFL dominated Burmese political life for a decade after independence, until it formally split into factions in 1958. The split led to a constitutional coup in which the civilian regime, led by Prime Minister U Nu, authorized a temporary military takeover, led by the commander of the armed forces, General Ne Win. The AFPFL contained a broad spectrum of political opinion but excluded two separate communist parties, both of which were in revolt.

The decade of civilian control between 1948 and 1958 was characterized by a series of ethnic and political revolts that severely restricted the capacity of the state to develop. The rebels included two communist parties and elements of most minority groups. The government was elected under a constitution adopted in 1947, which established a republic with a bicameral legislature: an upper house of nationalities (that is, ethnic groups) and a dominant lower house. All seats were elected. A president was chosen from among those elected; the office rotated among various ethnic groups. A prime minister was appointed by the party in power, which in this period was continuously the AFPFL. Opposition parties were tolerated, although the Burma Communist Party was banned because it was in revolt. The judiciary was relatively independent, and its senior members were well trained in British law. A career elite bureaucracy was fostered. Suffrage was universal, especially because women had traditionally wielded considerable power in the society. The press was relatively free. This period was the most democratic of any in Burmese history.

The military caretaker government lasted from 1958 until 1960, during which time it ruled by decree. Military leaders unsuccessfully attempted to improve the economy and eliminate the rebellions. They did, however, abide by the results of the 1960 election, which was widely heralded as a fair contest. Two components of the now dissolved AFPFL were the main contenders; former prime minister U Nu won, and a civilian, democratic government was again installed.

The Coup of 1962

Ethnic unrest continued. On March 2, 1962, claiming that Burma was about to disintegrate as a result of the conflicts, the military launched an almost bloodless coup. This time the military leaders—most of whom had taken part in the earlier military caretaker government—clearly intended to stay in power. They established a military Revolutionary Council and ruled by decree for more than a decade, until 1974. They centralized control and eliminated any threats to their power, abolishing both the legislature and the judiciary. The executive branch was staffed and controlled by the military. A statement of intent, called the Burmese Way to Socialism, was established soon after the coup, and by the following year Burma was characterized by military mobilization, centralized control, an absence of political and media freedom, and a socialist economy.

By 1974 the military, led by General Ne Win, had taken a cadre party founded in 1962, called the Burma Socialist Program Party, and expanded it into a mass organization. It was enshrined in the Constitution of 1974 as Burma's sole party. The military leaders had somewhat liberalized the extreme socialism that characterized the 1960s. The 1974 Constitution also created the Pyithu Hluttaw, or national legislature, whose members were elected by voting for designated candidates on single-party slates. A system of "people's justice" was established, in which party officials replaced lawyers. The military controlled the press and censored all media. There was an elaborate system of military intelligence and reporting. With the military in complete command, human rights and democracy were suppressed.

The Events of 1988 and After

By 1988 the people of Burma were suffering from political malaise and economic deprivation. That March a massive uprising began, which lasted several months. It began among university students in Rangoon, the capital, and soon spread to the rest of the country. Attempts by the military to appease the populace with piecemeal reforms came too late. There had been mass killings of students and demonstrators that had discredited the regime. In the midst of this ferment, on September 18, the military launched its third coup to shore up military control and to replace the earlier military regime.

The new leaders, the State Law and Order Restoration Council, brutally suppressed popular dissent. This group, originally composed of eighteen senior military figures, continued to rule in the early 1990s. Until August 1992 the State Law and Order Restoration Council ruled by martial law. It abolished the legislature and disbanded the Burma Socialist Program Party, establishing an even more autocratic military rule.

Promising an eventual move to a civilian, multiparty system, the State Law and Order Restoration Council allowed the formation and registration of political parties. The military promised to remain aloof from politics. Still, the National Unity Party was clearly the favored group. It had inherited many of the assets of the Burma Socialist Program Party. In all, 234 parties registered, and eventually 93 competed in the elections held May 27, 1990. An opposition party, the National League for Democracy, won 80 percent of the seats. It was led by *Daw* (Madam) Aung San Suu Kyi, whom the military had placed under house arrest. Taken aback by this sweeping rejection of the military's role in government, the State Law and Order Restoration Council refused to recognize the results of the election.

The council then promised to establish a multiparty civilian government under a new constitution and, in January 1993, began the long constitution-making process. The military called a national convention of more than 700 handpicked persons to establish guidelines for the constitution. No end date was set for the convention's deliberations. Following the convention, a new constitution would still have to be written (based, at least in theory, on the convention guidelines) and subjected to a national plebiscite, and then new elections would have to be held for the new government. The State Law and Order Restoration Council indicated that the military would continue in its traditional leadership role under any new government and would likely attempt to institutionalize its power.

Some members of the National League for Democracy held a rump, secret meeting in Mandalay of the majority of those elected to the Pyithu Hluttaw. They designated certain leaders to flee to a rebel-held area along the eastern (Thai) frontier. There they established, in December 1990, the National Coalition Government of the Union of Burma, a government claiming to represent the legitimate will of the people as expressed in the May 1990 elections. It was denounced by the Rangoon authorities.

Throughout its history Burma/Myanmar has been characterized by factional and personalized power. In the decades since independence the military has played the most conspicuous role and directly held power for more than three decades. The generation of leaders trained under the British in parliamentary democracy has grown too old to govern again.

International communications technology has kept the

military from closing off the country from outside influences, as happened after the 1962 coup. Moreover, the military leaders have tried to encourage foreign tourists and investment. In 1988, when the old political, authoritarian structure was collapsing, there were continuous cries for democracy. There is considerable dispute concerning how far the Burmese people and some of their leaders understand the nature of the democratic system, in contrast to its forms. Many Burmese advocate democracy. Short of a popular uprising backed by some of the military, however, the military leaders seem unlikely to give up political control, whatever the nature of the new constitution.

See also *Asia, Southeast.*

BIBLIOGRAPHY

Aung Cin Win Aung. *Burma: From Monarchy to Dictatorship.* Bloomington, Ind.: Eastern Press, 1994.

Gyi, Maurg. *Burmese Political Values: The Socio-political Roots of Authoritarianism.* New York: Praeger, 1983.

Shwe Lu Maung. *Burma, Nationalism and Ideology: An Analysis of Society, Culture, and Politics.* Dhaka: University Press, 1989.

Silverstein, Josef. *Burmese Politics: The Dilemma of National Unity.* New Brunswick, N.J.: Rutgers University Press, 1980.

Singh, Balwant. *Independence and Democracy in Burma, 1945–1952: The Turbulent Years.* Ann Arbor: Center for South and Southeast Asian Studies, University of Michigan, 1993.

Steinberg, David I. *The Future of Burma: Crisis and Choice in Myanmar.* Lanham, Md.: University Press of America, 1990.

C

Caucasus, The

The area, formerly part of the Soviet Union, in southeastern Europe between the Black Sea and the Caspian Sea. Within the Russian Federation the territories of Krasnodar and Stavropol and the republics of Adygey, Chechnya, Dagestan, Ingushetia, Kabardino-Balkaria, Karachay-Cherkessia, and North Ossetia are north of the Caucasus Mountains. South of the mountain range are Armenia, Azerbaijan, and Georgia. The boundaries of the Caucasus have been disputed for centuries. Ethnic and nationalist feelings—and economic hardship—have impeded the development of democracy in the region.

Historical Background

Until Russian conquests in the eighteenth and nineteenth centuries, the Caucasus was a region of constant struggle between nomads in the lowlands and farmers and herders in the highlands. The social structure of the highland people ranged from egalitarian tribal democracies to feudal principalities, but even the most authoritarian rulers had to tolerate and respect rights and customs in the peripheries of their domains, where their authority was recognized only nominally and conditionally. A few early attempts to restrict the absolute power of monarchs in the capitals of their kingdoms were unsuccessful. Centuries of invasions and civil wars prevented further democratic developments in the Caucasus until the 1980s.

In the late eighteenth century the Turks of the Ottoman Empire forced many Armenians to leave the area. During the Armenian diaspora ("dispersion"), when Armenians were scattered into the cities of Europe, Russia, and India, some attempts were made to devise a democratic British-style constitution for a future Armenian state. Although doomed to remain on paper, and little known even in Armenia, this effort nevertheless exerted some influence on the development of Armenian political thought and activity in the nineteenth century.

The Russians, who first invaded the Caucasus in 1763, finished absorbing it into the Russian empire in 1864. The institution of limited reforms in the early 1860s influenced later political thinking in Russia generally and in the Caucasus in particular. The Russian revolution of 1905 led to the creation of a number of political parties in the Caucasus. The main division lay between social democrats, who insisted on a socialist transformation of the whole empire, and various nationalists, who were concerned with the social and cultural development of their respective ethnic groups.

In April 1918 the Transcaucasian Provisional Congress declared the independence of the Caucasus as a whole. Several events prompted this declaration: the Bolshevik revolution in Russia in 1917; the Treaty of Brest-Litovsk in 1918, which ended Russian participation in World War I; and the retreat of demoralized Russian troops from eastern Turkey, which Russia had occupied during the war. The leaders of the various ethnic groups could not coordinate their efforts, however, and in late May the Democratic Republic of Georgia, the Armenian Democratic Republic, and the Republic of Azerbaijan declared their independence separately.

Three Independent Republics and the Soviet Period

Armenia, which was in the weakest position of the three, immediately became embroiled in conflict with Turkey; an unfavorable peace was followed by renewed war. The Armenian Dashnak (Socialist Federalist Party) government declared a number of democratic administrative reforms, but after facing economic and social disaster, the govern-

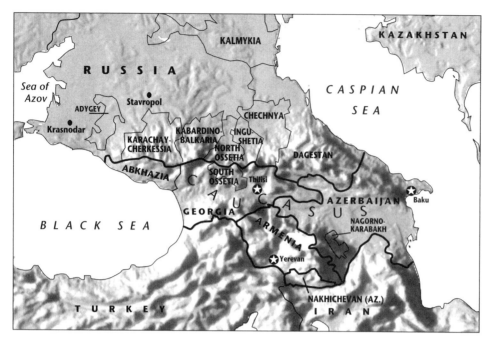

ment surrendered to an invasion by the Russian Federation at the end of 1920. Similar events took place in Azerbaijan, where the liberal-democratic Moussavat (Party of Equality) government was overthrown by the Soviets in April 1920. Armenia and Azerbaijan were incorporated into the Union of Soviet Socialist Republics in 1922.

Georgia also faced difficult economic and military problems but was aided by the British, who occupied Georgia at the end of 1918, after the Germans retreated. The British left in 1919. The Georgian government, under the leadership of the Mensheviks (a social democratic party), was able to conduct municipal elections in 1918 and national elections in 1919. More than 70 percent of the eligible voters cast ballots. The Mensheviks, who enjoyed the support of peasants and workers, won most of the seats in the Constituent Assembly. Several democratic reforms, including land reform, were carried out. On May 7, 1920, the Soviet Union signed a treaty renouncing all claims to Georgian territory. But in February 1921, on the pretext of unrest in the disputed district of Lori (the northernmost part of present-day Armenia), the Soviet army invaded Georgia. Within a couple of months the Menshevik government had to flee abroad. Georgia was absorbed into the Soviet Union, first as part of the Transcaucasian Federation in 1922; it became a separate Soviet Socialist Republic in 1936.

Despite their democratic vocabulary and serious attempts at reforms, these three governments were motivated chiefly by nationalist objectives. Armenia and Azerbaijan fought over the territories of Nakhichevan, a predominantly Azeri district within Armenia, and Nagorno-Karabakh, a largely Armenian district within Azerbaijan. The conflict was marked by atrocities on both sides clearly aimed at "ethnic cleansing." The Georgian government behaved equally brutally in suppressing any attempts at self-determination among ethnic Abkhazians and Ossetians. Its social reforms were arranged so as not to injure the property rights of ethnic Georgians but to take as much property as possible from rich farmers and urban bourgeoisie (mostly Armenians).

Prospects for democracy disappeared after the Soviets invaded the Caucasus. Dissidents who dared to mention the notion were arrested and sent to prisons or mental asylums. Although the reform efforts made by Soviet leader Mikhail Gorbachev in the 1980s should not be underestimated, the collapse of the Soviet Union in 1991—and the emergence of fifteen independent states and the end of communist rule—had never been his aim. True democratization came not from Gorbachev's reforms but from continuous popular pressure, especially from the intelligentsia. This pressure had been present long before Gorbachev, and it bore some early fruit in spite of repression. Popular demonstrations in Armenia in 1965, for instance, publicized the fiftieth anniversary of genocide by Ottoman Turks in western Armenia in 1915. And student demonstrations in Tbilisi, Georgia, in 1977 forced the inclusion of national language rights in the constitutions of all three

Transcaucasian republics. These actions paved the way for subsequent democratic developments.

Nationalism and Democratic Prospects

Since 1923 Nagorno-Karabakh had been an autonomous district within Azerbaijan; 75 percent of its people were Armenians and they wanted to be part of Armenia. In February 1988 Nagorno-Karabakh was declared separate from Azerbaijan. Azerbaijan responded by blockading Nagorno-Karabakh, starving it of food and fuel. Moscow was unable to control the situation; violence erupted, and many were killed or became refugees. In 1991, after mass rallies and strikes, Armenia proclaimed independence, though Nagorno-Karabakh remains disputed. Armenia's situation is difficult economically and politically. Not all the actions of its present government are democratic, but further democratic elections and reforms are possible, especially if tensions with Azerbaijan abate.

In Azerbaijan political developments still are motivated chiefly by nationalism. The National Front of Azerbaijan unified many factions ranging from neofascists to a tiny liberal Social Democratic Party. After many coup attempts, Azerbaijan finally had a democratically elected president, when Abulfaz Elchibey was elected in June 1992. But Elchibey's government failed to carry out any consistently democratic reform, and in June 1993 it was overthrown by military commanders, allegedly for inconsistency in carrying out the anti-Armenian policy in the war for Nagorno-Karabakh. The Azerbaijanis then elected as their president Heydar Aliyev. It would be naïve to expect any democratic action to be undertaken by Aliyev, the former first secretary of the Communist Party and chief of the KGB in Azerbaijan.

The most dramatic movement toward democracy in the early years of Gorbachev's tenure came in Georgia, where memories of a democratic past were stronger, the Social Democrats were less discredited in public opinion than were the Socialist Federalists, and democratic leanings among the intelligentsia were more robust. Various dissident groups gained momentum, and a number of political organizations opposing the Soviet government were created. In April 1989 demonstrations in Tbilisi, which began as a protest against Abkhazian separatism, turned into massive rallies for independence. In dispersing the protesters, special troops using toxic gas and tanks killed more than twenty people, mostly young women. From that moment on communism was doomed in Georgia. Two years later independence was proclaimed, and the collapse of the Soviet Union made it a reality.

Zviad Gamsakhurdia was elected president of Georgia, but he behaved inconsistently and often dictatorially and was overthrown. His main political opponent, former first secretary Eduard Shevardnadze, was then elected president of the parliament and head of state. Real power, however, was held by a junta of military commanders, who in August 1992 launched a military invasion of Abkhazia, which sought independence from Georgia. With the aid of volunteers from the northern Caucasus (mostly Kabardinian and Chechen), the Abkhazians threw the Georgian armed forces out of Abkhazia. Nearly 200,000 ethnic Georgian civilians fled Abkhazia in fear of mass murders. As long as the armistice between Abkhazia and Georgia remains shaky, and the authority of the central government in Georgia is disputed in nearly every town by local warlords, it is futile to talk about democratic progress in Georgia.

In most of the republics of the northern Caucasus, which are now part of the Russian Federation, the ruling groups are by and large the same party leaders as before. No opposing organization is strong or politically mature enough to challenge an establishment that shrewdly manipulates nationalist feelings and fears. Chechnya, which proclaimed independence and fought the Russian military to a standstill but is not recognized by other states, and Ingushetia, which willingly signed the treaty establishing the Russian Federation, are the exceptions: their leaders were elected with true popular support. Both nations, however, must struggle with rivalry between various clans.

There is thus little real prospect for democratic development in the Caucasus. Only Armenia holds some slight promise. Three groups of leaders are found in these societies: former party elites, military officers, and intellectuals. Before we can seriously talk about democracy in the region, we will have to wait for entrepreneurs, managers, lawyers, and economists to appear.

See also *Armenia*.

BIBLIOGRAPHY

Batalden, Stephen K., and Sandra L. Batalden. *The Newly Independent States of Eurasia: A Handbook of Former Soviet Republics.* Phoenix, Ariz.: Oryx Press, 1993.

Bremmer, Ian, and Ray Taras, eds. *Nations and Politics in the Soviet Successor States.* Cambridge and New York: Cambridge University Press, 1993.

Libaridian, Gerard, ed. *The Karabagh File.* Watertown, Mass.: Zoryan Institute, 1988.

Suny, Ronald Grigor. *Looking toward Ararat: Armenia in Modern History.* Bloomington: Indiana University Press, 1993.

———. *The Making of the Georgian Nation.* Bloomington: Indiana University Press, 1988; London: I. B. Tauris, 1988.

——. *The Revenge of the Past: Nationalism, Revolution, and the Collapse of the Soviet Union.* Stanford, Calif.: Stanford University Press, 1993.

Walker, Christopher. *Armenia and Karabagh: The Struggle for Unity.* London: Minority Rights Publications, 1991.

China

An East Asian nation formally known as the People's Republic of China since the advent of Communist rule in 1949. The Chinese tradition of democracy differs in both concept and form from the Western tradition. Whereas the Western tradition has placed a premium on individual rights, the Chinese tradition has sought harmony between the ruler and the ruled, placing a premium on the welfare of the people and the ability of the people to communicate their needs to the ruler without interference.

China's Confucian Tradition

Within this Confucian tradition, the right—indeed the obligation—of the moral person to remonstrate against corruption and misgovernment is enshrined in the story of Qu Yuan, a government minister of the fourth century B.C. who drowned himself when his entreaties were rejected by his king and disaster ensued. Yet this call to individual conscience was an appeal to the superior person as guardian of the kingly way, not to the articulation of individual, partial interests. Whereas the Western liberal tradition has assumed that a greater good will emerge from the competition of partial interests, the Chinese tradition has assumed harmony between the part and the whole. Just as the Confucian classic the Great Learning, written in the third century B.C., locates the basis of universal peace in the superior person's efforts to rectify his heart, the Confucian tradition has sought to harmonize the interests of the people under virtuous rulership.

In the late nineteenth and early twentieth centuries China was still under the sway of the Qing dynasty. Established in the mid-seventeenth century after the Manchu conquest of China, the Qing was suffering from both a demographic revolution and dynastic decline as the West began to assert its demands aggressively in the mid-nineteenth century. Forceful leadership was not forthcoming under the rule of the Empress Dowager Cixi, who died in 1908 after dominating Chinese politics for nearly half a century.

As democratic thought from the West began to enter China in the late years of the Qing dynasty, Chinese liberals responded largely within the constraints of their Confucian tradition, with two important exceptions. One was that Chinese liberals firmly located sovereignty in the people, thereby destroying the doctrinal basis of the monarchical system, which was so intertwined with Confucianism that the fall of China's last dynasty largely discredited Confucianism. The other was that Chinese liberals responded to the Western democratic message out of a sense of weakness and vulnerability; hence, nationalism and state building were an inherent part of the democratic enterprise. China had lost a series of wars with the Western powers, had been forced to sign unequal treaties, and appeared under imminent threat of dismemberment. Thus Chinese liberals looked to Western democracy as a key to understanding the source of Western wealth and power; their goal was not to promote individual rights and liberty but to restore Chinese greatness. Whereas Western democracy emerged as a response to absolutism, the modern Chinese democratic tradition looked to democracy as a way to enhance the strength of the state.

The Emergence of Modern Democratic Thought

Modern democratic thought in China emerged in large part as a reaction to China's defeat in the Sino-Japanese war of 1894–1895. This defeat by a nation that China had always regarded as inferior, and that had only begun its own reform efforts some seventeen years earlier, dispelled any illusions that the half measures that China had adopted to strengthen itself in the latter half of the nineteenth century would be sufficient.

The sense of imminent national disaster was captured by Kang Youwei, a brilliant and eccentric interpreter of the Confucian tradition. He organized some 800 of his fellow provincial degree holders, then in Beijing to take the metropolitan exam (the highest level of China's three-tiered traditional examination system), to sign a memorial to the throne demanding that the treaty with Japan be rejected and institutional reforms be implemented immediately. Three years later, in 1898, Kang and his precocious follower Liang Qichao were named advisers to the emperor. From this position they oversaw a radical reform effort aimed at transforming China's traditional monarchical system into a constitutional monarchy complete with a division of power between an executive, a legislature, and a judiciary.

The radical reform program of 1898 lasted only a hundred days before a coup d'état by the Empress Dowager sent Kang and Liang fleeing to Japan. In the ensuing years Liang overtook his mentor and became the undisputed leader of the reform movement. Liang, more than any other single person, defined modern democratic thought in

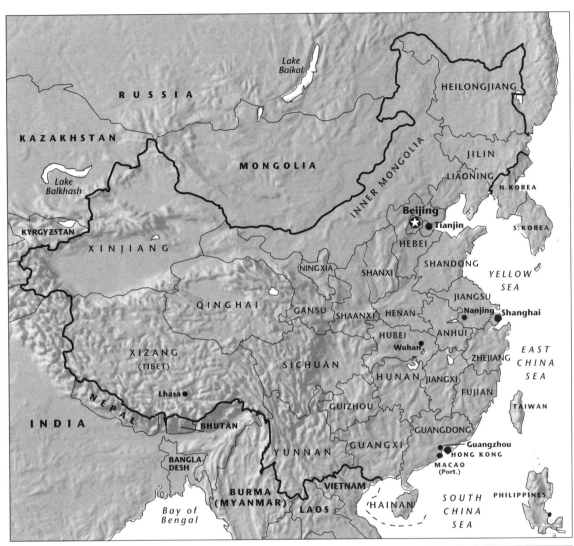

China. He excoriated the monarchy for regarding affairs of state as personal and private; instead, he identified sovereignty as residing in the people. Liang also urged the formation of such institutions as chambers of commerce and scholarly associations to enhance the flow of information between state and society and thereby improve policy formation.

Liang's thought, however, differed significantly from Western democratic ideas and often led him to misunderstand the writings of the Western democratic thinkers he so avidly introduced into China. In particular, Liang never understood one of the basic underpinnings of Western democratic thought—namely, that the pursuit of private, indeed selfish, interests could result in the common good. Such a notion of the "hidden hand"—the idea that the pull and haul of individual interests can result in the greatest good for society—was completely alien to the Chinese tradition, which placed a premium on the harmony of social interests. For a scholar such as Liang, bred in the tradition of the Great Learning, interests were to be reconciled on the basis of a higher good, not pursued at the expense of other interests. One searches Liang's work in vain for institutional mechanisms to reconcile divergent interests, for the assumption underlying such a need was simply alien to Liang's mental world.

Constitutionalists and Revolutionaries

If China's modern democratic ideas are inextricably linked with Liang Qichao, democratic practice finds its origins in the Constitutionalist Movement, which was closely linked with Liang. Following the antiforeign Boxer Rebellion of 1900 and the Qing dynasty's subsequent humiliation at the hands of an expeditionary force formed by eight foreign powers, the Empress Dowager finally agreed to a reform program. To win support from increasingly disaffected local gentry, the Qing court in 1905 yielded to pressures to move toward constitutional rule and sent a five-person observation team abroad to study the constitutions of other nations. After the mission returned the following year, the court announced a nine-year program to prepare for constitutional rule. This program included a call for the establishment of provincial assemblies as a first step toward full constitutional rule.

As a result, China held its first elections from February through June 1909. Only those with significant wealth or holders of higher education degrees were eligible to vote—requirements that restricted the electorate to less than one-half of 1 percent of the population. Moreover, the elections were indirect. The electorate chose an electoral college, which in turn elected members of the provincial assemblies.

Despite evidence of indifference and corruption in the election, some of the provincial assemblies boasted highly qualified members, and the assemblies quickly became forums for promoting local interests as well as for demanding more rapid reform and democratization from the Qing court. Since many began to feel that China was in imminent danger of partition, the provincial assemblies organized for joint action. In 1910 representatives from the provincial assemblies organized three petition drives—the last one allegedly collecting 25 million signatures—demanding an early convening of the parliament.

The representatives who made up the provincial assemblies were the last generation of China's traditional gentry. Met by resistance from the court, they turned toward revolution, and their support was one of the major reasons that the Revolution of 1911 succeeded quickly and without social turmoil.

As Liang was charting a reformist path and the Constitutionalist Movement was pushing for a constitutional monarchy, a revolutionary movement that rejected the Qing dynasty as beyond redemption was developing. Sun Yat-sen (Sun Zhangshan) established the Revive China Society in November 1894 to overthrow Manchu imperial rule, restore Chinese rule, and establish a federal republic. By the time Sun joined with other revolutionaries to establish the Chinese United League in 1905, he had formulated

the ideas embodied in his famous Three People's Principles—nationalism, democracy (sometimes translated as the "people's rights"), and the people's livelihood.

Sun's revolutionary aspirations met with success in 1911, when the tottering Qing dynasty responded ineptly to a prematurely launched revolutionary uprising in the central Chinese city of Wuchang. Most of the southern provinces, whose disgust with the central government had risen in the course of efforts to promote constitutionalism, responded by declaring their independence from the Qing and supporting the establishment of a republic.

This first effort at republican government was handicapped from the outset by the weakness of the democratic impulse that underlay the revolutionary movement. Anti-Manchu nationalism and local distrust of the corrupt Qing court contributed more to the overthrow of the dynasty than did the demand for democracy. Nevertheless, Sun and many other revolutionaries had been impressed by the combination of national strength and democratic institutions in Western nations, and they hoped that republican institutions would be the key to national strength and prosperity for China. Fear of foreign intervention, divisions within the revolutionary ranks, and the strong showing of northern military leader Yuan Shikai, however, led Sun and the revolutionaries to yield power to Yuan, who became the first president of the new republic.

Chinese hopes for democracy following the revolution thus centered on the reorganization of the United League as an open political party under the name Kuomintang (Guomindang), or Nationalist Party, and the development of an effective parliament to balance Yuan Shikai's authority. Largely through the efforts of Song Jiaoren, a young and articulate advocate of democracy and parliamentary government, the Kuomintang (KMT) emerged as the dominant party in the elections of 1912.

This optimistic beginning soured quickly, however, as the ambitious Yuan abandoned all pretense to democratic ideals, handily defeated the "Second Revolution" launched in 1913 to oppose him, and finally moved to make himself emperor. Widespread resistance quickly doomed Yuan's efforts as one province after another announced its independence. Yuan's monarchical ambitions collapsed, and he died in June 1916.

Warlordism became Yuan's legacy to China, as military commanders, many of them Yuan's former subordinates, carved out fiefdoms of their own and struggled for control of Beijing, the capital. Warlordism not only destroyed what little remained of constitutionalism but also undermined the belief that democracy could be achieved either quickly or directly through constitutional means. It also fueled the rise of the two revolutionary movements—the Nationalist and the Communist—that would dominate twentieth-century Chinese politics.

The May Fourth Movement

Although the period of warlordism marked the nadir of Chinese political development, it was nevertheless a period of remarkable social and intellectual ferment. In this period, while the West was embroiled in World War I, the Chinese economy expanded rapidly, even as Japanese pressures on China escalated at the same time. Both developments provided the impetus for popular nationalism, while the democratic ideals espoused by U.S. president Woodrow Wilson during World War I ignited hope and idealism among Chinese intellectuals.

Democratic ideals and nationalistic passion came together in the May Fourth demonstration of 1919, which was provoked by the news that the Versailles peace conference at the end of World War I had, contrary to Chinese popular hopes and expectations, awarded Germany's rights in Shandong province to Japan. Outraged students and faculty took to the streets to protest the decision as well as the news that the warlord government had betrayed China's national interests by agreeing to the transfer.

The protest movement that ensued combined the Chinese tradition of remonstration by the scholarly upholders of public morality with mass nationalism and an iconoclastic critique of Chinese tradition based on an ideal of enlightenment. It thus went beyond the visions of Liang Qichao, who never conceived of politics in anything but elite terms, by linking democratic demands with popular protest and cultural critique. Moreover, the sense of democracy held by many May Fourth intellectuals, especially those who had studied abroad, was more sophisticated than that of Liang Qichao.

Nevertheless, the driving force of the May Fourth Movement was nationalism, a passion that soon led to the revitalization of the Nationalist Party on the one hand and the founding of the Chinese Communist Party (in 1921) on the other. The ideal of enlightenment might in time have led to a more sophisticated understanding of democracy, but it was soon overwhelmed by nationalistic passions.

The Federalist Movement

A brief interlude that has generally received insufficient attention in Western and Chinese literature alike was China's federalist movement of 1920–1923. The federalist movement had its origins in the expansion of local authority in the late Qing period and in efforts to reform or overthrow the Qing. Sun Yat-sen, strongly influenced by the American example, appears to have been the first to advocate federalism, although he later denounced it as undermining nationalism. Participants in the constitutionalist movement, including Liang Qichao and others, looked to federalism as a way of resolving the conflicts between local and central interests. Federalist ideas grew in the aftermath of the 1911 Revolution, particularly in the southern provinces, which hoped to ward off a recentralization of authority in the hands of Yuan Shikai. Federalist ideas waned in the aftermath of the unsuccessful Second Revolution (1913) but revived after the collapse of Yuan's imperial ambitions, his death shortly thereafter, and the emergence of local warlords.

Federalist ideas in China also received a boost from Woodrow Wilson's proposal of a League of Nations and from the visit of John Dewey, the American philosopher of pragmatism, whose ideas bolstered those looking for ways to build democracy from the ground up and realistically address China's problems in a period of warlord division. American freedoms were widely perceived in China to be protected by its federalist system. At the same time, intellectuals looking for ways to end the fighting among warlords began calling for a constitutional convention.

The idealism and political activism unleashed by the May Fourth Movement contributed to this effort to convene a constitutional convention, but as the passions released by the movement began to wane, intellectuals began to look for ways to put their ideas into practice. Some of them turned to federalism. Perhaps no one better exemplified the convergence of these trends than Hu Shi, a May Fourth intellectual luminary and student of John Dewey, who became a strong advocate of federalism.

Federalism grew in opposition to militarism and in support of democracy, but ultimately it fell victim to continued militarism on the one hand and revolution on the other. The first and most important bastion of self-government and federalism was Hunan province, where local generals took advantage of shifts in warlord power to drive out the local warlord and invited prominent intellectuals to draw up a provincial constitution. Promulgated on January 1, 1922, Hunan's constitution was revised and diluted in 1923 and then set aside in 1924 amidst renewed warlord battles.

Other provinces also adopted federalist plans, but the

conflict between provincialism, which was a necessary foundation of federalism, and nationalism became clear when Chen Jiongming, the Guangdong warlord who supported federalism and hoped to make Guangdong a model province, rebelled against Sun, driving him from the province. The following year, however, Sun and his followers returned to Guangdong, defeating Chen and establishing their own revolutionary government. When the reorganized Kuomintang held its first congress in January 1924, supporters of provincial autonomy and federalism were scolded as presenting obstacles to national unification. The day of federalism had passed.

The Nationalist Government

Despite the corruption and ineffectiveness of parliamentary politics in the early republic and the deprivations of warlord politics, democracy remained a good word in China's political lexicon as well as one of Sun's Three People's Principles. The failed experiment with democratic politics, however, and the changing international climate (particularly with the Great Depression, which began in 1929, and the rise of authoritarian governments in much of Europe) made many think of democracy as a distant goal. The Kuomintang, reorganized with Soviet assistance in 1923, began to place greater stress on Sun's three-stage program for the realization of democracy: military conquest, political tutelage, and constitutional democracy. The Kuomintang announced in 1928 that the stage of political tutelage would last six years, but even many supporters of democratic politics soon began to view this goal as unrealistically optimistic.

The drift toward more authoritarian solutions was reinforced by the rise of Chiang Kai-shek (Jiang Jieshi), the former commandant of the Whampoa Military Academy, who had successfully outmaneuvered more senior members of the Kuomintang to become the successor to Sun following Sun's death in 1925. The success of the Kuomintang's Northern Expedition in 1926–1928 nominally reunified the country, although Nationalist authority was initially effective only in five provinces of eastern China. Chiang also faced challenges to his authority from members of the Kuomintang, from warlords who were nominally allied to the KMT, and later from an increasingly effective Communist movement based in the south-central province of Jiangxi. Given these challenges and his own predilection to rely primarily on military force, Chiang turned readily to authoritarian approaches and repeatedly postponed the stage of constitutional democracy.

Influenced by the rise of fascism and militarism in such countries as Germany, Italy, Spain, and Japan, at least some elements of the Kuomintang became quite attracted to fascist doctrines, although the party never developed the fascination with violence that characterized European fascist movements. At a minimum the theories of organic unity between state and society propounded by such movements resonated with Chinese concepts of societal harmony as well as with the needs of the Nationalist government.

Under such conditions, even longstanding proponents of democratic rule seem to have developed doubts about democracy, or at least about its applicability to China. Even Hu Shi, China's leading exponent of Western liberalism, defended democracy with the weak and convoluted argument that China could adopt democracy only because it was not yet ready for enlightened despotism—a form of government that Hu argued required more leaders of knowledge and ability than did democracy.

Given the government's increasing predilection for authoritarian solutions and the liberals' faltering defense of democratic ideals, the demand for democracy fell by default to the leaders of student movements, who repeatedly challenged the authority and authoritarianism of the government. The factor that lent passion and legitimacy to these student movements, however, was not so much the yearning for democracy as it was nationalism. Student movements were expressing the nationalistic feelings of Chinese frustrated by the government's corruption, inefficiency, and unwillingness to resist Japan's increasing encroachments on Chinese territory.

The Communist Movement

At the same time that a factionalized Kuomintang tried to exert effective control over China, the Chinese Communist movement capitalized on local grievances and nationalistic frustrations to build a highly organized and effective political movement. Though driven from their base in Jiangxi to the plains of the far northwest in the mid-1930s, the leaders of the Chinese Communist movement used its organizational abilities and appeals to nationalism to expand rapidly following the outbreak of the Sino-Japanese war in 1937 and the declaration of a second United Front with the Kuomintang.

Although the Communist Party rejected "bourgeois democracy" as a sham, democratic aspirations of a sort were recognized in the party's call for developing a higher level of democracy, one that was more "substantive" than its bourgeois counterpart. Moreover, in the course of the revolutionary movement, the Communists adopted a mobilizing technique known as the "mass line," which tried to combine the demands of a local population with the overall line of the party. At its best, the mass line mitigated the party's ideological rigidity and increased its popular support.

At the same time, the party developed the "unity-struggle-unity" formula for conducting intraparty struggle, an approach that rejected the wholesale use of secret police in purging party dissidents and placed a premium on forging group unity. Finally, in the course of the war years, the Communist Party cooperated with noncommunist forces in the areas it controlled, forming coalition governments through the so-called three-thirds system, in which party members would not occupy more than one-third of the government positions.

At their best, these organizational methods of the Communist Party greatly widened political participation, took into account local realities and divergent views, and forged solidarity both among participants and between the population and the party. In this sense, they marked a radical version of the late Qing and early Republican democratic ideal of a community of interests between state and society that would "awaken the people" on the one hand and make government responsive to the needs of the people on the other. The energies of the people could be mobilized, the state strengthened, and societal unity forged.

Following a devastating eight-year war against Japan, the Nationalist government squared off against a much enlarged Chinese Communist Party. In this fight, the Communists effectively utilized nationalist and democratic appeals, as well as superior organization and military tactics, to gain victory over the Kuomintang. The KMT, increasingly demoralized, collapsed rapidly and fled to Taiwan, as the Communists came to power in 1949.

Because the victory of the Communist Party was total and its dominance over society complete, the new government no longer had to compromise with other sources of power. At the same time, it placed emphasis on what it conceived to be overriding national priorities—strengthening socialist ideology, heavy industry, and national defense. These goals demanded ideological conformity and material sacrifice from the population, however, and thus undermined support for the party.

In 1957 Mao Zedong, chairman of the Chinese Communist Party, led an attempt to recapture the sense of unity between party and society when he launched the ill-fated Hundred Flowers Movement. Calling for the forthright expression of criticisms, Mao soon found himself beset with harsh criticism from China's intellectuals and a burgeoning student movement. The democratic expression of criticism, which resonated with China's longstanding tradition of remonstrance, outraged Mao and other party leaders. The Anti-Rightist campaign that followed sent more than 500,000 intellectuals to the countryside and ended the party's willingness to open itself to societal criticism until after Mao's death. Nevertheless, many of the intellectuals affected by this movement would emerge in the late 1970s and early 1980s as forceful advocates of democratization within the party.

New Pressures for Democracy

Two decades later, in its quest for a more democratic polity, the generation of intellectuals affected by the Anti-Rightist campaign was joined by a new generation of youth whose formative experience was the Cultural Revolution. The Great Proletarian Cultural Revolution (as it was known formally), launched in 1966, was anything but democratic in its inspiration and practice. It did, however, resonate with one longstanding tenet of democratic thought in China—antibureaucratism. For at least the past century, Chinese democrats had railed against a bureaucracy that stifled popular expression and hindered social mobilization on behalf of a stronger state. The Cultural Revolution unleashed a torrent of idealistic youth, most of whom had absolute faith in Mao and were convinced that he wanted them to break down the bureaucracy that had prevented unity between state and society.

Far from bringing about the utopian society the Red Guards thought they were called upon to build, the Cultural Revolution resulted in rampant factionalism, social chaos, and countless incidents of torture, murder, and suicide. Seeking to restore order, Mao turned to the People's Liberation Army in the summer of 1968. Millions of Red Guards were soon disbanded and sent to the countryside to "learn from the peasants." This action, which many viewed as a betrayal, was followed in 1971 by the report that China's minister of defense, Lin Biao, had died while trying to flee China after an abortive attempt to assassinate Mao. These events forced the once idealistic Cultural Revolution activists to rethink their ideological commitments and their understanding of Chinese politics. Thus did the Red Guard generation of Chinese youth become known as the thinking generation.

This reevaluation of politics marked an important new phase that would provide the shock troops of China's contemporary democratic movement. An important expression of this change can be seen in the famous "Li Yizhe" posters pasted on Guangzhou's city walls. In April 1974 a long essay entitled "What Is to Be Done in Guangdong?"—written under the pseudonym Li Yizhe—argued that only by restoring the democratic rights of the people could China repudiate Lin Biao and prevent a fascist dictatorship from recurring. Later that year another manifesto, on socialist democracy and the legal system, was posted. These protests skillfully skirted the border of permissible policy. While the posting of the original poster had violated party policy (a policy that was soon changed), it also led Zhao Ziyang, then Guangdong's party leader and later the general secretary of China's Communist Party, to consult secretly with the group in an effort to hitch its activities to the goals of the party's moderate faction.

The next major expression of democratic aspirations came in April 1976, when thousands of people took advantage of China's traditional day of mourning to pay honor to the country's recently deceased premier, Zhou Enlai. Mourners posted poems and essays in Beijing's Tiananmen Square that were sharply critical of the radical faction within the party, later known as the Gang of Four. The April Fifth Movement, as it was called, attracted thousands to Tiananmen Square, but the leaders appear to have been mostly disillusioned Red Guards like those who had participated in the 1974 movement in Guangzhou.

The death of Mao in September 1976 and the subsequent arrest of the Gang of Four ushered in—although not without considerable resistance—a more moderate phase in Chinese politics. In the spring of 1978, Hu Yaobang, who was later to become general secretary of the Communist Party, orchestrated a discussion on "practice as the sole criterion of truth," which was designed to loosen the ideological strictures of the party and pave the way for more pragmatic leaders, led by Deng Xiaoping, to return to power.

In this more relaxed ideological atmosphere, the democracy movement reemerged in the fall of 1978, not long before the party was to convene for a crucial work conference that would precede the historic Third Plenum in December 1978. Posters were pasted on a wall, which soon became known as Democracy Wall, near the heart of Beijing. Democratic activists began exploring heretofore forbidden topics in a variety of new journals. Such journals, while not strictly illegal (until later), circumvented China's publishing laws and opened up a new realm of public discourse.

Again, people inside the party aided people outside the party, the former providing inside information and appropriate themes while the latter provided the pressure of public opinion. Even Deng Xiaoping, in the heady days prior to convening the Third Plenum, declared that the posting of handwritten signs ("big-character posters") was normal and demonstrated the stability of China. However, as some within the democratic movement, most notably Wei Jingsheng, moved beyond the limits set by the regime, and as Deng successfully ousted his major rivals and consolidated power, the party moved first to curtail and then to suppress the movement. The new state constitution adopted in 1982 forbade the display of big-character posters.

As the regime began to pressure the democratic movement, participants frequently were forced to choose whether to work within the regime, sometimes accepting important advisorial jobs, or to remain on the outside. Some democratic activists called for cooperation between reformers within the regime and those on the outside; only thus, they believed, could democratic reform be achieved.

The structure of Chinese politics made that hope impossible to achieve. For instance, Yan Jiaqi, perhaps China's foremost political scientist, comments in his intellectual autobiography that he worked with democracy activists Wang Juntao and Chen Ziming in 1978 but ceased such activities after accepting an invitation to participate in the party's 1979 theory conference. Yan's predicament was understandable; contact with democratic activists outside the party naturally jeopardized the position and influence of reformers working within the party. In addition, many reformers in the party believed that the demands of democratic activists were excessive and that democracy in China could come only from the top down.

Calls for Democracy in the 1980s and 1990s

In the mid- and late 1980s demands for democracy in both the party and society reemerged with unprecedented force. Some party intellectuals tried to reinterpret Marxism in terms of humanism, while others began exploring democratic theory and institutions. At the same time, reforms released societal expectations and anxieties and stimulated a new generation of students to take the lead in demanding more freedoms. In the fall of 1985 students took to the streets to protest what they saw as Japan's economic invasion of China. The following year a student movement started in the east-central province of Anhui and quickly spread to other locations, including Shanghai, where more than 50,000 students took to the streets. In the ensuing crackdown, Hu Yaobang was removed from the nation's top party position and three prominent intellectuals—Fang Lizhi, Liu Binyan, and Wang Ruowang—were ousted from the party and criticized in a campaign as exemplars of bourgeois liberalization.

Such movements proved to be a prelude to the much larger protest movement of 1989, which had its origins in the confluence of many factors: rising expectations and frustration over rising costs, corruption, and fears of layoffs; a clash of generations with widely varying views of China's achievements and prospects; and elite conflict that pitted different visions of economic, social, and political development against each other. Although the movement demanded democracy, the content of its demands differed significantly from the aims of the democratic movements in Eastern Europe and elsewhere as well as from Western, particularly American, understandings of democracy. Students demanded that the regime recognize an independent, autonomous student organization and hold a dialogue on an equal basis with the student leaders. Such demands were difficult to accept explicitly, since they challenged the Communist Party's monopoly over political affairs and social organization.

In keeping with China's democratic tradition, the 1989 movement protested the corruption and bureaucracy that made the regime unresponsive to public opinion, rather than pushing demands for individual rights, which are usually seen as the basis for Western democracy. Moreover, the continuing force of China's tradition of moral remonstrance was palpable in the movement's use of moral symbols to present its demands. For instance, during the memorial service for deceased party chief Hu Yaobang, three students knelt for hours on the steps of the Great Hall of the People, waiting for one of the leaders to come out. (No one ever did.)

Critics of the students have pointed out that their unwillingness to compromise mirrored the government's own intransigence. For about a month, moderates on both sides searched for a way out, but various factors prolonged the protests: the glare of international media, the prospect of Soviet leader Mikhail Gorbachev's visit (on May 15, a month after the protests started), and severe division within the Communist Party. As the protests continued and even escalated, prospects for compromise dimmed. Students demanded explicit concessions from the government, while the government saw the movement as a challenge to its very existence. Finally, martial law was declared on May 20. On the night of June 3–4 the People's Liberation Army shot its way into the center of the city to recover Tiananmen Square, the site of mass demonstrations, killing hundreds.

The demand for democracy has been a constant element of modern China's effort to reconcile its traditions, its national aspirations, and its hopes for a government that truly serves the people. Chinese society, however, has been reluctant to recognize a genuinely private sphere, the force of law, and the legitimacy of interest group politics. Moreover, China's traditional political culture has depicted political power as monistic, unified, and indivisible. This conception has been reinforced continuously throughout modern Chinese history; most recently it contributed to the tragedy of Tiananmen. To date, this tradition has prevented the emergence of the type of politics of compromise necessary for democratic governance.

Some speculate that the societal changes currently under way—the growing strength of the provinces, the country's increasing economic and social diversity, and the increasing wealth and educational levels of many areas, especially in the east and southeast—will bring new pressures for democracy. These tendencies will likely be reinforced by the integration of Hong Kong's economy and society with that of south China. In addition, the efforts of other Confucian societies, particularly South Korea and Taiwan, to pioneer democratic transformations are certain to influence China. At the same time, however, other social issues and changes—the migration of peasants into cities, questions of law and order, the decline of state-owned enterprises, and the threat to Beijing's authority—are generating anti-democratic pressures.

Ultimately, the question is whether China's political traditions can be reconciled with democratic governance. Although the demand for democracy has been a major force throughout the twentieth century, even those demanding democracy have generally placed greater stress on unity between state and society, strong and effective rule, and antibureaucratism than on such requisites for democratic rule as institutionalization, procedure, law, division of power, and the willingness to compromise.

See also *Taiwan.*

BIBLIOGRAPHY

Chan, Anita, Stanley Rosen, and Jonathan Unger, eds. *On Socialist Democracy and the Chinese Legal System: The Li Yizhe Debates.* Armonk, N.Y.: M. E. Sharpe, 1985.

Chang, Carson. *The Third Force in China.* New York: Bookman Associates, 1952.

Chesneaux, Jean. "The Federalist Movement in China, 1920–23." In *Modern China's Search for a Political Form,* edited by Jack Gray. London and New York: Oxford University Press, 1969.

Des Forges, Roger V., Ning Luo, and Wu Yen-bo, eds. *Chinese Democracy and the Crisis of 1989: Chinese and American Reflections.* Albany: State University of New York Press, 1993.

Eastman, Lloyd. *The Abortive Revolution: China under Nationalist Rule, 1927–1937.* Cambridge, Mass., and London: Harvard University Press, 1974.

Goldman, Merle. *China's Intellectuals: Advise and Dissent.* Cambridge, Mass., and London: Harvard University Press, 1981.

Grieder, Jerome B. *Intellectuals and the State in Modern China.* New York: Free Press, 1981.

Hsu, Immanuel C. Y. *The Rise of Modern China.* 4th ed. Oxford and New York: Oxford University Press, 1990.

Liew, K. S. *Struggle for Democracy: Sung Chiao-jen and the 1911 Chinese Revolution.* Canberra: Australian National University Press, 1971.

Nathan, Andrew J. *Chinese Democracy.* New York: Knopf, 1985; London: I. B. Tauris, 1986.

Seymour, James D., ed. *The Fifth Modernization: China's Human Rights Movement, 1978–1979.* Stanfordville, N.Y.: Earl M. Coleman, 1980.

Tsou, Tang. "The Tragedy of Tiananmen." In *Contemporary Chinese Politics in Historical Perspective,* edited by Brantly Womack. Cambridge: Cambridge University Press, 1991.

Womack, Brantly. "In Search of Democracy: Public Authority and Popular Power in China." In *Contemporary Chinese Politics in Historical Perspective,* edited by Brantly Womack. Cambridge: Cambridge University Press, 1991.

Yan, Jiaqi. *Toward a Democratic China: The Intellectual Autobiography of Yan Jiaqi.* Translated by David S. K. Hong and Denis C. Mair. Honolulu: University of Hawaii Press, 1992.

Congo, Democratic Republic of the

A large central African state that has not known democracy since achieving independence from Belgium on June 30, 1960. The factors contributing to the absence of democracy include the country's colonial legacy, the crisis-ridden first five years of independence (1960–1965), the tyrannical presidency of Mobutu Sese Seko (1965–1997), and, until 1993, the firm political and economic support of Mobutu's external patrons and protectors—Belgium, France, and the United States. Because of the combination of these factors, democracy has never had a chance to succeed in this politically turbulent nation.

Historical Legacy and the Initial Crisis

Before the advent of formal colonial rule at the Berlin Conference in 1884–1885, the territory today known as the Democratic Republic of the Congo (Zaire until May 1997) was occupied by many different political forms. They ranged from highly centralized states such as the Kongo kingdom to decentralized village governments. These forms interacted with each other over the years in a long-term ebb and flow as people struggled to increase their autonomy. These struggles for political autonomy, however, were localized and were waged without the vocabulary of nineteenth-century European liberalism. While most villages and many precolonial kingdoms did have systems of checks and balances designed to prevent certain abuses of power, the democratic notions of competition among groups, inclusive political participation, and civil and political liberties were generally absent.

From 1885 to 1908 the Democratic Republic of the Congo, then the Congo, was the personal fiefdom of King Leopold II of Belgium. Vicious plunder prevailed until international outrage and pressure forced the elected Belgian government to take legal control of the colony in 1908. Belgium moderated some of the harsher aspects of Leopold's order, but forced labor, crop restrictions, and frequent imprisonment for violations of agricultural regulations remained. The state continued to extract wealth from those who produced it.

The population had no say in determining colonial policies. Political parties were not permitted until the end of the colonial period; educational policy emphasized primary education rather than secondary schooling or higher education; indigenous Christian groups such as the Kimbanguist Church and the Kitawalists were repressed because the colonial government saw them as subversive; and censorship ensured that no free interchange of political ideas could occur. The Belgian Congo was one of the most intensively administered states in Subsaharan Africa. It was, in many ways, the antithesis of democracy.

The colonial period also reshaped the way Congolese thought about themselves. Precolonial nationalities such as Kongo suddenly became "tribes" or ethnic groups. The Belgians permitted cultural organizations based on a single ethnic identity, but they banned political parties transcending ethnic lines. Congolese used ethnic identities, even if artificial, as a means of political mobilization in the colonial state. Consequently, when independence arrived, Congolese found it all too easy to perceive the new world of competitive politics in predominantly ethnic terms.

Civil and political order disintegrated from 1960 to 1965 for three main reasons. First, although the Belgians bequeathed their colony a constitutional and ostensibly democratic order when they left in 1960, Congolese were unprepared to run their newly independent country. There were few college graduates, and there had been no period of planned decolonization with training in the practices of democratic self-rule. The entire transition was hasty and ill conceived. The new institutions, simple copies taken from the Belgian system, quickly proved unworkable. The second reason was politicized ethnicity. It made trust and political legitimacy impossible to achieve, fostered the secession of the copper-rich Katanga/Shaba Province, and fueled an ethnic civil war in Kasai Province. The final reason was the cold war, which contributed to the interventions of the Belgians, Soviets, Americans, and the United Nations. Under such difficult circumstances, Mobutu and his soldiers staged a military coup in 1965 and seized power from the civilians who had shown themselves incapable of governing the country.

Mobutu's Tyranny

Wearied by the ceaseless strife, many Congolese welcomed the new regime because the civilian order had lost all legitimacy. Mobutu quickly tried to end instability by rebuilding the state. He created a rubber-stamp legislature and curbed pervasive ethnic conflict by decreasing the number of provinces, removing their political autonomy, and nationalizing their police. Provincial governors were named by the president. Single-party rule soon followed when Mobutu founded the Popular Movement of the Revolution in 1967. Although the constitution briefly permitted a second party, Mobutu would tolerate no other political organization, and he soon controlled all institutional arms of both state and party. A syndicate sponsored by the state absorbed trade unions; women's and youth groups found a home in the Popular Movement of the Revolution. Mobutu was president-founder of the party, president of the republic, and commander in chief of the armed forces. A cult of personality emerged as sycophants massaged Mobutu's ego in the state-controlled media.

Ill-advised economic policies, grandiose and unsuitable development schemes, and a generally mismanaged economic sector created pervasive scarcity. Moreover, Mobutu's policies to rebuild the state added to the insecurity of government officials whose tenure depended on Mobutu's whim. Since few had ventured into the private sector, they used public office to create private wealth. Corruption became endemic. The powerful felt impelled to use their state offices as a means of extracting wealth from their fellow citizens. Insecurity and scarcity thus fed on each other. When generals stole their salaries, soldiers raided villages. When teachers went unpaid, they charged students. When state-employed physicians could no longer survive, they charged patients. This vicious chain of extraction prompted a national search for survival in the economy's burgeoning informal sector.

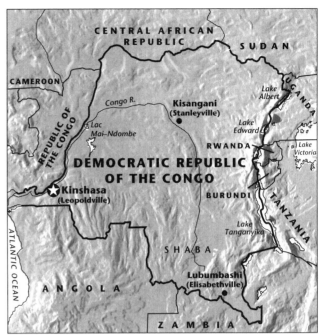

As the regime's legitimacy dwindled, Mobutu ruled increasingly through coercion. The army's primary purpose was to crush unarmed civilians. The civil guard, party youth wing, and political police also terrorized the citizenry. In 1982 some parliamentarians formed an opposition party, the Union for Democracy and Social Progress, but this movement was repressed at every turn. Until 1990 when Mobutu, under intense international pressure, opted to liberalize the system by legalizing political opposition, including the Union for Democracy and Social Progress, most Congolese remained silent for fear that they would be reported, jailed, or worse. For many years Amnesty International publicized the state's consistent abuse of fundamental human rights. It is no exaggeration to say that Mobutu's regime sustained a reign of terror: extortion, arbitrary arrest, detention without trial, and extrajudicial executions were all too common. Unsurprisingly, democracy did not flourish in this environment.

External Support

The final reason that democracy has not taken root in the Democratic Republic of the Congo pertains to Mobutu's external support. From the republic's earliest days the cold war fostered external intervention in the country's internal affairs while impeding the emergence of a democratic political order. The initial international interventions of the early 1960s accomplished the removal from power of Patrice Lumumba, the republic's first prime minister and the only politician who then had anything approaching a national following, because the West perceived him as a Soviet sympathizer. The rise to power of Mobutu, a strong anticommunist, was facilitated at certain key junctures by the U.S. government, and especially by the Central Intelligence Agency.

Throughout the cold war the United States and its European allies, France and Belgium, were quick to shore up the central government's political control whenever that became necessary. When, in 1964, a series of popular rebellions swept through two-thirds of the country, both Belgium and the United States provided military and logistical support so that the central government could defeat the insurgents. In 1977 and 1978 Congolese insurgents operating from Angolan and Zambian bases twice invaded Shaba Province in an attempt to topple Mobutu. Quickly, French and Belgian troops intervened to support the regime. Once again the United States provided logistical support.

By shrewdly playing his anticommunist card and pointing to "Kremlin-inspired" plots against him, Mobutu could shroud the deficiencies of his regime and get the attention of policymakers in Washington, D.C. Although these officials certainly knew that Mobutu's rule was substantially less than democratic, they rationalized their support for him because of his strong anticommunism and because—regardless of party affiliation—they did not wish to "lose" this country on their watch. External support enabled Mobutu to continue his ruthless regime even though it had lost all legitimacy at home.

When the cold war ended in the early 1990s, Mobutu's position became increasingly precarious. Long-suppressed internal dissent and global pressures toward democratization had weakened his hold on power and pushed the country toward a complete breakdown of civil and political order. In 1993 Mobutu lost his last vestiges of Western support. But by then the destruction of Congolese society had been complete. Decades of Mobutu's misrule and repression took an enormous toll—politically, economically, and psychologically.

Overthrow of Mobutu

Mobutu's rule came to an end in May 1997 as an indirect victim of the ethnic warfare that had broken out between Hutus and Tutsis in Rwanda three years earlier. The Rwandan fighting sent more than a million refugees into the Democratic Republic of the Congo, straining the economy as well as relations between Congolese Hutus and Tutsis. After hundreds of Congolese Tutsis were massacred in May 1996, allegedly by Rwandan Hutu refugees and Hutu Zairian troops, armed Tutsi rebel factions coalesced to form the Alliance of Democratic Forces for the Liberation of Congo-Zaire (AFDL). Led by Laurent Kabila, who had been fighting the Mobutu regime for more than two decades, AFDL sliced through the Congolese army in the early months of 1997, capturing the capital in May.

The first months of Kabila's rule were not inspiring from the perspective of democratic government. Although he professed a desire to build democracy and promised a new constitution and elections, his early steps included abolishing political parties and banning demonstrations.

See also *Africa, Subsaharan.*

BIBLIOGRAPHY

Callaghy, Thomas M. *The State-Society Struggle: Zaire in Comparative Perspective.* New York: Columbia University Press, 1984.

Kalb, Madeleine G. *The Congo Cables: The Cold War in Africa from Eisenhower to Kennedy.* New York: Macmillan, 1982.

MacGaffey, Janet. *Entrepreneurs and Parasites: The Struggle for Indigenous Capitalism in Zaire.* Cambridge: Cambridge University Press, 1987.

Schatzberg, Michael G. *The Dialectics of Oppression in Zaire.* Bloomington: Indiana University Press, 1988.

———. *Politics and Class in Zaire: Bureaucracy, Business, and Beer in Lisala.* New York: Africana, 1980.

Willame, Jean-Claude. *Patrimonialism and Political Change in the Congo.* Stanford, Calif.: Stanford University Press, 1972.

Young, Crawford. *Politics in the Congo: Decolonization and Independence.* Princeton: Princeton University Press, 1965.

———, and Thomas Turner. *The Rise and Decline of the Zairian State.* Madison: University of Wisconsin Press, 1985.

D

Dominant party democracies in Asia

Dominant party democracies in Asia have been a standard arrangement in which an entrenched, elite party asserts tutelary responsibility for guiding the country to economic and political development. Democratic development in Asia, with few exceptions, has taken a form in which a single, dominant party governs the country and is opposed by weak parties that only gradually come to have any hope of ruling. In one manner or another, the dominant party claims to have the dual mission of leading the country to rapid economic development and of teaching the people how their nation can become a modern democracy.

In performing its tutelary tasks, the dominant party's leadership usually claims that authoritarian practices are necessary and legitimate. The dominant parties have differed in the sincerity of their tutelary pledges and also in the length of time they have held on to their authoritarian advantages. Their tutelary pretensions or practices have set apart the Asian one-party-dominant systems from the ordinary autocratic one-party dictatorships found elsewhere.

Prevalence

Throughout Asia the dominant party tutelary pattern has characterized democratic development: from Japan, with its Liberal Democratic Party, across the continent to India and its Congress Party. In between, varying degrees of authoritarian government have been the experiences of South Korea, Taiwan, Singapore, Malaysia, Indonesia, and the military-dominated systems of Thailand, Burma (Myanmar), and Pakistan. Although the Marxist-Leninist one-party systems of Asia belong in a significantly different category of political systems, they share some characteristics with the noncommunist dominant party systems. Thus the Chinese, North Korean, and Vietnamese Communist parties have used some of the same justifications

for their monopolies of power as have the leaders of the other nations' dominant parties.

The claim that authoritarian ways can be used to advance democracy might seem a contradiction in terms, defying logic and democratic theory. Historically, many autocrats have cynically claimed that they were engaged in such an effort when in fact they have been interested only in maintaining power. Indeed, this is patently the case with some of the contemporary Asian governments, such as that of Burma. Yet for many of the Asian regimes there is evidence that the tutelary process has been carried out sincerely and that progress toward democracy has taken place.

Where the tutelage has been genuine, opposition parties have gradually become stronger over time. In South Korea and Taiwan the party systems have become more competitive. In South Korea the December 1992 election was the first in thirty years in which the military did not play an active and decisive role; the victorious Democratic Liberal Party took on the role of a dominant party that respects the rights of an opposition, much as the Liberal Democratic Party operated in Japan. In fact, following a 1995 party realignment, the Democratic Liberal Party lost control of the South Korean National Assembly in the April 1996 elections. In elections held in Taiwan in December 1992 the Nationalist Party (Kuomintang), which was the dominant party, won less than 60 percent of the vote, suggesting that the election was truly competitive. And in December 1995 the Nationalist Party won only a bare majority of seats: 85 of 164. In Indonesia the dominant Golkar organization (Joint Secretariat of Functional Groups)—which is effectively, although not officially, a party—established earlier the principle that to win more than 70 percent of the vote would reduce its electoral credibility; so the party has on occasion sought to hold in check its vote-getting machine.

Where such dominant party systems have prevailed, the test of progress in democracy has been less the changing of governments through elections than increased respect for human and civil rights—effectively, the extent to which opposition groups are free to operate. Thus, although for more than forty years the opposition had little hope of defeating the Liberal Democratic Party, Japan was rightfully recognized as being a truly democratic society. Because the authoritarian governments of South Korea and Taiwan had a history of arresting opposition leaders, only in the late 1980s were these countries seen as beginning to move toward democracy. The even more authoritarian and disciplined ways of Singapore's People's Action Party have kept that city-state from being classified as a complete democracy, even though it does have a parliamentary system and regular elections.

Origins

The Nationalist Party in China was the first Asian party to advance a coherent ideological rationale for its tutelary role. In his lectures on the Three People's Principles, Sun Yat-sen, the founder of the Nationalist Party, explicitly laid out the party's responsibilities for guiding China to democracy. While the Nationalists were in power on the mainland, there was relatively little progress toward democracy. After the Nationalist government was forced by the Communists to retreat to Taiwan, the Nationalist Party reinforced its claim for monopolizing power by establishing martial law as a defense against Communist attack and by asserting that the party had an obligation to reunite China as a "free" nation. In its tutelary role, the Nationalist Party initially refused to allow any genuine opposition parties; it tolerated only individual leaders who were not allowed any party identification. Finally, however, the Nationalist government withdrew martial law and permitted the formation of the Democratic Progressive Party in 1986 as a legitimate opposition.

The Asian one-party (or one-and-a-half-party) systems have originated in several ways. In some cases the dominant party—as in India, Malaysia, and Singapore—was the organized nationalist movement that had led the country to independence from colonial rule. The Congress Party of India long insisted that it had a mission to turn the religiously divided country into a secular democracy. Similarly, the military-dominated systems have claimed a tutelary rationale as part of their mission of nation building. And, of course, the Marxist-Leninist systems of China, North Korea, and Vietnam rationalized their monopoly of power as a means of carrying out the mission of revolutionary change.

During the cold war, fear of the expansionist tendencies of the nearby communist systems was used to justify the need for the discipline inherent in the dominant party systems of Taiwan, South Korea, and Singapore (and also the South Vietnamese regime before its defeat). Significantly, after the collapse of communism in the Soviet Union and the ending of the cold war, both South Korea and Taiwan moved rapidly toward becoming more competitive democracies.

Cultural Context

There are deeper cultural reasons for the Asian tendency toward one-party dominance. The traditional cultures of most Asian countries idealize harmony, hierarchy, orderliness, and discipline; they see little virtue in competitiveness, adversarial relationships, and individualism. People in such cultures like to think of authority as dignified, serious, and acting in the collective interest. To them, the confrontational and adversarial practices of Western, and especially American, democracy seem not only raucous and vulgar but also an unstable foundation for the realm of state affairs. The American ideal of checks and balances within the government is seen by most Asians as a guarantee for inefficiency.

In contrast, the Asian cultures generally accentuate group solidarity and consensus in decision making over self-assertion and individual rights. In the context of traditional authoritarian practices, any challenge to the collective leadership may be seen as disruptive and rude behavior, which may threaten the stability of the entire society. And stability is considered the necessary condition for rapid economic growth. Thus the preservation of the dominant party system has been justified as essential for improving the people's living standards. It is argued that improving the material conditions of life is a more fundamental obligation of government than the protection of individual human or civil rights.

Cultural tendencies did not, however, preordain the establishment of dominant party systems. In Japan, both in the early 1920s and during the American occupation after World War II, democratic institutions were created within multiparty systems similar to those in the West. The system established with the Taisho democracy (1912–1926) came to an end during the 1930s, when the Japanese military established a fascist government. The Liberal Democratic Party's iron grip on Japanese politics came about only after the socialists had won an election during the American occupation because the Liberal Party and the Democratic Party had split the popular and strongly conservative vote of the majority of the Japanese people. The leaders of these two parties decided that they should unite and form the Liberal Democratic Party as an uncontested majority party. Once the new party was established, however, the cultural bias apparently worked in favor of its dominance.

Justifications

In the early years of newly established governments, leaders of dominant party systems in Asia have often claimed that the people were not ready for democracy. They argued that mass communications were inadequate and that the people's level of education was too low for effective popular government. The more sophisticated argument advanced by such leaders as Singapore's Lee Kuan Yew (prime minister, 1959–1990) was that the process of creating the civic virtues associated with the rise of the middle class in the West took many generations; so if there was to be a forced pace of economic development in Asia there should also be a parallel program to teach the civic values of democracy. Prime Minister Lee liked to point out that the United States had been extremely successful in Americanizing its immigrants, making even those with no previous democratic experience into constructive, law-abiding citizens and effective participants in democratic politics. Lee further argued that after World War II the United States had abandoned the effort and made no comparable attempt to help the waves of rural blacks from the South adjust to urban life in the North. Therefore, he reasoned, the Asian countries should benefit from the American example and insist that their newly urbanized populations be taught systematically the civic virtues that are essential for both public safety and democratic participation.

By the 1980s the justification for the dominant and semi-authoritarian party was generally reinforced by the argument that rapid economic growth and continued improvement in the standard of living required the stability and disciplined direction of such a dominant party. This is the rationale that Singapore clings to as the People's Action Party continues to keep any opposition in check. The same rationale is used in Indonesia and to a lesser extent in Thailand. It is even advanced by the Chinese Communists to justify maintaining their Leninist system. The leaders of such dominant parties point to the Philippines, with its poor record of economic growth, its ineffectual government, and its corruption and lawlessness; they suggest that all these problems can be traced to that nation's commitment to multiparty democracy.

Business Ties

The linkage between dominant party rule and economic growth has frequently taken the form of close ties between party politicians and the business community. This relationship has had both positive and negative aspects. The close working relationship between politicians and business has meant that the governments have been the active friends of business, and state policies have played a major part in advancing national economies. In return for help in keeping their political power, the politicians of the dominant parties have sheltered companies from foreign competition and supported favored companies through various forms of industrial policies—actions that have expanded the economies and created jobs. On the negative side, the close ties between business leaders and politicians have fostered "money politics," that is, practices that would be seen as corruption in the West. In return for providing stability and a friendly economic environment for business, the politicians have expected business to protect their political stability through generous contributions.

In Japan the intimate relationships between party leaders and business leaders have resulted in scandals, one of which led to the downfall of the Liberal Democratic Party in 1993 and thus to the apparent end of the dominant party system in that country. Although the Liberal Democratic Party returned to government after the October 1996 elections, it had failed to win an absolute majority of seats in the lower house and was forced to form a coalition government. Electoral reforms enacted in Japan between 1993 and 1996, while the Liberal Democrats were out of power, should reduce politicians' dependence on outside money and thus change the parties' relationships with corporations.

In Taiwan the Nationalists built a huge corporate empire of their own, including both direct ownership and large investments. The revenue from such investments gives Nationalist candidates a virtually insurmountable advantage in campaign funds.

The grandest scandals of all involving political corruption and big business began to surface in South Korea at the end of 1995. Two former presidents, Chun Doo Hwan (1980–1987) and Roh Tae Woo (1987–1993), were convicted in August 1996 of accepting bribes worth hundreds of millions of dollars while in office. Their trials overshadowed serious allegations of election finance violations lodged against President Kim Young Sam (1993–   ).

Indeed, although per capita incomes are lower in Asian countries than in the Western democracies, politicians in the dominant party systems generally have been able to extract far more money from their societies than have Western politicians. The close ties between politicians, business, and government are no doubt part of the reason, but another factor is ethical. In some cultures it is considered more honorable to gain wealth through government office holding than by business dealings in the marketplace. Participants in the dominant party systems have shown great imagination, and often little shame, in coming up with ingenious ways of making private fortunes. For example, in some of the military governments, generals have used their government positions to establish profitable businesses, which they convert to their own use as they leave office.

Viability

The impressive economic successes of the East Asian dominant party systems, which have made them the model for countries that aspire to further development, have given some legitimacy to this form of "soft" authoritarianism. Initially, the Japanese model and more recently the experiences of South Korean and Taiwan have suggested to the leaders of other Asian countries that they should no longer look to Europe and America for examples of democracy to be copied.

Representatives of countries with such systems have argued that the Western model is only a parochial form of democracy and that the Asian dominant party model is equally legitimate and in many respects superior. They assert that the Western model fragments the society either into two contending but essentially identical parties, which can be easily captured by their fringe elements, or into a multitude of dogmatic, self-centered parties. In contrast, a single dominant party can represent the consensus of the mainstream of the society, making it into an effective instrument of governance, while isolating the political fringe elements into a variety of ineffectual parties. Those who argue in that way are convinced that the dominant party system is likely to become the principal model for the non-Western world. Prime Minister Mahathir bin Mohamad of Malaysia (elected in 1981 and still in office in 1997) formalized this view with his slogan of "Look to the East" for the best models for economic and political development.

In China before the suppression of the democratic movement by the Tiananmen Square massacre in 1989 there was considerable interest, especially among intellectuals, in the idea of neoauthoritarianism, by which was meant a form of progressive, one-party rule directed toward rapid economic modernization. By speaking of neoauthoritarianism, advocates were able to hold up the model of South Korea and Taiwan without mentioning those countries by name.

It seems likely that the pattern of one-party dominance will be followed in other non-Western countries eager to have the same impressive rates of economic development as the East Asian newly industrialized countries. Whether the dominant party in any particular country is only cynically rationalizing authoritarian rule or is genuinely practicing tutelary guidance can be determined by use of two key tests. First, is the authority of the dominant party being used to produce effective economic growth? And, second, are the conditions of human rights and political freedom improving at a rate appropriate to the pace of social and economic progress? These are the tests that separate the successful Asian tutelary efforts from, say, the African "one-party democracies" of the 1950s and 1960s, which produced only corrupt authoritarian rule.

It remains uncertain, however, whether there is a long-term future for such systems. The fact that in Japan the Liberal Democratic Party, after appearing to be unassailable, was suddenly defeated in 1993 because of corruption suggests that the dominant party systems may be destined to thrive only during a limited time span in Asian history. Indeed, the vigor of the opposition parties in both South Korea and Taiwan in the 1990s points to the prospect that these countries may evolve smoothly into multiparty systems. Thus the case can be made that the Asian dominant party systems have operated effectively to further both impressive economic growth and democratic development.

BIBLIOGRAPHY

Allison, Gary D., and Yasumori Sone, eds. *Political Dynamics in Contemporary Japan.* Ithaca, N.Y.: Cornell University Press, 1993.

Curtis, Gerald L. *Election Campaigning Japanese Style.* New York: Columbia University Press, 1971.

Diamond, Larry, Juan J. Linz, and Seymour Martin Lipset, eds. *Democracy in Developing Countries.* 4 vols. Boulder, Colo.: Lynne Rienner; London: Adamantine Press, 1988–1989.

Gold, Thomas B. *State and Society in the Taiwan Miracle.* Armonk, N.Y.: M. E. Sharpe, 1986.

Henderson, Gregory. *Korea: The Politics of the Vortex.* Cambridge: Harvard University Press, 1968.

Hrebenar, Ronald J. *The Japanese Party System.* Boulder, Colo.: Westview Press, 1986.

Ike, Nobutaka. *Japanese Politics: Patron-Client Democracy.* New York: Knopf, 1973.

Pempel, T. J. *Policy and Politics in Japan.* Philadelphia: Temple University Press, 1982.

Ramseyer, J. Mark, and Frances McCall Rosenbluth. *Japan's Political Marketplace.* Cambridge and London: Harvard University Press, 1993.

Weiner, Myron. *Party Building in a New Nation.* Chicago: University of Chicago Press, 1967.

E

Egypt

A predominantly Muslim republic located in the northeastern corner of Africa, with an Asian extension known as the Sinai Peninsula. Even though Egypt boasts a 6,000-year history of settled life along the banks of the Nile River that included 2,000 years under the Pharaohs, the country's contemporary cultural character can be traced to the years A.D. 639–641, when Egypt fell to the Muslim Arabs. Later, under the Fatimid and Ayyubid dynasties (969–1250), Egypt, and especially Cairo, became a culturally luminous part of the Islamic world.

In the early sixteenth century Egypt was conquered by the Ottomans but remained a semiautonomous unit. Fiscal and political control of the country passed into the hands of the British in the second half of the nineteenth century, until it was fully occupied by the British in 1882. Forty years later, on February 28, 1922, the British granted Egypt its independence.

In 1923 the country had its first constitution, declaring Egypt to be a hereditary monarchy with representative government. The legislative branch of government comprised a Senate, composed of members appointed by the king (two-fifths) and members elected for ten-year terms by universal male suffrage (three-fifths), and a Chamber of Deputies, whose members were elected for five-year terms by universal male suffrage.

The Monarchy

During the monarchical period (1922–1952), a number of political parties contested for power, but the Wafd Party, which had led the struggle for independence, dominated. During this time a democracy of sorts was practiced in which elections were held and parties competed for power. But some of the elections were rigged, and parliaments were sometimes suspended by the king, who at times exer-

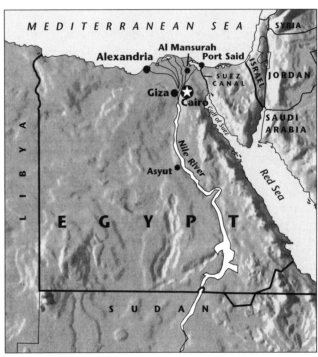

cised inordinate power over the political system.

The most impressive feature of this period was the freewheeling press, a testimony to the cosmopolitan nature of the educated segment of Egyptian society. In 1947, for example, Cairo boasted fourteen dailies and twenty-three weeklies, and Alexandria, Egypt's second largest city, had fourteen dailies and seven weeklies. Because of the constant efforts by the king to undermine parliamentary opposition to his authority, political debate and opposition tended to shift to the pages of the press.

The political system under the monarchy, however, was by no means truly democratic. There was too much interference by the king and too much domination of party politics by the Wafd Party. Nevertheless, the system was relatively tolerant. Opposing views were allowed to be aired, and enough checks and balances were exercised to stop any one person or organization from attaining dictatorial powers.

The monarchical period ended with a coup on July 23, 1952. The coup, executed by young army officers under the leadership of Lt. Col. Gamal Abdel Nasser, was supported widely. Within two years of taking power the army officers had dismantled the political system as it existed under the monarchy. The country was declared a republic, the 1923 constitution was abrogated, all political parties were dissolved and their funds confiscated, and the press syndicate was abolished. Spurred on by widespread popular support, a one-party system under the charismatic leadership of Nasser quickly emerged.

The popular support for the military takeover and the institution of authoritarian rule in all probability did not stem from the people's lack of interest in and understanding of democracy but from the foreign policy orientation of the monarchical regime. Egyptians increasingly thought of their government as hopelessly linked to that of Britain, the old colonial power, whose troops continued to be stationed in cities and towns along the Suez Canal. Moreover, the inability of Egypt (along with other Arab states) to prevent the establishment of the State of Israel confirmed the image of the monarchical regime as a client of the West. All this happened in an era in which intense anti-colonialism defined the political and ideological landscapes of developing nations. What was bound to follow therefore was a considerable loss of legitimacy not only for the monarchical regime but also for the political system it had fostered.

Nasser and Sadat

Under Nasser, Egypt's political system was strictly authoritarian. Nasser contended that if the eradication of colonialism and imperialism was the primary goal of the people and leaders alike, there was no need for a multiparty system. And, in any case, any confrontation with the imperialists, a daunting task, would leave neither the time nor the need for the endless political debates so characteristic of the legislative branch of government in pluralist societies.

Accordingly, Article 192 of the republican constitution promulgated in January 1956 decreed that all members of the National Assembly (the parliament) were to be nominated by the country's sole political party, the National Union, which itself was to be organized by the presidency. The electoral law that followed in March 1957 provided for a National Assembly of 350 seats. In the next elections the executive committee of the National Union, working closely with the presidency, screened all 2,528 applicants for nomination, rejecting 1,210 and leaving 1,318 actual contestants. In five constituencies all the original candidates were eliminated and replaced by regime-picked people; all cabinet members and some former army and police officers were elected unopposed.

This pattern continued through the 1960s. If anything, it became more ingrained after the collapse of the United Arab Republic, which came into being in 1958 with the merger of Egypt and Syria under Nasser's leadership. When, three years later, the Syrians seceded, Nasser became convinced that the secession was orchestrated by reactionary forces. In 1962 the National Union was replaced with the Arab Socialist Union, a party with a rigid socialist mandate and a mission to mobilize the masses.

Nasser's death in 1970 and the ascension to power of Anwar Sadat did not make much difference at first. Sadat seemed unable to free himself from the towering shadow of his predecessor. But the modest successes of the Egyptian armed forces against the Israelis in October 1973 proved to be the turning point in Sadat's presidency.

Once he was able to be his own man, Sadat changed Egypt's foreign policy from a Soviet to an avowedly American orientation. To make the most of this new relationship, and to create a legacy for himself that was distinct from Nasser's, Sadat radically changed Egypt's centrally planned economy to one that required the vigorous participation of the private sector. Concurrently, he dismantled Nasser's one-party system; in September 1971, a new constitution was adopted.

The process culminated in the general elections of October–November 1976, described as the freest in the country's history. Three platforms within the ruling party—representing the left, center, and right—were allowed to participate. After the elections the three platforms became independent parties: the Liberal Socialist Party, National Progressive Unionist Party, and Arab Socialist Party. In July 1978 Sadat formed the National Democratic Party (NDP) with himself as leader.

The formation of the NDP paradoxically signaled a new beginning as well as a return to old-style politics. Initially, it signified the end of the one-party system. Here was the president leading one party among many in a competitive political system. But the NDP soon became the vehicle by which the president would maintain his control of the country. In a sense the NDP became the structural heir to the National Union and the Arab Socialist Union. Sadat's countrywide roundup of opposition figures in September 1981 confirmed the impression that, while some change indeed had been instituted, in many ways the political system continued to be hostage to old-style authoritarian politics.

The Mubarak Regime

Anwar Sadat was assassinated by members of the militant underground Islamic group al-Jihad (holy struggle) in October 1981. He was succeeded by Vice President Hosni Mubarak, who had survived the assassination attempt. A former air force general, Mubarak had risen in the ranks of the NDP through unquestioning loyalty to Sadat and his programs. Upon assuming power he pledged to continue the process started by his predecessor by insisting that Egypt's democratic experiment would not stop.

Again there was much hope that the march toward democratization would continue and gather momentum. Because Mubarak lacked the charisma of his two predecessors, and thus seemed able to attain legitimacy only through concrete measures that would attract popular support, he was very receptive to broadening the ideological base by increasing the number of political parties. This resulted in a significant entry onto the political scene: the New Wafd Party.

It soon became apparent, however, that there were limits to Mubarak's political liberalism. The president was not about to see the domination of his National Democratic Party undermined in any way. The legislative elections of 1984 were conducted under a new electoral law that required parties to receive a minimum of 8 percent of the total vote in order to be represented in the parliament. Given the NDP's organizational dominance throughout the country, it was hardly surprising that the president's party won the elections with 73 percent of the total vote. Of the four other parties contesting the election, only the New Wafd passed the 8 percent threshold, receiving 15.1 percent of the votes cast.

By the end of the 1980s Egypt was encountering horrendous economic problems, and the government was fighting a major battle for survival against Islamic militants. As greater attention was focused on security, human rights suffered. By the 1990s it had become evident that the democratization process had stalled. Mubarak and his government were consumed by Egypt's many problems and consequently were unwilling to devote much time to further liberalizing the political system. Moreover, having ruled Egypt for more than a decade, Mubarak seemed to have acquired a penchant for the kind of political control enjoyed and exercised by Nasser and Sadat.

The people of Egypt, especially the middle classes, who had vigorously agitated for greater democracy and who had harbored great hopes at the beginning of Mubarak's rule, showed their disenchantment by withdrawing from the political process in the early 1990s. Thus the significant aspect of the legislative elections of 1990 was not the predictable landslide win by the NDP but the pitifully low voter turnout, estimated at just above 20 percent of those eligible to vote. In the legislative elections of November–December 1995, voter turnout rebounded to 48 percent, but the NDP continued to dominate the process. NDP candidates won 318 seats outright, and shortly after the election, 99 of 112 successful independent candidates joined the NDP faction in the legislature, giving the NDP 417 of 444 elective seats.

The electoral status of women also was reflected in this downward democratic trend. In 1984 thirty-one seats in the National Assembly had been allocated to women. But this allocation was abolished for the 1987 elections. As a result, only fourteen women were elected, with another four appointed to the Assembly by presidential decree. In the 1990 elections the number further decreased to seven women elected and three appointed, and in 1995 only nine women were elected. This decline in women's representation in the Assembly stemmed from a growing conservative trend in society as well as a general disillusionment with the political process.

Future Outlook

In light of these events, to what extent can Egypt be called a democratic state? If democracy is understood in terms of representation and accountability—the representative institutions that constrain state power and hold those who govern accountable to the governed—and if what is implied in these terms are certain essential features such as free, periodic elections, true separation of powers among the executive, legislative, and judicial branches of government, and respect for the right of the individual to free speech and religious and political beliefs, then present-day Egypt cannot be called democratic.

To some, this assessment may seem too harsh; after all, over the past two decades or so Egypt has introduced a number of democratic features into its once strictly authoritarian political structure. The government of Egypt boasts a multiparty system consisting of nine parties, holds periodic elections, allows opposition newspapers, and tolerates the kind of popular criticism that is unthinkable in some Arab states. Most important, in recent years Egypt's judiciary has stubbornly maintained its independence from the political authorities.

Even so, the political system has too many negative features for the country to be called truly democratic. For example, notwithstanding the multiparty system, political power is monopolized by the president's party, the NDP, and it is very likely that this monopoly will continue for the foreseeable future. Indeed, new parties can be authorized only by the NDP-dominated Committee on Political Parties. Furthermore, in contrast to the NDP, the opposition parties must contend with all kinds of obstacles designed to stunt their growth and undermine their ability to organize and advance their political and socioeconomic goals. In addition, much of the media is controlled by the political authorities, including radio and television as well as newspapers and magazines, which are under the guidance of the officially sanctioned Supreme Press Council. Three-fifths of the editorial boards of the mass-circulation national newspapers are appointed (including the chairs and the editors-in-chief); two-fifths are elected by staff members. And while opposition papers do criticize government policies and practices, the state is able, through a variety of means, to restrict their circulation. Consequently, the voice of the opposition often is drowned out by the all-pervasive official and semiofficial information dissemination machine.

Last, but by no means least, Egypt's military establishment remains a formidable power within the country, and the state's internal security apparatus is perhaps the most visible and abiding feature of Egypt today. The demands and concerns of the military-security establishment are always listened to and frequently acted on, and these concerns are very often at odds with democratic principles and prerequisites.

It is true that in recent years the increase in security measures and the decrease in concern for human rights have stemmed from the rising tide of Islamic militancy in the country. Indeed, the dramatic upsurge in terrorist activities by Islamic militants has had a negative effect on the move toward greater democracy. The political authorities have insisted that their priorities must be placed on internal security to the detriment of other considerations, including further liberalization of the political system.

As for the Islamic militants, they constitute the main threat to Egypt's political authorities precisely because opposing views remain unwelcome to the ruling elites. With the government's innate suspicion of opposing views, the opposition parties and groups find it difficult to organize properly and publicize their political and economic agendas. The Islamic militants, however, spread their message and attract followers through the thousands of mosques and their attendant social networks, which remain virtually outside governmental control. Consequently, the groups that seem to suffer most in the battle between the government and the Islamic militants are the secular, democratic-oriented opposition parties. Ultimately, the real loser might well turn out to be the very idea of democracy.

Thus far, of all the Arab and Islamic states, Egypt is perhaps the country that has traveled farthest along the road of political liberalization. But the journey seems to have come to a grinding halt, a long way from its ultimate destination. Recent events in Egypt do not augur well for greater democratization. The ruling elites, suspicious of what true democracy might do to their political control, are engulfed in a bloody and costly battle with an equally authoritarian foe. This indeed is an environment in which democratic ideals and practices are not likely to grow and prosper.

BIBLIOGRAPHY

Baker, Raymond W. *Egypt's Uncertain Revolution under Nasser and Sadat.* Cambridge: Harvard University Press, 1979.

Bianchi, Robert. *Unruly Corporatism: Associational Life in Twentieth Century Egypt.* New York: Oxford University Press, 1989.

Binder, Leonard. *In a Moment of Enthusiasm: Political Power and the Second Stratum in Egypt.* Chicago: University of Chicago Press, 1978.

Dawisha, A. I. *Egypt in the Arab World: The Elements of Foreign Policy.* New York: St. Martin's, 1976.

McDermott, Anthony. *Egypt from Nasser to Mubarak: A Flawed Revolution.* New York: Routledge Chapman and Hall, 1988.

Springborg, Robert. *The Political Economy of Mubarak's Egypt.* Boulder, Colo.: Westview Press, 1988.

Vatikiotis, P. J. *The History of Modern Egypt: From Muhammed Ali to Mubarak.* 4th ed. Baltimore: Johns Hopkins University Press; London: Weidenfeld and Nicolson, 1991.

G

Ghana

The first West African country to obtain independence from colonial rule. Ghana has a longstanding civil liberties tradition as well as extensive experience with democratic practices. Because of severe economic difficulties and the military's general hostility to multiparty competition, Ghana has moved back and forth between the poles of authoritarianism and democracy since obtaining its independence in 1957.

There have been four distinct periods of procedural democracy: the initial Kwame Nkrumah administration (1957–1960); the Kofi Busia government (1969–1972); the Hilla Limann regime (1979–1981); and the current period of managed multiparty competition, which enabled Flight Lt. Jerry Rawlings, who came to power following the December 31, 1981, military coup, to win a convincing victory over the combined opposition in the 1992 presidential election and to win reelection, also by a comfortable margin, in December 1996.

Independence and the Nkrumah Years

Before independence, Ghana (the former Gold Coast) had little formal opportunity to acquire experience with democratic institutions. In addition, the new democracy was also fragmented ethnically, with the Akan-speaking peoples—the Asante (Ashanti), Fante, Akwapim, Brong, Nzima, and smaller groups, based in the south—accounting for roughly 44 percent of the population. The Mole-Dagbani in the north accounted for about 16 percent; the Ewe in the east, for about 13 percent; and the Ga in the Accra region and many smaller groups made up the remainder.

Kwame Nkrumah's regime came to power in 1957 on an electoral majority and maintained a competitive multiparty system for a limited time. His militantly nationalist

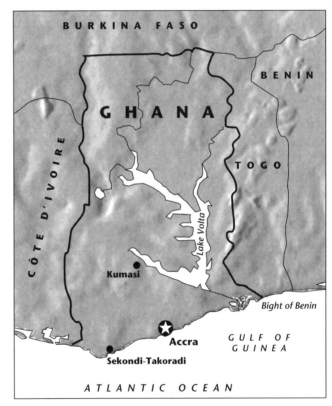

Convention People's Party successfully fought three election campaigns against the more conservative or ethnically and regionally based parties during the final decade of British overrule. The party's 1956 victory against the Ashanti-backed National Liberation Movement proved a critical juncture. The National Liberation Movement, with its call for a federal system, represented a major alternative to the Convention People's Party. By taking 71 of the 104 seats in the legislature, the Convention People's Party consolidated its control over the political order during the decisive period leading up to independence in 1957.

Nkrumah then moved increasingly toward the imposition of central control over societal affairs, establishing a single-party system and restricting civil liberties. Nevertheless, he held a plebiscite on the proposed republican constitution in 1960 and a referendum on a one-party system in 1964. The ability to secure majority agreement on both these measures represented, for Nkrumah, a broader mandate to speak in the name of the people.

From Military Rule to Limann's Government

In 1966 a military coup toppled Nkrumah. He was replaced during a transitional period by the National Liberation Council, a group of conservative military officers led by Lt. Gen. Joseph Ankrah. Although it believed strongly in no-party governance, the military junta nevertheless permitted a Constituent Assembly to meet and deliberate on a new basic law. With agreement reached on the return to parliamentary government, the National Liberation Council ended the ban on party politics. The military refused to allow some of the former leaders of the Convention People's Party to reenter the political fray. Otherwise, party competition proceeded relatively smoothly.

In 1969, in something of a return to the earlier traditions of Ghanaian politics, a largely rural and elitist Progress Party led by Kofi Busia competed with a primarily urban and populist National Alliance of Liberals under the leadership of Komla Gbedema, a former stalwart of the Convention People's Party. In contrast to former times, the ethnic support base of the urban nationalist party was Ewe, while that of the more professionally oriented and conservative Progress Party was pan-Akan. On the whole, however, the trends represented by past ideologies carried over into the present. In a relatively free and fair election, the public showed that it was ready to experiment with Busia's more market-oriented program. The Progress Party won 104 of the 140 seats in the legislature.

Although it was clearly committed in principle to the norms and values of democracy, the Busia administration took forceful action against the press, students, and trade unions. Minority resentment surfaced as the government passed an Aliens Expulsion Act, raising apprehensions among the country's Muslim population. The subsequent dismissal of more than 500 civil servants affected the Ewe and Ga peoples disproportionately. Professionals, civil servants, students and lecturers, and some military personnel criticized the government's partisanship and corruption. This disaffection became more pronounced as Busia, at-

tempting to deal with a serious foreign exchange crisis, announced an income freeze and a drastic 44 percent currency devaluation. Facing heavy cuts in military allocations, the army became increasingly discontented. In January 1972 Col. Ignatius Kutu Acheampong seized power.

Following Busia's fall, the pendulum swung to a six-and-a-half-year experience with three military regimes: Acheampong's National Redemption Council/Supreme Military Council, Lt. Gen. Frederick Akuffo's reconstituted Supreme Military Council, and Jerry Rawlings's Armed Forces Revolutionary Council. After a dogged drive to root out corruption, the Armed Forces Revolutionary Council, with no well-thought-out program to cope with the country's economic drift, organized a process of constitutional deliberations culminating in national elections in 1979. What ensued was a decisive electoral victory by Hilla Limann's People's National Party over a number of opponents. Limann, a northerner who embraced a modified Nkrumaist program, won handily in the presidential election over Victor Owusu, leader of the more conservative Popular Front Party. Limann's party won 71 of the 140 seats in the parliament, securing seats in every region.

Despite this auspicious beginning, Limann was unable to build a broad coalition behind his regime. His rather elitist cabinet members remained isolated from the former leaders of the Armed Forces Revolutionary Council, who resented their loss of budgetary allocations and political influence. Other alienated groups included the students and lecturers, labor unions, farmers, and certain ethnic interests (for example, the Akan peoples in the Ashanti and Brong-Ahafo regions). Moreover, for all its realism on economic issues, the Limann administration proved woefully inadequate in dealing with a steadily declining gross domestic product, rising food prices, high inflation, and heavy budget deficits and external debts. The government's efforts to encourage greater productivity through agricultural price supports and the development of industries linked to Ghana's natural resource base proved too cautious under the circumstances. Because the regime appeared unable to offer effective leadership in the face of its challenges, Rawlings intervened again, toppling another democratically elected government in December 1981.

Rawlings's Regime

Upon seizing power Rawlings governed the country arbitrarily, moving by stages from radical populism to structural adjustment to constitutional reform. Both the radical populist and structural adjustment phases involved considerable repression of civil liberties, including controls on freedom of assembly and expression, the dismissal of civil servants and judges, and the use of extralegal bodies to deliberate on policy and investigate corrupt practices as well as hand out sentences. After 1984 Rawlings was intent on combining populist rhetoric with conservative economic policies. He contained public participation in order to implement his economic reform program with its accompanying austerity measures. Repressive practices enabled public officials to control expenditures and public services and to reduce subsidies; the government divested itself of state-owned enterprises.

Encouraged by international donors, the Rawlings regime in the late 1980s concluded that it should link political reform with its Economic Recovery Program. Elections for district assemblies were held in 1988 and 1989, followed in due course by the appointment of a Committee of Experts and a Consultative Assembly to draft the constitution of a fourth republic. The guiding hand of Rawlings and the Provisional National Defense Council was readily apparent before the national elections of November 1992. Not only did the Provisional National Defense Council appoint the members of the Committee of Experts and heavily influence participation in the Consultative Assembly, but it controlled the agenda and timetable leading up to the elections. As a consequence, Rawlings had a distinct advantage over the various opposition parties: he had extensive state resources at his disposal for campaign purposes, and he could create jobs and raise civil service salaries just prior to the voting. In addition, Rawlings refused to open up the voting lists to those who had not registered in 1988 and 1989 (when the referendum was held on district assemblies) or in 1991 (when the voting lists were partially updated). This refusal effectively disenfranchised hundreds of thousands of his opponents.

Rawlings won 58.3 percent of the votes cast. Despite the austerity brought on by the structural adjustment program, Rawlings was able to overcome a history of military intervention and authoritarianism, becoming the first leader of an African military regime to win a multiparty election. The control the Provisional National Defense Council exercised over the election process partly accounted for this victory; however, it also was attributable to the public's perception that a change in government might interfere with the Economic Recovery Program, slow down rural development, reduce cocoa prices, and increase unemployment.

After initially refusing to accept the election results as free and fair, the opposition parties in February 1993 urged their supporters to give Rawlings's new government a chance to restore democratic institutions and practices. The Rawlings government subsequently met some opposition demands. Representatives of the opposition were included in a new Inter-Party Advisory Committee, created in March 1994 to advise the Elections Commission in advance of the 1996 legislative and presidential elections. And the government acquiesced to the opposition's primary objective: updating the voter registry.

The opposition received a boost in 1995 when widespread demonstrations and fissures within the government emerged over the imposition of a value added tax, which was rescinded within months. The issue gave the opposition a rallying point and contributed to the formation of the Alliance for Change. By the 1996 elections, however, the Alliance had changed membership and been rechristened the Great Alliance.

Rawlings won the December 1996 presidential election with 57 percent of the vote, but the opposition, which had boycotted the 1992 legislative elections in protest of the presidential election of that year, won 65 seats in the 200-seat Parliament. Although the governing National Democratic Congress retains a comfortable majority, the opposition now has a national platform from which to influence government policy and to promote further electoral reforms.

Despite the concessions of the Rawlings government and the successes of the opposition, tensions remain in evidence between the democratic and authoritarian tendencies of the political system, making the swing back to the democratic tradition in Ghana an incomplete one thus far. It is still unclear whether the current system of governance, which combines both authoritarian and democratic regime traditions, can promote economic and political reform.

BIBLIOGRAPHY

Austin, Dennis. *Politics in Ghana, 1946–1960.* London: Oxford University Press, 1964.

Chazan, Naomi. *An Anatomy of Ghanaian Politics.* Boulder, Colo.: Westview Press, 1983.

———, and Donald Rothchild. "Corporatism and Political Transactions: Some Ruminations on the Ghanaian Experience." In *Corporatism in Africa,* edited by Julius Nyang'oro and Timothy Shaw. Boulder, Colo.: Westview Press, 1989.

Gyimah-Boadi, E. "Ghana's Uncertain Political Opening." *Journal of Democracy* 5 (April 1994): 75–86.

Herbst, Jeffrey. *The Politics of Reform in Ghana, 1982–1991.* Berkeley: University of California Press, 1993.

Nkrumah, Kwame. *The Autobiography of Kwame Nkrumah.* New York: Nelson, 1957.

Rothchild, Donald, ed. *Ghana: The Political Economy of Recovery.* Boulder, Colo.: Lynne Rienner, 1991.

I

India

A vast country located in southern Asia, bordered on one side by the Himalayas and on two sides by the Indian Ocean. Extending 1,800 miles from north to south and approximately 1,650 miles from east to west, India is the most populous country in the world after China, having a population of more than 850 million people. Since achieving independence from British rule in 1947, it has had a parliamentary form of government, and each of its twenty-five states has its own elected legislature and government.

For theorists of democracy, India has been a source of bafflement. Low levels of income and literacy, a hierarchical social structure, and multiple ethnic cleavages are conditions considered inhospitable for the functioning of democracy. Almost half the people of India are illiterate; about 25 percent of them are below the poverty line. More than twenty languages and many more dialects are spoken in the country. The hierarchical caste system, although unraveling as groups at the lower end of the social scale begin to take their democratic rights seriously, has traditionally marked the social order of the Hindu community, which constitutes 82 percent of the Indian population. Religious and ethnic conflicts have erupted frequently. About 12 percent of the country's population is Muslim; 2.5 percent Christian; 2 percent Sikh; 0.7 percent Buddhist; and 0.5 percent Jain. Sikhism is an Indian religion born in the late fifteenth century; its followers are mostly concentrated in the state of Punjab. Jains are followers of an ancient faith. Small Jewish and Zoroastrian (pre-Islamic Persian) communities also exist, especially on India's western coast.

India has maintained its democratic institutions for five decades. The major exception was the brief period of "internal emergency" between 1975 and 1977, when Indira Gandhi, the prime minister, suspended democracy for eighteen months. In isolated states there have been periods of unelected governments, especially during times of insurgency. Apart from the eighteen-month emergency, however, the electoral process has never been suspended in the country as a whole.

Three factors go a long way toward explaining the longevity of India's democracy: (1) the historical background, especially some key characteristics of the nationalist movement and the implications of the British rule; (2) the role of the political leadership in the immediate pre-independence period; and (3) the structure of India's ethnic politics, which tends to localize ethnic conflicts.

History Before Independence

India was ruled by the British for nearly two centuries. The British arrived in India for commercial reasons in the seventeenth century, when the East India Company received permission from the British monarch to trade. After 1757 commercial interests evolved into a desire for political control as well. The East India Company conquered most of India by 1857, defeating the French, who were also vying for control of the country. In 1857 the British Crown replaced the East India Company as the sovereign power in India. In 1947, after three decades of an Indian nationalist movement, the British left and India became independent.

The story of India's democracy does not begin at independence in 1947. Rather, it goes back to the late British period. Two developments in this period turned out to be significant for the later period: the rise of the Congress Party, which led the nationalist movement, and the experience that indigenous politicians gained as the British allowed them to participate in the limited democratic governance of the country.

The Indian National Congress, popularly known as the Congress Party, was born in 1885. Its initial purpose was to provide a forum for the expression of India's political and economic demands to British rulers. Its first leaders were

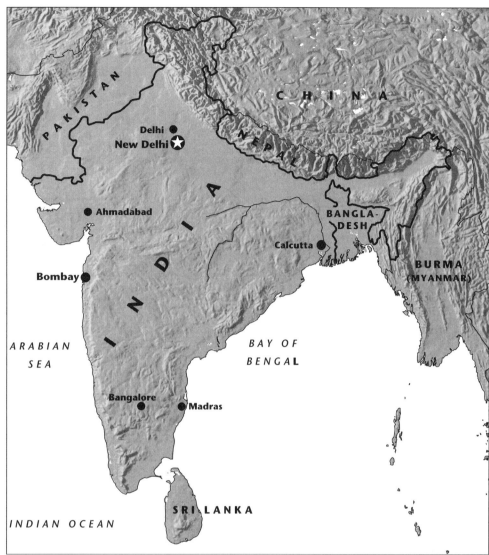

mostly lawyers who believed in constitutional politics and greater participation in local government. In the 1920s, under the leadership of Mohandas K. Gandhi, the Congress Party decided to involve the masses in the nationalist movement against the British. In the process the Congress Party was transformed from an elite club of lawyers into a mass party. The party opened district and provincial offices, launched a membership drive, and instigated intraparty elections for party leadership.

Under Gandhi's leadership the Congress Party launched a basically nonviolent campaign against the British. Civil disobedience was the principal method of protest. The party pledged to defeat the British through political, not violent, means. The party also operated on the principle of consensus. The dissenters within the party would not be forced out of the party; instead, they had the freedom to

persuade other members of the superiority of their point of view. Moreover, the Congress Party made an attempt to incorporate all ethnic and religious groups in India. In this task, however, it was not fully successful. Muslims, who constituted about 25 percent of the population, were eventually mobilized by the All-India Muslim League, a party founded in 1906. In the 1930s the Muslim League raised the demand for a Muslim homeland in the Indian subcontinent. It argued that in a democracy the Congress Party would primarily represent the interests of the majority community, not the interests of the Muslims. The Congress Party challenged this position and competed for the vote of Muslims but was finally defeated by the Muslim League. The result was India's partition and the birth of Pakistan as a Muslim homeland in 1947.

Other than the Muslim League, no nationwide parties

developed to challenge the Congress Party for the leadership of the nationalist movement. As a consequence of the party's emphasis on nonviolent means of struggle, the lack of strong alternative parties, and the formation of Pakistan, India was not troubled by fractious, internecine warfare, such as marked several nationalist movements in Africa and crippled democratic functioning after their countries gained independence.

The emergence of an elaborate party structure with an all-inclusive and nonviolent character was not the only important development of the late British period. In an effort to deal with rising nationalism, the British began to experiment with partial indigenous rule after the First World War. By 1919 indigenous politicians became participants in British governance of Indian provinces. In 1935 the British conceded provincial governance entirely to indigenous parties. The elections of 1937 were vigorously contested. The Congress Party swept the elections in the non-Muslim areas, forming governments in seven of eleven provinces. Between 1937 and 1939 the Congress Party thus acquired the experience of governing; some of its members had already acquired the experience of administration at the local levels.

The legacy of British rule was not all benign, however. The British gave Indian politicians a chance to acquire governing experience only after the Indian nationalist movement launched a struggle for self-rule. More important, although the British eventually permitted elections to be held, they created separate electorates for Muslims. This system weakened the incentives for Muslim politicians to build bridges with other communities and contributed to the partition of India.

In sum, the nationalist movement against British rule developed an important basis for India's democracy in the Congress Party. It was a party with an institutional structure in place all over the country; it sought to represent all ethnic groups; and it had experience in governing.

After Independence

India's historical advantage would have been wasted if the leadership after independence in 1947 had destroyed democratic norms. Jawaharlal Nehru, India's first prime minister, and his colleagues accepted democratic principles, even though these principles entailed considerable political inconvenience. The Congress Party regularly produced leaders who, unlike Nehru, did not want land reforms in agriculture and were opposed to state ownership of key industries and to socialism. After debates in party forums, Nehru and his supporters in the party won some policy battles but not all. Moreover, there were times when the powers of judicial review led the courts to overturn important policy legislation. Nehru and his supporters did not attack the judiciary or use coercion against their opponents within the party or in Parliament. Rather, they followed the accepted institutional procedures and norms to fight policy and political battles—winning sometimes but losing at other times. If the courts overturned legislation for land reforms, Nehru's government followed the constitutional requirement that the judiciary could be overruled only by a constitutional amendment, which called for a two-thirds vote in Parliament and approval by more than half of the state legislatures. If Nehru's opponents in the Congress Party succeeded in getting a majority vote against his plan for farm (as opposed to service) cooperatives, he accepted the verdict and dropped the plan. The result of Nehru's scrupulous adherence to constitutional norms and procedures was an increasing acceptance of these norms and procedures. This careful nurturing of India's democratic childhood bore good results later.

Since independence, eleven parliamentary elections and several more state assembly elections have been held. Peaceful transfer of power between rival political parties has taken place five times at the central (federal) level and many more times at the state level. Since 1967 nearly half the state governments have been run by parties that did not form the central government in New Delhi. India's press has remained vigorous and free; taking on the government of the day is viewed as a matter of right. Even a cursory perusal of the morning newspapers would indicate that the print media enjoy remarkable freedom. The judiciary, periodically pressed hard by the executive, refuses to bend fully, maintaining considerable institutional autonomy. The election turnout, which was 45.7 percent in the first general elections (1952), has risen since then to more than 60 percent, exceeding that in several Western industrial countries. For women, too, the turnout has gone up, from less than 40 percent in 1952 to between 55 and 60 percent during the 1980s and 1990s.

Adherence to democratic norms made the political system manageable. Because state-level leaders were elected, not appointed by the central government in New Delhi, the Congress Party regularly produced leaders who had stature, a base of their own, and considerable command over their states. They could manage regional political disorders. In the 1970s, when Indira Gandhi temporarily suspended these principles and sought to centralize the party under her governance, disorder, instead of being managed at the state level, traveled up to New Delhi for resolution. Some of the ungovernability of recent years is a result of the decline of the Congress Party and the inability of other parties to acquire the status that the Congress Party historically enjoyed.

Ethnic Conflicts and Their Political Management

Ethnic conflicts of all kinds—religious, linguistic, tribal, caste-based, regional—have been a pervasive feature of India's political life. Yet democracy has survived Hindu-Muslim riots; Hindu-Sikh violence in the state of Punjab; caste-based violence in various parts of the country; insurgency in the northeast and in Kashmir; sons-of-the-soil movements in the states of Assam, Andhra Pradesh, and Maharashtra; and language-based riots in the 1950s and 1960s.

Why did India's democracy not break down under these pressures? Two explanations can be given—one political and the other structural. The former has to do with the multireligious and multiethnic character of the Congress Party. Its electoral functioning did not depend on ethnic slogans but on bridging ethnic differences. The fact that the Congress Party lost this character beginning in the 1970s, and that no other party has replaced its vast machinery, is one of the causes of the ethnic eruptions that have occurred since then.

The structural explanation is that all ethnic cleavages in India, except for the cleavage between Hindus and Muslims, are regionally or locally specific. The Sikh-Hindu cleavage is confined basically to the state of Punjab and to parts of northern India. There has been an insurgence in Kashmir, based on demands for independence from India, but it has not spilled out of the Kashmir valley. Hundreds were killed in anti-immigrant riots inside the state of Assam in the early 1980s but not outside. The movement in Maharashtra in the 1960s to limit employment in the state to those born in the state, by definition, remained state-based. As a result, while Punjab and Assam were torn by violence, the administration in the rest of India continued to function more or less normally. Even the all-pervading caste system, intrinsic to the entire Hindu society, is locally based; castes are local, or at most regional, entities. Caste riots in one part of the country, therefore, do not necessarily affect life in other parts. Anti-Brahman movements in Tamil Nadu in the 1940s, 1950s, and 1960s, for example, threw a large number of Brahmans out of the state, but Brahmans elsewhere in India were not affected.

Dispersion of ethnic cleavages leads to a perceptual illusion: conflicts keep breaking out, giving the impression that the system is breaking down. Yet the center manages to hold. Parties that represent ethnic issues may create serious political turmoil in a given state, but they are unable to move beyond that state. Even when an ethnic party leading an insurgency confronts the central government, it is unable to mobilize sufficient support beyond the state. The insurgents end up facing the central government in its full coercive might. Deployment of coercion to deal with insurgency is not greatly resented by other parts of the country, although civil rights groups protest, sometimes quite effectively. Thus even an insurgency, the most extreme form of ethnic conflict, gets bottled up in a fragment of the country. Democracy is suspended in the area of insurgency while the rest of the country continues to function under routine democratic processes.

Another structural feature of India's political system, its federalism, contributes to its ability to withstand ethnic conflicts and insurgencies. If the country had been unitary, all antigovernment movements would have been directed at the central government, creating far greater systemic strains in the polity than have been witnessed so far. Whether the center would have been able to hold in that situation is open to question.

The Muslim Question: Implications for Democracy

Only one cleavage in India—that between Hindus and Muslims—is capable of ripping the country apart, should it come under more serious stress than it already has. Historians are aware of the hatred, violence, and disruption that can surround this cleavage. The 1947 partition of the country was not simply geographic. It is estimated that 200,000–300,000 people died in the riots set off by partition, and 12–15 million changed their places of residence in search of safety. Only about 12 percent of India is Muslim today, but that translates into more than 100 million Muslims, almost as many as in either Pakistan or Bangladesh.

The geographical distribution of India's Muslims gives their meager percentage a serious political meaning. There are significant concentrations of Muslims in virtually all parts of India. In the north, Muslims are in a majority in Jammu and Kashmir; in the east, they make up about 22 percent of West Bengal and nearly the same percentage of Assam; in north-central India, they form 16 percent of Uttar Pradesh and 14 percent of Bihar; in the south, Muslims constitute 21 percent of Kerala and 11 percent of Karnataka. Moreover, Muslims constitute more than their national average—in many cases up to a third or a fourth—of the populations of many cities in all parts of the country. Unlike the Hindu-Sikh problems confined to Punjab or the tribal insurgency limited to the northeast, a serious worsening of Hindu-Muslim relations, let us say in northern India, has the potential of affecting Hindus and Muslims all over the country.

The Muslim question is fraught with the pain of history in India. In the first two decades of India's independence, the pain lay dormant for two reasons: the migration of the Muslim middle class to Pakistan rendered the community leaderless in India, and the ruling Congress Party maintained a bridge-building character under Nehru's resolutely secular leadership. Since then a Muslim middle class has emerged, and the Congress Party is in decline. Moreover, no other party has been able to win the trust of Muslims all over India.

Two trends in particular make the situation somewhat shaky: a rise in majority chauvinism coupled with an ascending wave of minority communalism, and a proliferation of arms in the subcontinent. Majority chauvinism led by Hindu nationalists was most virulently expressed in the demolition of the Babri Mosque in the town of Ayodhya in December 1992. Majority chauvinism is not only affecting the political process; it also marks the behavior of the police. The everyday relationship between the machinery of law and order and the Muslim community has become quite adversarial in several parts of the country.

The newest political force in India is Hindu nationalism. Riding on the Hindu middle-class perception that secularism in India has degenerated into a pandering to minorities, making the state a prisoner of assertive minority communities, majority chauvinism is forcefully represented by the Bharatiya Janata Party (BJP). Since 1991 it has been the largest opposition party in the national parliament. It has also been in power in several states.

The BJP is a party of disciplined cadres. Many of its leaders and cadres believe that Muslims are disloyal to India, that Hinduism defines India's national identity, and that only a reassertion of Hinduism, not a proliferation of "pro-minority laws," will make India strong. Arguing that Babur, a sixteenth-century Muslim king, built the Babri Mosque in Ayodhya on a site where a temple commemorating the birth of the Hindu god Rama had stood, the BJP and other nationalist organizations mobilized the masses for the destruction of the mosque. The demolition of the mosque had two short-run results: widespread Hindu-Muslim riots, the worst since independence; and the BJP's

defeat in some important state elections in 1993. The latter indicated, among other things, the electorate's disapproval of the demolition of the mosque. Whether, in the long run, the electorate will continue to disapprove of the BJP or will embrace it as an alternative to the Congress Party in India remains to be seen.

The Future

Despite the odds, India has been remarkably successful in remaining democratic. Since 1947 there have been three moments of serious doubt about the country's democratic longevity: in the late 1960s, when several ethnic and caste conflicts erupted and the towering presence of Nehru was no longer available to calm passions; in the mid-1970s, when Prime Minister Indira Gandhi suspended democracy for a year and a half; and in the early 1990s, when Hindu nationalists tore down a mosque, touching off the worst Hindu-Muslim rioting since 1947. In similar circumstances, armies in other developing countries are known to have intervened in politics. India's army, however, continued to be professional, partly reflecting the legitimacy India's democracy still enjoys despite a noticeable decline since the 1950s.

There are two ways of looking at these moments of crisis. One is to suggest that India's democracy has developed some recuperative and self-correcting mechanisms. Politicians who go to an extreme, flagrantly violating democratic norms, are punished by the electorate or by institutions like the courts. Such corrections maintain a measure of normalcy. Another way to evaluate these crises is to contend that the system is in a long-term decline: each big crisis is pressing Indian democracy down to its eventual extinction. On the evidence so far, the latter claim does not appear to be valid. Problems exist, but democracy also seems to have established a vibrant and nonnegotiable political space.

Longtime observers of Indian politics have often emphasized that the biggest threat to India's democracy emerges from the deinstitutionalization of the party system—in particular, the weakening of the Congress Party and the inability of the opposition forces to provide a cohesive and effective alternative. The basic logic of this argument is simple: how can a democracy continue to function without solid and stable parties? At some point the bubble may burst.

In the 1990s a long-forgotten factor—religion in public life—reemerged as another threat. The BJP, a disciplined party with a solid organization, has brought religion explicitly into public life. The victory of religious nationalism is by no means certain, but if it does succeed, the hard work of the first generation of leadership and the many structural advantages of Indian democracy will be seriously tested. Either the Hindu nationalists will have to change, moving closer to the center and introducing moderation into their politics, or they will move the country to the extreme right, changing the political system beyond recognition. India's democracy can absorb a moderated Hindu nationalism, committed to an ideological agenda as well as a democratic framework within which to pursue that agenda. It will not survive the victory of communal bigotry. The victory of religious hatred seems unlikely and a democratic future more probable.

See also *Pakistan*.

BIBLIOGRAPHY

Kohli, Atul. *Democracy and Discontent.* New York and Cambridge: Cambridge University Press, 1990.

———, ed. *India's Democracy.* Princeton: Princeton University Press, 1988.

Kothari, Rajni. *Politics in India.* Boston: Little, Brown, 1970.

Rudolph, Lloyd, and Susanne Rudolph. *In Pursuit of Lakshmi.* Chicago: University of Chicago Press, 1987.

Varshney, Ashutosh. "The Self-Correcting Mechanisms of Indian Democracy." *Seminar* (Delhi), January 1995.

Weiner, Myron. *The Indian Paradox.* Delhi and London: Sage Publications, 1989.

Indonesia

A nation located on an archipelago between the Indian Ocean and the Philippine Sea, a member of the Association of Southeast Asian Nations, and the world's fourth most populous country. The pluralism of Indonesia is spectacular. Represented among the estimated 193 million people who live on its roughly 6,000 inhabited islands are some 300 different ethnolinguistic groups and all the world's major religions. The largest group, the Javanese, make up roughly half the population and are concentrated on Java, the archipelago's economic, cultural, and political center.

The political pluralism of democracy might seem the natural way to express and protect these diverse identities. Instead, the presence of so many differences has been used to justify authoritarian rule, as if political monism were the only way to prevent social pluralism from breeding stalemates and conflicts powerful enough to deadlock or destroy the state through secession or civil war.

Dutch colonialism in Indonesia left competing legacies. The Dutch presence spread and evolved from coastal trading relationships into an economic monopoly and coerced production under the United East Indies Company (1602–1799). The company gave way to a fully official colonial state, which by 1911 had established Dutch sovereignty throughout the archipelago. The company's corrupt patrimonialism and its successor state's antipathy to popular representation later enabled some observers to blame the Dutch for the corruption and authoritarianism that marked public life in postcolonial Indonesia.

The Dutch company communicated with local leaders in the Malay language, and after 1917 the Dutch government decided to publish cheap reading material in Malay. As a would-be national tongue, Malay had two advantages over Javanese: first, it lacked the gradations of deference intrinsic to the speech levels of "feudal" Javanese; second, it was the first language of a small ethnic group living not on Java but on the east coast of Sumatra, a main outer island. Had Javanese become the national language, Indonesians would likely have experienced much more anti-Javanese violence and even less democracy than they have.

Independence

During World War II, Japan occupied the Indies (1942–1945). In 1945, after Japan had surrendered to the Allies but before the Dutch could retake the archipelago, the nationalist leader Sukarno declared an independent Republic of Indonesia. The Dutch then offered a federal system defined by ethnic and regional groups as an alternative to the unitary republic. That system reserved, for example, a state of Pasundan for the Sundanese, the second-largest ethnic group. Despite the merits of federalism as a means of managing diversity, Indonesian nationalists saw the Dutch offer as a ploy to divide their country the better to rule it. By stimulating ethnoregional sentiments that later fueled a civil war (1958–1962), the profederal strategy of the Dutch discredited federalism among Indonesian nationalists and confirmed their view of the need for a centralized state powerful enough to hold the archipelago together.

The sovereign country born on August 17, 1950, took over the Dutch-drawn borders of the Indies, with one exception: the Dutch kept control over the easternmost part of their colony, West New Guinea. They did so partly on the grounds that its Melanesian inhabitants were too un-

like the Malayo-Polynesian peoples to the west to be included in Indonesia. Implicit in that argument was a desire to protect West New Guinea's darker skinned and mostly Christian inhabitants from Indonesia's Muslim Javanese.

In 1961–1962, infuriated by Dutch efforts to move the excluded territory toward its own independence, President Sukarno launched a military campaign. In 1962, thanks in part to U.S. diplomatic pressure, the Netherlands ceded the area to the United Nations, which passed it on to Indonesia on the understanding that within five years an unspecified "act of free choice" would express the local population's wishes. Sukarno was ousted and replaced by an army general, Suharto, in 1966–1968. In 1969 the new leadership selected, persuaded, and convened 1,025 tribal leaders who ratified, without a formal vote, the absorption of their territory, renamed Irian Jaya, into Indonesia.

Nationalism

Not until 1907 did the Dutch begin a general program of elementary education for their colonial subjects. By 1942 only some 230 Indonesians had attained higher education. But ideas about democracy could hardly be kept

out of the colony, and the few Indonesians who studied in the Netherlands, including the Sumatran economist Mohammad Hatta, the republic's first vice president (1945–1956), saw at first hand the contrast between Dutch democracy and the authoritarianism of the Indies.

Under the Japanese occupation and the revolution that followed it in 1945–1949, nationalism and populism swept the archipelago. The Japanese mobilized large numbers of Indonesians against the West and, by association, against Western ideas, including liberal democracy. Within the Indonesian revolution, proponents of parliamentary government struggled against more authoritarian-minded nationalists and communists, while advocates of an Islamic state for Indonesia pursued their own agenda. Within months of its adoption, the constitution of 1945, which provided for a strong president, was replaced by a parliamentary regime.

First under Japanese encouragement and then to combat the returning Dutch, a variety of military and paramilitary units sprang up. The guerrilla origins of the armed forces left a legacy of popular mobilization that army leaders later used to justify intervention in Indonesian public life. After Suharto's "New Order" replaced the "Old Order" of Sukarno in the mid- to late 1960s, army leaders codified that rationale as the "dual function" of the military to perform both military and nonmilitary tasks. But the guerrilla background of the armed forces also contributed to their disunity in conflicts between anticommunist and left-wing officers. The former wanted to equip Indonesia with a hierarchically organized professional army, while the latter resisted betrayal of the egalitarian values of the 1945 revolution.

Democracy

For its first nine years as a sovereign republic (1950–1959), Indonesia was a constitutional parliamentary democracy. Free nationwide elections were successfully held in 1955 for a new legislature and for a constituent assembly charged with drafting a new constitution. But the experiment with democracy failed. Using proportional representation—with the whole country, in effect, one district—the 1955 elections yielded fragmented bodies without clear majorities. Despite repeated votes, the constituent assembly could not agree on the principles of a new constitution. Unstable cabinets and rotating prime ministers could not stop ethnoregional and religious tensions from escalating into civil war. Weak and divided governments could not implement policy. The army and President Sukarno grew less and less willing to play secondary roles.

In 1959, with army backing, President Sukarno dispersed the assembly and returned Indonesia to the strong-executive constitution of 1945, calling his new system "guided democracy." In 1960 he banned the largest Muslim party, the Consultative Council of Indonesian Muslims (Masyumi), for having backed the rebels in the civil war. In 1963 he had himself named president for life.

Guided democracy (1959–1966)—later termed the "Old Order"—was in theory a tripod with Sukarno at the top. The legs were nationalist, religious, and communist, each with its own main political party: respectively, the Indonesian National Party, the Islamic Scholars' Revival, and the Indonesian Communist Party. At the apex, Sukarno played one group off against another while insisting on national unity, as if by manipulation and exhortation he could bridge the country's pluralism with a single nation-state.

In the end Sukarno could only postpone a showdown between the army and the communists. In 1964–1965 his regime faced multiple threats. These included communist efforts to seize land and infiltrate the armed forces, the restlessness of senior army officers alienated from the president's increasingly leftist line, and a rapidly deteriorating economy. In addition, Sukarno was in bad health.

On October 1, 1965, six army generals were assassinated by leftist officers. This coup enabled Maj. Gen. Suharto to assume control of the army, blame the murders on the Indonesian Communist Party, and preside over that party's destruction. Hundreds of thousands of real and suspected leftists died in the transition to Suharto's New Order.

The New Order

Suharto's regime might appear to be an extension of Sukarno's. Suharto did decide to keep the constitution of 1945 in force, including the article that assigns lawmaking authority to the president, subject to legislative assent. He also chose as the centerpiece of his New Order a formula—*pancasila,* or the five principles—that Sukarno himself had set forth in 1945. In 1985 all social and political organizations in Indonesia were obliged to endorse the five principles: monotheism, humanitarianism, unity, democracy, and justice.

Institutionally and procedurally, however, the New and Old Orders differed in major ways. The 1945 constitution vests the exercise of popular sovereignty in a People's Consultative Assembly comprising a People's Representative Council (the national legislature) and delegates from unspecified regions and groups. In 1960 Sukarno appointed the assembly and the council; under guided democracy no elections were held.

By the mid–1990s, in contrast, six national elections to these bodies had been held under Suharto's *pancasila* democracy—in 1971, 1977, 1982, 1987, 1992, and 1997. The government's vote-gathering vehicle, Golkar (Functional Groups), originally launched by the army in 1964 to support anticommunist social organizations, collected roughly two-thirds majorities of the votes cast in these polls. As in 1955, proportional representation was used, but the province replaced the country as the basic electoral district. In deference to sensitivity over Javanese domination, representation from the outer islands was given greater weight; so Java, with two-thirds the population, would fill fewer than two-thirds of the elected seats.

In the fragmenting elections of 1955, twenty-eight different parties had won at least one seat in the People's Representative Council, and each of the two biggest winners—the Indonesian National Party and Masyumi—had filled only 22 percent of the seats. In the council appointed by Sukarno in 1960, and again in the first one elected under Suharto in 1971, only eight parties were represented. But in 1973 Suharto reduced this number to two by amalgamating the Muslim parties into a Unity Development Party and the nationalist and Christian ones into an Indonesian

Democracy Party. After 1973, only Golkar and these two sponsored opposition parties were allowed to compete in national elections. Voters, especially civil servants and villagers, were discouraged from choosing an opposition party.

The Muslim Unity Development Party was barred from advocating an Islamic state, and any reference to Islam was kept out of its name. In 1986 Suharto also disallowed the party's use of the sacred stone of Mecca as a ballot symbol. In 1984 the party's largest constituent organization left. The party's vote share fell from 28 percent in the 1982 to 16 percent in 1987 and 17 percent in 1992 before rebounding slightly to 23 percent in 1997. Meanwhile, the Indonesian Democracy Party, over those same elections, improved its showing from 8 percent to 11 percent to 15 percent, drawing nearly even with the Unity Development Party before dropping to 3 percent in 1997. Some leaders of the Indonesian Democracy Party were inclined to press cautiously for more openness and respect for the rights and freedoms associated with liberal democracy. Others, however, emphasized the nationalist tradition of Sukarno.

Suharto surrounded his regime with the power of the armed forces, especially the army. He used the "dual function" doctrine to justify military intervention on almost any matter. The army exercised control through its penetration of the state at all levels. The army's combat units, intelligence apparatus, and hierarchy of territorial commands paralleled the civilian bureaucracy down to the villages. The army could be relied on to quell perceived threats to political order from, for example, liberal-democratic university students and theocratically minded Muslims. In July 1996 the army shot and killed a number of citizens who were demonstrating against the storming of an opposition party's headquarters by security forces.

In 1997 President Suharto's vice president was an army general, as every vice president had been since 1983. Retired or active-duty military men also held many cabinet posts, governorships, and other offices. In 1987 and 1992 only 400 of the 500 seats in the People's Representative Council were filled by election; in 1997, 425 of 500 members were directly elected. The remainder of the seats were reserved, by appointment, for the armed forces. (Their representation being thus guaranteed, military personnel were denied the right to vote.) Even if an opposition party had won all 400 elective seats in the council, it could still have been a minority within the 1,000 seat assembly because the assembly included, in addition to the 500 council members, another 500 delegates who were appointed or only indirectly elected. Empowered by the 1945 constitution to do so, the assembly elected Suharto president in 1968 and reelected him in 1972, 1973, 1978, 1983, 1988, and 1993.

Suharto legitimated his regime through economic growth. By reinvesting receipts from oil and gas in agriculture and manufacturing, Indonesia was able to move away from dependency on hydrocarbon exports and toward self-sufficiency in food. With an average annual 4.3 percent rise in per capita gross national product (GNP) in 1965–1988, Indonesia tied Japan for eighth place in the World Bank's ranking of countries on this measure. Nor did this growth significantly skew the distribution of income in Indonesia compared with its neighbors.

The Role of Capitalism

Capitalism may prove more conducive to democratization in Indonesia than other factors, such as pluralism, colonialism, Javanism, and nationalism. By the early 1990s Indonesian society under the New Order had been transformed by economic growth. A middle class had grown up. Private voluntary organizations had proliferated. Workers had grown bolder in demanding better conditions and higher wages. Despite periodic government crackdowns, the limits of press freedom had been enlarged. Suharto himself had endorsed the idea if not the practice of greater openness. It seemed that Indonesia might follow the examples of South Korea, Taiwan, and Thailand, countries whose dynamic economies had unleashed irresistible pressures for political liberalization.

Yet future rulers of Indonesia would still be able to argue, however self-servingly, that only a strong government could prevent the country's pluralism from splitting it up. Regional resentments still existed in East Timor (which Suharto's army had invaded and annexed in 1975–1976), Irian Jaya, and the strongly Muslim province of Aceh. Colonial rule in Indonesia, unlike in the neighboring Philippines, had left a legacy of autocracy. Javanese culture, though complex and nuanced, had not been conducive to belief in liberal democracy, egalitarian norms, or individual rights. Indonesian nationalists had fluctuated between accepting democracy as a means to popular sovereignty and rejecting it as a Western invention ill suited to local conditions.

See also *Asia, Southeast.*

BIBLIOGRAPHY

Anderson, Benedict. "Old State, New Society: Indonesia's New Order in Comparative Historical Perspective." *Journal of Asian Studies* 42 (May 1983): 477–498.

Body for the Protection of the People's Political Rights Facing the 1992 General Election. *"White Book" on the 1992 General Election in Indonesia.* Ithaca, N.Y.: Cornell Modern Indonesia Project, 1994.

Bouchier, David, and John Legge, eds. *Indonesian Democracy, 1950s–1990s.* Clayton, Australia: Monash University Center for Southeast Asian Studies, 1994.

Crouch, Harold. *The Army and Politics in Indonesia.* Rev. ed. Ithaca, N.Y.: Cornell University Press, 1988.

Feith, Herbert. *The Decline of Constitutional Democracy in Indonesia.* Ithaca, N.Y.: Cornell University Press, 1962.

Liddle, R. William. "Indonesia's Democratic Past and Future." *Comparative Politics* 24 (July 1992): 443–662.

Reeve, David. *Golkar of Indonesia: An Alternative to the Party System.* Singapore: Oxford University Press, 1985.

Schwarz, Adam. *A Nation in Waiting: Indonesia in the 1990s.* St. Leonards, Australia: Allen and Unwin, 1994.

Sundhaussen, Ulf. "Indonesia: Past and Present Encounters with Democracy." In *Democracy in Developing Countries: Asia,* edited by Larry Diamond, Juan J. Linz, and Seymour Martin Lipset. Boulder, Colo.: Lynne Rienner; London: Adamantine Press, 1989.

Young, Kenneth, and Richard Tanter, eds. *The Politics of Middle Class Indonesia.* Clayton, Australia: Monash University Center for Southeast Asian Studies, 1989.

Iran

An Islamic republic located between the Middle East and South Asia, bordered on the west by Turkey and Iraq; on the north by Armenia, Azerbaijan, and Turkmenistan; and on the east by Afghanistan and Pakistan. Iran was the first country in the Middle East and the Muslim world to have a constitutional revolution. But unlike constitutionalism in other Middle Eastern countries, which was largely an elite phenomenon, Iran's constitutional movement was a popular phenomenon that had its roots in all segments of Iranian society.

The Constitutional Revolution of 1906 and Its Roots

Iran's long history—more than 3,000 years—has witnessed periods of tremendous glory but also periods of decline and decadence. Indeed, in terms of imperial expansion, Iran's record has been matched only by that of Rome. After the country's defeat by the Arabs in A.D. 642, its vast lands were ruled by a number of minor dynasties. Yet, although Iran was Islamized, it was never Arabized. By the ninth century A.D., a literary and cultural renaissance was under way. Over the course of the next six centuries, Iran would exert a great influence in shaping Islamic civilization.

By 1502 Iran was united once more and had nearly reached its pre-Arab invasion borders under the Safavid dynasty. The beginning of the nineteenth century, however, found Iran again in a weakened state. The extent of its decline became quite clear during two series of wars with Russia (1804–1812 and 1824–1828). These ended with the loss of Iran's lands in the Transcaucasus. The wars also opened Iran up to Russian influence. Because Britain was engaged in a fierce rivalry with Russia over a vast area that extended from the Balkan states to the Persian Gulf, Iran became a battleground for the imperial powers and suffered grievously.

In the nineteenth century foreign economic and political penetration into Iran reached an extremely high level. In fact, the country was divided into colonial spheres of influence between Russia and Britain. Both imperial powers worked hard to frustrate reform efforts and to undermine reformist leaders, such as Amir Kabir, who was Iran's prime minister in the 1850s and who began Iran's first attempt at modernization. His reforms included the introduction of a European-style education and studies abroad, as well as modest economic and technological advances. As a result of these efforts, the European notions of constitutionalism and liberal democracy, as well as socialist philosophy, gradually trickled into Iran. Its proximity to Russia, which by the mid-nineteenth century was undergoing significant political mutations, accelerated Iran's political development as well. Iranian developments, however, were not spearheaded solely by the penetration of secular and Western ideas; they also had a very strong indigenous and Islamic dimension—no small point in light of the evolution of Iran, including its Islamic revolution.

The constitutional revolution of 1906 found Iran in its weakest economic and political position since its reunification in the fifteenth century. Two factors contributed most to the revolution: first, internal weakness and the lack of governmental accountability and, second, foreign penetration and the country's steady loss of independence. In the minds of most Iranians these two factors were closely related: the prevention of foreign encroachment required governmental reform and curbs on royal powers.

An important event in the process of reform was the so-called tobacco revolt of 1890. For some time the Iranian king had been granting large-scale concessions to foreign, especially British, concerns. These concessions, if main-

tained, would have put all Iran's natural resources under foreign control and ownership. Each time the king granted such concessions, however, he had been forced to cancel them at considerable cost because of popular protest. The crisis over the granting of a total monopoly of the country's tobacco trade to a British concern acquired dimensions never seen in previous cases. In particular, the religious establishment and the merchant community led in efforts to force the cancellation of the concession. Leading Iranian clerics issued a religious order banning the use of tobacco. This ban, which was widely observed by the people, involved them directly and massively in the protest movement. The tobacco monopoly was then canceled, but Iran's problems continued to worsen, leading to increased demands for political reform and the establishment of the rule of law.

The Iranian reformists, however, were divided on the question of whether the government that they wished to see emerge should be religious or secular. The Iranian secularists wanted to create a constitutional monarchy modeled on the European monarchies and to introduce European legal systems. The religious factions wanted the strict application of Islamic law—that is, an Islamic state.

The constitution adopted in 1906 after the victory of the constitutionalists was a compromise between these two extremes. It reflected the balance of political power between the two groups, as well as Iran's essentially Islamic character. In theory the 1906 constitution turned Iran into a con-

stitutional monarchy. It established a bicameral parliament with a lower and an upper house, an executive branch headed by a prime minister and a cabinet responsible to the parliament, and an independent judiciary. A body of supplementary fundamental laws approved in 1907—a kind of bill of rights for the Iranian people—provided for freedom of the press, speech, and association, and for security of life and property.

The religious influence was reflected in Article 6 of the constitution, which stipulated that at all times five prominent clerics were to be present in the parliament to ensure that all legislation was compatible with Islamic law. Personal freedoms also were limited by the provision that such freedoms should not contravene Islamic law and morality. In addition, the monarch and all high government officials had to be of the Islamic faith. The three main religious minorities—the Zoroastrians, Christians, and Jews—had the right to elect one representative each to the parliament. If democracy is equated with absolute secularism, the constitutional revolution of 1906 was not the beginning of democracy in Iran.

Despite these early advances, constitutionalism has had a rocky history in Iran. In 1908 the new Iranian king, with Russian help, bombed the parliament building, arrested many deputies, and closed down the assembly. His actions, however, led to armed resistance in major Iranian cities. In July 1909 constitutional forces marched into the capital, deposed the king, and reestablished the constitution.

Despite continued economic weakness, political strife, and foreign intervention, political life in Iran became more active from 1906 until the late 1920s. Political parties were formed, syndicalist and other ideas related to workers' movements spread, and a lively press emerged. Throughout this period the parliament functioned effectively, although not always in Iran's political and strategic best interests. But between 1925 and 1943, while the outward manifestations of constitutionalism remained, Iran gradually reverted to monarchical absolutism, beginning with the reign of the first Pahlavi king.

Between 1943 and 1953 Iran's political process was again revitalized and liberalized. However, a number of internal and international factors, notably the rise of Iranian nationalism, the growing influence of the left, the cold war, and increased Soviet activity in Iran, led to the British- and American-sponsored coup d'état against Iran's constitutionalist and nationalist prime minister, Mohammad Mossadegh, in 1953. This move stifled the development of Iran's young democracy.

From 1953 to 1979, while the outward trappings of constitutionalism continued, both the extent of monarchical power and the level of foreign influence in Iran increased. Consequently, neither the political parties nor the other civic institutions that had developed after the constitutional revolution succeeded in putting down strong roots in the society. Lack of adequate freedom of expression also hampered Iran's political maturation and led to the spread of clandestine political activity.

Nevertheless, between 1953 and 1978 a series of economic and political reforms were introduced in Iran—among others, land reform, voting rights for women, expansion of education, and a more egalitarian system of recruitment to government office—all of which created more solid bases for future consolidation of democratic institutions. But these reforms also caused social dislocation and social and political tensions, in part by raising expectations.

This reform process also unraveled the religious-secular compromise embodied in the 1906 constitution, thus increasing polarization between the religious establishment, on the one hand, and the more secularized political elites, on the other. This polarization, as well as the undermining of the nationalist, mostly secular, constitutionalism in Iran, led to the articulation of new ideas of society and governance based on Islamic principles.

The Islamic Republic

With the revolution of 1979, a 2,500-year tradition of monarchy ended in Iran. Once more the political forces that joined together against the monarchy differed on the character of the political system that should replace it. The secular forces wanted a democratic republic; the Islamists preferred an Islamic republic. In the referendum held in March 1979, the people were offered a narrow choice of voting for or against an Islamic republic. They chose the former.

Iran's current political system is based on the constitution of 1979 and minor amendments that were effected in 1989. The present system could be characterized as a theocracy, with elements of participatory democracy and a presidential executive.

Article 1 of the 1979 constitution stipulates that the form of government in Iran is an Islamic republic. Article 2 elaborates that the Islamic system of government is based on the belief that God has sole sovereignty and the right to legislate; the role of leadership and guidance in ensuring the continuity of the revolution of Islam; the dignity and value of man, joined to responsibilities before God; and the continuous interpretation of Islamic law by religious clerics.

In the Islamic republic, those who have mastered Islamic jurisprudence occupy an influential place. The key position within the system is that of the supreme jurist council—the leader who exercises guardianship. This leader is chosen from among a number of prominent clerics by an assembly of experts, whose members are elected by the people. The leader is aided in his duties by the guardian council, who ensures that all legislation is compatible with Islamic law.

The main legislative body is the Islamic Consultative Assembly, whose members are elected by universal suffrage. In addition, municipal councils function at the city and village levels. Executive power initially was divided between the president and a prime minister. This double-headed executive, however, proved extremely ineffective, and, following the constitutional reforms of 1989, the post of the prime minister was eliminated.

Articles 19–42 of the constitution elaborate the rights of the Iranian people. Article 19 stipulates that, regardless of their ethnic group or tribe, all the people of Iran enjoy equal rights and that such factors as color, race, and language do not bestow any privilege. Articles 20 and 21 deal with women's rights, which, they state, are equal to those of men in accordance with Islamic criteria.

Article 13, on the rights of religious minorities, states that Zoroastrian, Jewish, and Christian Iranians are the only recognized religious minorities. As such, they have the right to perform their religious ceremonies freely within the limits of the law and to live according to their own customs in matters of personal status and religious education.

Articles 22, 23, and 24 deal with the security of life and property, and with freedom of opinion and the press. All these rights are limited by the provision that they should not conflict with Islamic principles.

According to Article 14, the formation of political parties and of professional associations and societies is allowed, provided again they do not violate the principles of independence, freedom, and national unity; the criteria of Islam; or the basis of the Islamic republic. In practice, however, political parties, with few exceptions, have not developed in Iran. Moreover, during the period of revolutionary turmoil, individual rights and personal freedoms were seriously compromised.

Yet a number of grassroots associations and various local councils and committees have developed, and the people's political and social consciousness has risen considerably. A very lively press also has developed in Iran, enjoying more freedom than is found in most Muslim countries. Nevertheless, those publications that openly challenge the ideas of the revolution are periodically harassed. In the 1990s efforts were made toward rectifying violations of people's rights and establishing law and order, but Iran still has a way to travel on the road to the rule of law.

Since 1979 the Islamic republic has discovered the limitations of a theocratic system in dealing with the requirements of a vastly complex society and world. Contradictions between Islamic principles and democratic principles also have become evident. The result has been a gradual but steady move away from theocracy. This move is reflected in a reassertion of the supremacy of state interests over religious principles, the questioning of the relevance of the guardianship of the jurist council, and a trend toward Islamic reformation and the gradual separation of church and state.

If external conditions allow Iran to continue these reforms, the promise of constitutionalism and democracy in a form compatible with Iranians' culture and spiritual values may yet be fulfilled. Opponents of greater openness and a more enlightened and democratic Islam, however, are still strong in Iran, and the promise of democracy may yet elude the Iranians for some time to come.

See also *Middle East*.

BIBLIOGRAPHY

Hamid, Algar. *Religion and State in Iran, 1785–1906.* Berkeley: University of California Press, 1969.

Hunter, Shireen T. *Iran after Khomeini.* New York: Praeger, 1992.

Sharong, Akhari. *Religion and State in Contemporary Iran.* Albany: State University of New York Press, 1980.

Shaul, Bakhash. *The Reign of the Ayatollahs.* New York: Basic Books, 1984.

Iraq

An Islamic republic located in southwestern Asia at the northern tip of the Persian Gulf. Iraq's 6,000-year history dates back to the rise of the Sumerians, who established a thriving civilization in Mesopotamia, the ancient name for Iraq. With the Sumerians followed by the Akkadians, Babylonians, Assyrians, and Chaldeans, Mesopotamia contin-

ued to be the seat of great indigenous civilizations until foreign forces began to invade the area.

In terms of their lasting influence, the most relevant of these forces were the Muslims of the Arabian Peninsula, who conquered Iraq in A.D. 636. During the 'Abbasid dynasty (750–1258), Iraq, and especially its capital, Baghdad, became the center of the most glittering of Muslim civilizations. The country then began a gradual decline until its conquest by the Ottomans in 1534.

After the defeat of the Ottomans in World War I, Iraq came under British control, and in 1920 the country was placed under a League of Nations mandate, to be administered by Britain. In 1921 Emir Faisal ibn Hussein was proclaimed king of Iraq, and the British guaranteed Iraq's independence after a probationary period. The British passed on their system of government to the Iraqis, and, as such, a law calling for the establishment of a parliament—a Senate nominated by the king and an elective Chamber of Deputies—was adopted. The British mandate ended in October 1932, when Iraq became fully independent.

The Monarchy: 1921–1958

The period between 1921 and 1945 was marked by chronic instability. Although about 80 percent of Iraq's population was Arab, a significant Kurdish minority, ethnically and linguistically different from the rest of the Iraqis, lived in the north of the country. The Kurds launched a series of rebellions demanding independence. The Arab population itself was divided along sectarian lines with the majority belonging to the Shi'a sect of Islam (Shi'ites). The government in Baghdad, however, drew mainly on members of the minority Sunni sect. These divisions were exacerbated by the increasing tension between the essentially tribal nature of Iraqi society, on the one hand, and the rising tide of all-inclusive Arab nationalism (fueled by the German and Italian models) among city dwellers, on the other.

As a result, the country was difficult to govern. The central government in Baghdad expended much of its energy trying to extend its authority through the rest of the country. But it was challenged repeatedly by Kurdish and Shi'ite rebellions, and this instability encouraged other minorities to rise against the Baghdad government. It was hardly surprising, then, that governments came and went with bewildering rapidity and that the army began to intervene in politics.

Yet chaotic as it was, the political system boasted a Chamber of Deputies, whose members, elected periodically, met and debated government policies. The electoral process and the Chamber may have been dominated by feudal lords and a number of influential urban politicians who belonged to powerful, rich families, but in the final analysis some limits were set on the power of the central government. There were even attempts at political associations. Political coalitions, such as the Ikha and Ahali groups, provided opposition and participated in the political process.

Immediately after the Second World War the monarchy allowed the formation of political parties. Five parties then came into being, four of which were genuine opposition parties. Three of these parties later were suppressed because of national turmoil over Iraq's relations with Britain. Nevertheless, in a few years Iraq again had five parties, three of which formed a vociferous opposition to the government.

Although many of the periodic elections suffered from tampering, they invariably placed in the Chamber of Deputies a number of independent-minded opposition figures, who vigorously and continually probed governmental goals and policies. The September 1954 election, however, the last under the monarchy, was so fully rigged that no opposition figure won. At the very least, the Chamber of Deputies generally provided a forum for discussions with and criticism of leading governmental personalities, thus tending to restrain the latter from excessive abuse of power or from total political control.

Until the demise of the monarchy in July 1958, Iraq boasted a vigorous press. Although radio and television were controlled by the government, newspapers either were independently owned or belonged to the various political parties. In 1957, for example, fourteen newspapers were published in Baghdad, five in Mosul, and four in Basra. And although every now and then the government would ban a newspaper for a particularly strident attack, the ban would last for no more than a few days, and the paper would duly reappear.

According to the strict criteria of Western liberal democracy as practiced in Europe and the United States, monarchical Iraq could hardly have been called a thriving democracy. Nevertheless, at various times in its history, the monarchical political system exhibited a number of democratic features—periodic elections, political parties, and a press that was not government controlled. Compared with what was to succeed it, Iraq under the monarchy was at least a democracy of sorts.

Personal Authoritarianism
After 1958

The military coup of July 1958 set the political pattern for the next three and a half decades when its head, Gen. 'Abd al-Karim Kassem, acquired the title "sole leader." But Kassem lasted fewer than five years, to be followed by two other military leaders over the next five years.

Ten years of authoritarian, personalized rule by army officers backed by the armed forces set the scene for the next military takeover, which proved to be far more resilient: the July 1968 coup by members of the Ba'ath Party, one prominent leader of which was the young and ruthless Saddam Hussein. Hussein quickly came to dominate not only the party but also the whole spectrum of Iraqi politics.

Supporters of the Ba'ath Party argued that their government would be different from the ones that had preceded it. There would be no place for the cult of personality in such a long-established, prestigious party as the Ba'ath. Indeed, the party had been politically active in Iraq, albeit in a clandestine fashion, for more than two decades, and all of its leaders were committed, loyal followers. That any one person could rise above the party was allegedly impossible.

Moreover, the Ba'athists contended that true democracy would be practiced in Iraq through the organizational structure of the Ba'ath Party. Party cells would permeate

Iraqi society at all levels—in schools, villages, factories, agricultural compounds, professional associations—and these cells, which were to represent the true interests of the people, would filter societal concerns and demands upward in a pyramidal fashion to be acted on by a leadership that would be constantly revolving.

Even if these claims were genuine and well intentioned, those who expounded them soon realized the folly of excluding competitive parties from the political arena. By the very logic of their reason for existence, one-party systems are highly susceptible to domination by a charismatic or ruthless figure or by a small and closely knit oligarchy. And so it was in Ba'athist Iraq. By the late 1970s Hussein dominated the party, and by extension the country, to such an extent that a personality cult was created, the likes of which Iraqis had never experienced before. He became president of Iraq in 1979. The party itself, which its founders and supporters had projected as the Arab democratic alternative to the supposedly corrupt model of Western liberal democracy, was reduced to a cheerleading role, never missing an opportunity, no matter how inappropriate, to applaud and lionize Hussein. For example, the June 1982 deliberations of the party's Ninth Regional Congress—undertaken when Iraq's military strategy in its war with Iran, which had been devised personally by the president, was proving to be an unmitigated disaster, and when Iraq's economic performance was beginning to founder—not only proclaimed the Congress's ecstasy about Iraq's achievements under Hussein but also transformed all the manifest failures into glittering successes that were attributed to the president alone.

Given Hussein's absolute dominance over the political system, it was clear that any initiative, no matter how anemic, to liberalize the political system would have to come from the president himself. In 1980 Saddam Hussein allowed elections for a National Assembly, the first to be held since the end of the monarchy in 1958. The new electoral law, however, contained so many stipulations and conditions that it was hardly surprising when the Ba'ath Party ended up with a massive victory. The process was repeated in 1984 and again in 1989 with the same predictable results. Thirty-three women, however, were elected in 1984 and twenty-seven in 1989.

More promising initially was Hussein's announcement in November 1988 of a political reform program, which included the introduction of a multiparty political system and a new, permanent constitution. Indeed, a new draft constitution was completed in January 1990 and approved by the National Assembly in July.

The process came to a grinding halt on August 2, 1990, when Iraq invaded Kuwait. Undertaken totally on Hussein's initiative, the invasion and later Hussein's obstinate determination not to withdraw from Kuwait pitted the Iraqi army against an awesome coalition under U.S. command. The result was a foregone conclusion. The Iraqi army suffered a catastrophic defeat, and the country's economic and industrial infrastructure was severely damaged.

Perhaps still feeling the shock of the disaster of the Gulf war, Hussein initially allowed his reformist prime minister, Saadoun Hammadi, to introduce in September 1991 legislation providing for the establishment of a multiparty political system in accordance with the constitution approved a year earlier. Later in the month, however, Hammadi was dismissed, and the notion of a multiparty democracy was soon laid to rest.

Under the political structure devised and led by Hussein, democratic institutions clearly have no chance of being introduced in Iraq. Hussein's Iraq is the quintessential totalitarian state. The president, who treats the country as his personal property, is kept in power by a pervasive security machine, unparalleled in its cruelty, and by an elite military force, the Republican Guard, drawn almost exclusively from his kith and kin from the town of Takrit. Moreover, the president and his cronies control the dissemination of information. Of Baghdad's few daily newspapers, all government-controlled, the most influential is edited by Hussein's eldest son, Uday. The papers are distinguishable from each other only by their names, and the only competition between them seems to center on how much of the front page is devoted to Hussein's picture.

Accustomed to many years of undisputed leadership, President Hussein considers any kind of opposition, no matter how tame, to be unacceptable, even a traitorous act. He brooks no argument and consults with few people. It is therefore highly improbable that such a man would willingly open up the system and take the risk, no matter how minute, of relinquishing power.

Democracy may have a chance of putting down roots in Iraq after the demise of Hussein and the political system he has fostered, but the successful adoption of some form of democracy cannot be predicted. It is unclear what kinds of psychological and cultural scars have been left by the brutalization of Iraqi society over the past quarter of a century. Moreover, since the beginning of the Iraq-Iran war, sectarian tensions have gradually come to the fore, and the Gulf war exacerbated them considerably. The longer these schisms are allowed to acquire political and geostrategic dimensions, the more uncertain the hopes for ultimate reconciliation become.

BIBLIOGRAPHY

Baram, Amatzia. *Culture, History, and Ideology in the Formation of Baathist Iraq.* New York: St. Martin's; Basingstoke: Macmillan, 1991.

Batatu, Hanna. *The Old Social Classes and the Revolutionary Movements of Iraq.* Princeton: Princeton University Press, 1978.

Hiro, Dilip. *Desert Shield to Desert Storm.* London: HarperCollins, 1992.

Khadduri, Majid. *Independent Iraq, 1932–58: A Study of Iraqi Politics.* 2d ed. New York: Oxford University Press, 1960.

al-Khalil, Samir. *Republic of Fear: Saddam's Iraq.* Berkeley: University of California Press, 1989.

Marr, Phoebe. *The History of Modern Iraq.* Boulder, Colo.: Westview Press, 1983.

Israel

A republic in the Middle East on the Mediterranean Sea. The main features of Israel's system of government are its multiparty parliamentary democracy, its pure proportional representation system of elections, its coalition government, its lack of a formal constitution, and the centrality of Judaism in its legal structure and public life. All these features add up to a unique political entity that occasionally appears less than fully democratic.

Questions are often raised about the monopoly of Orthodox Judaism over key public and private domains, about the inequality of Israel's Arab citizens, and about the lack of a bill of rights. Like several other newly created democracies that suffer from similar problems, the explanation for many of these deficiencies is historical.

Israel's founders, most of whom immigrated to Palestine from eastern Europe at the beginning of the twentieth century, had neither prior knowledge of the Western liberal tradition nor any experience with its democratic practice. For many years the most critical problem faced by the Zionist community was survival. The conflict with the Arabs and the question of physical security consumed much of the nation's attention. The political organization of Israel has therefore evolved through a lengthy process of trial and error in which questions about its democratic quality were very rarely asked. Only in the last decade has the very question of democracy emerged as an issue of meaningful public concern, and Israelis have only started to demand democratic reform. In 1990 Israel began a program of constitutional reform that has begun to change much of its democratic processes and institutions.

Historical Background

The Jews, who were exiled from the land of Israel between A.D. 70 and 135, always wanted to return, but present-day Israel came into being as an unprecedented twentieth-century rescue operation from the threat of European anti-Semitism. In 1897 the first Zionist Congress resolved in Basel, Switzerland, that the Jews should establish a state of their own. The resolution was a result of the Zionist conviction that anti-Semitism was insurmountable and that unless saved by their own hand Jews were bound to suffer individual and collective destruction. Neither Theodor Herzl, the movement's great leader, nor any of his colleagues ever doubted that the newly created Jewish state would be democratic. Because the Jews had been a persecuted minority for two millennia, Jewish nationalists could imagine themselves working only within the framework of democracy.

Israel's embryonic democracy came into being in the 1920s. The British, who had ruled Palestine since 1917 through an arrangement recognized by the League of Nations as the British mandate, allowed the newly created polity to develop its autonomous representative institutions. These included about ten political parties, an emerging national executive, and several highly politicized development agencies. Because there was not a large private economy, the political parties, through the skills of early Zionist politicians, expanded their scope of activities. The typical Zionist party was directly involved in several economic and cultural institutions. It provided jobs, education, and housing and became the central institution for most of the newly arrived penniless immigrants. Because the community was small and the ideological parties were prominent, the method adopted in the 1920s for electing delegates to the national assembly was pure proportional representation. People voted for parties, not personal representatives, and the entire country was a single electoral district.

The State of Israel was formally established on May 14, 1948. Its establishment was made possible by a special resolution of the United Nations in 1947 and a reluctant agreement by the British to terminate the mandate. The survival of the state was secured only after a lengthy war with the Palestinians and several Arab states, who invaded the country on the day the British left.

The system of government underwent few substantial changes when the new state was established. The state maintained the parliamentary nature of the prestate government, as well as its electoral system and coalition politics. It failed to draw up a written constitution, which was promised in the nation's Declaration of Independence, and paid little attention to the countervailing power of the judiciary.

One reason for the lack of change was the intensity of the 1948 war with the Arabs, which made everything else almost irrelevant. Another was the satisfaction of the nation's dominant party, Mapai (Israel Workers' Party), with the functioning of the existing system. The party's leader, David Ben-Gurion, saw no need to alter a political system that had served his party well in the past. He was especially uninterested in a written constitution and a bill of rights that could impose checks and controls on his government. Using the pretext of the war and the reluctance of his religious coalition partners to adopt a secular constitution, Ben-Gurion managed to postpone the restructuring of the government for two years. In 1950 the Knesset, Israel's legislature, resolved that Israel's future constitution would develop gradually through the enactment of "basic laws." The difference between ordinary and basic laws was never made clear, and in the nation's first forty years little progress was made toward a written constitution, a bill of rights, and a more suitable electoral system.

Institutions and System of Government

Israel is a parliamentary democracy. Its one-chamber, 120-member Knesset is constitutionally the supreme organ of the nation and the sole representative of the people's will. The lack of a formal constitution makes the Knesset an all-powerful body that can make any law it pleases. The members of the Knesset are elected every four years through a vote that is general, equal, and secret. Each of the parties offers the voters a list of 120 candidates. The number of Knesset seats the party obtains is determined according to the percentage of the general vote that it wins.

Prior to adoption of a 1992 constitutional law (which was implemented for the first time in 1996), Israel's president, the nation's nominal head, selected one of the Knesset members to form a government following a general election. The designated person, usually the leader of the largest party, became prime minister if he or she secured the support of sixty-one members of the Knesset. Under special circumstances it was possible to form a minority government that remained in office as long as no Knesset majority votes against it. Beginning in 1996, the position of prime minister became subject to direct election by the voters, with tremendous implications for government formation and the relationships among the president, prime minister, and Knesset.

The Israeli government is accountable to the Knesset and can be brought down by a Knesset vote of no confidence. Once a government is formed, especially a stable government that enjoys a comfortable majority, the Knesset as a whole loses much of its political power. The government is in a position to pass or stop almost any legislation. Israeli law requires all Knesset coalition members to vote with the government, if and when the prime minister wants them to. The country's official head, the president, is elected by the Knesset for a term of five years. The presidency is mostly a symbolic office devoid of real power.

Israel's electoral system is responsible for the multiplicity of political parties. Any list of candidates that gets the support of 1.5 percent of the Israeli voters enters the Knesset. In each general election, more than twenty lists try their luck, and about eight to ten are successful. The advantage of this system is that the Knesset accurately reflects the nation's diverse opinions and social groupings. The disadvantage is that the formation of a stable government is very difficult. A significant feature of Israel's polity has been the historical inability of a single party ever to win a majority of the seats in the Knesset. The best that Israel's largest parties, Likud and Labor, have ever done has been to get about 40 percent of the vote. That has created the need to form coalitions and to rely heavily on very small political parties, some of which may have no more than two Knesset seats. Thus the entire government (and the nation) is often dependent on the desires of a tiny minority.

Although the coalition politics of Israel has always created problems of governability, the system was relatively stable before 1977. There was only one dominant party, Labor, and no other political bloc had enough electoral support to form an alternative coalition. This limited the bargaining power of the small political parties. The situation changed with the rise to power in 1977 of the Likud Party, which meant the passing of Labor dominance and the presence of two large parties capable of coalition formation. This electoral shift has resulted in an enormous rise in the bargaining power of the small and pragmatic political parties that have no ideological inhibitions about joining either the Likud or the Labor bloc. The art of coalition making has occasionally turned into ugly horse trading, giving a large national role to shrewd and unprincipled political operators. The need to compromise constantly has also made it increasingly difficult for the nation's large parties to carry out their original platforms.

Israel's judiciary, having gradually separated itself from politics and become independent—as well as highly professional—has evolved into a major pillar of the nation's democracy. The judiciary comprises three court levels: magistrate, district, and supreme court of appeal. The most important factors in the high quality and independence of the nation's judges are their nomination for life, their relatively high pay, and their exceptional selection process. All of Israel's judges are selected by a committee composed of three supreme court justices, two government ministers, two Knesset members, and two representatives of Israel's bar association. The committee conducts its business in total secrecy and is perceived by the public to be politically impartial.

The most important institution of Israel's judiciary, with respect to the nation's democracy and rule of law, is Bagatz, Israel's Supreme Court of Justice. Bagatz is, for all practical purposes, Israel's informal constitutional court. It is called upon by all those wishing to challenge the authorities on illegal or unjust activities and is especially instrumental in stopping ongoing government policies that it finds to be unjust. The Israeli lawmakers who in the 1950s instituted Bagatz as just another legal function of the supreme court never intended to create a powerful judiciary. However, the lack of a bill of rights and the initiative of outstanding justices have gradually turned Bagatz into a bastion of legality and a guardian of the rights of ordinary citizens.

Political Parties and Ideologies

As a national community that was a vision before it even existed, Israeli society and politics have always been intensely ideological. Roughly speaking there are four distinct ideological blocs: the left, the right, the ultra-Orthodox, and the Arabs. Between the 1920s and the 1950s the left-right polarity in Israel was a dichotomy involving two diametrically opposed socioeconomic visions. Since the 1967 Six-Day War, left and right have implied opposed positions on the territories occupied by Israel in that war and on their attitudes toward the Palestinians. The Israeli left believes in territorial compromise and is increasingly certain of the Arab readiness to live in peace with Israel. The Israeli right is profoundly opposed to territorial compromise and is certain of the ultimate Arab intention to destroy the Jewish state. The territories of the greater land of Israel, according to the right, belong to the nation for religious and historical reasons. They also bring greater security.

Israel's leading leftist party is the Labor Party. A direct descendant of the old Mapai of David Ben-Gurion, the Labor Party is deeply entrenched in the social, cultural, and economic life of the nation. It is closely associated with the Histadrut (the large general federation of labor unions), with several kibbutz organizations, and with many other cultural and financial organizations. The Labor Party, which in 1977 lost the political hegemony of the nation, returned to power in 1992 under the leadership of Yitzhak Rabin and Shimon Peres. Forming a dovish coalition government, it recognized the Palestine Liberation Organization (PLO) and started negotiations for a major territorial compromise and the acceptance of a Palestinian entity in the occupied territories. Although Labor outpolled Likud by twelve seats in the May 1996 elections, Likud's Binyamin Netanyahu won the first-ever direct election for prime minister and formed a coalition government that excluded the Labor Party.

Israel's second-largest leftist party and Labor's closest ally is Meretz, a bloc of three smaller left-wing parties. Meretz's attitude toward the Palestinians is more liberal than Labor's and is marked by a readiness to return to the pre-1967 borders and to allow the establishment of an independent Palestinian state. In the 1992 elections, Labor received forty-four Knesset seats, and Meretz received twelve. In 1996, Labor and Meretz won thirty-four and nine seats, respectively.

The Israeli right is made up of the Likud, its largest party, and several small radical rightist parties. The Likud Party is the descendant of the Herut (Freedom) Party, established in 1948 by Menachem Begin. A champion of the expansion of Israel, Begin brought the party to electoral victory in 1977 after nearly thirty years in opposition. His other great achievement was the peace agreement with Egypt in 1979. But Begin and Yitzhak Shamir, his post-1983 successor, were also responsible for opening up the occupied West Bank to massive Jewish settlement, thereby creating an enormous block against future Israeli peace with the Palestinians. Israel's radical right parties, one of which is Jewish Orthodox, are more extreme than Likud on the territorial question and the Arabs. They are vehemently opposed to the establishment of a Palestinian state in the occupied territories and demand, instead, their annexation to Israel. In the 1996 legislative elections, Likud received twenty-two seats; and its allies, Gesher and Tzomet, won five seats each.

The two other political blocs are smaller than the left and the right and do not subscribe to the Zionist ideology. They are made up of Jewish ultra-Orthodox parties and of Israel's Arab minority parties. Ultra-Orthodox Judaism represents those religious Jews who have never accepted the validity of the Zionist thesis. The ultra-Orthodox consider the Jewish Diaspora (the exile from the land of Israel) as an existential state and an indication that God has not yet forgiven his people for the sins that made him send them into exile two thousand years ago. The reason ultra-Orthodox Jews do nevertheless participate in the politics of the Jewish state is that they have a community to care for, most of whose members escaped from European anti-Semitism.

There are presently two ultra-Orthodox parties in Israel. Their conviction that the future of the Jewish people and their territories will be determined exclusively by God makes the ultra-Orthodox good coalition partners. None of the great debates between the Israeli left and right really matter to them, and they feel comfortable with both leftist and rightist governments. The price of gaining ultra-Orthodox participation in a coalition is generous financial allocations for their private schools and legislation making the country "more Jewish."

Israeli Arabs make up 18 percent of the country's population, but the Democratic Arab Party won only four seats in the 1996 elections. Although the Arab parties do not oppose Israel's right of existence, they have never subscribed to Zionism. In recent years these parties have expressed increasing support for the PLO and for the demand to establish a fully independent Palestinian state in the occupied territories. The small number of the Arab Knesset members and their pro-PLO position explain their relative political weakness. Their political orientation makes Israeli Arabs impossible coalition partners for Likud, a situation that greatly reduces their bargaining power with Labor. Their incomplete legitimacy in view of most Israeli voters further reduces Labor's ability to offer them positions of influence and power.

Sociocultural Cleavages

Although the integrity of Israeli democracy has never been seriously challenged, it has had to cope with three major cleavages: between Ashkenazi Jews (Israelis of northern European descent) and Sephardi Jews (immigrants from the Middle East and North Africa), between secular and religious Jews, and between Jews and Arabs. The conflict between the Sephardim and the Ashkenazim first erupted in the 1950s, when most of the Sephardim immigrated, and lasted into the 1980s. It involved a perception by the Sephardim of institutionalized socioeconomic and political discrimination and was expressed in several waves of unruly protests and riots. A major reallocation of national resources beginning in the early 1970s, aimed at addressing the problem of the disadvantaged Sephardim, as well as an intense recruitment of young Sephardi leaders by Israel's major political parties, seems to have reduced the cleavage significantly.

The root cause of the cleavage between religious and secular Jews in Israel is the claim of Jewish Orthodoxy to be an all-inclusive state and communal religion and the partial acceptance of this claim by the Israeli political system. The claim is manifested in the exclusive, state-supported position of Orthodox institutions in the country and in the political inability of liberal forces to introduce a more pluralistic approach to their functioning. According to a Knesset law, all Israeli Jews must have their marriage, divorce, and burial ceremonies conducted by an Orthodox rabbi. Public transportation on the Sabbath is prohibited by law, and most restaurants must serve kosher food or face state-backed rabbinical sanctions. Every community in Israel has an official Orthodox rabbinical council that is financed by the state and is actively involved in the life of the community. These provisions, which leave little room for full secular freedom or for less demanding organized interpretations of Judaism, do not represent the will of the majority and infringe upon its fundamental rights.

The dilemma of Israel's Arabs was born simultaneously with the State of Israel. About 85 percent of Palestine's Arabs escaped—or were driven out—in 1948. Those who remained became, as stated in Israel's Declaration of Independence, "full and equal" Israeli citizens. They were, however, part of a large Arab world that in 1948 launched a "war of extermination" against the Jewish state and that, upon losing the war, vowed to continue the struggle until the state's final destruction. For this reason, Israeli Arabs were put, in 1948, under the "military government," a special emergency regime. The military government may have been beneficial for a while, separating the defeated Arabs from the Jews and thus helping them to cope with the omnipresence of the Israeli state, but it had horrendous long-term effects. The situation was maintained for nearly eighteen years, far beyond any security need of Israel. It led to the creation of two classes of Israeli citizens, Jews and Arabs.

For many years, Israeli Arabs led a regimented life full of military and security restraints and were made to feel like second- or third-class citizens. Their total dependence on the Jews delayed the evolution of genuinely independent Arab parties. It blocked the development of Arab political power capable of lobbying effectively for Arab cultural and economic interests. Even in the 1990s, and long after the rise of Arab political parties and effective extraparliamentary groups, most of the Arab towns and villages lagged behind similar Jewish settlements in economic well-being and in the availability of social services.

Democratic Reform

The lack of direct contact between voters and Knesset members, the enormous power of the party machine compared with that of individual legislators, the inflated blackmail power of Israel's small religious parties, and the lack of a bill of rights have long disturbed observers of Israeli democracy. Yet until 1990 there was little public support for reform, and calls for change remained politically meaningless. Israel's government crisis in 1990, involving three months of ugly coalition bargaining, finally produced popular support for reform. Tens of thousands of angry demonstrators protested against the corrupt politicians and called for an overhaul of the system.

The first reform bill to be passed by the Knesset, in 1992, was that instituting direct election of the prime minister. The bill introduced a strong presidential component to Israel's parliamentary system, with the expectation that it would strengthen the Israeli prime minister and have a significant effect on the working of the entire system. A second electoral bill considered by the legislature but not adopted was to combine direct and proportional representation for the Knesset. The Knesset also moved in the direction of enacting a bill of rights, passing in 1992 two basic laws: Human Dignity and Liberty, and Freedom of Occupation. In that same year the Knesset also passed Israel's Parties Law, which requires that all the business of the nation's political parties be conducted in open and democratic procedures and that parties no longer be involved in profit-making operations.

The spirit of reform, in fact, went beyond Knesset legislation. Following the growing popularity of the notions of accountability and direct elections, both the Labor and the Likud parties introduced primary elections. For the first time in Israel's history all candidates for national office were elected directly by party members.

See also *Middle East.* In Reference Material section, see *Israeli Declaration of Independence (1948).*

BIBLIOGRAPHY

Arian, Allen. *Politics in Israel, the Second Generation.* Chatham, N.J.: Chatham House, 1988.

Galnoor, Itzhak. *Steering the Polity.* Beverly Hills, Calif.: Sage Publications, 1982.

Horowitz, Dan, and Moshe Lissak. *The Origins of the Israeli Polity: Palestine under the Mandate.* Translated by Charles Hoffman. Chicago: University of Chicago Press, 1978.

———. *Trouble in Utopia.* Albany: State University of New York Press, 1989.

Medding, Peter. *The Founding of Israeli Democracy, 1948–1967.* New York: Oxford University Press, 1990.

Sachar, Howard M. *A History of Israel.* Vol. 1. New York: Knopf, 1976; Vol. 2. Oxford and New York: Oxford University Press, 1987.

Sprinzak, Ehud, and Larry Diamond, eds. *Israeli Democracy under Stress.* Boulder, Colo.: Lynne Rienner, 1993.

J

Japan

An island country in northeast Asia with the second largest economy in the world. Japan's democracy is of particular importance for several reasons. Japan was the first country in Asia to establish democratic institutions—and probably the first outside the Western European cultural sphere. Undermined by military rule in the 1930s and early 1940s, democracy was reestablished in new form under the American occupation (1945–1952) after World War II.

Because Japan is the greatest economic power in the world after the United States and the major industrial country in the fastest developing region of the world, the operation and outcomes of its democratic polity affect many people around the world. Japan's political system appeared to reach a turning point in the early 1990s. Perhaps the world's most stable industrialized democracy, with the same party in power for thirty-eight years, Japan in 1993 seemed to be entering a new phase of major political change or at least greater instability. A split in the ruling Liberal Democratic Party (LDP) led to a vote of no confidence in the government. In the ensuing general elections, the LDP lost its legislative majority. This outcome paved the way for coalition governments that excluded the LDP, some lasting only a brief period, for the first time since 1955. By the time the LDP regained government in 1996, the reform coalitions had written into law a new electoral system with great implications for the political landscape.

Historical Background

The evolution of Japan's state goes back to about the seventh century A.D. The imperial institution, which emerged at that time, was legitimized by myths attributing the founding of the dynasty to the grandson of the sun goddess Amaterasu about a thousand years before. The next thousand years of Japanese history were characterized by the borrowing and adaptation of many elements of culture from China, including a writing system, the Buddhist religion, and the martial arts. In those centuries Japan was governed by successions of aristocratic families and military conquerors who maintained the imperial institution to legitimize their rule.

From the beginning of the seventeenth century until after the middle of the nineteenth, Japan was ruled by a shogun, or generalissimo, of the Tokugawa family. The emperor remained on the throne but in obscurity, playing no role in governing the country. Hundreds of feudal lords governed their local domains under the watchful eye and control of the shogun's government in Edo (later renamed Tokyo). The Confucian class system was introduced from China but modified to make the warrior class—called samurai—the hereditary elite. These warriors were fiercely loyal to their feudal lord. Subordinate to the samurai were the other hereditary castes: the peasants who made up the overwhelming majority of the population, the artisans, and the lowest class, the merchants. Under this hierarchical system, order was imposed on the country for more than 250 years. The shogunate enforced Japan's isolation from foreign contacts, which also helped to maintain the shogun's control.

By the end of this period (called the Tokugawa period, 1603–1868), several factors led to a movement to overthrow the shogun. Among these factors were the economic decline of the samurai, the prosperity of the merchants, the rise of a national consciousness, and the forced opening of Japan to the West with the arrival of foreign warships. In 1853 Commodore Matthew Perry arrived on a mission from the American president to open up Japan to Western trade. By that time Japan's once stable system of Tokugawa

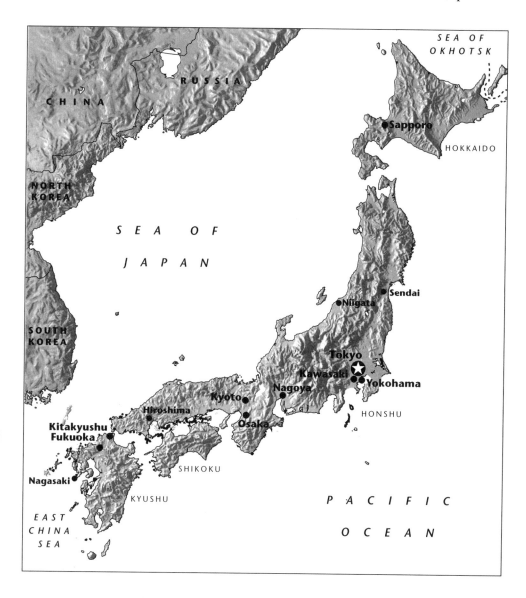

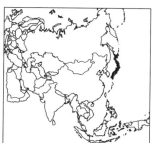

rule was already in crisis. In 1868 a rebellion succeeded in "restoring" the emperor to his rightful place as the chief figure of the political system. This event, called the Meiji Restoration (after the young emperor Meiji), brought to power a new generation of talented leaders. They quickly united the country, abolished the feudal system, and embarked on a rapid program of economic and social modernization to save Japan from Western colonialism. Within the first decade of the new regime, demands for more democratic government modeled on the West had arisen and could not be resisted.

After studying Western countries, one of the young leaders of the government wrote Japan's first constitution, promulgated in 1890 and modeled on the Prussian state. It established a parliament with a house of representatives, elected by limited male suffrage of property owners, and

an appointed house of peers filled with a newly created "aristocracy." Like the Prussian assembly after which it was modeled, the national Diet had very limited powers. The source of sovereignty was the emperor. All authoritative decisions were made in the emperor's name—not in the name of the people. The cabinet, military, and civilian bureaucracy were all directly responsible to the emperor, not to the Diet. But the emperor did not make decisions; rather, decisions were made by his advisers, former leaders of the Restoration who now occupied cabinet posts. The official ideology made the emperor a sacred institution in whose name all laws and decisions of government had to be obeyed.

Despite the restrictions of the Meiji constitution, democratic developments continued into the 1920s. Competitive political parties formed and ran candidates for election. The prime minister and cabinet became responsible to the Diet. Universal manhood suffrage was adopted in 1924. Gradually the position of the emperor became something like that of a constitutional monarch in the West.

Beginning in the 1920s, however, a series of internal and external shocks undermined Japan's fragile democratic institutions. Military dissatisfaction increased with the disarmament policies of the 1920s, and citizen alienation grew with perceptions of political corruption and the economic hardships of the Great Depression. In this atmosphere nationalism, terrorism, and military insubordination flourished. In 1931 the Japanese military took over part of Manchuria, souring relations with the Anglo-American powers. This added a crisis in foreign relations to Japan's other problems.

Gradually, the military took power from within, repressing democratic processes and mobilizing the economy and state under its control. In 1937 Japan invaded China, a step that led to a long and brutal attempt to conquer that country. The invasion further damaged relations between Japan and the United States. Ultimately, it led to the attack on Pearl Harbor (December 7, 1941) that caused the United States to enter World War II. In August 1945 the United States dropped one atomic bomb on the Japanese city of Hiroshima and another on Nagasaki. Japan quickly surrendered. It remains the only country ever to be the target of atomic warfare.

The American Occupation

In 1945, after the end of its disastrous Pacific war, Japan was occupied by a foreign power for the first time in its long history. The Allied occupation was primarily led and directed by the United States. U.S. general Douglas Mac-Arthur served as the Supreme Commander Allied Powers, or SCAP (the term also referred to occupation headquarters in general). SCAP's twin goals were democratization and demilitarization. The two aims were seen as linked: the more democratic Japan became, the less militaristic it was likely to be. Conversely, if Japan was demilitarized, its democratic institutions would be less vulnerable.

A new, democratic constitution was put into effect in 1947. It marked the end of the long tradition of the sacred emperor who was the source of political sovereignty. Under this constitution, sovereignty derived from the people, and the emperor was nothing more than a "symbol of the State and of the unity of the people." The parliamentary system with its bicameral Diet was retained, but the House of Peers was changed to a democratically elected House of Councillors. Women were granted the right to vote. The prime minister had to be a civilian and a member of the Diet, and the cabinet members the prime minister appointed also had to be civilians, a majority of them from the Diet. The constitution provided for a fifteen-judge Supreme Court, modeled on the American institution, with the power of judicial review and a guarantee of judicial independence. Mayors and governors were to be elected rather than appointed by the central government as in prewar days. Under Article IX of the constitution, Japan was forbidden from engaging in war or maintaining a military for that purpose.

The Americans attempted to democratize all aspects of Japanese society, not only its government. Education and police organization were decentralized to the local level. The Shinto religion, which had provided symbolic support for the prewar imperial system, was disestablished. Freedom of religion, assembly, press, and speech was guaranteed. Women were given legal equality with men—an "equal rights" provision that, ironically, is not part of the U.S. Constitution. The widespread problem of tenant farming was solved by a land reform that redistributed land from large owners to small farmers. The right to unionize was guaranteed, and the formation of unions was encouraged. The large family trust firms (*zaibatsu*) that had largely controlled Japan's prewar economy were partially broken up.

These structural changes were accompanied by a massive reorientation of people's attitudes through the mass media. The media campaign encouraged belief in democracy as the best form of government, in the emperor as merely a constitutional monarch, and in the right of the people to determine their government.

All these enormous changes were put into effect in the first two to three years of the occupation. After 1948, however, the emphasis of the occupation began to change. With the onset of the cold war, SCAP began to envision Japan as a stable ally, rather than an unarmed, neutral nation. The plans for economic decentralization were never completed, and attempts were made to purge communists from government and labor unions, to stabilize the economy, and to promote economic growth. With the outbreak of the Korean War in 1950, Article IX also was reinterpreted to allow Japan to maintain "Self-Defense Forces" for its own protection.

With the end of the occupation in 1952, the newly sovereign Japanese government partly undid at least two reforms by recentralizing education and police organization.

It retained the other democratic reforms, however, as well as the American-inspired constitution, which remains, unamended, the law of the land in Japan.

Elections and Parties

Two striking and related facts stand out concerning the democratic electoral and party system in postwar Japan. The first is that the Japanese electoral system for the House of Representatives was until its reform in 1994 nearly unique in the world. The second is that one party, the conservative LDP, won the plurality of votes and controlled the Diet and the cabinet uninterruptedly from 1955 until 1993 and regained power in 1996.

The House of Representatives is the most important chamber of the bicameral national Diet. In the postwar decades, elections were held at the discretion of the prime minister but had to be held at least once in four years. Members of this chamber were elected until 1994 through a system of medium-sized, multimember districts. In contrast with the system of proportional representation common in Europe, the Japanese system had voters casting their ballots for a person, not a party. And unlike the system of single-member districts common in Anglo-American democracies, more than one representative could be elected from each district. The number of representatives elected per district ranged from two to six; the less populous districts elected two or three representatives, while the more densely populated districts elected four to six. Voters, however, cast only one ballot apiece, and the candidates with the most votes won, up to the total number for that district. For example, twenty candidates might run for the four seats available in a certain district; each voter would cast a ballot for one of the twenty candidates, and the four candidates who received the most votes would win seats. Therefore, even the most popular candidates did not receive much more than 20–25 percent of the constituency vote, and some were elected with less than that.

This electoral system resulted in a multiparty system: for most of the postwar period in Japan, there have been between three and seven major national parties. The larger parties, such as the Liberal Democratic Party and the largest opposition party, the socialists, had enough support to run more than one candidate in a district. Accordingly, competition in elections was often between members of the same party rather than between parties. Such campaigns focused on individual candidates rather than on party differences. Diet members in office focused on providing services and benefits to their constituents, be-

cause this was often the chief way in which they could distinguish themselves from their colleagues in the same party and thus win reelection.

The electoral system also encouraged intraparty factionalism in the larger parties. The LDP, for example, was divided into a half-dozen or so factions, each led by a party and Diet veteran who desired to become prime minister. A candidate running for a Diet seat for the first time usually joined a faction and received financial and other aid from that faction as well as from the party as a whole. Once in the Diet, the member repaid the faction leader for this help by supporting the leader to become the party's president and thus—since the LDP had a majority of seats in the Diet—the prime minister.

This unusual electoral system had one other important characteristic: it was not fundamentally adjusted to reflect population shifts through most of the postwar period. Consequently, as the country became urbanized, rural districts were greatly overrepresented, while urban and suburban districts were underrepresented. The Supreme Court declared some elections unconstitutional on this basis (a violation of the constitutional provision for "equality under the law"). It did not, however, order the Diet to alter the system fundamentally. The justices—all appointed by LDP prime ministers—obviously were reluctant to take firm action to correct this malapportionment, at least in part because it might result in the LDP's loss of its majority.

There are several reasons why the LDP was able to stay in power for the longest continuing period of any governing party in the democratic world. First, a plurality of Japanese voters preferred its policies to those of the other parties. Second, the malapportionment of the electoral system favored the party because of its strength in the overrepresented rural areas. Third, divisions and conflicts among the opposition parties prevented them from presenting a united front, and therefore an effective alternative, to the LDP. Finally, the LDP's longevity in office led many voters to see it as the party that was most capable of governing.

In 1992 and early 1993 the LDP itself was beset by serious infighting among its factions and was rocked by financial scandals. As many as two hundred politicians were implicated in a bribery scheme estimated to involve some 70 billion yen (approximately US$560 million), and a senior LDP official was arrested for tax evasion. On June 18, 1993, Prime Minister Kiichi Miyazawa lost a no-confidence vote, and in the elections of July 18 the LDP lost its parliamentary majority for the first time since 1955. The new government, an odd, seven-party coalition of conservatives and socialists, passed an electoral reform law in early 1994 intended to foster a more competitive electoral system, to reduce the influence of corporate donations on elections, and to stabilize government (that is, to reduce the likelihood of unwieldy coalitions coming to power.)

The "upper" but less important house, the House of Councillors, has 252 members, 152 of whom are chosen in multimember local district contests similar to those for the prereform House of Representatives. The other 100, however, are "national" representatives elected at large by a system of list proportional representation. In this system each voter casts two ballots: one for a local candidate, the other for a party for the national seats. Councillors serve a six-year term, and half the House is up for election every three years.

Elections, Leadership, and "Money Politics"

One of the most important consequences of the pre–1994 Japanese electoral system was "money politics." The system required individual candidates to raise large sums of money to finance their campaigns, to maintain personal support organizations among constituents, and to provide constituency services to gain support at the expense of their opponents both in other parties and in their own. This practice made it a very expensive business to become and remain a national politician in Japan.

The LDP raised its funds from big business and attempted to help out its candidates, but the party provided only about half the amount needed for a candidate to be elected. Further, the party had to give equal amounts to all its nominated candidates, but since there were often several LDP candidates competing in a district, each also had to come up with his or her own source of funds in order to gain an advantage over the rival LDP candidates. One major source of these extra funds was the candidate's faction leader within the party. The faction leader was expected to maintain extensive contacts with businesses and to raise a great deal of money to distribute to members of the faction.

Leadership of the government in Japan was determined primarily by the politics of the personal factions in the LDP. Each faction leader attempted to recruit to the faction as many members as possible, to advance his goal of becoming party president and thus prime minister. The factions were not informal and temporary groups. They were hierarchical, well organized, and enduring. New Diet members recruited to a faction became eligible for higher

positions in the party and government only by rising through the faction's ranks in a predictable pattern based on seniority in the faction. Factions had histories, as well: all of the major factions could trace their lineage back to earlier, prewar leaders. Usually when a faction leader retired as prime minister or died, one of the lieutenants would inherit the factional leadership.

None of the major factions came close to having a majority of LDP Diet members, who determined by balloting who would lead the party and thus the government. For this reason, faction leaders had to wheel and deal and form coalitions with their counterparts in order to gain the necessary votes of their colleagues. A successful faction leader who became prime minister selected a cabinet in part on the basis of considerations of factional balance. Thus to all intents and purposes these personal leadership factions determined recruitment to the top posts in government.

In effect, the faction leaders had a relationship of exchange with their followers. They provided the extra funds necessary for followers to maintain support organizations in their constituencies and to run campaigns against their LDP and other party rivals in their district. They also held out to followers the possibility of rising eventually to cabinet rank. In return, followers were expected to vote loyally for the faction leader in the race for party president.

There were frequent national scandals involving money and politicians in Japan. These scandals became a source of dissatisfaction with politics among the public and the press. For example, in the 1970s former prime minister Kakuei Tanaka was indicted for having accepted a bribe, while prime minister, from the American aircraft manufacturer Lockheed. Prime Minister Noboru Takeshita had to resign in the 1980s because of allegations that a company executive had bought influence with the government through unethical, if mostly legal, campaign contributions. And, as mentioned earlier, Prime Minister Miyazawa and the LDP stranglehold on government were felled by scandal.

By changing the electoral system from small, multimember districts to a combination of three hundred single-member districts and two hundred national list seats, the reformers hoped to disrupt the old style of business. Members of a party are less likely to compete against one another in single-member districts, hence faction should become less important as a source of campaign support; therefore, factions should be weakened and party cohesion enhanced in the House of Representatives by the electoral reform.

Governing

Policy making was never a major function of the factions. The most important actors in policy making were the national bureaucracy and senior LDP politicians, whose source of power was not necessarily related to factional membership. The higher civil servants of the national bureaucracy are recruited from the best graduates of the most prestigious universities in Japan. They form a small but elite core of respected public administrators. (Japan has the smallest proportion of bureaucrats to population among the major industrialized countries.)

The bureaucracy plays a much greater role in policy making in Japan than is true in the United States; its role is similar to that of civil servants in France. For example, most legislation introduced into the national Diet by the government (constituting most of the legislation passed into law) is formulated in the ministries by bureaucrats. Societal groups also have an input into those proposals through the many advisory councils (shingikai) attached to the ministries and agencies. These are composed of "experts," including academics; representatives of societal groups affected by policy, such as business and labor leaders; and former bureaucrats. These experts advise the bureaucracy on policy, and their recommendations are often incorporated into changes in law.

But the bureaucrats do not have the final say in whether laws get passed and which laws get passed. This role fell instead to the elected representatives of the people. All policy proposals had to go through the ruling party's specialized organ for policy making, the Policy Affairs Research Council. In the many divisions, subdivisions, and research committees of this body, party representatives screened, amended, rejected, or supported all policy proposals brought by the bureaucracy, interest groups, or individual representatives. The bills that passed this body went to senior party leaders and then to the cabinet for final approval before being introduced into the Diet.

The long tenure of the LDP as governing party gave experienced veterans of the Policy Affairs Research Council the opportunity to wield great influence in specific policy sectors. Working their way up through positions in the Policy Affairs Research Council and in Diet committees concerned with the same policy area, veteran LDP politicians eventually came to have expertise rivaling or surpassing that of bureaucrats, as well as connections to both interest groups and the bureaucracy in that policy area. Called policy tribes (zoku), the experienced LDP Diet members thus gained at least as much influence over policy and policy making in many areas as did the bureaucrats.

Responsiveness

The perpetual dominance of one party, through competitive free elections in a multiparty system, is unusual but not unique among the industrialized democracies. For various periods, Sweden, Italy, and Israel also have had such "dominant party democracies." But the lack of alternation in power raises several important questions concerning the role of opposition parties and the responsiveness of the ruling party to the people.

Japan had, at different times, four major opposition parties to the LDP. The Democratic Socialist Party, a moderate trade union–based party that supports the alliance with the United States, and the Clean Government Party, a center party originally founded by a Buddhist organization and a proponent of the expansion of welfare programs and world peace, merged in November 1994 with seven other opposition parties to form the New Frontier Party (NFP). The NFP was the runner-up in the October 1996 elections, winning 156 seats to the LDP's 239. The Japan Socialist Party (which now calls itself the Social Democratic Party in English) was for a time the largest opposition party. It mobilizes the support of public labor unions and until recently adamantly opposed the existence of the self-defense forces and the alliance with the United States. It won 15 seats in 1996. The Japan Communist Party is a "Eurocommunist"-style party that attempts to take power through the ballot box. The Communists won 26 seats in 1996. Historically, the Japan Socialist Party and Japan Communist Party (the left) together usually gained no more than a third of the popular vote and less than a third of the seats in the lower house. The center parties, the Democratic Socialist Party and Clean Government Party, together obtained about half that.

For most of the postwar era, this disparate and disunited group of opposition parties had little hope of unseating the LDP, but it was able to perform at least part of the important democratic function of limiting the power of the governing party. The Japanese government usually made some minor concessions to at least some of the opposition parties in order to gain their support on most bills. In the lower house the combined number of seats of the opposition came close to that of the LDP during the late 1970s; in the upper house the opposition surpassed the LDP during the early 1990s. This situation forced the LDP to take opposition party sentiments into account more than it had formerly. Further, when the opposition adamantly opposed a particular bill on grounds of principle, that stand was often enough to postpone or kill the legislation. Thus the opposition had a de facto veto power on some types of legislation. Rather than the "serial" influence of parties alternating in power in the textbook version of democracy, the Japanese opposition had limited "simultaneous" influence on the perpetually ruling party.

The LDP also was responsive to societal needs and interests for reasons other than opposition pressure. To maintain its electoral dominance, it had to put together a broadly based social coalition of interest groups. With the partial exception of organized labor, almost every type of interest group—big and small business, agriculture, urban parent-teacher groups, and neighborhood associations—was incorporated under the party's umbrella. Further, competition among LDP candidates in the pre–1994 multimember districts prompted the ruling party's representatives to be particularly attuned to their constituencies' demands for concrete benefits, such as roads, dams, schools, and other "pork barrel" goods.

Finally, when the government's policies proved unpopular, the LDP showed the ability to change direction in response to the popular will and media pressure. The classic example is the issue of environmental pollution. The party's rapid industrialization policies of the 1950s and 1960s produced horrendous pollution problems. These problems aroused widespread media attention and public concern, gave rise to locally organized citizens movements against pollution, and caused the electoral loss of many local executive positions in urban areas. In response, in the late 1960s and early 1970s the LDP passed laws to clean up and prevent pollution and adopted nationwide some of the policies of popular local executives in the opposition. Welfare is another case in point. During the early postwar period of rapid economic growth, Japan lagged far behind Western countries in social welfare programs. Beginning in the 1970s, however, the LDP responded to the growing popular desire for such programs and began to initiate and implement them.

The active and multifaceted media in Japan are always ready to remind the ruling party of what is perceived to be the popular will at any time. National newspapers with giant circulations keep Japanese citizens extremely well informed. As with environmental issues, the media can help to put important issues on the public agenda. In addition to the newspapers, a respected public broadcasting service—the second largest in the world after England's BBC

—and a full range of commercial stations supply the well-educated Japanese citizenry with political information.

Because of the close relations between journalists and officials, the mainstream press can be slow to unearth scandal and corruption—a function more likely to be performed by those outside the establishment press. Once a scandal has been revealed by other sources, however, the media are often instrumental in keeping the issues in the front of public consciousness. This is probably one reason why Japanese citizens are cynical about politicians and the ability of the average citizen to influence the government, even though public opinion surveys show them to be supportive of democracy and its institutions in general.

Strengths and Weaknesses

Like other democracies, Japan's system exhibits characteristic strengths and weaknesses that stem from the nature and development of its institutions. Since the American occupation, Japan has enjoyed constitutional guarantees of civil rights, competitive elections and a multiparty system, and an active free press. The citizenry is highly educated and well informed on public affairs. Electoral dominance by the LDP provided stability and prosperity as well as a more equal distribution of wealth and income than in almost any other industrialized democracy except Sweden. The party distributed public goods to a wide range of interest groups and local constituencies and was responsive to changing public sentiment nationwide. The opposition parties, although shut out of power but for the brief period of coalition rule in 1993–1996, still managed to have some influence.

The political system that produced these accomplishments, however, also led to major weaknesses in democratic life. The malapportioned electoral system gave rural voters disproportionate representation compared with urban voters. As a result, agricultural interests received more attention and had their inefficiency protected, while the interests of urban consumers and organized labor were neglected. Because the electoral system pitted members of the same party against each other, it created an insatiable need for money in order for candidates to retain their seats—money that could not always be raised within the bounds of the law and without giving its donors undue influence in politics.

The perennial money scandals of Japanese politics, the factional struggles to become prime minister, and the problems of the electoral system came together in 1993 to mark a milestone in postwar Japanese democracy. When the prime minister appeared to renege on a promise of electoral reform that would diminish the role of money in politics, about a fifth of the members of his own party bolted and formed a new party. Previously, other conservatives dissatisfied with "money politics" had also formed their own party. In the elections that followed in July 1993, the LDP lost its parliamentary majority but managed to maintain a plurality, and the new reform-minded parties increased their strength.

As a result the unprecedented occurred. A seven-party coalition of reform-minded conservatives and the opposition parties (except the Communists), united only by their opposition to the LDP, took power with a majority of seats. Led by a personally popular young reform conservative, Prime Minister Morihiro Hosokawa, the new coalition vowed to clean up money politics and change the electoral system. It did manage to pass the electoral reform bill in early 1994 that did away with Japan's multimember district system and placed limits on corporate contributions to individual candidates. Instead, the House of Representatives would be elected by a combination of single-member districts (300 seats) and proportional representation (200 seats). Coincidentally, this hybrid system is similar to one adopted recently in Italy, also in an attempt to reform corrupt politics.

This bill was all the coalition accomplished. Hosokawa was soon forced to resign over allegations of financial improprieties in his own political past and objections to his tax policies lodged by his socialist coalition partners. The coalition selected as prime minister Tsutomu Hata, whose government lasted only fifty-nine days. The coalition broke up when the socialists bolted to form their own coalition with the LDP and an LDP offshoot, New Party Harbinger. Thus the two old rivals for most of the postwar period were able to patch up their ideological differences—mostly by the socialists abandoning some of their long-held leftist policies, such as maintaining the unconstitutionality of the self-defense forces. The new three-party partnership came to power in a governing coalition in June 1994, with Tomiichi Murayama becoming the first socialist to hold the post of prime minister since the 1940s.

The Socialist–LDP–New Party Harbinger coalition held together under Murayama until January 1996 and then under Ryutaro Hashimoto of the LDP until early elections were held in October 1996. In those elections, the first to be held under the new electoral law, the LDP won 239 of the 500 seats in the lower house. The LDP formed a minority government on the basis of an agreement with the Social Democratic Party and New Party Harbinger to consult on policy in return for support in the House.

Japan is probably entering a period of transitions: new parties forming and re-forming, governing partners shifting. On the basis of a single election, it is not possible to know whether the new electoral and party systems will be able to clean up politics, respond to popular sentiment for more open and responsive policies, and produce effective governments.

In Reference Material section, see *Constitution of Japan (1947)*.

BIBLIOGRAPHY

Curtis, Gerald Leon. *Election Campaigning, Japanese Style.* New York: Columbia University Press, 1971.
———. *The Japanese Way of Politics.* New York: Columbia University Press, 1988.
Hayao, Kenji. *The Japanese Prime Minister and Public Policy.* Pittsburgh: University of Pittsburgh Press, 1993.
Hrebenar, Ronald. *The Japanese Party System.* Boulder, Colo.: Westview Press, 1992.
Ishida, Takeshi, and Ellis S. Krauss, eds. *Democracy in Japan.* Pittsburgh: University of Pittsburgh Press, 1989.
Kawai, Kazuo. *Japan's American Interlude.* Chicago: University of Chicago Press, 1960.
Krauss, Ellis S., Thomas P. Rohlen, and Patricia G. Steinhoff, eds. *Conflict in Japan.* Honolulu: University of Hawaii Press, 1984.
Pempel, T. J. *Politics and Policy in Japan: Creative Conservatism.* Philadelphia: Temple University Press, 1982.
———, ed. *Uncommon Democracies.* Ithaca, N.Y.: Cornell University Press, 1990.
Pharr, Susan. *Losing Face: Status Politics in Japan.* Berkeley: University of California Press, 1990.

Jordan

A predominantly Muslim constitutional monarchy located in southwest Asia and bordered on the west by Israel, on the south by Saudi Arabia, on the east by Iraq, and on the north by Syria. As Transjordan (the area east of the River Jordan), the country was part of the Ottoman Empire, but in 1917–1918 British forces, with Arab support, defeated the Ottomans and occupied the area. British control was formalized when Transjordan and Palestine were placed under British mandate in 1920.

In 1921 the British nominated Abdallah bin Hussein, a member of the Hashemite dynasty of Hejaz, to be emir of Transjordan. The mandate was terminated in 1946, and Abdallah was proclaimed king. After the first Arab-Israeli war in 1948, Palestinian territory on the west bank of the

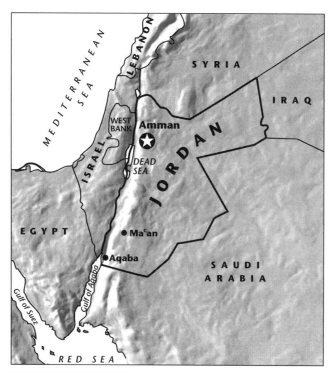

Jordan, including East Jerusalem, was annexed by Jordan, and the new country was renamed the Hashemite Kingdom of Jordan. After the assassination of King Abdallah and the abdication of Abdallah's eldest son, Talal, the crown passed to Hussein bin Talal, then sixteen years of age. Hussein formally assumed power as king in May 1953.

Years of Turmoil

A small country of fewer than two million people, the vast majority of whom were Palestinians radicalized by the Arab-Israeli war and the rising tide of militant Arab nationalism, Jordan would experience considerable turmoil in the years to come. It was a rough beginning for the child-king, who, to survive, had to deal quickly with his country's basic predicament: Jordan was a small nation with bigger Arab neighbors whom it could not antagonize and bordered on Israel, a powerful enemy whom it could not afford to befriend. Its people's loyalties were largely elsewhere, and its economy was almost totally dependent on Western powers, who were the current enemies of the Arab nationalist tide led by the charismatic Gamal Abdel Nasser of Egypt.

This was indeed a hostile environment for the growth and prosperity of democratic ideals. Nevertheless, in the first four years of King Hussein's rule Jordan was a constitutional monarchy with a functioning parliament. The parliament consisted of a Senate, the smaller house, whose members were appointed by the king, and a forty-seat House of Representatives, elected by secret ballot in periodic direct elections.

In the early 1950s one or two loose political coalitions were formed, but it was not until 1956 that full-fledged parties emerged. And it was in the period between October 1956 and April 1957 that the country witnessed the spectacular flowering of democracy to be followed by its equally spectacular demise.

In the October 1956 elections, seven parties, along with a host of independent candidates, ran for the forty-seat House of Representatives. Described as the quietest and most fairly conducted elections in the country's history, the elections saw the independents win thirteen seats. The remaining twenty-seven seats went to the various parties, the biggest of which, with eleven seats, was the leftist and pro-Nasser National Socialist Party. The king duly entrusted the leader of that party with the formation of the new cabinet.

In more tranquil times this could have been an auspicious beginning for true Jordanian democracy. But times were not tranquil. Nasser was leading a revolutionary Arab nationalist crusade that resonated throughout the Arab world and which, in the case of Jordan, resulted in periodic demonstrations, riots, and disturbances. The new prime minister, whose sympathies were clearly with the Egyptian leader, found himself increasingly at odds with the young king. But the monarch had the army, most of whose units came from Jordanian tribal stock fiercely loyal to the king. In April 1957 King Hussein made his move. He dismissed the government, and, after widespread rioting in favor of the dismissed prime minister and his government, he proclaimed martial law, dissolved all the political parties, demanded numerous arrests, and even purged the civil service of opposition supporters.

Period of Direct Monarchical Rule

The post-1957 period was characterized by direct monarchical rule. The king had decided that in the highly polarized and conflictual Arab political environment, argument and debate within a democratic setting would inevitably turn into violence that would undermine the stability of the country and his own rule. From then on, power was to be the monopoly of the king. Hussein allowed elections to be held, but they were accompanied by such restrictive regulations that only supporters of the regime were returned to the parliament. In any case the loss of the West Bank to Israel in the June 1967 Six-Day War and the resultant radicalization of Jordan's Palestinian population were used by the king as an excuse to stop holding elections.

Then, in 1974, a summit of the Arab heads of state, meeting in Rabat, Morocco, gave the Palestine Liberation Organization, not Jordan, sole responsibility for the West Bank. Responding to the summit resolution, the king dissolved the Jordanian parliament (which had equal representation for the East and West Banks) and postponed elections indefinitely.

The political situation remained essentially unchanged until April 1989, when rioting occurred in several Jordanian cities in response to steep government-imposed price hikes on basic goods and services. The riots were so widespread and serious, particularly because they occurred among the native Jordanians—supposedly the king's most loyal constituents—that not only did the prime minister and his cabinet resign, but the king decided to cut short an official visit to the United States and return to the capital, Amman.

A Softening of Monarchical Rule

The king's response was as dramatic as it was surprising. While refusing to make any concessions in the price increases, Hussein announced that a general election would be held for the first time since 1967. And indeed six months later, 647 independent candidates (the ban on political parties had not been lifted) ran for the expanded eighty-seat House of Representatives. When the results were counted, thirty-eight seats had gone to Islamic fundamentalists and their sympathizers.

What was behind the king's change of heart? First, after years of prosperity Jordan was suddenly faced with economic hardships, necessitating tough and unpopular decisions. It was hardly in the king's interest to be the focus of all the blame. Second, and perhaps more crucially, the king had been at the helm for more than thirty-five years. A seasoned and astute leader, he quickly grasped the lesson of what was happening in Eastern Europe, where popular discontent quickly turned into popular revolutions. His action thus could be seen as a preemptive move against the forces of revolution.

And King Hussein knew that he could not stop there. In April 1990 he announced the appointment of a sixty-member commission entrusted with drafting a national charter that would legalize political parties. In June 1991 the king signed the charter, declaring that pluralism was the only safeguard against tyranny. The charter guaranteed the opposition greater freedom of political activity as well as the right to organize formally into parties. It also expanded political rights for women (who first gained the right to vote in 1974), provided for broader freedom of the press, and placed curbs on the internal security forces.

The next month the House of Representatives passed a law that would put into effect provisions of the charter relating to political parties. A year later the Senate approved the law and so ended the thirty-five-year ban on the formation of political parties in the kingdom. By 1993 a number of parties had been formed and allowed to organize. More than five hundred candidates representing twenty-two political parties ran for the eighty seats in the House of Representatives in the November 8, 1993, elections. Eleven parties, representing diverse viewpoints, won seats; no one party won more than sixteen seats.

It must be remembered, however, that just as King Hussein was single-handedly responsible for the creation of the multiparty system, he could also single-handedly undo the system in as dramatic a fashion as it was created. Although there certainly are now more argument and debate in the political system, more constraints on the executive's freedom of maneuverability, and more perceptible sharing of power, the king continues to be the dominant figure in Jordanian politics.

Any judgments and prognostications about the permanence and future direction of Jordan's latest democratic experiment would be premature. Reverses might well occur in the ever fluid environment of Jordanian politics, which continues to be beset by many uncertainties, among them the Palestinian issue, post–Gulf war Iraq, and the rise of Islamic militancy. Thus far, however, at least the kingdom seems to have taken significant steps toward a democratic system.

See also *Middle East*.

BIBLIOGRAPHY

Day, Arthur. *East Bank/West Bank: Jordan and the Prospects for Peace.* New York: Council on Foreign Relations, 1986.

Gubser, Peter. *Jordan: Crossroads of Middle Eastern Events.* Boulder, Colo.: Westview Press, 1983.

Lunt, James. *Hussein of Jordan: From Survivor to Statesman.* New York: Morrow, 1989.

Schlaim, Avi. *Collusion across the Jordan.* New York: Oxford University Press, 1988.

K

Kenya

A republic in East Central Africa that gained independence from Great Britain in 1963. Kenyan political history is an odyssey from multiparty politics to a single-party system and back again.

Between 1963 and 1964 Kenya had a Westminster parliamentary system of government, modeled on that of Britain, in which executive powers are vested in a group of legislators who command a majority in the lower house of the bicameral legislature. Two main parties, the Kenya African National Union (KANU) and the Kenya African Democratic Union (KADU), contested the first elections from which KANU emerged victorious. Like many new African governments that inherited a Westminster parliamentary system when they gained independence, Kenya moved swiftly to increase central power by creating a republican government. In 1964 Jomo Kenyatta became the country's first elected leader. Thereafter Kenya became a de facto single-party state with KANU in control. Only in 1982 under the country's second president, Daniel arap Moi, did Kenya move to a de jure single-party system, which lasted nearly ten years.

At the end of November 1991, under pressure from foreign donors, the Moi government legalized opposition political parties. It sponsored multiparty elections a year later. Thus Kenya tentatively joined the ranks of the many other African countries that had started to broaden political participation, reversing the trend of the previous thirty years.

The Kenyatta Period

Kenya won independence in part as a result of a much earlier decision by the British government to decolonize. Pressures for independence were heightened by the Mau

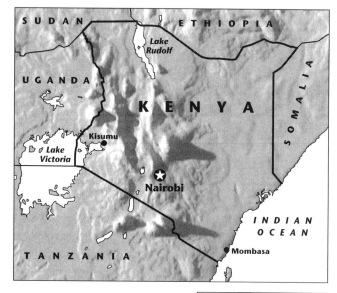

Mau rebellion, a class conflict that raged largely within the Kikuyu, Kenya's largest ethnic group, in the 1950s.

The initial structure of the Kenyan political system was negotiated at Lancaster House in England, the product of discussions among representatives of new political parties. There was widespread agreement that a multiparty parliamentary system was most suitable for the country. Whether Kenya should have a unitary government or a federal system attracted the most debate. KADU, which comprised many of the smaller ethnic groups that feared incursions by Kikuyu settlers, backed a federal system. KANU, which prevailed, supported a unitary system. KANU politicians won a majority of seats in the legislature in the country's independence elections, and Kenyatta became head of the government.

Initially, Kenyatta sought to use KANU as a forum for compromise, steering it away from a strong mobilizational role and tolerating diverse points of view within the ranks. This relative openness of Kenyan political life in the very early days most likely stemmed from the challenges Kenyatta faced upon assuming office. At independence, Kenyans were divided economically. Unlike many African countries, Kenya had an active class of commercial agricultural entrepreneurs who grew coffee, tea, and other crops. These emerging economic elites had been the earlier carriers of nationalist ideas. At the same time many Kenyans lacked access to land. Both groups were represented among the Kikuyu, Kenyatta's community.

To complicate matters, Kenyans also were divided culturally, although in a distinctive manner. First, no one group held numerical superiority. The Kikuyu constituted 17 percent of the population. The Luo, Kamba, Luhya, Kalenjin, and Masai also commanded significant numbers, alongside many much smaller groups such as the Samburu, Rendille, Gusii, and Giriama. Second, most of the country's wealthy entrepreneurs were Kikuyu, and the coincidence of economic and ethnic cleavages increased the likelihood that ethnicity would become salient in political life. Third, there was no broad-based nationalist movement before independence to help Kenyatta knit together a broad, coherent political base.

Most likely as a response to these conditions, Kenyatta initially refused to give KANU a strong role in maintaining social control. The ruling party remained loosely organized, a vehicle for managing political debate. It possessed limited representative functions. Moreover, it had no internal structures for resolving differences among members or for forging a common party platform. This situation opened the party to divergent viewpoints and made it a poor forum for aggregating interests. KANU also had little influence over policy because most legislative initiative lay with the office of the president.

Kenyatta's refusal to turn KANU into a strong vehicle for political and social control on the model of the Convention People's Party in Ghana was made possible in part by the success of the extraparliamentary bargaining system he established. The government quickly tried to deflect the attention of politicians from the national to the local level. It introduced the notion of *harambee,* or self-help development, a system that encouraged community members to construct local infrastructure and amenities instead of relying on the central government to do so. The president encouraged politicians to contribute to these projects and told residents to vote only for those who did, not for candidates who stayed in Nairobi and concerned themselves with national affairs. Through harambee, Kenyatta discouraged newly elected officials from pressing sectional demands at the national level, and he was able to limit demands for development programs that were more extensive than the budget could support.

Repression also played a role in the government's strategy for maintaining order, although it was used less under Kenyatta than under Moi or in many other countries of subsaharan Africa. Backbenchers as well as senior ministers periodically overstepped the bounds Kenyatta had tried to establish. Kenyatta had difficulty controlling some of these activities, even on the part of those close to him. To eliminate electoral opposition, some politicians framed others for criminal activity or occasionally resorted to political violence and assassination. J. M. Kariuki, a one-time junior minister who had a broad political following and was well positioned to launch his own party, was murdered. At other times the government forces tried to change the rules of the game by seizing control of party institutions or by securing passage of laws to restrict the activities of others. In the Kenyatta period these tactics met with opposition from the Backbenchers' Group and from some of the junior ministers in Kenyatta's cabinet, many of whom were not affiliated with the "Family." By marriage or blood, many senior politicians were related to Kenyatta, and they had developed a strong coalition within KANU.

The Nyayo Period

In 1978 Kenyatta died, and Daniel arap Moi, his vice president, won election as his successor. In the succession KANU party elections assumed special importance because Moi's opposition came mainly from the Family faction within the party. For several reasons the Family doubted Moi's support for the unitary system. Moi hailed from the Tugen, a small community from the Rift Valley, nominally part of the Kalenjin ethnic group. And he had once been a member of KADU, which had backed a federal structure for the country in the independence negotiations. Moi's victory in the party elections was a result of the efforts of Kikuyu technocrat Mwai Kibaki and non-Family member Charles Njonjo to broker a broad, multi-ethnic slate with a slightly populist cast.

Although Moi's slogan was "Nyayo"—follow in the footsteps—his tactics for maintaining political order differed considerably from Kenyatta's and precipitated a deepening of authoritarian rule. For example, Moi used harambee patronage to support candidates who opposed senior politicians whom he feared. He used provisions for harambee licensing, introduced by Family politicians in the later Kenyatta years, to punish critics and reward supporters. These interventions eventually undermined the harambee system, which had served as a vehicle for keeping all politics local.

Other tactics of Moi's undermined the government's effectiveness. For instance, Moi displaced many officials and technocrats in favor of backers with few qualifications for their new jobs. Key gatekeeping positions in the economic ministries as well as internal security posts went to the Kalenjin. Moreover, the extensiveness and magnitude of political corruption increased, reaching an estimated $300 to $500 million in 1992 alone. Aid monies from several countries, most notably Sweden, could not be accounted for and ultimately provoked the donors to cut off assistance in 1991. Furthermore, Nicholas Biwott, a close associate of the president, was implicated in the 1991 murder of Foreign Minister Robert Ouko, who allegedly had protested against the scale of corruption.

Other tactics restricted contestation and participation, threatening the vibrancy of political life. The Moi government resorted increasingly to restrictions on speech and association. Rules requiring the registration of all political gatherings were extended and enforced with greater regularity. In 1982 the government outlawed political opposition, making Kenya a de jure single-party state for the first time. Although these measures provoked some public ire and triggered a coup attempt in August 1982, the regime became increasingly authoritarian as time passed. In 1986 and 1988 Moi won passage of constitutional amendments that eliminated security of tenure in office for the attorney general, the controller, the auditor, and the judges of the High Court and Court of Appeal. These amendments removed some of the few remaining checks on the power of the president.

For the preliminary round of voting in the 1988 elections, the government used a queuing system, in which voters lined up behind candidates of their choice, instead of a secret ballot system. Furthermore, candidates who received at least 70 percent of the vote in this round were elected unopposed. The Moi government also set out to weaken or eliminate interest groups and voluntary associations that might mobilize for reform. Although the churches were largely spared such restrictions and became important bases for the defense of civil liberties, the government deregistered or dissolved many other groups.

Pressures for Democratization

Domestic opposition to KANU grew during the mid- to late 1980s. Some of the growing criticism came from diffuse movements such as Mwakenya, an underground neo-Marxist group whose membership and dangerousness were exaggerated by the government as a pretext for detaining intellectuals. The most potent opposition came from business and religious leaders.

During 1989 and 1990 the principal figures in the main, elite-directed opposition were Charles Rubia and Kenneth Matiba. Rubia was an old-time politician who had played a moderate role as a quiet defender of civil liberties in parliament during the later Kenyatta period. He had supported the church's opposition to the queuing system that replaced the secret ballot, and he alone had dissented openly when parliament had passed the bill to eliminate the independence of the attorney general, controller, and auditor. He was tainted by a career as a Nairobi machine politician, however, and the leadership of the elite opposition rested more heavily on former minister Kenneth Matiba, a wealthy entrepreneur who had entered politics only in 1979. Matiba had resigned from the cabinet in protest in 1988, after the president's supporters manipulated party elections in his district in an attempt to remove him from power. Rubia and Matiba publicly attacked government corruption and repression as the sources of the country's growing economic problems. In July 1991 the Moi government detained both of them. Thereafter, dissident lawyers Paul Muite and Gitobu Imanyara led the opposition fight.

Although pressures for greater political openness had their origins in domestic movements and interest groups, it took international pressure to yield change. Alarmed at the waste of their resources, bilateral and multilateral donors agreed on November 26, 1991, to suspend assistance to Kenya for six months, pending political reform. Within days Moi legalized opposition parties.

During the last weeks of 1991 the opposition formed the Forum for the Restoration of Democracy (FORD). Over the ensuing months, however, differences of opinion and style fragmented this coalition. When elections were called for December 29, 1992, ten parties registered to contend for seats in the legislature and sponsored presidential candidates. The principal opposition to KANU split into three parties: FORD-Asili (the Kiswahili word for *original),* led by Kenneth Matiba; FORD-Kenya, led by independence-era Luo politician Oginga Odinga; and the Democratic Party, led by Mwai Kibaki and composed of a number of KANU defectors. The fragmentation allowed Moi to be reelected with 36.3 percent of the vote. KANU also secured 100 of the 188 elected seats in parliament and picked up 12 seats through a provision in Kenyan law that allows the president to appoint a dozen nominated members. Opposition parties challenged the results, arguing that serious irregularities had taken place in the design and conduct of the elections.

Although international observers found the electoral process seriously flawed, they concluded that the opposition was too fragmented and too divided by ethnic appeals to constitute a viable government. For this reason they urged the opposition to accept the election results and use the period leading up to the next campaign to reorganize.

A year later no coherent opposition had formed despite the death of Oginga Odinga, the head of FORD-Kenya, and the continued efforts of Wangari Mathai's "Middle Ground Group" to forge an alliance. In the months after the elections, Moi suspended parliament, then reconvened it, and opposition leaders and supporters were subjected to harassment and arrest. In 1994 fifteen opposition members of parliament were detained, thirteen of whom were charged with sedition. By mid–1997, on the eve of scheduled December elections, the opposition to Moi was still inchoate.

BIBLIOGRAPHY

Barkan, Joel D. "Kenya: Lessons from a Flawed Election." *Journal of Democracy* 4 (July 1993): 85–99.

———. "The Rise and Fall of a Governance Realm in Kenya." In *Governance and Politics in Africa*, edited by Goran Hyden and Michael Bratton. Boulder, Colo.: Lynne Rienner, 1992.

Holmquist, Frank, and Michael Ford. "Kenya: Slouching toward Democracy." *Africa Rights Monitor* (third quarter 1992): 97–111.

International Republican Institute. *Kenya: The December 29, 1992, Elections.* Paper prepared for the U.S. Agency for International Development. New York: IRI, spring 1993.

Widner, Jennifer. *The Rise of a Party-State in Kenya: From Harambee! to Nyayo!* Berkeley: University of California Press, 1992.

Kuwait

A predominantly Muslim constitutional monarchy located in the Middle East at the northern end of the Persian Gulf. Like many other contemporary Arab states, Kuwait became part of the Ottoman Empire in the sixteenth century, but the country generally was left to its own devices. Although Kuwait was settled by various tribes, the Sabah clan of the Utub tribe had gained political control by the middle of the eighteenth century. Over the next century this clan increasingly operated autonomously from the Ottoman authorities in Iraq.

In 1899 Kuwait's ruler signed a treaty with Britain, accepting British protection while surrendering control over external relations. The sheikhdom remained a self-governing British protectorate until 1961, when Britain and Kuwait terminated the 1899 treaty by mutual agreement. The ruler took the title *emir* and assumed full executive power.

Immediately upon independence, Kuwait, a tiny country rich in petroleum surrounded by vastly more powerful states, experienced the quicksand of Arab politics. No sooner had the new national flag been raised than neighboring Iraq made its first claim on Kuwait. Iraq's strongman at the time, Gen. ʿAbd al-Karim Kassem, declared Kuwait to be part of Iraq and appointed the emir, who was thought to be making more than $200,000 a minute from oil, mayor of the "Iraqi city" of Kuwait at a salary of $120 a month.

British troops entered Kuwait at the request of the mortified emir, to be replaced later by an Arab force from Egypt, Jordan, and Saudi Arabia. The crisis subsided when Kuwait was granted full membership in the Arab League and in the United Nations.

Kuwaiti Democracy, 1961–1976

That unpleasant experience, coupled with gentle British pressure, prompted the Kuwaiti sheikhs to try the democratic route. It was expected that genuine popular support for the emir and his family would minimize the possibility of external subversion of the country. Thus, on December 30, 1961, elections were held for a constituent assembly that would draw up a constitution for the infant state.

A new constitution was drafted and duly approved a year later. Under its provisions executive power was vested in the emir (always a member of the Sabah family), who would appoint the prime minister and, on the latter's recommendation, other ministers. Legislative power was entrusted to a fifty-member National Assembly. Only literate adult male Kuwaiti citizens were eligible to vote. Political parties were not legally permitted. Under this limited franchise, elections were held in January 1963. Since no political parties could participate, candidates ran as independents. Nevertheless, a few known opponents of the Sabah family were elected.

During the 1960s petroleum production and revenue expanded considerably, making the tiny sheikhdom the

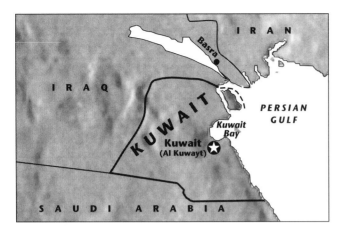

most prosperous country in the Arab world. Moreover, through periodic free elections Kuwait could boast a stable and relatively open political system, which stood in stark contrast to the sea of authoritarianism that surrounded it. Nationals from other Arab countries flocked into Kuwait to partake in its phenomenal economic growth, and the country's relative liberalism attracted the educated and the intellectuals. By the 1970s the capital, Kuwait City, had become a thriving, culturally active metropolis, with a press that could compete with the Lebanese as the freest in the Arab world. It was indeed a paradox: Kuwait was a relatively free and democratic country, yet it was still ruled by a feudal family who instinctively regarded the country as personal property.

By the mid-1970s the ruling Sabah family was becoming increasingly alarmed at the extent of criticism leveled against it in the National Assembly and in the press. The Assembly, backed by some of the radical press, constantly agitated for a reduced role by the Sabah family in Kuwaiti politics. And in foreign policy it demanded that Kuwait's rulers take a more nationalistic and radical posture, implying less dependence on the West. As a result, not only the Kuwaiti sheikhs but also, perhaps more significantly, the rulers of Saudi Arabia, the most implacable enemies of democratic reforms, were troubled by what they considered to be excessive freedom in Kuwait. Indeed, throughout the first half of the 1970s the Saudis continually complained to the Kuwaiti rulers about the attacks being made by Kuwait's press and National Assembly against Saudi policies.

By 1976 relations between the Sabah family and the As-sembly had become totally polarized. In August of that year the emir dissolved the Assembly, suspended four articles of the constitution, and severely curtailed the freedom of the press. The next day the pro-Palestinian weekly *al-Watan* was banned for one month for describing the emir's action as a "watershed for democracy" and questioning whether it was necessary. In succeeding days other newspapers and periodicals were banned.

Kuwaiti Democracy, 1976–1990

During this period the tension between the ruling family's patrimonial instincts and its recognition that democracy was perhaps the surest means for the family's political survival came to the forefront. Initially, the emir ruled by decree, supported by the large Sabah family and backed by the army, most of whose members were drawn from indigenous Kuwaiti stock loyal to the Sabah family. Essential backing came from the king and princes of Saudi Arabia. Although Kuwait did not emulate the rigid authoritarianism or the coercive control of some of its neighbors such as Iraq, Iran, and Saudi Arabia, it nevertheless restricted individual rights and placed significant limits on the freedom of the press. Essentially, the emir and his family were emulating the Saudi rulers in treating the country as a family concern.

There was a difference between Saudi Arabia and Kuwait, however. Saudi Arabia, by virtue of its dominant position in the Persian Gulf as well as in the Organization of Petroleum Exporting Countries, had always been and will continue to be treated as critical to the security of the Western world. The Saudi rulers, therefore, could always count on Western, especially American, protection in times of crisis. Kuwait—threatened to a far greater degree by Iraq and Iran, two large and irredentist states (that is, they had ambitions to restore ethnically related groups then under Kuwaiti control)—historically had not had that kind of blanket security assurance from the West. Kuwait's leaders, therefore, had long understood that their survival, and that of their country, would ultimately depend on them and their own policies and practices.

The February 1979 "Islamic revolution" in Iran was watched with considerable alarm by Kuwait's rulers. And this fear continued to mount as Tehran's revolutionary government became increasingly aggressive and avowedly expansionist. It was then that the need of Kuwait's rulers for full public support became paramount. The emir issued a decree in August 1980 for the restoration of the parliamentary system. Elections took place in February 1981 for the National Assembly, which had been dissolved in 1976.

For the next five years the National Assembly returned to its earlier vigorous life, virulently attacking incompetence and corruption within the Council of Ministers and forcing the resignation of a number of ministers, some of whom were senior members of the Sabah family. And, as in 1976, the rulers grew increasingly wary and restless over the Assembly's attacks on the executive. Nor were the rulers any more sanguine about the press. In late 1985 the crown prince spoke of his anguish and bitterness at the Assembly's charges against the government. He warned that if the charges continued, they would harm the security and stability of the country. He also warned the news media to take a more responsible attitude, adding that if the ruling family had tolerated excesses in the past, the time had come to put them right.

The handwriting was on the wall. In the tug of war between patrimony and democracy, this time patrimony was beginning to pull harder. In July 1986 the emir again dissolved the National Assembly and proceeded to rule by decree, a state of affairs that continued until the sudden Iraqi invasion of Kuwait in August 1990.

After the Iraqi Invasion

In the months after the invasion, Kuwaitis and others lost no time in pointing out to the emir and his family that Iraq's primary public relations thrust was to characterize Kuwait as an archaic and authoritarian country, even as a family-owned enterprise, undeserving of international support. During the seven-month Iraqi occupation, while the emir and his family lived opulently in neighboring Saudi Arabia, Kuwaiti nationals fought and suffered under Iraqi occupation. Outside Kuwait, the emir, his brothers, and cousins met regularly with Kuwaitis, many of them identified with Kuwait's opposition groups, to publicize national solidarity and to try to work out an acceptable formula for the political future of Kuwait. Time and again the emir unequivocally pledged a quick return to democracy and absolute respect for human rights and for freedom of the press. He even promised to look into the problem of female suffrage, until then denied by the constitution.

The first few months after the liberation of Kuwait in March 1991 did not augur well for the future of democracy. In September the respected human rights organization Middle East Watch accused the highest level of the Kuwaiti government of flagrant human rights abuses and charac-terized Kuwait's human rights conduct since liberation as deplorable. The emir also seemed to be dragging his feet on the question of elections, finally announcing that they would be held in October 1992.

The first half of 1992 was no more promising. Law and order virtually broke down, with regular abductions and shootings of expatriates, particularly Palestinians. But the domestic situation calmed down sufficiently for the elections to take place as scheduled on October 5.

Even though only 14 percent of Kuwaiti citizens could vote (men over age twenty-one whose families had lived in Kuwait before 1921), the elections produced a majority for loosely organized opposition groups, which gained thirty-one of the fifty seats in the National Assembly (parties remained formally proscribed). Subsequent to the elections, vigorous debates were held in the National Assembly over granting the right to vote to women and to Kuwaitis who immigrated to the country after 1921, legalizing political parties, allowing freedom of the press, and dealing with the thorny issue of the still immeasurable powers and privileges enjoyed by the emir and the ruling family.

The new parliament represented a wide range of societal elements: pro-democracy advocates, business interests, moderate Sunni fundamentalists, Shiʿites, and religious activists opposed to the government. Although the 1992–1996 parliament was not fully representative of society and did not resolve the big issues of universal suffrage or legalization of parties, it did make life difficult to the ruling family. The legislature asserted control over financial and budgetary matters and vigorously investigated government corruption and malfeasance.

Significantly, regularly scheduled elections were conducted in October 1996, at the end of parliament's four-year term. Again, the franchise was highly limited and parties prohibited, but opponents of the regime claimed a significant number of seats.

In the ongoing struggle between patrimony and democracy, it should be recognized that Kuwait's latest move toward a democratic order occurred not because of the rulers' commitment to democracy but because of their grudging recognition of the political preferences of those countries that restored them to power. The country's total dependence for its survival on the United States and the West in the era after the Iraqi invasion and the Gulf war that restored its sovereignty might very well constrain the recalcitrant rulers from trying to reverse the process of democratization as they have done twice in the past.

See also *Iran; Iraq; Middle East.*

BIBLIOGRAPHY

Finnie, David H. *Shifting Lines in the Sand.* London: I. B. Tauris; Cambridge: Harvard University Press, 1992.

Hay, Sir Rupert. *The Persian Gulf States.* Washington, D.C.: Middle East Institute, 1959.

Mansfield, Peter. *Kuwait: The Vanguard of the Gulf.* London: Hutchinson, 1990.

Rush, Alan. *Al-Sabah: History and Genealogy of Kuwait's Ruling Family, 1752–1987.* London: Ithaca Press, 1987.

Winstone, H. V. F., and Zahra Freeth. *Kuwait: Prospect and Reality.* London: Allen and Unwin, 1972.

Kyrgyzstan

A mountainous, landlocked republic in Central Asia, bordered by China, Kazakhstan, Uzbekistan, and Tajikistan. With a population of approximately 4.5 million (about 54 percent of whom are Kyrgyz, 20 percent Russian, and 13 percent Uzbek) in an area of 76,640 square miles, this is one of the smallest and least industrialized of the Soviet successor states. The Kyrgyz are a Turkic people, most of whose ancestors probably came to the area with the armies of Genghis Khan, in the thirteenth century.

The northern Kyrgyz are similar to the Kazakhs; after Russian conquest in the eighteenth century, the two were administered as a single people. The southern Kyrgyz, separated from the north by high mountains, most resemble their Uzbek neighbors. In the czarist period (until 1917) the Kyrgyz were nomads, who did not even have a written language. Attempts to draft the Kyrgyz and other Central Asians into the czarist army, as well as persistent economic deprivation, sparked the uprising of 1916, which was savagely repressed. As many as 40 percent of the Kyrgyz in the north were killed or driven into exile in China. During the years of the Soviet period (about 1920–1989), Kyrgyzstan was used as a place of exile; ultimately it became a quiet, politically dependable backwater.

Prelude to Statehood

In 1989 Kyrgyzstan surprised observers by leaping to the forefront of Soviet leader Mikhail Gorbachev's attempts to restructure the Soviet Republic. The original impetus for democratization in Kirgizia (as it was called in Soviet times) was economic; persistent housing shortages in the capital (then called Frunze, now Bishkek) led people in May 1989 to begin seizing building plots. Zhypar Zheksheyev, a painter, organized these squatters into an informal organization which took the name Ashar (Help).

Riots in the southern city of Osh in June 1990 brought about the next stage in Kyrgyzstan's political development. The cause this time was ethnic. Southern Kyrgyzstan has nearly a half-million Uzbeks, one-third of the local population, who are economically and culturally integrated with nearby Uzbek cities. By contrast, the capital of Kyrgyzstan is physically remote from Osh, reachable only by airplane or by a high mountain road that is impassable in winter. The riots, which began over a market squabble, lasted three days and may have claimed several hundred lives. (A believable official account has never been released.)

When news of these riots reached Frunze, mobs of Kyrgyz youth assembled, preparing to burn out Uzbeks there. Zheksheyev, working closely with the head of security forces in the city, Feliks Kulov, was able to prevent further violence. The government, headed by Gorbachev appointee Absamat Masaliyev, attempted to portray the disorders as being in part the fault of the Kyrgyzstan Democratic Movement, which Zheksheyev and others had founded in late May. However, prominent figures in the Kyrgyz Communist Party supported the Democratic Movement.

By fall 1990 there was strong opposition to the Masaliyev government, both within and outside the party. A hunger strike was begun in front of the government building, demanding Masaliyev's resignation, among other things. The strikers kept a constant vigil on the street while the Supreme Soviet met inside. Following the practice of Gorbachev, Masaliyev had submitted himself to the parliament for ratification as republic president. However, a splinter bloc of members kept him from getting the necessary number of votes.

After some maneuvering, Askar Akayev, a physicist and president of Kirgizia's Academy of Sciences, was put forward as a dark-horse candidate. He was elected on October 27, 1990. His presidency would be reaffirmed by popular vote, on October 12, 1991, after Kyrgyzstan had declared its independence. Akayev was the first leader of a Soviet republic who had not been appointed by Moscow and who had not come up through the ranks of the Communist Party (though he was of course a Communist Party member).

Akayev moved rapidly to dissociate the administration of his republic from the Communist Party, and he tried to foster as much democratization as was possible in what proved to be the last year of the Soviet Union's existence. A number of prominent Kyrgyzstanis resigned from the

Communist Party during that year, including Topchubek Turgunaliyev, who founded the democratic party Erkin (Freedom). Erkin and another newly founded party, Asaba (Banner), together made up the bulk of the Kyrgyzstan Democratic Movement. In parliamentary elections in October 1990 the Democratic Movement had succeeded in getting five of its candidates elected; they were the first non-Communist members of the parliament in Kyrgyzstan's history.

When the August 19, 1991, attempted coup came in Moscow, Kyrgyzstan's administration believed (mistakenly, as it turned out) that troops were being sent from Moscow to uproot their experiment in self-rule. This belief sparked a spontaneous preparation for resistance. Crowds kept vigil around the government building, while Kulov, who was now minister of the interior, made preparations for brave but desperate guerrilla-style resistance. Although the quick collapse of the coup attempt made these preparations unnecessary, the republic responded to the general wave of euphoria by declaring independence on August 30, 1991.

Independence

Kyrgyzstan was among the first ex-Soviet states to achieve international recognition, including recognition by the United States in January 1992. The republic's reputation for democracy was enhanced by its unusually adept diplomatic corps, exemplified by Roza Otunbayeva, who served as ambassador to the United States and Canada. Widely regarded as the best and most active of the new states' representatives, Otunbayeva was recalled in May 1994 to serve as foreign minister.

With broad support from the Kyrgyzstan Democratic Movement and most of the parliament, Akayev embarked on an ambitious program to make Kyrgyzstan into an "Asian Switzerland," a bastion of economic prosperity and political freedom. With almost no restrictions on their activity, political parties flourished; by 1993 there were at least ten legally registered parties, on a philosophical spectrum from the democratic-nationalist Freedom Party, Banner Party, and Ata-meken (Fatherland, which grew out of Freedom) to the Communist Party of Kyrgyzstan, which was allowed to reconstitute itself in September 1992. Even more striking was the flourishing of independent newspapers, which quickly created an atmosphere of virtually complete public openness, with all affairs of state exposed to public scrutiny.

Efforts to create a post-Soviet constitution for Kyrgyzs-

tan continued through most of 1992. There was general agreement that the republic would have a unicameral elected parliament (the Supreme Soviet), an elected president who would have power of appointment for lower level executive posts, and a judiciary also appointed by the president. Despite concern about the great power it gives to the president, the constitution was adopted by the parliament in March 1993.

Threats to Democratic Hopes

Unfortunately, Kyrgyzstan's bright hopes and brave beginnings have been considerably damaged by its economy, which has essentially collapsed since independence, and by a steady succession of corruption and malfeasance scandals that involved government officials. Fueled by extensive press coverage and a high-profile parliamentary investigative commission, a scandal about how gold mining concessions (the republic's major potential source of income) had been awarded brought down the government of Prime Minister Tursunbek Chyngyshev in December 1993.

Kyrgyzstan's faith in democracy was also tempered by the civil war in Tajikistan, which came to a conclusion only in December 1996, and by the bellicosity of Uzbekistan. In December 1992 Uzbek KGB agents arrested three human rights activists who were attending a conference in Bishkek. The government also refused to allow publication of an Uzbek newspaper in Osh, out of fear of Uzbekistan's reaction. The civil war in Tajikistan made President Akayev, like all the Central Asian presidents, determined to maintain civic order even at the cost of democracy, if necessary.

The result was a general hardening of political positions in the republic. Most of the parties of the Kyrgyzstan Democratic Movement moved from Akayev's side to the opposition. The escalating criticism of the government, including Akayev, led to a temporary reimposition of censorship in the fall of 1993, then again in January 1994, in anticipation of a nationwide vote of confidence in Akayev. The republic's single, state-owned printing plant refused to print any but pro-Akayev newspapers. The referendum resulted in a Soviet-style 99 percent approval rating for Akayev and his government, but democratic activists in the republic were badly disillusioned.

After the referendum the government concentrated on coping with the republic's vanishing economy and showed little interest in continuing to foster its early democratic impulses. Difficulties in working with the 350-member legislature, elected in 1990 while the republic was still part of the Soviet Union, prompted Akayev to dissolve the parliament in September 1994. He proposed creation of a bicameral legislature, with an upper house that would rarely meet and a smaller, "professional" lower house that would be in constant session. Akayev himself, in a move not allowed for in the constitution, scheduled a fall 1994 referendum on the proposal; it was approved by 70 percent of the voters. This change in government structure enhanced the president's executive power.

Elections to the seventy-member upper house (the Assembly of People's Representatives) and thirty-five-member lower house (the Legislative Assembly) were held in February 1995. None of the twelve parties contesting the seats won a commanding position in either house, further strengthening the president's hand. Akayev won reelection by a wide margin in early presidential election in December 1995. Subsequently, he orchestrated a referendum in February 1996 that vastly increased presidential powers.

Beginning in 1994 the government became less tolerant of the press. Even the government's own newspaper received no state funds, and in September 1994 three opposition newspapers were ordered shut. Little effort has been made to adhere to the constitution, especially in the localities where presidentially appointed governors have abused their power. The accelerating economic collapse, combined with rampant corruption, has created an atmosphere of wide distrust that will make the democratic impulses of 1989–1991 difficult to sustain.

See also *Asia, Central.*

BIBLIOGRAPHY

Akaev, Askar. "Kyrgyzstan: Central Asia's Democratic Alternative." *Demokratizatsiya* 2 (1994): 9–24.

Allworth, Edward, ed. *Central Asia: 120 Years of Russian Rule.* Durham, N.C.: Duke University Press, 1989.

Chukin, Almas. "Free Kyrgyzstan: Problems and Solutions." *Current History* (April 1994): 169–173.

Fierman, William, ed. *Soviet Central Asia: The Failed Transformation.* Boulder, Colo.: Westview Press, 1991.

Pryde, Ian. "Kyrgyzstan: The Tragedy of Independence." *Journal of Democracy* (January 1994): 109–121.

L

Lebanon

A constitutional republic located on the eastern end of the Mediterranean Sea, bordered on the east by Syria and on the south by Israel. For more than three decades—from independence in 1943 until the collapse of civil order in 1975–1976—Lebanon had the only continuous democratic political system in the Arab world. To be sure, Lebanese democracy was limited and flawed in many ways, but it could boast regular, free, and competitive elections and an impressive degree of open political debate and activity. The ruinous civil war that claimed at least 120,000 lives between 1975 and 1990 ended with the restoration of the old parliamentary system, considerably modified, and with the country's politics dominated by its bigger neighbor, Syria.

Although modern Lebanon, in terms of territory and political structure, is a recent creation—dating only to the establishment of the French mandate in 1920—historic Lebanon, according to the mythology of some Lebanese nationalists, is rooted in ancient Phoenicia and early Christianity. Traditional "Mount Lebanon" encompassed the area from the Mediterranean just north of Beirut and south of Tripoli to the Lebanon mountain range. Owing in part to its rugged terrain (useful for defensive purposes), Lebanon became the refuge and home of numerous Christian and Muslim sects: Maronites, Greek Orthodox, Greek Catholics, Roman Catholics, Sunnis, Shi'ites, Druze Muslims, and many other smaller communities. It also developed a complex quasi-feudal social structure during the Ottoman Empire.

Because of its many sects and complex society, Lebanon was not a place that could be governed, even by a powerful empire, without mechanisms for balancing the various communities and interests found there. It was perhaps this diversity rather than any common orientation that set

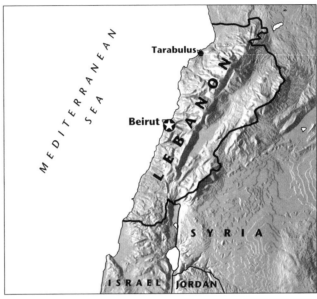

Lebanon apart from neighbors and gave it a kind of "negative identity."

In 1920, after World War I, France created two new states in former Ottoman territory: Lebanon and Syria. "Greater Lebanon" comprised the traditional Mount Lebanon as well as the territories now known as North Lebanon, the Biqa, South Lebanon, and Beirut—territories that, significantly, were composed overwhelmingly of Sunni or Shi'ite Muslims. France's political control over Lebanon came to an end in 1943, allowing a coalition of Lebanese nationalists (Christians and Muslims) to achieve a relatively bloodless independence. An act of creative statesmanship by two liberal politicians (Bishara al-Khuri, a Maronite Christian, and Riyad al-Sulh, a Sunni Muslim) produced in 1943 the National Pact, often dubbed Lebanon's "real" constitution.

The National Pact

The National Pact solved the problem that had paralyzed politics under the French mandate: it brought the Muslims back into the system. It did so by allocating major offices according to a more equitable formula than had previously been used and by stipulating a foreign policy that would avoid entangling alliances with either the Christian West or the Arab-Muslim East. The National Pact ensured that the president would always be a Maronite Christian, the prime minister a Sunni Muslim, and the president of the Chamber of Deputies a Shi'ite Muslim. It also provided that legislative and executive positions would be allocated on a 6 to 5 basis between Christians and Muslims, with an equitable distribution among the various Christian and Muslim sects as well.

Thus the National Pact, a constitution in 1926, and subsequent electoral laws brought about a fairly faithful replication of the consociational democracy model, in which elites representing mutually hostile ethnic groups share power according to fixed rules. Sects were represented proportionally within the government, and the system encouraged the integration of all sects at the elite level. It also furthered elitism within the sects. Landowners, business leaders, and lawyers were able to manipulate the electoral system so as to enhance their prestige and power in the emerging Lebanese state.

For three decades Lebanon's consociational arrangements ameliorated the problem of sectarian insecurity and rivalry. But Lebanon's politicians were never able (nor indeed was it in their interest) to eliminate political sectarianism altogether. By the mid-1950s the demographic rationale for Christian (especially Maronite) predominance was widely thought to have evaporated. The only formal population census had been taken under the French in 1932. But higher Muslim birthrates and higher Christian emigration after that time led many to think that non-Christians were now a majority. Compounding the problem was the rise of Arab nationalism in the 1950s. Lebanese Muslims felt that the Christian president was siding with the "imperialist West," while Lebanese Christians feared a Muslim-led, pan-Arab takeover that might extinguish the country's Christian character, if not its very existence. Socioeconomic tensions also were growing, driven by uneven development and rapid urbanization. The carefully calibrated sectarian system made it difficult for government to respond to these challenges.

In theory, the president should have been able to provide dynamic and creative leadership because his powers exceeded those of any other politician or institution, including the prime minister and the Chamber of Deputies. In practice, however, independent Lebanon's first two presidents, Bishara al-Khuri (1943–1952) and Camille Chamoun (1952–1958), concentrated their energies on consolidating their winning coalition in Parliament and in the country, and both sought to renew their terms despite a constitutional prohibition. In both cases disgruntled notables—traditional leaders of sects or regions—banded together to challenge the president and drew on the increasingly radicalized young people from the middle and lower classes to rally around their "reformist" opposition. President al-Khuri was replaced after a constitutional crisis in 1952, and President Chamoun precipitated a brief civil war in 1958. An American diplomat, Robert Murphy, helped to negotiate Chamoun's resignation and his replacement by the commander of the Lebanese army, Gen. Fu'ad Shihab.

The 1958 crisis revealed the fragility of Lebanon's consociational democracy. A formula designed to neutralize sectarian divisions was unable to adapt to changing demographic and social conditions, nor could it bridge the growing divide between Lebanese Christians and Muslims over Lebanon's position in the "Arab cold war" between Western and Arab nationalist orientations. The "military solution" to the 1958 crisis, in the person of General Shihab, resembled more the Turkish model of temporary corrective intervention than the Arab model of intervention by military figures in nationalist garb who often seek to make the presidency a lifetime position. Shihab's reform program, however, began to run out of steam by the end of his term in 1964, and his handpicked successor, Charles Hilu (1964–1970), lacked the authority and leadership to regain the momentum.

The traditional politicians, mostly Christian, who had been shoved aside by "Shihabism" gradually recovered and were able to exploit the inefficiency, corruption, and occasional repressiveness of the Shihabists. The regional turmoil churned up by the defeat of neighboring Arab regimes at the hands of Israel in the 1967 Six-Day War stimulated the growth of the Palestinian resistance movement in Lebanon and elsewhere. Many Lebanese Christians feared that the growth of this movement threatened Lebanon's delicate sectarian balance. For their part, many Lebanese Muslims (and some Christians) lent enthusiastic support to the Palestinian guerrillas who had emerged in the wake of Arab government defeats in 1967. While the leading Palestinian group, al-Fatah, emphatically denied any interest in becoming involved in Lebanese affairs,

Palestinian leaders felt it prudent to cement relationships with friendly Lebanese Muslims in order to offset growing Lebanese Christian hostility. Lebanese Muslim politicians feared that right-wing Christians might control the Lebanese army, and they also observed that Christian politicians were building their own militias. Because they lacked comparably powerful militias, they turned to the well-organized and well-equipped Palestinians.

Driven by worst-case, self-fulfilling prophecies, all these players found themselves marching toward civil war. Between 1970 and 1975 the coherence, authority, and relevance of the Lebanese state dwindled. Not only was the multisectarian consociational Lebanese elite disintegrating, but the masses too were increasingly riven by sectarian fear and hatred. The parliamentary election of 1972, though broadly representative of the sects and major traditional leaders, was unable to bridge the growing cleavages.

There would not be another such election for twenty years. In 1975 Lebanon was plunged into a fifteen-year civil war that wrecked the country's economy and society. Armed militias displaced the authority of the state; democratic processes were paralyzed. Complicating matters was the involvement of external actors, notably Israel, Syria, Iran, and the Palestinians.

Ta'if Accords

The civil war was formally brought to an end with the signing of the National Accord Document for Lebanon, issued in Ta'if, Saudi Arabia, on October 24, 1989. The Ta'if accords, composed with the active participation of Syria, Saudi Arabia, and the United States and signed by nearly all of the surviving members of the 1972 Chamber of Deputies, were the blueprint for the restoration of the Lebanese state.

The accords may have modified the rules of the game of the First Republic, but they did not alter the basic character of the rules. Postwar Lebanon—in form—is still more or less a consociational democracy. Sectarian proportionality remains in place, but the proportion of Muslim to Christian legislators and officials has been increased to 50-50. For the foreseeable future the president of the republic remains a Maronite Christian, but the powers of the office have been substantially reduced. The prime minister remains a Sunni Muslim, but the powers of the Council of Ministers, chaired by the prime minister, have been increased. The office of president of the Chamber of Deputies still goes to a Shi'ite, but the term has been increased

from one year to four and the influence of the office has also increased. The power of the Chamber itself was increased by the elimination of the old provision allowing the executive to pass "urgent" legislation without parliamentary involvement. At the same time, the Ta'if accords explicitly called for a gradual phasing out of political sectarianism.

Other provisions of the Ta'if accords relating to Lebanon's external relations were more controversial. For example, in proclaiming that Lebanon was Arab in identity, the accords went farther than the 1943 National Pact and thus alarmed some Christians. Even more alarming was the provision authorizing a special relationship between Lebanon and Syria, which would give Syria a privileged position in certain matters, including national security. Moreover, a pledge by Syria to redeploy its forces in Lebanon east of the Lebanon mountain range within two years of the formal ratification of the Ta'if accords (in 1990), the holding of a new presidential election, and the formation of a new cabinet also were conditional on the approval of political reforms (by which was meant the beginning of the process of desectarianization). Two years later, in 1992, with a new president and cabinet in place, the Syrians refused to redeploy on the grounds that not all of the political reforms had been achieved. Furthermore, as long as Israel controlled its self-styled "security zone" in southern Lebanon, Syria could justify keeping its own military presence in the country.

Many Maronite Christians either opposed the Ta'if accords outright or accepted them with great reluctance. They also opposed holding new parliamentary elections in August and September 1992, but Syria refused all requests to delay them, even for technical reasons such as the difficulty of updating the electoral rolls after the vast demographic upheavals of the previous seventeen years. The elections were held, notwithstanding the shadow of Syria and a boycott in much of the Maronite heartland of Mount Lebanon. The new Parliament was welcomed in most other parts of the country as an important, if flawed, step on the road back to stable representative government.

There were several striking trends in the political make-up of the new Chamber of Deputies. Some 47 percent of the new deputies were affiliated with a political party or movement (as opposed to a traditional grouping or independent status), compared with 31 percent in the 1972 Parliament. Some of the parties showed continuity—for example, the Ba'ath, Druze leader Kamal Junblat's Progressive Socialist Party, and the Armenian Revolutionary Federation (Dashnak). More striking was the disappearance of many traditional Maronite actors. Absent too were the prominent anti-Syrian militia chiefs of the civil war. Many Maronites of Mount Lebanon looked upon these results as depressing evidence of the end of Maronite hegemony. But not only were traditional Christian players missing, there also were new Islamic actors on the parliamentary scene. The Shiʿite parties Amal and Hizballah now constituted the largest blocs in Parliament—twelve seats for Hizballah and twenty for Amal. There also was small but significant representation from two Sunni Muslim Islamist parties.

Even Lebanese observers who detested Syria's involvement in Lebanese politics admitted that Damascus had on the whole acted skillfully to implant its influence in postwar Lebanon while allowing quite a broad spectrum of traditional and new political forces a place on the stage. But if Lebanon was to emerge definitively from its past agony, the traditional Christians of Mount Lebanon would have to be brought back into the formal system in one way or another.

The parliamentary elections of 1996 were an important test of the inclusiveness of the postwar order. The elections, held in August and September and conducted at the normal expiration of parliament's four-year term, provided evidence of somewhat greater acceptance of the postwar order. Voter turnout rose from 13 percent in 1992 to 44 percent in 1996, thus leading to a more inclusive and representative legislature. Amal and Hizballah continued to be major forces in parliament. Both demonstrated a willingness to abide by the rules of parliamentary practice.

The Lessons Learned

Modern Lebanon has exhibited a limited form of liberal democracy because of its exceptional cultural and social diversity. As perhaps the most heterogeneous region in the Ottoman Empire it was too hard to rule directly. There was a functional imperative for institutionalized procedures for consultation and representation. As a quintessentially plural society, Lebanon developed pluralist political structures long before it emerged as a modern state. The liberal bourgeois founders of independent Lebanon sought with considerable success to integrate traditional pluralism with a European parliamentary model.

In the early 1950s, when liberal experiments in neighboring Arab countries such as Syria, Egypt, and Iraq were giving way to anti-Western nationalist authoritarianism,

Lebanon's Christian-dominated elite managed to deflect similar tendencies, but only with great difficulty. The 1958 crisis, in retrospect, should have sounded the alarm that the system was insensitive to internal socioeconomic pressures that were undermining the sectarian formula, and that regional ideological challenges were growing. The failure of the Shihabist reforms and the resurrection of the parochial Maronite leaders paved the way for the total collapse of the system in 1975.

What are the lessons of the civil war? The first reaction might be that Lebanon has given democracy a bad name. If democracy failed in Lebanon—the only Arab country where it had worked—why should anyone recommend its application elsewhere in the region? Indeed, why should anyone recommend a return to democracy for postwar Lebanon itself? This issue has been hotly debated in Lebanon, with some arguing that the civil war was almost totally the result of outside pressures and others insisting that the domestic sociopolitical order was the principal weakness. Without minimizing the complexity and multiple causes of the war, one might propose that Lebanon's problem was not too much democracy but rather too little. More precisely, the built-in sectarianism that defined Lebanon's elitist, consociational democracy carried the seeds of future disaster. The consociational medicine that relieved immediate sectarian tension lost its potency as Lebanon's society and demography changed. Furthermore, the side effects—parochialism and a certain immobilism and insensitivity in policy making—tended to impede effective responses to many other issues that were threatening social order and political stability. To blame Lebanon's troubles simply on "democracy," then, would risk throwing out the democratic baby with the consociational bathwater.

See also *Middle East.*

BIBLIOGRAPHY

American Task Force for Lebanon. "Working Paper: Conference on Lebanon." Washington, D.C.: American Task Force for Lebanon, 1991.

Baaklini, Abdo I. *Legislative and Political Development: Lebanon, 1842–1972.* Durham, N.C.: Duke University Press, 1976.

Hudson, Michael C. *The Precarious Republic: Political Modernization in Lebanon.* New York: Random House, 1968; Boulder, Colo.: Westview Press, 1985.

Khalaf, Samir. *Lebanon's Predicament.* New York: Columbia University Press, 1987.

Salibi, Kamal. *The Modern History of Lebanon.* London: Weidenfeld and Nicolson, 1965.

M

Malaysia

A federation, located in Southeast Asia, of Malaya, Sarawak, and Sabah, which has been independent from the British since 1957. In contrast to neighbors who fought wars of independence, Malaysians had the advantage of not having to struggle against the return of their colonialist ruler, Great Britain. Independence was granted peacefully and was received with some reluctance by the Malaysians, who feared their country's continued existence would be jeopardized without the support of Great Britain.

When Malaysia received its independence from British rule on August 31, 1957, the new country was called Malaya and consisted of the peninsular area south of Thailand to Singapore. The country's multiethnic nature was reflected in its politics. Ethnic Malays constituted nearly half the population, and the Chinese made up about one-third. Indians, aborigines, and Europeans were smaller minority groups. The Chinese and Indians had been brought to Malaya by the British in the nineteenth century to work on fruit plantations and in the tin mines.

Malaya was transformed into the Federation of Malaysia in 1963, when Sabah, Sarawak, and Singapore were incorporated. The creation of the federation was due in part to the communal (multiethnic) nature of Malaya. Sabah and Sarawak, on the island of Borneo, were populated by ethnic Malays and hence balanced the new Chinese from Singapore. The new federation lasted only two years in that form. In 1965 Prime Minister Tunku Abdul Rahman, the leader of Malayan independence, requested that Singapore leave the federation. With its overwhelmingly Chinese population, Singapore threatened the fragile balance achieved by the Malaysian government, which promised the ethnic Malays political dominance.

Postindependence Government

The Malaysians adopted the British model of governance, including regular competitive elections, a representative parliament, separation of powers, civilian supremacy, and civil liberties. This choice is especially noteworthy because Malaysian elites tend to hold a formalized view of democracy, which crumbles when it faces more deeply held values; stability and security, for example, take precedence over democratic values. In terms of the achievement of democracy, political stability, and economic development, Malaysia is the most successful country of Southeast Asia.

The distinctive Malayan contribution to the constitutional arrangements was the creation of the position of paramount ruler (*yang di-pertuan agong*), selected from each Malay state in turn every five years. Nine states in the federation have hereditary rulers, known as sultans, and together these constitute the Council of Rulers. The paramount ruler is chosen from this body. This king, who has ceremonial and religious duties and powers of appointment, can delay (but not kill) certain legislative bills; the parliament can overrule the veto.

The most traumatic event of the postindependence period occurred in 1969, when ethnic riots erupted in the capital city, Kuala Lumpur. Dozens of people were killed in the racial violence. To bring order to the country, democratic institutions were temporarily disbanded, and total authority was granted to a National Operations Council. It was clear that a return to parliamentary rule would be disastrous unless significant changes were made in Malaysian politics. To preserve stability, several pieces of legislation were passed that limited the rights of Malaysians. These acts provided Malays with special rights and prohibited discussion of "sensitive issues," such as the prerogatives of the Malay rulers and the official status of the Malay lan-

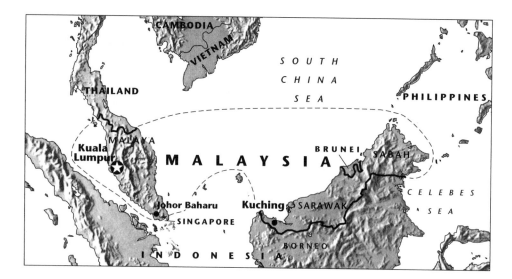

guage. Malay was required to be used in all the nation's schools; no debate was allowed regarding its official status, despite the views of many academics that English should also be allowed in the schools.

A modified parliamentary government returned to Malaysia in 1971. Political stability was restored, and a new united front, called the National Front, was established among the major political parties. The National Front consisted of the leading Malay, Chinese, and Indian political parties and continued to dominate every election in the following years.

In 1981 Mahathir bin Mohamad was elected the first "commoner" prime minister—that is, the first leader with no roots in the traditional aristocracy. Mahathir became a vigorous symbol of the modern Malaysian technocrat. He set forth a "Look East" economic policy, arguing that the Western nations were not appropriate models for Malaysia to follow. Mahathir's policy emphasized adoption of the work ethic and methods of Japan and South Korea; a market-oriented economy featuring the privatization of public utilities, communications, and transportation; and increased trade with Asian neighbors. Mahathir viewed the authoritarian societies of South Korea and Taiwan, in particular, as worthy of emulation. He argued that at Malaysia's stage of development, authoritarian leadership was more effective than Western-style democratic government. The success of these programs led economists to predict that Malaysia would be the next newly industrialized country, joining Singapore, Taiwan, South Korea, and Hong Kong as Asia's fifth "tiger." Mahathir continued to serve as prime minister in mid–1997, his political party, the United Malays National Organization, having been re-

turned to office in every election through the most recent—that of April 1995.

Communalism, Religion, and Ethnic Identity

During Mahathir's administration, communalism continued to be the central issue in Malaysia. This was especially so because of the rise of Islamic fundamentalists who demanded an Islamic state. The excellent economic growth among most sectors during Mahathir's term, however, provided a cushion for the Malaysian government. Communal tensions remained beneath the surface because the people perceived that their needs were being met.

In the early 1990s Malaysia continued to be ruled by the National Front. Fourteen parties contested the April 1995 parliamentary elections as members of the National Front, including the United Malays National Organization, the Malaysian Chinese Association, and the Malaysian Indian Congress. These parties accepted the alliance formula in order to legitimize the interests of the three major ethnic groups, which they represented. The formula required that each group accept the basic societal division: Malays dominate the political sphere, and Chinese and Indians dominate the economy. Every Malaysian prime minister has reached that position because he led the United Malays National Organization.

In Malaysia, all Malays are Muslim by legal definition. Islam provides Malays with both legal and political privileges. The loss of these privileges would amount to renunciation of the Malay way of life. Islam, which does not separate secular from religious activities, is tightly organized from the village up to the state level. Muslim youth, many of whom are fundamentalist, call for rigid codes of conduct and the implementation of Islamic law. This increase in Islamic militancy is viewed as threatening by the non-Muslim population.

The religious element is central to the political party orientations of Malaysians. During the independence period some of the parties that were formed were defined almost exclusively in terms of their degree of Islamic orthodoxy. Through the mid–1990s moderate Islamic parties were dominant in the ruling alliance. The principal opposition parties have been made up of Islamic fundamentalists, who used their religious doctrines for political objectives.

Chinese citizens also join political parties that reflect their ethnicity. Most Chinese have joined moderate parties, such as the Malaysian Chinese Association. Radical parties have also arisen, out of fear of Islamic militancy and as a reaction to economic policies that threaten the leading Chinese role in the economy.

Quasi-Democracy

Since independence, Malaysia has held nine national elections. Four orderly successions of power have taken place. Despite this record, Malaysia is regarded as a quasi- or semidemocracy because of limitations on civil liberties. The explanation given for the necessity of quasi-democracy is that the communal situation in Malaysia is unique. In the context of communal issues, an election loss by the National Front would mean the perceived end of the primary rights of the Malays.

Malaysia's Official Secrets Act, Internal Securities Act, and Sedition Act have imposed a culture of silence on citizens. Newspapers, television, and radio are controlled by the government or the United Malays National Organization and are generally compliant with regard to all communalism issues. Newspapers that raised "sensitive issues" were shut down when Prime Minister Mahathir invoked the Internal Securities Act.

Mahathir moved toward authoritarian rule in 1987, when factionalism arose in the National Front. His administrative style was characterized more by confrontation than by consensus. His opponents responded in kind, thereby departing from the traditional ways of leading the nation. By 1993 Mahathir had succeeded in taming the bureaucracy, the political parties, the judiciary, the press, and the state rulers (sultans).

Malaysia's economic growth was among the highest in the world during Mahathir's terms in office. As a result, Malaysians appeared willing to let him rule in a more au-

thoritarian manner than his predecessors. With a gross domestic product (GDP) of almost $3,000 per capita, Malaysia surpassed the European nations of Portugal and Hungary in the world rankings. The standard of living had clearly continued to improve since independence. Clean water, electricity, televisions, and education were universally available. In 1966 just 4 percent of Malay families owned a television; in 1990 more than 90 percent owned one. In this same period, dirt roads were paved, telephone lines were installed, and schools were built.

Under Mahathir, Malaysia emphasized a market-oriented economy. Formerly public enterprises were privatized. Malaysia became integrated into the world capitalist system, as the world's largest exporter of semiconductors and one of the largest exporters of air conditioners, textiles, and footwear.

The April 1995 parliamentary election continued the established pattern of authoritative decision making, with the National Front leading an alliance of parties. Malaysia continued to prosper, and there was a general perception that the government was meeting the needs of the people. It appeared that Malaysians would continue to achieve political stability in the context of a quasi-democracy.

See also *Asia, Southeast; Singapore.*

BIBLIOGRAPHY

Jomo, Kwame Sundaram. *A Question of Class: Capital, the State, and Uneven Development in Malaya.* New York: Oxford University Press, 1986.

Mauzy, Diane K. *Barisan Nasional: Coalition Government in Malaysia.* Kuala Lumpur: Marican and Sons, 1983.

Ness, Gayle D. *Bureaucracy and Rural Development in Malaysia.* Berkeley: University of California Press, 1967.

Roff, William R. *The Origins of Malay Nationalism.* New Haven: Yale University Press, 1967.

Scott, James C. *Weapons of the Weak: Everyday Forms of Peasant Resistance.* New Haven and London: Yale University Press, 1983.

Tilman, Robert O. *Bureaucratic Transition in Malaysia.* Durham, N.C.: Duke University Press, 1964.

Von Vorys, Karl. *Democracy without Consensus: Communalism and Political Stability in Malaysia.* Princeton: Princeton University Press, 1975.

Middle East

The countries that stretch from northeast Africa and the coast of the Mediterranean Sea down to the Persian Gulf, including Egypt, Iran, Iraq, Israel, Jordan, Lebanon,

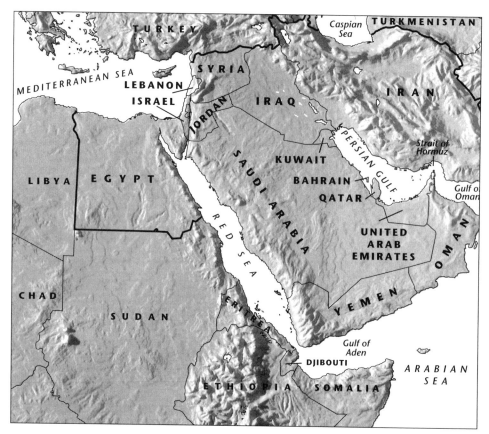

Saudi Arabia, Syria, Yemen, and the Gulf states of Bahrain, Kuwait, Oman, Qatar, and the United Arab Emirates. The political systems of the Middle East include monarchies (Jordan, Saudi Arabia, and the Gulf states); dominant, authoritarian party structures (Iraq, Syria); an Islamic republic (Iran); a reunified nation (Yemen); a rebuilding consociational state (Lebanon); and an advanced multiparty pluralist state (Israel). With the exception of Israel, two features characterize the region: the powerful influence of Islam as a religious and political movement and the limited nature of democracy. This conjunction has inevitably led to an examination of the relationship between Islam and democracy.

On the one hand, Islam is regarded as an obstacle to the establishment of democracy mainly because of the incompatibility between the absolute rule of God (Allah) and the secular forms of political expression that rest on representation and accountability. One strand of Islamic thought associates democracy with secularism, with the consequence that democracy becomes a deliberate violation of God's law. Islam's total view contains social, political, and economic creeds enshrined in Islamic law and based on interpretations of the Quran. This view precludes the need

for other political movements and militates against the full participation of Islamic groups in competitive multiparty politics.

On the other hand, some find within Islam an Islamic agenda for democracy. These ideas center on the notion of the wider Muslim community, the *umma*, and the need for consultation, *shura*. In large states, *shura* takes place in a form of national assembly, *majlis*. In this context, Islamic parties may stand for election to national assemblies, and they can deliberate, advise, discuss, and consult with individual leaders. Yet the central features of liberal representative democracy—freedoms of speech and association, accountability, legitimate opposition, rights of the individual, and adequate information and debate—are not included. The reasons that so few Islamic countries appear to be democratic are linked to the defining characteristics and demands of Islam, but other factors are also important.

The Middle East's diverse cultures—Jewish, Arab, Iranian (Persian), and Christian—have given rise to a number of political movements: Zionism, Pan-Arabism, Arab nationalism under Egyptian president Gamal Abdel Nasser (1918–1970), state socialism under the Ba'ath parties, and

Islamic revivalism. Conflicts since the end of World War II—including the Arab-Israeli wars of 1948–1949, 1967, 1973; the Iraq-Iran war of 1980–1988; the invasion of Kuwait by Iraq in August 1990 and the subsequent Persian Gulf war of 1991—contribute to a view, prevalent in the West, that political instability, tension, divisiveness, and military preparedness are endemic features of the area.

Impediments to Democracy

In spite of varying degrees of electoral activity in Iran, Jordan, Lebanon, Syria, and Yemen, lack of governmental accountability and full voter enfranchisement are major barriers to fully functioning democratic political systems. It can be argued that Middle Eastern states have rejected the liberal democratic option largely because of where it came from rather than what it contained. Certainly the impact of imperialism did much to foster anti-Western sentiments. Under a system of mandates established after World War I, France and Britain extended a system of colonial rule over the area, arbitrarily dividing territory and stifling political development. The cold war, the post–World War II competition between the United States and the Soviet Union, further polarized opinion in the Middle East. Rivalry between the superpowers and political and military interference in the region exacerbated tensions.

Division and conflict between North and South Yemen was deepened by the institution of a Marxist government in South Yemen under the reorganized Yemen Socialist Party. South Yemen signed a twenty-year friendship pact with the Soviet Union in 1979 and declared the country a people's democratic republic. (North and South Yemen reunited in 1990.)

The decision of the United Nations in 1947 to recommend the partition of Palestine into two states, one Jewish, the other Arab, went against Palestinian wishes and caused much hostility. Israel was not recognized by members of the Arab community, who saw creation of the state as an act of imperialist intervention in land taken without their agreement. The creation of Israel set in motion a series of events that provoked some of the more enduring problems of the region: the plight of Palestinian refugees, the occupation of land, the recurrent conflicts and wars, and spiraling military expenditures.

The economic benefits of oil and its massive increase in price during the 1970s did little to encourage democratization. Rather, oil wealth led to increased power for regimes in Kuwait and the other Gulf states, which became benevolent autocracies, allocating the wealth through welfare schemes. In such *rentier* states, the nation accrues income not through traditional domestic taxation and economic programs, which often become associated with popular demands for political reform and legitimacy, but from such external sources as stocks, rents—or, in this case, oil exports. The oil-rich states are under no pressure to become democratic. State distribution of goods and services—that is, the allocation of oil wealth in the form of welfarism—meets societal needs, and the people therefore have no need to form trade unions, political parties, or any other economic or political organizations.

The Iranian Islamic revolution of 1979 introduced another dynamic into the region, that of theocratic politics—public affairs carried out in accordance with the belief that governance proceeds from divine authority. Under the stewardship of Ayatollah Ruhollah Khomeini (1901–1989), the popular revolt against the powerful Western-backed autocracy (1941–1979) of the shah, Mohammad Reza Pahlavi, contributed to the rise and importance of Islam as a strong political movement. The revolt also provided great momentum for anti-Western sentiment. Any possibility of introducing liberal democratic practices into the region seemed remote.

Indeed, Western countries did not want to see liberal democracies arise in the Middle East. Their dependence on oil, and the prevalence of strong communist parties in Iran, Iraq, South Yemen, and Syria, caused them to regard puppet regimes such as the shah's as preferable to, and potentially more stable than, democratic regimes. As the cold war was played out in the Middle East, the countries of the region became strategic assets. Coups engineered by the U.S. Central Intelligence Agency and military pacts with the Soviet Union were not the best ways of developing political structures and democratic processes. Furthermore, the Palestinian-Israeli conflict debilitated political advancement in the area as the ebbs and flows of stateless people affected the politics of surrounding states.

Iraq and Syria can both be described as authoritarian states, although they operate differently. In Iraq the president is the head of state with executive power and appoints the council of ministers. In Syria elections to the People's Assembly (parliament) are held every four years, and the president stands for reelection every seven years. Yet the controlling force and preeminent political organization in both countries has been the split, secular Ba'ath Party, one faction of which operates in Syria, the other in Iraq. Syria's constitution defines the country as a socialist popular democracy, while the Iraqi Ba'ath Party looks to a more powerful role at the vanguard of Pan-Arabism, an effort to achieve unity among Arab peoples beyond the constraints of national boundaries. One political feature that has differentiated Syria from Iraq is the National Progressive Front, an umbrella organization of various socialist parties that was formed in 1972 to broaden the Ba'ath Party's political base and to create an appearance of opposition.

Bahrain, Oman, Qatar, Saudi Arabia, and the United Arab Emirates have no political parties. In Saudi Arabia the king holds supreme power, and in Bahrain Sheik 'Isa ibn Salman Al Khalifa dissolved the National Assembly in 1975 for an indeterminate period on the grounds that it interfered with the administrative affairs of government. Oman has no constitution or modern judicial system. Final legal and administrative power is vested in the sultan, and all authority emanates from him. Qatar is an absolute monarchy. The emir is head of state, appoints the cabinet, and occupies the office of prime minister. There is an advisory council but no legislature. In these states, there is no semblance of contemporary democratic political institutions.

Citizenship

The concept of citizenship is crucial in any analysis of democratization processes within Middle Eastern countries. In liberal democratic theory, which emphasizes that the individual's rights and responsibilities lie within a legal framework, the citizen assumes a primary position. In the Middle East, citizens may be enfranchised and participate in the political process, but they are under a duty to accept being ruled. A pluralist society, which recognizes all interests, enables its citizenry to form pressure groups to petition the government, thereby permitting a structured form of participation.

The role of the citizenry can be both stable and responsible, but there are difficulties in regions that experience a high degree of population mobility for either political or economic reasons. The countries of the Middle East have high levels of population mobility partly because of the Palestinian-Israeli dispute but also because of migrant labor, which reflects the uneven economies in the region. The support given to Iraq by the Palestine Liberation Organization during the 1991 Persian Gulf war resulted in the immediate expulsion of Palestinians working in Kuwait. Stateless Palestinians became as much of a security risk in Arab states as in the Jewish state of Israel.

Immediately before the invasion by Iraq, Kuwait had an estimated population of 2.2 million, of which approxi-

mately 70 percent was non-Kuwaiti. Population movement and citizenship affect the essential nature of nation-statehood and majority-minority apportionment within a society; both are vital elements in sustaining a democracy. In nations in which the majority of the population falls into noncitizen or semicitizen categories, democratization poses difficulties, in that political participation usually is confined to the minority. Palestinians living in Jordan are granted Jordanian citizenship and have participated in political procedures since 1950. The Jordanian constitution divides cabinet and parliamentary seats equally between Jordanians and Palestinians. In a sense the move toward the establishment of Palestinian autonomy, with the prospect of eventual statehood, presents a challenge to the region as well as to Palestinians living in the Diaspora. Palestinians who choose not to live in their sovereign territory may seek greater representation and influence in the political processes of their host states. For that reason or others, host countries may have to decide whether to grant citizenship and political rights to Palestinians.

Possibilities of Political Reform

Although some states felt internal pressure for democracy building during the 1980s, democratization was more widely discussed in the Middle East after the Persian Gulf war of 1991 and the end of the cold war. The changed global political environment, the disintegration of the Soviet Union, and the inefficiency of state-controlled economies led to some political reform, although not in every country of the region. Distinctions between the nation-states of the Middle East are such that a move toward democratization in one country may be symbolized by the removal of the ban on the formation of political parties or the introduction of a national assembly. In another country, it might be characterized by the establishment of a more equitable parliamentary system. A government decree passed in Jordan in 1992 permitted the formation of political parties, and elections were held for the National Assembly in November 1993. In Lebanon elections were reintroduced in 1992 after a twenty-year absence, mainly because of that country's civil war, and were held as scheduled in 1996.

By the end of the 1980s demonstrations, bread riots, and strikes had occurred in Iran and Jordan, and petitions calling for representative government appeared in Kuwait. In Jordan the population's grievances were twofold: a reaction against the dissolution of the parliament and changes in electoral laws and resentment of an economic reform plan that increased prices of basic foods and services. Government reforms that had aroused pleas for social justice and democracy had come in response to demands from the International Monetary Fund (IMF) that Jordan repay its foreign debt more quickly and effectively. In 1989 community leaders demanded changes in election law to provide democratic parliamentary representation, more political freedoms, a freer press, and formulation of a national economic program. Because it was bound to the IMF economic program, the government of Jordan had to create an atmosphere of confidence in the credibility of government policies by relaxing the curbs on freedom of expression and political rights.

The situation in Jordan showed that international organizations may exert pressure on a country to become democratic, but internal pressures may exist, too. The two elements are not mutually exclusive.

In Kuwait, beginning in 1989, three years after the dissolution of the National Assembly, a series of pro-democracy street rallies took place, and senior officials were involved in circulating secret petitions calling for a return to parliamentary life, or what passed as such. Suffrage had been confined to male citizens twenty-one and older who could prove Kuwaiti ancestry prior to 1920. Only 6.4 percent of the population was eligible to vote in the 1981 elections.

Although Kuwait is the only Gulf state in which a national assembly is elected entirely by popular vote, the restrictions on citizenship and enfranchisement make the term something of a misnomer. Nevertheless, the imprisonment of opposition leaders who demanded the reinstitution of the National Assembly and the glare of international publicity during the Persian Gulf war created a sensitivity about political processes. The emir announced that elections to a new parliament would be held, the question of women's participation in parliamentary life would be studied, and the status of naturalized "second category" citizens, previously denied the vote, would be reviewed. Kuwait learned from the war that the rights and responsibilities of citizens have as much to do with a nation's defense as with its maintenance of representative institutions. Denying the status of citizenship to people who have been residents in a country for decades undermines the fabric of a nation-state and renders it vulnerable both internally and externally.

Consociational Democracy

One promising model of democracy in countries with deep social cleavages and political or religious differences is consociational democracy. Consociationalism permits politicians representing sectional interests to govern at a national level in coalition with the leaders of other parties and groups. Through a system of proportional representation it is possible for leaders of all groups to participate at the decision-making level. This procedure permits all sectors of society to have a stake in the political institutions of the country. The political system of Lebanon between 1943 and 1975 fitted the consociational format.

Consociationalism can bring about a workable political system, but it does have disadvantages. The process may contribute to the continuing segregation of groups. Equally, it can allow an elite cartel to emerge that represents particular interests and exchanges favors for votes. In Lebanon it is estimated that twenty families have dominated the political arena since French colonial rule began after World War I.

The central difficulty with consociational forms of government is not necessarily that they are less democratic than conventional forms of liberal democracy but that decision making can be slow or can become immobilized. The larger the coalition, the more difficult it is to avoid stagnation and inefficiency.

Although the adversarial two-party system can be more decisive in policy making—largely because one party is in office at one time—animosity and suspicion may arise in parties excluded from government. The consociational model, even with its deficiencies, may create a climate more conducive to democracy. In the case of Lebanon, elections were held again in 1992 under a constitutional amendment that increased National Assembly membership and changed the division of seats from a 6:5 to 6:6 ratio—that is, an equal ratio—between Christians and Muslims. Of nine new seats available to Muslims in 1992, three were to be allocated for Shi'ites, and two each for the Sunni, Alawi, and Druze communities.

Lebanon's consociational electoral system may help ensure democracy and put an end to concerns about the participation of Islamic organizations in democratic exercises. Many fear the possible ulterior motives and ambitions of Islamic parties and doubt their true commitment to democracy. Consociationalism may offer a process of controlled democratic participation that will help preserve stability.

Economic Factors

The signing of the Declaration of Principles (the Oslo accord) between Israel and the Palestine Liberation Organization (PLO) on September 13, 1993, in which both parties agreed to end decades of confrontation and conflict and to recognize their mutual political rights, raised the prospect of peace in the Middle East. The agreement signed on May 4, 1994, finalizing plans for Israel to hand over the administration of Gaza and Jericho (the West Bank) to a Palestinian autonomous authority created an awareness in the region that economic advancement and cooperation may be the key to stability, peace, economic well-being, and political reform.

The Islamic Development Bank, the financial agency of the Islamic Conference Organization (the international body that coordinates and furthers the interests of Muslims), has called for an increased and more dynamic private sector and greater regional trade. The bank, however, does not connect economic change with political reform.

International experts agree that poor economic management and unpredictable governance are this region's chief liabilities. Influential bureaucracies, government control of production, a regulatory environment that stifles private initiative, public business sectors that are unresponsive to demand, and systems of governance that lack accountability and accessibility are seen as responsible for disappointing economic growth figures and high levels of unemployment. The World Bank, the German Development Agency, and Britain's Overseas Development Administration have all recommended that attention be focused on economic liberalization and cooperation between states in the region so that resources can be better utilized and greater efficiency and effectiveness can be promoted. Development of human resources through training, education, health care, and employment has been strongly emphasized. If these policies are implemented, pluralism can emerge in the form of economic, social, and labor groups that will be distanced from state structures.

In short, a civil society may develop in the Middle East that will demand political rights and freedoms. As the role of the state in the economy diminishes, businesses and organizations will be able to articulate their interests. Because competition is believed to be vital for the success of the private sector, a process of economic privatization, or *infitah* ("opening up"), was begun in Egypt. It is hoped that, through economic liberalization and increased trade and cooperation, greater bonds will develop between states in the region, hostilities will diminish, polities will stabilize, and political reform may be introduced.

Despite attempts at political reform in some states, it would be misleading to underestimate the formidable challenges confronting the successful introduction of lib-

eral democracy in the area. Still, the ending of the cold war created a climate of opportunity for states in the Middle East to enjoy political autonomy. In a sense the onus is now on these states to become democratic. Some may follow a consociational pattern or reintroduce elections; others may remove bans on political parties and tinker with electoral processes; still others may resist reform altogether. The people of the region may make significantly greater demands on their governments. Increased participation is an important move toward democratization, but the next steps, if they are taken, must be in the direction of pluralism and accountability.

See also *Egypt; Iran; Iraq; Israel; Jordan; Kuwait; Lebanon.*

BIBLIOGRAPHY

Ayubi, Nazih. *Political Islam: Religion and Politics in the Arab World.* London and New York: Routledge, 1991.

Choueiri, Yousef M. *Islamic Fundamentalism.* Vol. 2 of *Twayne's Themes in Right-Wing Politics and Ideology.* London: Pinter; New York: Macmillan, 1990.

Deegan, Heather. *The Middle East and the Problems of Democracy.* Boulder, Colo.: Lynne Rienner; Buckingham: Open University Press, 1993.

Diamond, Larry, Juan J. Linz, and Seymour Martin Lipset, eds. *Democracy in Developing Countries: Asia.* Boulder, Colo.: Lynne Rienner, 1988; London: Adamantine Press, 1989.

Fischer, Stanley, Leonard J. Hausman, Anna D. Karasik, and Thomas C. Schelling. *Securing Peace in the Middle East: Project on Economic Transition.* Cambridge, Mass., and London: MIT Press, 1993.

Hudson, Michael C. *Arab Politics: The Search for Legitimacy.* New Haven and London: Yale University Press, 1977.

Lijphart, Arend. *Democracy in Plural Societies: A Comparative Exploration.* New Haven and London: Yale University Press, 1977.

Luciani, Giacomo. *The Arab State.* Berkeley: University of California Press, 1989; London: Routledge, 1990.

Owen, Roger. *State, Power and Politics in the Making of the Modern Middle East.* New York: Routledge, 1992.

Piscatori, James P., ed. *Islamic Fundamentalism and the Gulf Crisis: A Fundamentalism Project Report.* Chicago: University of Chicago Press, 1991.

Morocco

A constitutional monarchy situated on the northwest coast of Africa, where the effective political authority remains in the hands of a monarch. King Hassan II combines political power with authority derived from religion. (He is known as the supreme religious ruler or "commander of the faithful.") The monarch is skilled at playing off competing elites, manipulating electoral politics to ensure that only representatives of political parties loyal to the throne serve in government, and, after abortive military coups in 1971 and 1972, maintaining tight control of the military. Periodically, the king uses repression and imprisonment to silence critics.

The centrality of the monarchy in politics reflects Morocco's unique position at the crossroads between the West, Middle East, and Subsaharan Africa. From its position in the northwest corner of Africa, Morocco is separated from Europe only by the Strait of Gibraltar. Historically, Morocco was settled by Berbers, colonized by Rome, and conquered by Arabs, before being incorporated as an autonomous province of the Ottoman Empire in the early nineteenth century. King Hassan II uses these linkages to play a key role in international relations among Western, Middle Eastern, and African countries, while seeking increased economic integration with the European Union. Economically, Morocco relies heavily on remittances from workers abroad, including more than a million in Europe, and on Western trade and tourism.

Morocco was partitioned by France and Spain into formal protectorates in 1912, commencing forty-four years of colonial rule. But political traditions were preserved throughout the colonial era, and the local monarchy reemerged after independence in 1956. Hassan's father, who assumed the title of King Mohammed V in 1957, reigned until his death in 1961.

After Spain withdrew from Western Sahara in the mid-1970s, Morocco fought against a nationalist movement, popularly known as the Polisario Front, for control of the territory. Although the Polisario Front won recognition from more than sixty nation-states as the Saharan Arab Democratic Republic, by the mid-1980s Morocco had gained effective control over most of the territory. Morocco's campaign to annex the Western Sahara was costly (military costs ran $1 billion annually), but it enjoyed widespread popularity at home. The king repeatedly used this support and the international stalemate to his political advantage. For example, in the 1970s, when the monarchy faced social and labor unrest, it used the idea of a "Sahara consensus" to postpone parliamentary elections until 1977. When parliamentary elections were postponed again in 1989, the need to allow King Hassan to settle the Sahara conflict was cited.

The king also uses his constitutional authority to maintain power. The first constitution, ratified in a national ref-

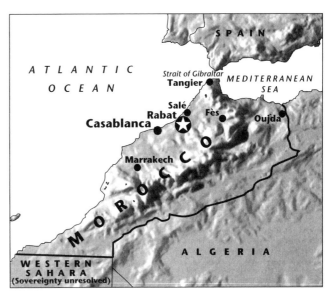

erendum in 1962, codified the constitutional monarchy, guaranteed personal and political freedoms, and recognized Islam as the official state religion. Although opposition leaders participated in the first postindependence government, King Hassan II, after assuming the throne in 1961, moved quickly to consolidate his power. In 1962, while removing critical opposition party members from government, he outlawed single-party rule in Morocco. He instituted a state of emergency and direct rule in 1965, permitting normal political activities to resume only gradually in the late 1960s. Throughout the 1970s no major political parties participated in the government.

The current constitution was approved in a national referendum in 1972 over the objections of the major political parties, trade unions, and student organizations. This constitution reaffirmed the king's role as chief executive, the supreme civil and religious authority, and commander in chief of the armed forces. The king appoints most important officials, including the prime minister and the governors of the forty-three provinces (including four in the Western Sahara) and the two urban prefectures of Casablanca and Rabat-Salé. The king also dominates the legislative process and retains broad powers, including the power to initiate constitutional amendments, to pass laws subject to ratification in national referendums, and to declare a state of emergency during which the king rules by decree.

In the early 1990s the king promised a series of political changes that he claimed would make Morocco the boldest democratic experiment in the Arab world. He sponsored a series of legislative changes, including the requirement that the government submit its program to a vote by the Chamber of Representatives and seek legislative approvals to extend states of emergency beyond the first thirty days. The king also sponsored constitutional changes, including amendments to enhance basic political rights and the creation of a constitutional council to review new laws. These constitutional changes were approved in a national referendum in 1992. The official results, however, raised doubts about the integrity of the process: 99.96 percent of all voters, including 100 percent of all voters in the main cities and in three of the Western Sahara provinces, approved the king's proposals.

The majority of representatives elected to the unicameral parliament in 1977 and 1984 represented center-right parties willing to support strong monarchical rule. In June 1993, after acrimonious local elections and voter registration campaigns, parliamentary elections were held once again. Representatives from center-right parties again won a slight majority. The opposition made its strongest showing to date, winning 99 of 222 elective seats compared with 80 seats in the 1984 elections. The elections also were notable in that the victorious candidates included the first two women to serve in the parliament.

Two socialist opposition parties, the Socialist Union of Popular Forces and the Independence Party, together hold the largest bloc of seats in the 1993–1998 parliament. These parties have used their increased electoral strength to press for improvements in the country's observance of human rights and for reforms in the governing system.

Further constitutional amendments were adopted by national referendum in September 1996. These amendments created a second legislative chamber, the House of Councillors, and made the existing lower house wholly elective beginning with the 1998 elections. The new upper house is to be indirectly elected. The amendments also expanded the legislature's powers to include the right to censure the government.

Critics of recent reforms, including leaders of the main opposition political parties, remain skeptical about whether top-down multiparty system reforms can lead to meaningful democracy. Some observers predict major political changes after Crown Prince Sidi Mohammed, who is reported to favor a more ceremonial role for the monarchy, assumes the throne. But the status quo is also threatened by the fundamental economic, social, and political trends evident throughout North Africa today: high unemployment in an increasingly youthful population (two-thirds of Moroccans are under twenty-five), declining standards of living for laborers, growing awareness of elite corruption and mismanagement, an increasing gap between the wealthy urban elite and the three-quarters of Moroccans who still earn their living by farming, and rising expectations fueled by comparisons with European living standards. These trends will continue to foster demands for political freedoms and support for Islamic fundamentalism.

BIBLIOGRAPHY

Amin, Samir. *The Maghreb in the Modern World.* Harmondsworth, England: Penguin Books, 1971.

Hodges, Tony. *Western Sahara: The Roots of a Desert War.* London: Croom Helm, 1983.

"Morocco." In *The Middle East and North Africa.* 39th ed. London: Europa Publications, 1993.

Munson, Henry, Jr. "Morocco's Fundamentalists." *Government and Opposition* 26 (summer 1991): 331–344.

Nelson, Harold D. *Morocco: A Country Study.* Washington, D.C.: Library of Congress, 1986.

Zartman, I. William, ed. *The Political Economy of Morocco.* New York: Praeger, 1987.

———, and William Mark Habeeb, eds. *Polity and Society in Contemporary North Africa.* Boulder, Colo.: Westview Press, 1993.

N

Namibia

An African country that has overcome more than one hundred years of authoritarian colonial rule to establish a democratic system of government. Called South West Africa prior to its independence from South Africa in 1990, Namibia now has free elections and an independent judiciary.

Historical Background

Before the creation of South West Africa as a colony in the late nineteenth century, indigenous political systems predominated, including seven powerful Ovambo kingships in the far north-central regions, the Kavango in the northeast, and the highly centralized authority systems of the Mafwe and Basubia in the far northeast. A number of important Nama clans ruled over the southern regions, while a dozen pastoral Herero chieftainships dominated the eastern regions and competed with Nama groups for control of central areas.

Smaller groups had already been dispersed to isolated regions before the eighteenth century. German colonial rule (1884–1915) and South African colonial rule (1915–1989) destroyed most of the indigenous political systems and perpetrated relentless violence against the Namibian people as a whole. South Africa had been granted control over South West Africa in 1919, when the League of Nations accorded political rule of the country to Britain after Germany's defeat in World War I, and Britain passed on this responsibility to South Africa.

The Germans initiated and the South Africans consolidated a rigid division of the country along racial and ethnic lines for the benefit of the white settlers. The far northern and eastern regions were called "communal" areas, and they remained politically divided from the rest of the country, although the Ovambo-dominated northern areas were exploited as labor reserves for the mining industry. Meanwhile, an immense police zone was established, comprising the central and southern regions, within which blacks were forced off their land to make room for large, white-owned farms that raised livestock. South African authorities imposed strict military and police rule over the black populace in this zone, where serf-like conditions prevailed for farm workers. Pass laws curtailed the mobility of urban and rural blacks. In the populous northern regions outside the police zone, traditional black leaders became subservient to South African officials. The black majority, comprising 94 percent of the populace, enjoyed no political or human rights.

End of Colonial Rule

In 1960 an anticolonial political party was established—the South West Africa People's Organization (SWAPO). Six years later it began an armed struggle to liberate the colony. South Africa's modern military forces, however, easily held SWAPO's tiny guerrilla army at bay and terrorized the peoples of the northern regions in an effort to force them to curtail their support of SWAPO. Also during the 1960s and 1970s puppet governments were erected in all communal areas to represent the different ethnic groups. This ethnically based political division of the country gave rise to a political party, the Democratic Turnhalle Alliance (DTA).

South Africa now sought to construct a democratic façade in South West Africa in response to SWAPO's anticolonial political movement. National elections in 1978 were boycotted by SWAPO and manipulated by the South African authorities. These elections resulted in the creation of a DTA-dominated, ethnically constituted National Assembly that remained under the authority of the

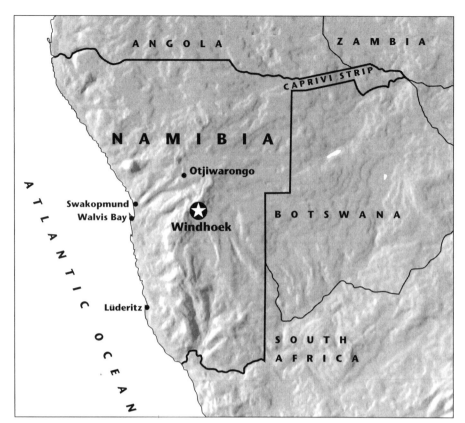

South African–appointed administrator general. The legislature, temporarily abolished in 1983, was reconstituted in 1985 as the Transitional Government of National Unity—a nonelected body with circumscribed legislative powers.

Meanwhile, international factors played an increasingly important role in pushing South West Africa toward a genuinely democratic future. The United Nations in 1966 revoked South Africa's right to rule South West Africa and in 1978 passed a resolution urging free and fair elections and full independence. After a decade of international negotiations aimed at resolving both the Angolan civil war and the anticolonial struggle in Namibia, South Africa agreed in 1988 to United Nations–supervised elections in Namibia in preparation for full Namibian independence (while Cuba agreed to withdraw its troops from Angola). As a result, 1989 witnessed the ending of SWAPO's armed rebellion, the return from abroad of the SWAPO leadership, and an active electoral campaign on the part of SWAPO, the DTA, and eight minor political parties.

Independence

National elections, administered by South Africa and tightly monitored by the United Nations, were held in November 1989. Ninety-seven percent of the eligible voters (totaling about 700,000 people) selected the party of their preference in the balloting. There was some violence and intimidation, purportedly by the South African military (which supported the DTA) and SWAPO supporters, but the elections as a whole were declared free and fair by a wide range of observers. A party list system of proportional representation was used. SWAPO, with 57 percent of the national vote, received 57 percent of the seventy-two seats in the Constituent Assembly (that is, forty-one seats). SWAPO's chief rival, the DTA, won 28 percent of the vote and thereby twenty-one seats. Five minor parties also won legislative representation: the United Democratic Front (four seats), National Christian Action (three seats), the National Patriotic Front (one seat), the Federal Convention of Namibia (one seat), and the Namibia National Front (one seat).

This first free and fair election marked the country's historic passage to democratic rule. The resultant Constituent Assembly negotiated a constitution that is among the most democratic in the world, codifying a large number of political rights and human rights. The bargaining that took place among SWAPO, the DTA, and minority party members of the Parliament from November 1989 to

February 1990 set the stage for a political culture of compromise and tolerance that has characterized both the Parliament and Namibian politics more generally since that time. This is remarkable in light of the brutal oppression and racial intolerance that characterized Namibia's colonial experience. Moreover, SWAPO has demonstrated an impressive capacity to shift roles from that of a liberation party directing a guerrilla war to that of a parliamentary party overseeing a democratic republic. Similarly impressive is the DTA's willingness to step peacefully out of its former role as ruler of the Parliament into its new role as the official parliamentary opposition.

From among its members the Constituent Assembly elected SWAPO leader Sam Nujoma as president in February 1990. Then on the day of independence, March 21, 1990, South West Africa became Namibia. The Constituent Assembly, reconstituted as the National Assembly, expanded to seventy-eight members to accommodate six nonvoting members appointed by the president, as stipulated by the constitution. Between April 1990 and November 1994 the National Assembly held eight full sessions, lasting three to four months each. The Assembly continues to serve as a forum for intensive political debate.

Consolidation of Democratic Institutions

Democratic institutions in Namibia were further strengthened by direct popular elections from November 30 to December 3, 1992. These elections, the first carried out by the SWAPO-run government, established fifty new local authorities (mostly town councils) and thirteen regional councils. Despite some organizational problems with registration, almost all eligible voters were able to participate. The councils preside over a redistricted nation with the new constituencies based on geographic and economic factors (rather than on ethnicity, as was the case under South African rule).

The election of the new regional councils made possible the creation of Namibia's second house of Parliament, the National Council, as mandated by the constitution. In December 1992 each of the regional councils elected two members to serve six-year terms in a twenty-six–member National Council, which was officially inaugurated in February 1993. The principal function of the National Council is to review bills passed by the National Assembly and to recommend revisions where necessary.

The National Council is the weaker house of Parliament, but it can influence national decisions. Its regional bases provide it with a grassroots linkage that the National Assembly lacks. With a two-thirds majority vote, the National Council can force the National Assembly to reconsider a bill that it has passed.

The democratic principles and tolerance that have predominated in the legislature are also reflected in Namibian society as a whole. The half-dozen daily and weekly newspapers are intensely critical of government policies much of the time. Political interest groups, several minor opposition political parties, and influential church groups are essentially unrestricted in their activities, and basic democratic rights have been upheld. The judicial system is independent from the legislative and executive institutions, and its decisions have been respected (if not always appreciated) by both ruling and opposition political parties.

Many divisions and inequities created by colonial rule persist, however, despite an official government policy of national reconciliation. Most land in southern and central Namibia remains in the hands of a few thousand white farmers, and black Namibians await a clear land reform policy by the government. Although the ethnic communal area governments were abolished at independence, ethnic divisions could become more prominent if the economy fails to improve. In the long run such problems, if unattended, could threaten the stability of Namibia's new democratic institutions.

The national elections held December 7–9, 1994, however, strengthened the country's democratic promise. The president was chosen through direct suffrage on separate balloting for the first time (henceforth the election will be every five years). Incumbent president Sam Nujoma defeated DTA leader Mishake Muyongo, with Nujoma receiving 74.46 percent of the vote and Muyongo receiving 23.08 percent. Balloting for the National Assembly was again held according to the party list system (as it will be henceforth). SWAPO received 72.72 percent of the vote, augmenting its majority to fifty-three seats, and the DTA received 20.45 percent of the vote total, with its preliminary seat total declining to fifteen. Also winning National Assembly seats were the United Democratic Front (two seats), the Democratic Coalition of Namibia (one seat), and the Monitor Action Group (one seat). This election provided SWAPO with a two-thirds majority in the National Assembly, enabling it to revise the constitution with a straight party vote.

These national elections represented an impressive step toward the consolidation of Namibian democracy. Continuing progress, however, will depend in large part on the new government's ability to moderate lingering socioeconomic inequities.

See also *South Africa*.

BIBLIOGRAPHY

Bley, Helmut. *South West Africa under German Rule.* London: Heinemann, 1971.

Cooper, Allan D. *The Occupation of Namibia: Afrikanderdom's Attack on the British Empire.* Lanham, Md.: University Press of America, 1991.

Drechsler, Horst. *Let Us Die Fighting: Namibia under the Germans.* Berlin: Academie Verlag, 1966; London: Zed Books, 1980.

Du Pisani, André. *SWA/Namibia: The Politics of Continuity and Change.* Johannesburg: Jonathan Ball, 1986.

Forrest, Joshua Bernard. "Namibia: The First Postapartheid Democracy." In *Journal of Democracy* 5 (July 1994): 88–100.

Goldblatt, I. *History of South West Africa from the Beginning of the Nineteenth Century.* Cape Town: Juta, 1971.

Katjavivi, Peter H. *A History of Resistance in Namibia.* London: James Currey, 1988.

Sparks, Donald L., and December Green. *Namibia: The Nation after Independence.* Boulder, Colo.: Westview Press, 1992.

Nigeria

The most populous country on the African continent, and one of the wealthiest in natural resources, lying at the inner corner of the Gulf of Guinea in West Africa. The Nigerian experience with democracy has been paradoxical and ambiguous.

Three times the country has undertaken to govern itself under liberal democratic constitutions, and each time it has failed. The first two republics (1960–1966 and 1979–1983) were overthrown by military coups after they were widely discredited by corruption, election rigging, and undemocratic conduct. The transition to a third republic (1986–1993), also characterized by extensive corruption and controversy, was never completed: a cynical military regime kept extending the deadline and changing the rules, until it finally annulled an otherwise successful presidential election and was forced out of power. Another military coup displaced the transition process altogether on November 17, 1993, leaving the country in a quagmire of political illegitimacy and ethnic tension. This latest military regime promised a return to civilian government by October 1998 and has taken a few steps toward that goal, but the outcome is by no means assured.

Although the military controlled the government for twenty-seven of the first thirty-seven years of independence, Nigeria has never accepted indefinite authoritarian rule, and no military regime that has not committed itself to a transition to democracy has been able to survive. Through ten national governments, six successful military coups, a civil war, and a dizzying economic boom followed by a crushing depression—not to mention repeated assaults by military regimes on human rights and associational life—Nigerians have maintained a passionate commitment to personal freedom and political participation. Pressure for democratization continues to emanate from the country's many ethnic groups and from a battered but still vigorous civil society. Nigeria boasts the largest, most pluralistic, and most resourceful independent press in black Africa, as well as a wide array of human rights groups, trade unions, business groups, student and professional associations, women's groups, and other organized interests.

The Ethnic and Regional Setting

Home to some 250 distinct linguistic groups, Nigeria has been prone to the intense politicization of ethnic differences. Although most of its ethnic groups are relatively tiny, three groups constitute somewhere between 60 and 67 percent of the population. (No authoritative population figures exist because there has been no reliable and broadly accepted census since independence in 1960.) These are the Yoruba (whom different censuses have placed at anywhere from 16.6 to 20 percent), the Igbo (16.6 to 18 percent), and the Hausa-Fulani (28 to 30 percent).

Regional location and religion have served to reinforce this tripartite cleavage. The Hausa-Fulani, located in the north, are predominantly Muslim. They have a history of centralized, theocratic kingdoms, or emirates, owing political and religious allegiance to the Caliph at Sokoto. The Igbo, who attempted to secede in 1967 as the Republic of Biafra, occupy the east and are almost exclusively Christian; their political traditions are very egalitarian. The Yoruba, in the west, have an extensive tradition of monarchical but more limited political authority. They are roughly evenly divided between Muslims and Christians and generally are more tolerant in religious matters than are other ethnic groups.

Numerous ethnic minority groups make up the remaining one-third of the population. These are concentrated in the oil-producing areas of the midwest (the largest group here being the Edo) and southeast (the Ibibio, Efik, and Ijaw), in the "Middle Belt" of the country (the Tiv), and in the northeast corner, just below Chad (the Kanuri, who are Muslim and the largest single minority group). The Middle Belt has been a zone of particularly keen political rivalry, where Christians have resisted the domination of the Muslim emirates of the far north.

British colonial rule reinforced these regional and cultural differences. To be sure, precolonial history did feature warfare among rival Hausa states and rival Yoruba kingdoms; an Islamic jihad (1804– 1830) that extended the Fulani empire, or Sokoto caliphate, over the Hausa states and most of the rest of the north; and myriad other conflicts. However, trade and peaceful interchange also featured prominently in the contacts between peoples.

The British initially established separate protectorates for Northern and Southern Nigeria in 1900; they continued to rule the two parts separately even after formal amalgamation in 1914. In the north, a Native Authority system was constructed to rule indirectly through the centralized structures of traditional authority in the emirates. In the south, indirect rule was less successful. Western commerce, religion, and education spread much more rapidly there than in the north (particularly the emirates), where Western practices were severely restricted. This unequal exposure to Western influences and resources under colonial rule gave rise to enormous and enduring disparities in income, education, and entrepreneurship between north and south. These disparities have been a source of political tension and instability ever since.

Early Democratic Steps

Democratic politics began in Nigeria during the final decade of colonial rule. The 1951 constitution designated the western, eastern, and northern provinces as regions in a quasi-federal system and provided for indirectly elected assemblies in each to participate in governance. This decade of pre-independence electoral politics further crystallized the tripartite ethnic cleavage, as ethnically based political parties rose to dominance in each region. These were the Northern Peoples' Congress (led by Sir Ahmadu Bello, holder of the powerful traditional title, sardauna of Sokoto), the Action Group (led by Chief Obafemi Awolowo), and the National Council of Nigeria and the Cameroons (NCNC, led by Dr. Nnamdi Azikiwe, a major nationalist leader).

The NCNC (which was renamed the National Convention of Nigerian Citizens in 1961) sought with some success to reach out nationally beyond its Igbo base, and the Action Group later also campaigned aggressively in other parts of the country (particularly the minority areas). In contrast, the Northern Peoples' Congress presented itself as strictly a northern party and was mobilized hurriedly in defense of the class and ethnic interests of the traditional ruling class of the emirates. Challenging it on its own turf was the Northern Elements Progressive Union (led by Mallam Aminu Kano), a party of radical young northern com-

moners who sought to dismantle the "feudalistic" structures of the emirates. Several parties representing ethnic minority groups also ran candidates in local elections within each region.

Although political alignments were to shift constantly thereafter, the basic ethnic and political axes of party competition for the next four decades can be traced to this initial configuration of electoral politics in 1951. This structure consisted of a party of the traditional northern establishment, which sought to extend its hegemony throughout the north and (beginning in the First Republic) to pick up some allies among minority groups in the southeast opposed to Igbo domination; a political party dominated by the Yoruba and seeking to mobilize a national coalition of "progressive" forces opposed to political domination by the northern establishment; and an Igbo party oriented to the "progressive" cause but shifting pragmatically in its alliances.

The identity between region, party, and ethnicity deepened in 1954 with a constitutional change that created a fully federal system: it devolved enormous autonomy and control over resources to each of the three regions. Intense struggle ensued along the cumulative fault line of region, party, and ethnicity, over such issues as the distribution of socioeconomic resources, the timing of self-government, and efforts by the Northern Peoples' Congress to purge southerners from the northern bureaucracy and economy. Most intense of all was electoral competition, which progressively tightened the grip of each ruling party over its region, and which was marred by considerable violence, repression, intimidation, fraud, intolerance, and blatant appeals to ethnic prejudice.

Abuses reached new levels in the federal election of 1959, called to select the national government for the forthcoming independence. The northern region was to have half the seats in parliament. The Northern Peoples' Congress won an enormous plurality and formed the new government in coalition with the NCNC. The prime minister was Abubakar Tafawa Balewa, the Northern Peoples' Congress vice president who had headed a broad coalition cabinet since 1957.

Although British colonial rule had produced constitutional reform and a brief but staged transition to self-rule with significant indigenous participation, it left behind deep contradictions that would devour constitutional democracy within a few years. Most seriously, the colonial authorities steadfastly resisted eloquent Nigerian appeals to scrap the awkward and unstable three-region system in favor of a more balanced federal system with more constituent units and autonomy for minority groups. This type of system would have been more fluid and competitive, with better protection for minority rights and interests. With the breakup of the huge Northern Region, it would have been impossible for the northern elite simply to convert hegemonic control of their own region into control of the entire federation.

The British also bequeathed a political economy in which the indigenous capitalist producers were few and weak, while the state controlled the most important sources of capital accumulation: the marketing of cash crops, mineral production, numerous industries, and a sizable bureaucracy. Through corruption and clientelism, which grew rapidly in scope and scale, the state quickly became the principal means for the accumulation of personal wealth and the achievement or consolidation of dominant class status. Few avenues of upward social mobility existed independent from politics. With so high a premium resting on control of the state, no party was willing to tolerate opposition or accept defeat.

The First Republic

Nigeria achieved independence on October 1, 1960, under a formally democratic parliamentary system that was the object of high hopes domestically and internationally.

As part of the coalition arrangement, NCNC leader Azikiwe became the first head of state (initially, governor general and then president after Nigeria became a republic on October 1, 1963). Constitutionally, power was separated and rights were protected. A partisan but vigorous and diverse press assured pluralism outside the party system as well.

Democracy in the First Republic, however, quickly fell victim to its own contradictions. Political competition was increasingly restricted to the federal arena as one-party states emerged in each region. The center was rocked by five successive crises that progressively deepened ethnic and regional polarization.

The first crisis began in 1962, when a political split developed within the Action Group between Chief Awolowo, now opposition leader in the Federal House, and his successor as western premier, Chief S. L. Akintola. Although the latter was voted out of power by Awolowo's larger faction, the ruling federal coalition of the Northern Peoples' Congress and NCNC seized upon the conflict to declare emergency rule in the Western Region; they restored Akintola to power and destroyed their mutual rival, Chief Awolowo, through the dubious device of a treason conviction.

The second crisis, over the 1962 national census, underscored the determination of the north to preserve its political power. When the census showed a southern population majority, a subsequent "verification check" found 8 million more northerners (thus restoring the north's population majority). A fresh census conducted in 1963 reconfirmed the northern population majority, and its results were accepted over bitter protests from the Eastern Region's NCNC government.

Highlighting widespread public disillusionment with the political class, a general strike brought the country to a standstill for thirteen days in June 1964. Although the strike was resolved by government concessions, a fourth crisis, the 1964 general elections, soon arose. In what would become the principal, enduring bifurcation of Nigerian politics, the NCNC joined in alliance with the politically devastated Action Group, the Northern Elements Progressive Union, and the ethnic minority party of the Middle Belt to form the United Progressive Grand Alliance. The Northern Peoples' Congress drew in the accommodationist political party of the Yorubas, under Chief Akintola, and a few southern minority parties to form the Nigerian National Alliance.

With the consolidation of the parties, politics was reduced to a bipolar struggle, dominated then by the Igbos of the east and the Hausa-Fulani of the north. The election campaign was disfigured by unprecedented levels of political thuggery and by official obstruction and repression. A United Progressive Grand Alliance boycott provoked a tense showdown between the Northern Peoples' Congress prime minister and the NCNC president during which, for several days, the country seemed close to civil war. Unable to rally military and police support to his side, President Azikiwe finally yielded and the NCNC took a diminished role in a new coalition government more than ever dominated by the Northern Peoples' Congress.

The fifth and final crisis was triggered by the Akintola government's resort to massive, wholesale electoral fraud to award itself victory in the October 1965 Western Regional election. With the party's victory announcement, the region erupted into popular rebellion. Public disgust was intensified by a spate of corruption scandals during the year and the growing arrogance, pomposity, waste, and incessant political crisis associated with the politicians as a class. When a group of young army majors and captains seized power on January 15, 1966, assassinating Prime Minister Balewa and Premiers Ahmadu Bello and Akintola, the public welcomed their coup in an outpouring of joy and relief.

The First Military Interregnum

As would prove to be the case repeatedly in the future, the military was even less capable than the politicians of managing the country's ethnic and political tensions. The perception of the coup as being an Igbo affair (no leading Igbo politician was killed) and the insensitive handling of ethnic concerns by the Igbo major general (Johnson Aguiyi-Ironsi) who took control of government prompted a countercoup six months later. Aguiyi-Ironsi and other Igbo officers were killed and a compromise choice, Lt. Col. Yakubu Gowon (a northern Christian from a minority group), became head of state.

Although Gowon sought constitutional dialogue and reform, ethnic tension spun out of control later in 1966, with a wave of Igbo massacres in the north and a massive migration of Igbo settlers back to the east. In May 1967 the Eastern Region, under the leadership of Col. Odumwegwu Ojukwu, seceded, declaring itself the Republic of Biafra. Thirty months of civil war began in July, claiming perhaps a million lives and devastating the Eastern Region.

Nigeria emerged from the war in January 1970 with a hopeful future, as large-scale oil production was commencing and Gowon pursued a policy of reconciliation with the defeated Eastern Region. His earlier division of the country into twelve states now took full effect. With the quadrupling of oil prices in 1973–1974, an economic boom began, but corruption, another census debacle, and Gowon's indefinite postponement (on October 1, 1974) of the promised return to civilian rule produced broad disaffection. Nine years after he had assumed power, on July 29, 1975, Gowon was toppled by a coup of senior officers led by Brigadier Murtala Muhammad.

Muhammad purged the army and bureaucracy in an anticorruption campaign. On October 1, 1975, he launched a detailed and imaginatively staged four-year timetable for democratic transition. At the peak of his popularity, he was assassinated in an abortive coup attempt on February 13, 1976. However, his successor, Gen. Olusegun Obasanjo, implemented the transition timetable with skill and efficiency. Under Obasanjo's rule, the federal system was developed into nineteen states, new local governments were elected, an elected Constituent Assembly debated and adopted a new constitution (with an American-style presidential system), and civilian legislatures and executives were elected at the state and federal levels.

The Second Republic

Although many thought the Second Republic largely reproduced the party system of the First Republic, there were significant differences. The presumed successor to the Northern Peoples' Congress, the National Party of Nigeria, was still dominated by the northern Muslim elite, but it had the broadest national base of any Nigerian party to date, having won control of several ethnic minority states. The Unity Party of Nigeria, led again by Awolowo, was viewed as a successor to the (mainly Yoruba) Action Group; the Nigeria Peoples Party, led again by Azikiwe, as successor to the NCNC; and the Peoples Redemption Party, led by Aminu Kano, as successor to the radical Northern Elements Progressive Union. In addition, there was a Kanuri-based party, the Great Nigeria Peoples Party, which resulted from a split in the Nigeria Peoples Party.

Each of these five parties became dominant in its ethnic base, winning at least two of the nineteen states. But there was more cross-cutting support than in the First Republic and less partisan solidarity than before in the Hausa and Igbo heartlands in particular. The nineteen-state system and other provisions of the new system (such as the requirement that parties eschew ethnic symbols and have national political bases) seemed to be generating a more complicated politics. Although the National Party of Nigeria candidate, Alhaji Shehu Shagari, won a clear plurality of the vote over runner-up Awolowo, the legitimacy of his election was tarnished by a dispute over whether he had satisfied the requirement that a presidential candidate win 25 percent of the vote in at least two-thirds of the states.

There were other echoes of the First Republic. A working alliance developed between the Hausa-led National Party of Nigeria and the Igbo-led Nigeria Peoples Party within the National Assembly. Gradually, a "progressive" alliance emerged against the National Party of Nigeria, involving first the nine state governors from the Unity Party of Nigeria, Peoples Redemption Party, and Great Nigeria Peoples Party, and then eventually the three Nigeria Peoples Party governors as well.

Gradually, this transethnic and somewhat ideological cleavage between self-styled progressive and more conservative, traditionalist forces seemed to be reorganizing politics and bridging multiple ethnic divisions. Advanced by a number of events—including the controversial impeachment of a militant Peoples Redemption Party governor in June 1981 and an orchestrated riot against the other Peoples Redemption Party government the following month—this political division held promise of maturing into another "grand alliance" or even a party merger for the 1983 presidential elections.

The progressives, however, were unable to unite behind a single candidate (both Awolowo and Azikiwe ran again). An effort of the dominant factions of the Nigeria Peoples Party and Peoples Redemption Party to unite with the Great Nigeria Peoples Party in a new, broad party was refused in a baldly partisan ruling of the electoral commission. The five weeks of state and national elections in August and September 1983 witnessed the most blatant election rigging since the 1965 Western Regional election, as the National Party of Nigeria entrenched its political control with margins of victory that grew more incredible by the week.

By 1983 public disillusionment with the Second Republic was intense and pervasive, fed by an unending succession of breathtaking financial scandals, endemic political corruption, rising levels of political violence and intolerance, increasing disarray within the political parties, and a broad economic collapse. A second oil boom went bust, cutting the country's peak oil earnings of $24 billion in 1980 by more than half. Schools, clinics, and other government services ceased functioning.

Blocked from achieving change by legal means, the Yoruba areas in particular erupted in violence, and the country seethed. Once again when the soldiers seized control of government, on December 31, 1983, the people celebrated.

The Second Military Interregnum

In avoiding the polarization of ethnic conflict and generating broader forms of political cleavage and identity, the Second Republic made significant progress over the first. The major reasons for its collapse were corruption, abuse of power, and electoral fraud, rather than ethnic conflict. Many saw bad politicians as the problem and hoped the military might purge the system and quickly withdraw. The government of Maj. Gen. Muhammadu Buhari and Maj. Gen. Tunde Idiagbon moved quickly to punish corruption and eliminate waste, detaining hundreds of former politicians and seizing huge sums of cash from their homes. Their popularity from these moves abruptly waned, however, as the regime acted with unprecedented harshness and impunity to silence criticism and dissent. Journalists were arrested and prominent associations banned (along with any discussion of the country's political future). In response to the new cycle of bitter public disaffection, deepened by the inability of the Buhari government to come to grips with the economic crisis it inherited, high-ranking officers, led by Maj. Gen. Ibrahim Babangida, seized power in a bloodless coup on August 27, 1985.

Rejecting the authoritarian tactics of his predecessors in power, Babangida was enthusiastically welcomed by Nigerians. His popularity rose when he repealed repressive decrees and released from jail detained journalists and many civilian politicians. In a brilliant political maneuver, he even managed to launch a far-reaching structural adjustment program while neutralizing public opposition by rejecting the International Monetary Fund loan that was to have accompanied the program.

The most skillful, corrupt, wily, and manipulative military politician in the country's history, Babangida managed to rule for eight years through three tactics: co-optation of prominent civilians and military officers (through the prodigious dispensation of cash and other favors), repression and intimidation of opposition (repeatedly closing down publications and associations and arresting critics), and constant manipulation of the political game. By continuously holding out the prospect of a return to civilian rule, and by leading a wide range of politicians to believe they enjoyed his secret support, Babangida managed to prevail through a period of enormous political turbulence and economic suffering.

At the beginning of 1986 Babangida promised a return to civilian democratic rule in 1990. But when he announced a formal timetable for the transition in 1987, the return was deferred until 1992. The transition plan called for a sequential phasing in of democratic politics, beginning with local elections in 1987, formation of parties in 1989, state elections in 1990, and national elections in 1992. Babangida revised the timetable repeatedly, first in 1989, then in 1990, after the regime announced that it would establish the two political parties called for in the new constitution, rather than register any of the thirteen parties that applied.

The two parties were to be "a little to the left" (the Social Democratic Party) and "a little to the right" (the National Republican Convention). When they took shape in 1990 they reproduced to a considerable degree the progressive-conservative fault line that had been developing through the previous two republics. For the first time, however, the progressive and more southern-based party, the Social Democratic Party, emerged as the stronger political force, controlling a majority of states and local government areas.

Protest against official manipulation of the transition deepened in November 1992, when the regime seized upon chaos and fraud in the presidential primary elections of both parties to disqualify all presidential candidates, dissolve the party structures, and postpone the hand over of power yet again, from January 2 to August 8, 1993. To rally support from segments of the political class, Babangida reversed his policy of banning the old politicians from competing during the transition. The lift of the ban generated a new rush of presidential candidates.

By then there was general skepticism that Babangida intended to hand over power at all. As the first Nigerian to establish a personal dictatorship, Babangida was the object of increasing scorn for his brazen mismanagement of public funds, his repression of dissent, his inability to reverse the economic crisis, and his costly concessions to the demands of various interest groups. These included swelling the federal system to thirty states and doubling the number of local governments. Christian political militancy rose in reaction to the perception that he was favoring Muslim interests, and religious conflict reached unprecedented levels of intensity and violence.

The 1993 Elections and Aftermath

Surprisingly, to many skeptics, the presidential election process did go forward in early 1993. At the two party conventions one of the country's wealthiest industrialists, Moshood Abiola, emerged as the Social Democratic Party presidential candidate. A relatively young and unknown banker, Bashir Tofa, became the National Republican Convention nominee. Like Shehu Shagari of the Second Republic, Tofa was a Hausa Muslim from the far north. By contrast, as a Yoruba Muslim (and generous philanthropist) whose name was known around the country, Abiola was able to mobilize political support of an ethnic and regional breadth never before seen in Nigeria.

In the June 12, 1993, presidential election, Abiola won a decisive victory, capturing nineteen of the thirty states (including Tofa's home state of Kano) and scoring well in virtually every section of the country. The election was considered the freest, fairest, and most peaceful since independence, perhaps partly because of the light turnout and the doubts about whether its results would count. (Babangida supporters had filed in court to halt the election.)

Abiola became the first southerner (and the first Yoruba) ever elected to head a Nigerian government. But before the results were officially announced, the military embargoed their release and annulled the election. Southerners (in particular Yorubas) were outraged—noting the continuous control of government by northern Muslims since 1979—and intense, sometimes violent, public protest ensued. The National Republican Convention and a faction of Abiola's own Social Democratic Party, however, accepted the annulment in pursuit of their own political interest in new elections.

Fearing arrest, Abiola fled the country. Tension mounted. After weeks of controversy and extensive negotiations among the military and several political factions, President Babangida was forced to resign on August 25, 1993, handing over power to an interim national government headed by a Yoruba businessman, Ernest Shonekan, who had been the figurehead chairman of the Transitional Council since January. All previously elected officials (including the National Assembly) remained in place. But real power remained with the military, now commanded by the long-time defense minister, Gen. Sani Abacha (another northern Muslim).

Once again, as in the first and second republics, the politicians proved unable to bridge their political differences in response to a national crisis. With the country deadlocked over the legitimacy of the June 12 election and the economy reeling from protracted strikes, financial mismanagement, swelling debt, and 90 percent inflation, the Shonekan government floundered. On November 17,

1993, the military reclaimed total power, dismissing all elected officials, suspending the 1989 constitution, and liquidating the transition process.

Although the new military dictator, General Abacha, promised a new democratic transition process and filled his cabinet with civilian politicians from across the political (and regional) spectrum, he seemed intent on trying to prolong his stay in office. A promised Constitutional Conference commenced months later than promised and quickly adjourned in June 1994 because of inadequate housing for delegates. During that June and July the political crisis deepened as disaffected Yorubas and other southerners warned of a breakup of the federation if power was not allowed to rotate among ethnic groups.

On the first anniversary of his election, Abiola was about to declare himself president when he was arrested and charged with treason. Workers in the strategic oil sector went out on strike in support of his claim, and protests spread around the country. The strike was broken after several weeks, but popular discontent with the regime intensified.

This volatile political impasse underscored the deterioration of the country's democratic prospects. Although the military was more discredited and hated than ever—unable to legitimate its rule even with broad civilian participation—it was also reluctant to surrender control over the nation's oil wealth. And the politicians, driven by the same corrupt ambitions as ever, were unable to unite behind a clear alternative. Despite the courageous mobilization for democracy by human rights organizations and other groups in civil society and the vigorous coverage and commentary by the press, the country remained adrift politically. It was less and less capable of managing its profound ethnic, regional, and religious divisions.

It was in this context that the Constitutional Convention reconvened. After nearly a year of work, the convention submitted a draft constitution to the Provisional Ruling Council (PRC) on July 27, 1994. The proposal paid somewhat more attention to regional sensitivities on the selection of the president—under the draft, the presidency would rotate between the north and south—but the conference was strongly resented by many Nigerian democrats, particularly in the southwest. Moreover, in deference to the military regime, the Constitutional Conference proposed no timetable for the transition to civilian, constitutional rule.

Under severe domestic and international pressure to proceed toward democratization, Abacha created his own timetable. In October 1995 he announced a three-year transition that would culminate in civilian rule on October 1, 1998. Only one month after the announcement, however, the regime showed its true nature by hanging dissident activist Kenule Saro-Wiwa and eight of his associates on murder charges that few outside the ruling regime thought credible. International condemnation of the regime followed the executions, from the United Nations, the European Union, the British Commonwealth, and many individual nations.

Despite steps on the path to civilian rule—including the establishment of a National Electoral Commission; March 16, 1996, local elections; and the legal recognition of five political parties in September 1996—it is not certain that the planned end of military rule will come to fruition. The draft constitution remains in limbo, and political repression continues largely unabated.

See also *Africa, Subsaharan*.

BIBLIOGRAPHY

Coleman, James S. *Nigeria: Background to Nationalism.* Berkeley: University of California Press, 1958.

Diamond, Larry. *Class, Ethnicity, and Democracy in Nigeria: The Failure of the First Republic.* London: Macmillan; Syracuse: Syracuse University Press, 1988.

———. "Nigeria: Pluralism, Statism, and the Struggle for Democracy." In *Democracy in Developing Countries: Africa,* edited by Larry Diamond, Juan J. Linz, and Seymour Martin Lipset. Boulder, Colo.: Lynne Rienner; London: Adamantine Press, 1988.

———, and Oyeleye Oyediran. "Military Authoritarianism and Democratic Transition in Nigeria." *National Political Science Review* 4 (1994): 221–244.

Ekeh, Peter P., and Eghosa E. Osaghae, eds. *Federal Character and Federalism in Nigeria.* Ibadan, Nigeria: Heinemann, 1989.

Ekeh, Peter P., Patrick Dele Cole, and Gabriel O. Olusanya. *Politics and Constitutions.* Vol. 5 of Nigeria since Independence: The First Twenty-Five Years. Ibadan, Nigeria: Heinemann, 1988.

Joseph, Richard A. *Democracy and Prebendal Politics in Nigeria: The Rise and Fall of the Second Republic.* London: Cambridge University Press, 1987.

Kirk-Greene, Anthony, and Douglas Rimmer. *Nigeria since 1970: A Political and Economic Outline.* New York: Holmes and Meier, 1981.

Lewis, Peter. "Endgame in Nigeria? The Politics of a Failed Democratic Transition." *African Affairs* 372 (July 1994): 323–340.

Sklar, Richard L. *Nigerian Political Parties: Power in an Emergent African Nation.* Princeton: Princeton University Press, 1963.

Suberu, Rotimi. "The Democratic Recession in Nigeria." *Current History* 93 (May 1994): 213–218.

P

Pakistan

A constitutionally Islamic country of South Asia, founded in 1947, and a test case for Islamic democracy. In its experience with democracy, Pakistan compares well with other constitutionally Islamic states. But when measured by the extent of popular participation, the effectiveness of representative institutions, and commitment to a constitutional order, democratic rule in Pakistan has been inconsistent and shallow.

For more than half the time since its founding, Pakistan has experienced military rule. A parliamentary vote in 1970 was the first conducted under universal suffrage, and the election of 1988 was the first in which a transfer of power occurred smoothly, without military interference. As of the mid-1990s, no government had completed its term of office since the lifting of martial law in 1985. In 1990 a popularly chosen prime minister was dismissed, and the federal legislature was dissolved, by a president who had been chosen indirectly. When, in 1993, the same president again attempted to remove a government, his action was overturned by Pakistan's Supreme Court.

This very mixed picture of democracy in Pakistan raises two questions, which may be related: Why has Pakistan failed to emulate its neighbor India in that country's relative success with democratic institutions? And how instructive are Pakistan's problems in understanding the transition to democracy, especially the compatibility of an Islamic state with liberal democratic institutions?

The Partition and Later Divisions

Pakistan was created in August 1947 as the British, hurriedly departing, partitioned colonial India. The accession to Pakistan of the provinces and districts with the largest concentrations of Muslims met the demands of Muslim nationalists seeking self-determination apart from India's Hindu majority. The two-nation solution left Pakistan itself divided geographically into east and west wings, more than a thousand miles apart. The west encompassed the ethnically distinct provinces of Punjab, Sindh, Baluchistan, and North-West Frontier. The more populous eastern province was dominated by Bengali Muslims.

The two wings were culturally and linguistically distinct and marked by wide economic disparity. For nearly twenty-five years they struggled for political ascendance. After the 1970 elections the eastern wing, led by Mujibur Rahman, was denied the parliamentary control it had won. East Pakistan agitated for sovereignty, only to be brutally suppressed by Pakistan's army. Indian military intervention late in 1971 defeated Pakistani forces and paved the way for Bengali independence as Bangladesh. Still unresolved in Pakistani eyes, however, has been the status of Kashmir. Although predominantly Muslim, at the time of independence Kashmir had a Hindu ruler who brought the state into the Indian union. Three wars later, the issue continues to poison relations between India and Pakistan.

The Decades After Independence

The mass movement that resulted in a separate Islamic state was led by Mohammad Ali Jinnah, who became Pakistan's first head of state. A charismatic leader who had earlier expressed misgivings about parliamentary government, Jinnah was nonetheless committed to free and open elections and to the rule of law in Pakistan. He died in September 1948, just thirteen months after independence. The country's only other political figure of national stature, Liaquat Ali Khan, was assassinated in October 1951. The deaths of these leaders dimmed hopes for legitimizing participatory institutions and building a political consensus through a national party.

For at least the first twenty years of the republic, none

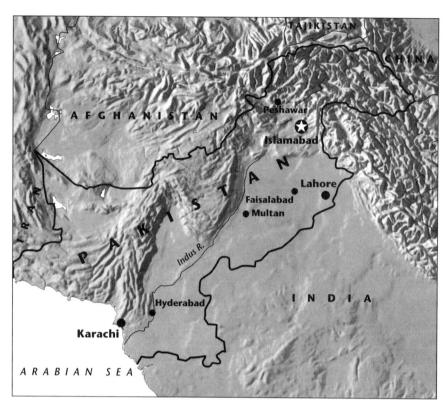

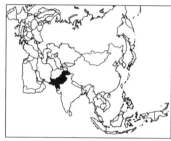

of Pakistan's leaders saw a need to cultivate popular support. The people, in turn, had little understanding of the kind of vigilance necessary for citizens to hold political leaders accountable. Little attention was given to educating the people to practice democracy through meaningful participation in their political affairs. In the absence of effective public opinion, the political system was open to ambitious, corrupt leaders. Power was concentrated in the hands of an elitist bureaucracy and an overbearing military. The semifeudal system on which so much of the country's politics was based was not conducive to building a democracy. Large, wealthy landowning families remained the traditional power brokers, prepared to lend support to any leader who promised to protect their interests.

Jinnah's successors were unable to resolve several basic constitutional issues, the most important of which was provincial autonomy. For example, much dissension followed the decision to impose the Urdu language on the mainly Bengali-speaking population of the eastern province. Politicians from East Pakistan also argued for a proportional system of representation to ensure that Bengali interests would be heard in a future federal legislature. Since Pakistan lacked a formal, written constitution until 1956, precedents were created in the meantime that rapid-

ly undermined parliamentary and democratic norms. For example, in the early years there was a practice of appointing nonparty prime ministers who owed their position to the head of state rather than to a constituency of voters. This contributed to the country's political instability and the failure of its parliamentary system.

Heads of state after Jinnah came from the ranks of the bureaucracy rather than from the Parliament. Having little feel for democratic politics, they often governed in an arbitrary fashion. The concept of impartiality that Jinnah had tried to instill was damaged by the appointments and dismissals of Ghulam Mohammad as governor general. Ghulam Mohammad, a former civil servant and a Punjabi, had replaced a Bengali, Khwaja Nazimuddin, who became prime minister in 1951. Ghulam Mohammad's removal of Nazimuddin from that position in 1953, while the prime minister still commanded a majority in the Constituent Assembly, revealed the governor general's disdain for parliamentary procedures and his determination to expand the powers of his office. Ghulam Mohammad's decision the following year to dissolve the Assembly and impose central rule, or governor's rule, in the provinces further undercut democratic practice.

As a consequence, lines of authority became increasingly vague. With legislators locked in constitutional debate, the running of the country fell to the permanent bureaucracy. Meanwhile, the Muslim League, which had spearheaded the independence movement, degenerated in the public's eyes from a body of men speaking for the whole nation to a collection of squabbling, self-aggrandizing politicians.

Martial Law

Pakistan, like India, inherited a tradition of the military's detachment from active involvement in politics. Within a decade after partition, however, civil-military relations in the two countries sharply diverged. In India, the practice of having regular elections took deep root in the political culture. India also had the benefit of retaining the leadership of Jawaharlal Nehru for sixteen years after independence. Over those years democratic practices became institutionalized, and India was able to avoid a highly personalized system of government. The supremacy of the civil authority established under India's constitution of 1950 contrasts with Pakistan's constant struggle to head off military rule and revive disintegrating political institutions.

In 1958 weak parties and unelected, ineffective governments gave way to the martial law regime of Gen. Mohammad Ayub Khan. As president, Ayub Khan in 1962 offered a constitution that called for a system of "Basic Democracies." The constitution, adopted that same year, centralized national political power in the presidency, leaving the legislature little control over finances and legislation. It established a pyramidal, four-tiered system, providing for administrative responsibilities and local government, as well as national development. Local bodies acted as electoral units in contests for the presidency and National Assembly. In Ayub Khan's view, the only sound political system was one that was home-grown. The system supposedly had older roots in the *panchayats*, or local governing bodies, of historic India. Democracy's failures in Pakistan were seen as resulting from the importation of alien institutions from the West. Parliamentary democracy, Ayub Khan believed, tended to divide people when Pakistan needed unity and singleness of purpose.

Besides serving to legitimize Ayub Khan's regime, the system of Basic Democracies was expected to help mobilize people and educate them to participate in local affairs. Its localized, indirect system of elections was said to be particularly well suited to largely illiterate rural populations, making the government process more meaningful to them. In practice, the system severely limited popular par-

ticipation. Eighty thousand "Basic Democrats" were designated to elect the National Assembly. Local units fell under the influence of government officials and council chairmen, and ordinary citizens were kept out of politics.

Ayub Khan's constitution, and with it his regime, came to a turbulent end in March 1969. Student-led demonstrations, backed by a new political organization headed by former government official, Zulfikar Ali Bhutto, spread from West Pakistan to East Pakistan. The protests against restrictions on political activity and the press and against the government's educational policies led Ayub Khan to resign in favor of Gen. Agha Mohammad Yahya Khan. As president, Yahya Khan reimposed martial law and promised a new constitution. He also scheduled for December 1970 Pakistan's first general election among the entire adult population. In contests for a National Assembly, Bhutto's Pakistan People's Party was dominant in the western provinces, but Mujibur Rahman's Awami League held a clear majority of legislative seats and moved into a position to draft the new constitution. Bhutto and his supporters, however, prevented the convening of the Assembly the following March. This failure to honor the election led to a general strike and administrative paralysis in East Pakistan, which provoked the army's crackdown against a fast-growing independence movement. After the Indian army's invasion and quick defeat of Pakistan in December 1971, Yahya Khan was forced to quit. He transferred the presidency of the now truncated country to its most popular politician, Zulfikar Ali Bhutto.

Bhutto and Zia

The 1970 election did more than legitimize Bhutto's ascension to power. It marked the first time that a party in Pakistan could claim to reflect the will of a majority of the people, at least in the western provinces. Offering a quasi-socialist program, Bhutto's Pakistan People's Party achieved the mass mobilization of the electorate, communicating effectively with rural voters for the first time. The election set the standard in Pakistan for orderly and honest balloting.

In 1973 legislators, under Bhutto's leadership, approved Pakistan's most democratic constitution, which contained guarantees for fundamental rights. Although Bhutto initially emphasized the supremacy of the people and asserted civilian control of the military, in time he abandoned this populist ideology. Rather than work through participatory institutions, he strongly personalized his power. To deal with his enemies, Bhutto resorted to constitutional changes, and he came to rely on military and paramilitary forces. In maneuvering for the March 1977 elections, he restored ties with the landed families that were still locally powerful. Pakistan had made some progress toward increased participation, but Bhutto had failed to deliver a liberal state, one that was able to tolerate a legitimate political opposition. At the same time, the regime's opponents were never fully willing to trust the system.

The parliamentary elections of March 1977 that officially returned Bhutto to office as prime minister were delegitimized by evidence of widespread fraud. Demonstrations organized by a coalition of opposition parties nearly brought the country to a standstill. As a result, Bhutto's handpicked army chief, Gen. Mohammad Zia ul-Haq, was able to seize power in July 1977 with claims of restoring order and instituting truly Islamic rule. As president, Zia repeatedly refused to hold promised elections. Not until 1985 did he agree to share power with an appointed civilian government and allow a nonparty election for the legislature. Zia had legitimized his continued hold on the presidency with a national referendum in December 1984 and through revisions of the 1973 constitution. Most important was the eighth amendment, which he pressed on legislators in 1985. This amendment assured wide discretionary powers for the president in post–martial-law governments. Zia was then able to dissolve the federal legislature and call fresh elections as well as to make senior government and military appointments. Critics charge that the eighth amendment perpetuates the kind of arbitrary rule that undercuts the authority of elected officials and renders a democratic mandate nearly meaningless.

Contemporary Politics

Zia ul-Haq's death in an airplane crash in August 1988 paved the way for a party-based election in which the Pakistan People's Party under Benazir Bhutto assumed power. Bhutto is the daughter of the former prime minister. The Zia regime, fearing her father's return to power, had had him executed in 1979 for complicity in the murder of an opposition politician some years earlier.

Benazir Bhutto promised to strengthen constitutionally protected liberties, notably for women. Once in office as prime minister, however, she found her policies constrained by military and religious leaders. After just twenty-one months, she was dismissed by President Ghulam Ishaq Khan and replaced by a caretaker government. Initially, it seemed that democracy had been dealt a severe blow. These concerns were eased, however, when elections

were held as promised in October 1990, and Bhutto and her party were allowed to compete in a reasonably honest contest. Bhutto's party lost the election.

Although marked by some demagoguery and violence, the elections of 1988 and 1990 had seemed to signal a gradual strengthening of the democratic system. This was again cast in doubt by President Ishaq Khan's attempt to oust Prime Minister Mian Mohammad Nawaz Sharif in April 1993, followed nearly three months later by the resignation of both men, under pressure by the military. Military leaders were impatient with the political struggle and resolved to hold army-supervised parliamentary elections.

Rather than instituting a martial-law regime leading up to new elections, the military supported an interim civilian government headed by Moeen Qureshi, a former senior vice president of the World Bank. An outsider without political debts to pay, Qureshi implemented bold economic and anticorruption measures, although not all his ordinances survived the necessary parliamentary approval. In national elections on October 6, 1993, Benazir Bhutto's People's Party captured eighty-five seats. With the support of thirty-six other legislators, Bhutto formed a coalition government in the National Assembly. Soon after, in provincial assembly elections, and in a combined vote of national and provincial legislators that chose the country's new president, her followers tightened their political control.

Although the election results appeared to leave Prime Minister Bhutto with a freer hand than she had had in her earlier term to chart policy and stabilize Pakistan's democracy, she disappointed many. She tolerated corruption, permitted abuse of political opponents, and acquiesced in discrimination against minorities. Citing these factors as well as allegations of mismanaging the economy, President Sardar Farooq Ahmad Khan Leghari dismissed Bhutto on November 5, 1996. Malek Meraj Khalid was named her successor, and new elections were scheduled for February 1997. More than six thousand candidates representing thirty parties contested the 217 seats in the legislature. Four parties won 9 or more seats. Bhutto's Pakistan People's Party won only 17 seats amid allegations of election fraud. But Bhutto did not press the allegations. The Pakistan Muslim League, with 134 seats, had a comfortable ruling majority.

The Issue of Islamic Democracy

A history of weak democratic accountability in Pakistan raises the question of who or what is to blame. Many observers cite a poor quality of leadership and failures of institutional design, while others point to the absence of a supportive, participatory political culture. Ayub Khan claimed that because Muslims historically had never known real sovereignty in the predominantly Hindu subcontinent, they had difficulty adjusting psychologically to their new freedom as Pakistanis.

Still others trace the problem specifically to education and the Islamic religion. The most common assertion is that Islam, by basing ultimate authority in God's word, must reject the principle that sovereignty lies in the will of the people. The Sunni branch of Islam recognizes the concept of elevating rulers by election. Nonetheless, regimes in the Islamic world have so far derived little of their legitimacy from authentic popular forces expressed through representative institutions. Likewise, they have not tempered their authority with tolerance for those who disagree with them. To many critics, Islam fails to support democratic values because it makes no provision for legitimate opposition and allows only second-class citizenship to non-Muslims. Islam is also said to have a particular reverence for the military. The concept of holy war gives the military the kind of prestige that inevitably leaves civilian-run democratic rule vulnerable.

At a minimum, a religiously prescribed constitution for Pakistan would place certain prohibitions on the majority's lawmaking powers. Whether such restrictions, along with limits on the civil rights of minorities, would fatally compromise a modern democratic system is debatable. It is notable that Pakistan's radical Islamic parties have never gained wide popular support. Pakistan could in fact be a test case for determining whether extensions of democratic practice can accommodate and moderate militant Islamic political movements.

Elected officials in Pakistan have had difficulty competing with a military that is integrated, disciplined, and respected. Pakistan's institutions are sufficiently weak and discredited, and its politicians are held in enough contempt, that the military has easily dislodged them. Civilian regimes were subject to military dominance from 1962 to 1968 and from 1985 to 1988, and the country came under complete martial law during 1958–1962, 1969–1971, and 1977–1985. From the mid-1950s on, the influence of the military was bolstered by assistance from China, Saudi Arabia, the United States, and other nations. Especially during the Afghan conflict, from 1979 to 1989—when Pakistan acted as host to about 3.2 million Afghan refugees and largely orchestrated the activities of exiled party leaders—the weapons and training received strengthened the military's confidence and status. When in power, military regimes—most effectively the Zia government—contained political activity while scoring some economic successes. Full legitimacy has continued to elude the military, however, when it has grasped a governing role in Pakistan's politics.

The military's restraint after Zia's death, as seen in its willingness to abide by the constitution, appeared to be a serious attempt to respect elected governments. In the ongoing power struggle between feudal families and bureaucrats, on the one hand, and industrialists and the middle class, on the other, the military became an arbiter. But not all military leaders are reconciled to losing direct management. The military carved out for itself areas of policy dominance—management of the Afghan war, nuclear development, and the conflict over Kashmir. Civilian governments faced with ethnic crises in the provinces found themselves dependent on military forces to restore law and order. To keep the loyalty of the military, governments have had to allocate a large segment of the country's resources to defense expenditures.

For democracy to prosper in Pakistan, it must survive the elites that subvert it in pursuit of economic interests, ideologies, and personal ambitions. Democracy must also ensure reasonable security from external enemies who are widely perceived as threatening the state, especially now, in the region's nuclear age. The tensions that threaten a major war between Pakistan and India may severely test the proposition that democracies do not fight one another. Over the long haul, liberal civilian governments must demonstrate their ability to function as well as or better than authoritarian ones. They will have to overcome wide economic disparities, allow for sustained development, and avoid corruption and mismanagement.

Pakistan's democratic institutions and elected leaders may be judged most of all by their solutions to the country's disruptive ethnic and regional problems. Despite the common religious identity that justified the state's creation, its varied population—Punjabi, Sindhi, Pathan, and Baluchi—has yet to shed the resentments and distrust that deny Pakistan its full nationhood.

See also *India.*

BIBLIOGRAPHY

Callard, Keith. *Pakistan: A Political Study.* London: Allen and Unwin, 1957.

Khan, Mohammad Ayub. *Friends Not Masters.* London: Oxford University Press, 1967.

Richter, William. "The 1990 General Elections in Pakistan." In *Pak-*

istan 1992, edited by Charles H. Kennedy. Boulder, Colo.: West-view Press, 1992.

Rizvi, Hasan-Askari. "The Legacy of Military Rule in Pakistan." *Survival* 31 (May–June 1989): 255–268.

Rounaq, Jahan. *Pakistan: Failure in National Integration.* New York and London: Columbia University Press, 1972.

Safdar, Mahmood. *A Political Study of Pakistan.* Lahore: Sh. Muhammad Ashraf, 1975.

Wriggins, Howard W., ed. *Pakistan in Transition.* Islamabad: University of Islamabad Press, 1975.

Ziring, Lawrence, Ralph Braibanti, and Howard W. Wriggins, eds. *Pakistan: The Long View.* Durham, N.C.: Duke University Press, 1977.

Philippines

A nation of Southeast Asia spread over an archipelago of some 7,000 islands, which gained independence from the United States in 1946. Although large numbers of Muslims live on the southern Philippine island of Mindanao, about 90 percent of Filipinos are Catholic Christians. The Spanish brought Catholicism to the Philippines during their centuries of colonization. After the United States colonized the Philippines, English became the language of the educated. Eventually it became the main language in the school system and in official Philippine government documents. English is the language Filipinos use when they meet other Filipinos who speak a different dialect of the national language, Pilipino.

After independence, the Philippines became known as Southeast Asia's "showcase of democracy." In terms of the formal institutions of government, that description is accurate. In the postindependence period, up to the time of martial law, which began in 1972 under Ferdinand Marcos's administration, and since the administration of Corazon Aquino, who was elected president in 1986, the Philippine government carried out its functions on the basis of constitutional guidelines, the separation of powers, and adherence to a bill of rights.

Colonialism and Dynastic Politics

The reality is different from the formal structure. The Spanish colonized the Philippines almost five hundred years ago, and ever after the nation was ruled by a few family dynasties that controlled both the economic and the political sphere. The Philippines is the only country in Southeast Asia that was colonized before indigenous institutions had been established. From the great haciendas of the Spaniards to the patronage politics during the American period, through the period of independence and continuing in the early 1990s, these dynasties ruled in a baronial, feudal manner, each controlling a particular area of the archipelago.

Even after the People's Power revolt of 1986, which ousted the authoritarian government of Ferdinand Marcos and installed the democratic Corazon Aquino as president, a group of provincial barons commanded the rural areas. In Cebu Province, for example, the governor, the mayor of Cebu City, and the national member of Congress were all named Osmena. All were members of a politically powerful clan once led by a former president. That system remained essentially the same throughout Filipino history.

The nature of the country—spread over thousands of islands, many of them quite small—was partly responsible for its decentralized, dynastic system. In addition, pervasive poverty taught the poor to rely on their wealthy patrons. Dynastic families sponsored the weddings of their laborers and tenants, paid for children's education, and cared for the sick. This kind of aid formed a relationship of dependence that kept the poor deferential and loyal. In the absence of strong government institutions, patron-client relations developed to meet the needs of the poor people who made up the majority of the population.

Culture also helped shape the dynastic character of Philippine politics. A Filipino's loyalty is directed first to family, then to close friends, then to the local community, then to personally known political leaders, and finally to distant, impersonal governmental agencies. All these concentric circles of allegiance place emphasis on the personal nature of loyalty. Still, an individual's family and "patron family" demand the deepest loyalties.

As a result of colonialism, Filipinos often tend to feel that everything Filipino is second-rate, while everything Western is first-rate. Thus many Filipinos have a feeling of national inferiority, so their support for the nation's governmental system is weak compared with support for family and patrons. Filipino elites are often alienated from their roots and from the masses of the people, most of whom they scorn. The first priority of the elites is self-interest, not the public good. Such values are not conducive to democratic rule, a form of government that requires mutual trust and respect for different points of view.

Party Politics from Marcos to Aquino

For democratization to take root in the Philippines, the formal institutions of government will have to become more than façades for oligarchical rule. From independence to Marcos's declaration of martial law in 1972, the Philippines had a two-party system. The Liberal and Nacionalista parties held power in alternation, with neither party able to reelect its presidential nominee. The ideological differences between the two parties were negligible, and neither party appeared to represent the interests of the vast majority of Filipinos. For the most part, the two parties served to get out the vote for specific candidates.

Under Marcos, one party dominated the political scene. Marcos's New Society Movement was a noncompetitive, authoritarian party devoted to keeping Marcos in power. In the post–martial-law era after 1981, the New Society Movement continued to dominate politics. Opposition parties began to emerge, however, the most important of which was the United Nationalist Democratic Organization (Unido), an alliance of establishment politicians. Unido eventually supported Aquino when she became a candidate for president in 1986. Parties played little role in the 1992 election, when seven candidates vied for the presidency.

The remarkable grassroots movement called the People's Power revolt included Filipinos from every socioeconomic class. In February 1986 they succeeded in ousting Marcos and installing Aquino. Nonetheless the election of Aquino was more a restoration of certain families (and the demise of a few who had aligned with Marcos) than a revolution. The overwhelming majority of newly elected senators and representatives in 1986 were members of families that had dominated Filipino politics for centuries. Although the persons in charge of the government changed, the people's power movement marked no fundamental change in the character of the Philippine political system.

The inability of Aquino to restructure the feudal socioeconomic system in the Philippines detracted somewhat from her success in reviving constitutional rule, free elections, freedom of the press, and autonomous institutions accountable to the public. Although personalism remained an integral part of Filipino politics under Aquino, corruption and cronyism declined, compared with the era of Marcos.

Past and Present Problems

Aquino inherited a profoundly difficult and complex situation, one that could not easily be resolved even by the outstanding economists she brought to her administration. The problems that beset the Philippines under Aquino were the same as those of the past: economic in-

equality, land disputes, monopolistic industries, corrupt leadership, and an elite class concerned more with self-interest than with the public good. Such problems could be resolved only by fundamental changes in all areas of Filipino life, including the social, economic, cultural, and political realms. For most Filipinos, the standard of living remained the lowest in the Association of Southeast Asian Nations. This was a galling fact for a people who live in a country with rich natural resources, who are highly literate and well educated, and who have more experience with democratic rule than other nations in Southeast Asia.

Aquino's rise to power was the quintessential example of democratization in 1986 and may have indirectly encouraged the people of Burma (Myanmar) to stage their own version of "people's power." The triumphs and travails of the Aquino regime, however, were a product of indigenous culture and behavior. The demise of communist states and the new international era played little role in

Philippine domestic politics. Only in the realm of foreign relations, particularly with regard to military bases, did the end of the cold war influence Philippine policy making.

The overriding unmet challenge in the Philippines is to fashion a stable political structure that is predictable enough for the development of external economic ties and domestic entrepreneurship. In the past the Philippines has been a model for how not to develop economically. The growth of the gross domestic product (GDP) in the Philippines has been negligible for almost two decades. In 1992 the GDP grew 1 percent in the Philippines, compared with 8 percent in the other countries in the Association of Southeast Asian Nations. The nation's high population growth (2.6 percent per year) also limited real economic growth.

The country's economic difficulties resulted in part from the Marcos years, when the economy was characterized by crony capitalism. Coveted contracts were frequently given to incompetent presidential clients rather than to effective contractors. Marcos gave his best friends monopoly control over the sugar and coconut industries, thus allowing them to amass fabulous riches that ended up in Swiss and U.S. bank accounts. The flight of capital subverted the national economy and brought it to the brink of disaster.

In Thailand, Malaysia, Singapore, and Indonesia, capital from Japan, Taiwan, South Korea, and the United States stimulated and sustained economic growth. Such foreign investment, however, never took off in the Philippines. Seven military coup attempts against President Aquino, from 1986 to 1992, frightened away trade, aid, and investment. Thus, even after the fall of President Marcos, the democratic Aquino administration was not able to solve the nation's problems. President Aquino was not a strong enough leader to transform the democratic façade of Philippine government into democratic practice. That goal could be attained only through fundamental changes made by political leaders willing to undercut their own privileged positions.

In the 1980s and early 1990s natural calamities, including floods, hurricanes, and volcanic eruptions, devastated the islands and hampered efforts to build needed infrastructure. Such disasters added to the economic and political morass. The government's inefficient response to the crises also undermined citizen support for the system.

The Philippines is an example of a state that intervened in the economic system with ruinous results. The Philippine government critically hurt the economy through its corrupt intervention and its subservience to the traditional economic dynasties. For their part, the dynasties, with their power bases in the provinces, were often at odds with state authorities.

Domestic insurgency is another of the many problems that subverted political stability in the Philippines in the postindependence period. Although there was evidence of a decline in the number of New People's Army insurgents after President Aquino's election victory, the dire economic conditions suggested that the decline might be temporary. The armed forces managed to capture or co-opt leaders of the New People's Army, and the military became more professional in counterinsurgency activities. And the decision by the Philippine Senate in 1992 to remove U.S. troops from Subic and Clark military bases deprived the insurgents of a principal point of their propaganda: the claim that the Philippine government was a lackey of "imperialist America." Nonetheless insurgency could rise again in the face of economic decline and administrative incompetence.

Still another cause of domestic instability in the Philippines was the excessive administrative centralization of government, which crushed entrepreneurial and creative efforts by the citizenry. The oversized bureaucracy strangled every area it controlled, including such basic services as electricity, water, garbage collection, telecommunications, police protection, and education.

The Ramos Presidency

Fidel Ramos was elected president in May 1992 for a six-year term. Like Aquino, he faced the ubiquitous corruption that undercut the legitimacy of every postindependence government. Waiting for the propitious moment to intervene was the army, whose commitment to professionalism and civilian rule was nominal.

In his campaign against six other major candidates for president, Ramos won only 24 percent of the vote. Many of the supporters of losing candidates believed that Ramos was elected through fraud. Six weeks elapsed before a final vote tabulation was announced; the interval provided numerous opportunities for cheating. Moreover, because Ramos's party supporters in the Senate and House constituted a small minority, there was little chance that a coherent program could be enacted. The new president lacked charisma that would help lift the spirit of Filipinos and mobilize them to enact fundamental changes. Furthermore, Ramos did not have the loyal backing of the factionalized armed forces.

Thus after the 1992 elections the chances for needed reform were not good. To pull the Philippines out of its predicament, Ramos needed to reform the economy. Reforms would mean opening the country to foreign investment, ending cronyism by basing economic decisions on merit, eliminating corruption, and creating a workable tax system. The nation's infrastructure, especially the production of power, needed to be overhauled to end the constant electrical brownouts that sapped industrial output. State-owned enterprises needed to be privatized.

Politically, the new president had to modernize the bureaucracy, decentralize decision making, and find ways to make the dynastic families contribute to the nation's best interests. He also needed to reinvigorate ties with the United States, which had deteriorated following rejection of the Military Base Agreement by the Philippine Senate. U.S. aid programs were greatly reduced, and only a diplomat of middle rank (the director of the Peace Corps) was sent to attend Ramos's inauguration. Without support from abroad, the massive problems of the Philippines could not be solved.

Five years into his six-year term, Ramos had made no more than marginal progress on any front. Muslim extremists continued to challenge the government despite ceasefires negotiated with a few of the smaller factions. Food shortages and tax increases led to sporadic strikes and demonstrations in 1996, and government corruption remained endemic. More than a decade after the fall of the Marcos regime, the economic, social, and political foundations of Philippine democracy were still shaky.

See also *Asia, Southeast.*

BIBLIOGRAPHY

Bonner, Raymond. *Waltzing with a Dictator.* New York: Times Books, 1987.

De Guzman, Raul P., and Mila A. Reforma, eds. *Government and Politics of the Philippines.* Singapore: Oxford University Press, 1988.

Greene, Fred, ed. *The Philippine Bases: Negotiating for the Future.* New York: Council on Foreign Relations, 1988.

Hawes, Gary. *The Philippine State and the Marcos Regime: The Politics of Export.* Ithaca, N.Y.: Cornell University Press, 1987.

Johnson, Bryan. *The Four Days of Courage.* New York: Free Press, 1987.

Kerkvliet, Benedict. *Everyday Politics in the Philippines.* Berkeley: University of California Press, 1990.

Kessler, Richard J. *Rebellion and Repression in the Philippines.* New Haven and London: Yale University Press, 1989.

Lande, Carl H. *Rebuilding a Nation: Philippine Challenges and American Policy.* Washington, D.C.: Washington Institute, 1987.

Steinberg, David Joel. *The Philippines: A Singular and Plural Place.* 2d ed. Boulder, Colo.: Westview Press, 1990.

Wurfel, David. *Filipino Politics: Development and Decay.* Ithaca, N.Y.: Cornell University Press, 1988.

S

Senegal

A democracy in West Africa dominated by a single party, now the Socialist Party. The French colony of Senegal emerged in the mid-nineteenth century from a handful of trading posts on the Atlantic shoreline: St. Louis, Dakar, Rufisque, and Gorée. Before then the area was dominated by powerful chiefs and Muslim religious leaders, especially of the Wolof or Fulani groups. The Wolof now account for 44 percent of Senegal's population; Fulani speakers, 23 percent; and the Serer, 15 percent, according to the 1988 census. Muslims account for 85 percent of the population; Catholics, 5 percent; and African traditional religions, 5 to 10 percent. Senegal became independent in 1960, about the same time most of the states of France's African empire gained their independence.

Historical Background

Electoral democracy in Senegal dates to 1848, when the inhabitants of the French colony in this West African territory were awarded the right to elect a deputy to the French National Assembly. This was a year of revolutionary enthusiasm in France. Senegal's electoral right was withdrawn by Napoleon III in 1851, but it was restored under the French Third Republic in 1875. From then on Senegal had not only an elected deputy in Paris but also elected municipal governments in the coastal communes. A legacy of 1848 was suffrage for all adult males born in the communes, regardless of race, making Senegal a pioneer of voting rights in black Africa.

Democratic politics in the colonial communes was, to be sure, a corrupt enough tradition, dominated by the money of the French trading companies and the political weight of the colonial administration. The ordinary voter was usually glad to sell his vote at a very modest price. The

deputies were all white Frenchmen until 1902, and the Senegalese seat was seen as being in the gift of the French government of the day. In 1902 a Senegalese trader of mixed race, François Carpot, was elected deputy, and from 1914 to 1934 Blaise Diagne, the first black African to serve in the French Parliament, was regularly reelected deputy. Diagne was the master politician of the commune tradition, corrupt on a grand scale but also a man with enough independent power to bring about the nomination of a colonial governor of Senegal in 1930.

The revival of democratic politics in Senegal after World War II extended the electorate beyond the coastal towns into the rural hinterland. The dominant Senegalese politician in this postwar period was Léopold Sédar Senghor. In 1948 Senghor created the Senegalese Democratic Bloc, a political party that was based on his recognition of the indispensable role of rural notables in reaching a rural electorate. The notables in question, particularly the leaders of the country's Sufi Muslim brotherhoods, were often in a position to deliver the votes of their clienteles: this system was democracy based on the patronage principle.

Thanks to the support of these rural notables, who in turn enjoyed the support of their own clienteles, the Senegalese Democratic Bloc won the elections of 1951 and 1952, assuring its lasting hegemony. Since that time the dominant party has changed its name three times and its leader once, but it has never failed to win an election.

The First Years of Independence

Léopold Senghor's presidency during the first twenty years of Senegalese independence (1960–1980), and the domination of his party, were contested at first (1960–1966) by politicians and parties of the left or extreme left. These parties were in general based in urban areas, and Senghor's strategy was to portray them as representatives of urban privilege. (He relied on his own excellent connections with the rural Muslim aristocracy.) Senghor's tactic was also to work toward the incorporation of political opposition within his own party, picking out particular opposition leaders and offering them cabinet positions. This tactic appeared to have reached its logical conclusion in 1966, when the last legally recognized opposition party, the African Congress Party, joined the governing party, then called the Senegalese Progressive Union; three leaders of the African Congress Party then joined the government. Within this process of incorporation, a mediated democracy was at work: politicians usually did not receive an offer from the government unless they enjoyed substantial popular support and thus had something of value to contribute to the governing coalition.

The gentle art of coalition building was accompanied by occasional measures of severity against opponents who were considered to be dangerous. For example, Mamadou Dia, Senghor's first prime minister, spent thirteen years in detention after allegedly leading a coup d'état in 1962. When severe action by the president was needed (during this attempted coup in 1962 or the general strike in 1968), it was more than useful to be able to call on support from the French army, which since independence has maintained a base in the Senegalese capital and elsewhere in valued former colonies in Africa. A French armed presence has helped to ensure the survival of civilian regimes in Côte d'Ivoire and Cameroon as well as Senegal.

The decade from 1966 to 1976 was a period of de facto single-party government in Senegal, although clandestine opposition survived, notably in the capital city of Dakar.

This opposition, in general coming from the left, was centered at the University of Dakar. Although sometimes derisively labeled the politics of the "little groups," or *groupuscules,* the opposition could assume threatening proportions, as in June 1968 when protesting students and striking trade unions nearly brought down the Senghor regime. Supplementary patronage expenditures together with a hint of coercion saw the regime through that particular crisis.

A form of electoral democracy survived even under these single-party conditions. The governing Senegalese Progressive Union held elections to choose the party candidates for the National Assembly (or municipal council). These internal elections were contested by factional groupings—"clans" in local parlance. Clan politics focus on personalities rather than on ideologies or political programs. Elections are often bitterly contested, with all eyes fixed on the prize of office and the expected rewards of victory. The sale of party cards in an annual membership drive to known supporters is fundamental to building a winning clan, together, of course, with the denial of cards to the enemy. This style of factional politics has a genuinely adversarial quality; violence is deployed as well as supernatural sanctions (the semi-Muslim magic of *maraboutage).*

Multiparty Politics

Beginning in 1974, multiparty politics revived in Senegal, perhaps because Senghor wanted to prepare the political conditions for his own retirement. A 1976 constitutional revision specified the creation of a tripartite political structure, with one party to the left (Marxist-Leninist or communist), another party to the right (liberal and democratic), and a third party in the center (socialist and democratic). Suitable candidates then declared themselves for these ideological slots: Mahjmout Diop's African Independence Party, banned since 1961 as a subversive communist organization, took up the position to the left; Abdoulaye Wade's Senegalese Democratic Party under some ideological protest took up the position to the right; and the governing party, soon to be renamed the Socialist Party, took the strategic center ground.

The first elections to be held under this new dispensation came in 1978 and gave the Socialist Party its expected majority (82 seats out of 100), with the Senegalese Democratic Party taking the remaining seats (18). Since that time the Democratic Party has consistently been the principal challenger to the governing party. When Senghor resigned as president at the end of 1980, the constitution designated the prime minister, Abdou Diouf, his successor. One of Diouf's first important initiatives, in April 1981, was to open up the field of multiparty electoral competition. Henceforward there was to be no ideological restriction to the registration of political parties, and any number could be legally recognized provided that they were not based on primordial identifications such as language, region, or religion. The early years of Diouf's presidency were marked by general popular approval of this youthful leader of apparent integrity and energy.

Many aspiring political leaders came forward after Diouf unblocked party registration, but most of the new parties were university based, the *groupuscules* in legal form. Marxism, in effect, went legal and appeared to have little audience outside the capital city, indeed beyond the university precinct. But Wade's Democratic Party was another matter, with branches throughout most of the country, even in regions previously considered to be part of the governing party's heartland. This party could present itself as a viable reformist alternative to the governing Socialist Party, with new faces if not such strikingly new policies, and with a flair for the effective electoral campaign.

Prospects for Change

The Senegalese Democratic Party distilled its message to a single telling word in the 1988 campaign, the word *change,* taken up by the party's supporters in the streets. The officially declared results gave little indication of the party's surge: 103 National Assembly seats went to the Socialist Party, and the remaining 17 seats to the Senegalese Democratic Party, while Diouf received 74 percent of the vote for president and Abdoulaye Wade received 26 percent. Serious rioting followed the declaration of these results. Cars were burned and buildings looted. Wade and his principal associates were jailed for several days.

The Senegalese Democratic Party vehemently denounced the following examples of electoral malpractice in the 1988 campaign: the secret ballot was no more than "optional"; the polling card came with no photograph attached (allowing multiple voting); and the vote was counted in the capital city by civil servants behind doors that were closed to all observers from the opposition parties. Most of those civil servants were members of the governing party, and they were in a position to make up their own electoral result. It would appear in this case that the Senegalese Democratic Party did very much better than the official results indicated and may even have won in some of the cities.

Wade lost much of his crowd appeal when he accepted a position in the Diouf government (April 1991–October 1992), a position he said was essential to win reform of electoral procedures. The next elections, in February 1993, were for the presidency, with Wade and Diouf as the main candidates. Although the principal defects of the electoral system appeared to have been eliminated, the result was the usual crushing victory for the government candidate (Diouf received 58 percent; Wade received 32 percent). Protests this time were lame, and it appeared that the opposition had run out of belief in its principal candidate. In addition, the patronage resources of the governing party were, as usual, formidable at election time.

Despite the continuing electoral advantages of the Socialist Party and further allegations of fraud, the Socialist Party lost 19 seats in the National Assembly elections of May 1993. The Senegalese Democratic Party gained 10; still, it was outnumbered by the Socialists 84 seats to 27 in the 120–seat body. (Four minor parties split the remaining 9 seats.) The Democratic Party should have been invigorated by achieving a greater voice in the national legislature. To the contrary, it was in such disarray that Wade accepted a cabinet post in August 1995, and, along with two other opposition groups, the Democratic Party joined the Socialist government.

Senegalese democracy thus remains without an opposition electoral victory. Although the country's economic stagnation has made the government unpopular, most evidently in the capital city, its downfall at the polls appears unlikely. Senegal remains fortunate in being able to call on substantial foreign economic assistance, particularly from France, while living under the tightened financial discipline of structural adjustment policies since 1979–1980. And the country's democratic reputation appears to stimulate the generosity of international donors. Because its agricultural sector is stagnant, and local industry is hopelessly uncompetitive, democracy may have become the country's most reliable source of foreign exchange.

BIBLIOGRAPHY

Coulon, Christian. "Senegal: The Development and Fragility of Semidemocracy." In *Politics in Developing Countries: Comparing Experiences with Democracy,* edited by Larry Diamond et al. Boulder, Colo.: Lynne Rienner, 1995.

Cruise O'Brien, D. B. *Saints and Politicians: Essays in the Organisation of a Senegalese Peasant Society.* Cambridge: Cambridge University Press, 1976.

———, and C. Coulon. "Senegal." In *Contemporary West African States,* edited by D. B. Cruise O'Brien, J. Dunn, and R. Rathbone. Cambridge and New York: Cambridge University Press, 1989.

Diop, M. C., ed. *Sénégal: Trajectoires d'un état.* Dakar/Paris: Codesria/Karthala, 1992.

Fatton, Robert, Jr. *The Making of a Liberal Democracy: Senegal's Passive Revolution, 1975–1985.* Boulder, Colo.: Lynne Rienner, 1987.

Gellar, Sheldon. *Senegal: An African Nation between Islam and the West.* Aldershot: Gower; Boulder, Colo.: Westview Press, 1986.

Kanté, Babacar. "Senegal's Empty Election." *Journal of Democracy* 5 (January 1994): 96–108.

Vaillant, Janet G. *Black, French, and African: A Life of Léopold Sédar Senghor.* Cambridge, Mass., and London: Harvard University Press, 1990.

Singapore

An island city-state in Southeast Asia at the southern end of the Malay Peninsula, which gained independence in 1965 and has undergone rapid modernization. Singapore's principal resource is its people. The 3.1 million citizens are about 77 percent Chinese, 14 percent Malay, 7 percent Indian, and 2 percent other ethnic groups. Singaporeans, who live in a densely populated city, are the wealthiest, best housed, and healthiest people in Southeast Asia. They also enjoy the most Westernized conveniences and public services of the region.

In the 1960s Singapore was still little more than a swampy port facility for the British, who had begun colonizing the area in the early 1800s. Sir Stamford Raffles, an agent for the British East India Company, first established British control over Singapore in 1819.

Occupied by the Japanese during World War II, Singapore became a British Crown Colony in 1946. It attained self-rule in internal affairs in 1959 and in 1963 joined Malaya, Sarawak, and Sabah in the Federation of Malaysia. The incorporation of Singapore into Malaysia was intended to ensure economic stability by providing an agricultural base and to ensure national security against perceived communist advances. Malaysia ousted Singapore in 1965, however, because it feared Chinese dominance over politics in the new federation.

Lee Kuan Yew, who had been educated at the British universities of Oxford and Cambridge, became prime minister of Singapore in 1957. He led his country to complete independence in 1965, amid much concern on the part of the nation's leaders that Singapore would not be able to cope on its own. Lee led Singapore to economic heights unparalleled in the rest of Southeast Asia. He stepped down as prime minister in 1990, allowing his deputy, Goh Chok Tong, to become prime minister, while Lee became the "senior minister." Goh emphasized Lee's style

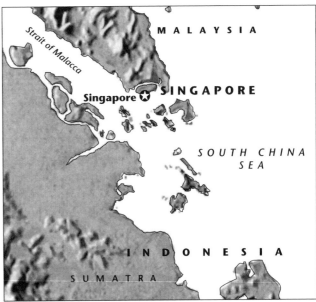

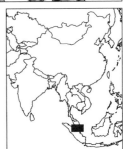

of consultation and consensus and remained in Lee's shadow. Goh remained in office through the legislative elections of August 1991 and January 1997.

A One-Party State

Politics in Singapore is based on the British parliamentary model, although the parliament is unicameral rather than bicameral. Legislators are elected to five-year terms, and almost all are members of Lee's People's Action Party. From the late 1950s on, the People's Action Party continually won parliamentary election victories. Until 1991 only an occasional, single seat was won by opposition-party candidates; in that year the opposition won four seats.

The People's Action Party has continued to win large majorities in parliamentary elections both because the opposition is fragmented and because the party controls the entire bureaucracy, including the lowest levels of precincts. In addition, most voters see the dominance of the People's Action Party as the best chance for Singapore's continued political and economic stability and growth. The opposition has been co-opted by Singapore's economic growth, passage of popular social-welfare legislation, low level of unemployment, and noncorrupt government. From a Western perspective, a one-party state is neither competitive nor democratic. From the perspective of Singaporeans, paternalistic government provides law and order and achieves economic growth.

The People's Action Party has kept potential opposition parties from mounting effective campaigns. The leaders accept in principle the concept of a critical, competitive opposition—they do so as long as that opposition remains weak. The party has mobilized the civil service to carry out its programs and thus consolidate its rule. To many citizens of Singapore, the party is synonymous with the state. Singaporeans saw the phenomenal economic growth that touched virtually every person during the postindependence period as an accomplishment of the People's Action Party. With its clean sweep of every election, the party has been transformed into a state institution.

The dominance of the People's Action Party also results to a great extent from the leadership of Lee Kuan Yew. Brilliant, energetic, and motivated, Lee appeared as the consummate pragmatist, concerned with efficiency and results. He showed himself to be ruthless upon occasion, as when he ordered political adversaries to be imprisoned. At the same time, he took credit for the high standard of living that Singaporeans enjoy.

The case of Singapore raises the question of whether a one-party state can be democratic. The governmental system of Singapore does not meet the criteria of full civil liberties and competitive choices of leaders. From the Chinese perspective, however, Western-style majority rule leads to chaos, instability, dissension, and inefficiency.

Prime Minister Lee argued that in the Chinese tradition there is no concept of a loyal opposition. For example, it is not possible for people to support an opposition candidate without withdrawing their total support from the government. This tradition is based on Confucian philosophy, which stresses the principles of centralized authority. Obedience to those in authority was the cement of the Confucian order. As long as the authorities met the needs of the people and led them according to moral principles, the ruler was considered to have the mandate of heaven and was therefore deemed legitimate by the public. Given this cultural perspective, a strong one-party system is most conducive to effective rule. As might be expected, Singaporeans do not swing back and forth from opposition to support for the People's Action Party.

One-party systems can provide policy alternatives in the case of differences in opinion among the party leaders. Moreover, if two-way communication between the government and the people is established, the citizenry can influence public policy. In Singapore, intraparty factionalism is prevalent, and varying points of view are aired publicly. In addition, the People's Action Party has established vari-

ous grassroots organizations, including Citizens' Consultative Committees designed to elicit ideas from the public. Singapore's semidemocracy has provided the republic with effective and accountable government, consistent with its traditions and history and supportive of the goals of development, order, and merit.

Communitarianism Versus Individualism

Singaporeans do not enjoy the kind of civil liberties expected by citizens in Western democracies. Indeed, Lee Kuan Yew has expressed disdain for the Western value of "individualism," which he contrasts with Singaporean "communitarianism." He consistently has criticized the absence of discipline in Western societies (as well as in developing countries) and has noted Singapore's excellent record of public safety as compared with the dangers of crime-ridden U.S. cities. Tight controls have made it possible for Singaporeans to walk the streets in any place and at any time; graffiti, gangs, and criminals are almost unknown. Furthermore, Singapore has a superb educational system and has achieved a 99 percent literacy rate. The high standard of living and the low level of homelessness compare favorably with the high levels of poverty and homelessness in "democratic" societies.

Lee's critics have complained about censorship and other constraints on individual freedoms. Lee himself emphasizes the advantages of a country that is free from pornography; free from corrupting influences, such as prostitution, gross materialism, and drug abuse; and free from foreign ideas that are contrary to Confucian values and that undermine the people's respect for authority.

Most Singaporeans have been willing to accept the tight discipline because the state has achieved such high levels of economic growth. Nevertheless, Singapore faces significant problems. Worldwide protectionism could undermine the economic growth of countries, like Singapore, that depend on exports. Moreover, wage increases have reduced the number of cheap local laborers available. Multinational corporations increasingly are turning to nations with cheaper labor than Singapore.

More important, the rapid modernization of Singapore has undermined the traditional values of its people. Housing projects, for example, have subverted the former emphasis on the extended family, in which several generations lived together in housing compounds. Once characterized by spirit, heart, and vitality, Singapore seems cold and materialistic to many. The extraordinary cleanliness of the city seems sterile, and even the perfect landscaping appears antiseptic rather than lush. For tourists, shopping is the main attraction.

The standard of living in Singapore is equal to those of New Zealand, Ireland, and Spain; Singapore has an income of more than $10,000 per capita. There is virtually no unemployment, and with few exceptions poverty has been eliminated. A public housing scheme, cheap health care, and universal public education have enhanced the living standards of Singaporeans. Perhaps no other city in the world can claim as high a degree of modernization as Singapore.

Singapore has achieved such a high level of economic development because the interventionist state is involved in all aspects of the national economy. By structuring the economy toward high-technology industries, emphasizing exports, and establishing conservative fiscal policies, the government achieved a phenomenally high growth rate of 8 percent in the 1980s and early 1990s. Many of the exports are products of multinational corporations. Foreign capital plays a major role in the domestic economy as well.

The unique aspects of Singapore make it difficult to compare it with developing countries. Its status as a city-state with virtually no agricultural base, its small population, and its remarkably high standard of living make Singapore an anomaly among its Southeast Asian neighbors. Thus the urban island-state is not a useful model for other nations to emulate because its conditions are so unusual.

Yet despite Singapore's uniqueness, many leaders of developing countries have looked with favor at the "Asian style of democracy" found there. Singapore, Taiwan, and South Korea are Asia's most successful developing nations in terms of economic growth. All three adopted a pattern of government featuring one-party dominance, hierarchical and centralized rule, emphasis on communitarian values rather than individualism, strong state intervention, and discipline. Such a system may not meet Western criteria for democracy, but it is appropriate for the cultures and traditions of the citizens of Singapore.

See also *Asia, Southeast; Dominant party democracies in Asia; Malaysia.*

BIBLIOGRAPHY

Bellows, Thomas J. *The People's Action Party of Singapore: Emergence of a Dominant Party System.* New Haven: Yale University, Southeast Asian Studies, 1970.

Chan, Heng Chee. *The Dynamics of One-Party Dominance: The PAP at the Grassroots.* Singapore: Singapore University Press, 1976.

George, T. J. S. *Lee Kuan Yew's Singapore.* London: Andre Deutsch, 1973.

Josey, Alex. *Lee Kuan Yew.* Singapore: Asia Pacific Press, 1968.

Rodan, Garry. *The Political Economy of Singapore's Industrialization: National, State, and International Capital.* New York: St. Martin's; London: Macmillan, 1989.

South Africa

A former white-ruled republic, situated on Africa's southern tip, that held its first nonracial elections in April 1994. Race had long polarized South Africa's 40 million people (30 million blacks, 5 million whites, 3.4 million "colored" people, and 1 million Asians), and the country was known for its system of apartheid, a form of racial segregation and minority rule. A decades-long ideological experiment had entrenched white dominance and sought to create separate "homelands" for black ethnic groups. The most populous were the 8 million Zulus, the 6.8 million Xhosa speakers, and 5.6 million Sotho speakers.

In February 1990 South Africa's white government, headed by Frederik W. de Klerk, had signaled its intention to negotiate a democracy with the hitherto outlawed black nationalist opposition. Although the government expressed willingness to negotiate, the historical background against which this attempt was launched presented obstacles to democracy more formidable than those encountered by many democratizing societies.

South Africa, however, had an advantage denied some countries hoping to become democracies—a limited democratic tradition. Whites (13 percent of the population) had enjoyed regular competitive elections since 1910, when four white-ruled states agreed to form a union under British colonial rule. The 1910 Union of South Africa was an attempt, imposed by British conquest, to incorporate into a common polity two hostile white blocs: Afrikaners (people of Dutch descent) and English speakers. Like other British colonies, they adopted the Westminster parliamentary system, and until the 1990s whites enjoyed the trappings of pluralist democracy. But the roots of union ensured that democracy remained oligarchic and that, even for the minority, it increasingly became a matter of form rather than content. The colored (mixed race) and Asian minorities (together 11 percent of the population) were granted a vote for separate and subordinate parliaments only in 1984; black Africans (76 percent of the population) were denied the franchise until 1994.

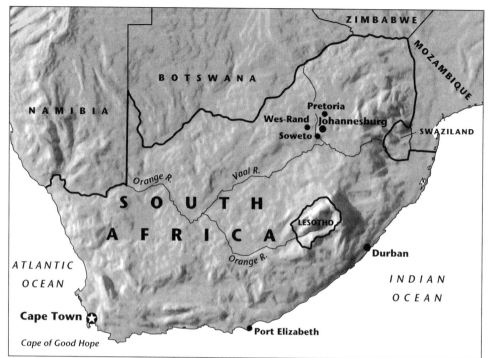

Seeds of Oligarchy and Resistance

In 1652 the Cape of Good Hope, Africa's southernmost shoreline, was colonized by the Dutch. After conquering the indigenous Khoi and San peoples, the Dutch penetrated into the interior. Great Britain formally established a colony at the Cape in 1806, and in 1820 the first British settlers landed on its shores. The settlers clashed repeatedly with the authoritarian colonial rulers. Those of Dutch descent, who proclaimed their attachment to their new continent by labeling themselves Afrikaners, were particularly resistant to colonial rule. But this resistance, which nurtured a democratic ethos within the settler community, was accompanied by a strong antipathy to the indigenous tribes and to Malay slaves imported to work in the colony. The strength of opposition to British rule and enthusiasm for white democracy usually coincided with support for racial dominance.

These tensions crystallized in the 1830s. Conflict with tribes on the Cape's eastern frontier and continued resentment of colonial rule prompted Afrikaner settlers to migrate. For the rest of the century, the Afrikaner, or Boer (farmer), settlers penetrated inland, subduing the resident black tribes. They established independent Boer republics that were governed democratically; however, for the conquered black inhabitants they proclaimed the principle of no equality with whites in church or state. The exclusivity of this policy contrasted with the paternalism of the Cape

colony, whose authorities extended the franchise to a few blacks who met education and property qualifications.

Boer sovereignty ended in 1902, after a brutal three-year war between Britain and the Boer republics. When the Boer forces surrendered, British authorities sought to cement their victory with a campaign to suppress the Boer language (Afrikaans) and culture. This policy stiffened an Afrikaner nationalism with twin objectives: independence from colonial rule and hegemony over the black majority. When a whites-only national convention convened in 1909, the more compliant Afrikaner leaders dominated; even then the price of unity was agreement that the limited franchise for black Africans not be extended outside the Cape. Within three years the Union Parliament enacted the 1913 Land Acts, depriving Africans of land ownership rights outside some 7 percent of the country set aside as reserves.

Two issues dominated parliamentary politics for much of the rest of the century. The first was the attempt by the Afrikaner elite (60 percent of the white population) to wrest power from the economically dominant English speakers (40 percent of the white population). This effort culminated first in the victory of the National Party in 1948 and then in the establishment of a republic in 1960. The second was the means by which white supremacy was to be maintained: the paternalism that had created the limited Cape franchise clashed with the aggressive exclusivism that had developed in the Afrikaner republics. But the 1913 land ownership laws that consolidated white hegemony also triggered the other force in twentieth-century South African politics: organized black resistance to white rule.

By 1912 tribal units had been conquered, and white rule was consolidated. The political aspirations of blacks now hinged on inclusion in common representative institutions. Their vehicle was the South African Native National Congress, launched in 1912 to defend land rights and to press for political rights. Eight years later the group became the African National Congress (ANC), the chief organization of the African nationalist movement for the rest of the century.

The ANC initially was moderate in methods and goals. Its leadership was an African intelligentsia educated in the Christian liberal tradition brought by British missionaries. Their mission education nurtured a respect for liberal values and an abiding belief that moral appeals to the colonial power would ensure the extension of political rights to the disenfranchised. Among the first acts of the Congress was the sending of a delegation to London to urge the monarch to intervene on behalf of his loyal black subjects. For the next three decades the moral appeal was the ANC's primary weapon. The ANC elite did not seek the overthrow of the union but incorporation within its democratic institutions—gradually if need be. They cherished the hope that the extension of political rights to some would begin a process that would eventually extend to them all.

Route to Polarization

The ANC moderates were ignored. The Crown was concerned with developing the British Westminster model of democracy among the white settlers. Blacks' demands were irrelevant or inimical to this task. Concessions to local demands for political autonomy were made to the strong white lobbies, not the weak black ones. And the inexorable move of colonial policy toward white self-rule ensured an equally inevitable drift away from black enfranchisement.

White democracy produced two sorts of government. The first was an alliance of English speakers and Afrikaner leaders who had made their peace with the empire; it favored a paternal "trusteeship" over black Africans. The limited Cape franchise for blacks was abolished by such a government in 1936. An elected advisory body, the Native Representative Council, was established in its stead. (Evidence of the ANC's enthusiasm for even limited democratic institutions was its willingness to contest elections for, and serve in, this body.) But this type of government was less rigid in its insistence on social and economic segregation.

The second kind of government was based on Afrikaner nationalism. When Afrikaners first won power, in alliance with white labor in 1924, their government reserved skilled work for whites. When they triumphed in 1948, they abolished even advisory representation for black Africans and initiated a program of rigid racial segregation in pursuance of a proclaimed policy of "white mastery." The trend in white politics was toward this second, more racist form of government. Only twice in white democracy's eighty-four-year history (1910–1994) did power change hands at the polls; each time Afrikaner nationalism and stricter racial exclusivism triumphed.

These trends ensured the failure of ANC moderation, which by the 1940s was discredited among young African intellectuals. Control of the ANC's Youth League passed to militant nationalists such as Oliver Tambo and Nelson Mandela (both later to become presidents of the ANC). These nationalists were convinced that white goodwill was a scarce or fictional commodity. Their goal was not incorporation into the white-ruled polity but national liberation; their preferred method was mass mobilization. After the 1948 election, their argument became compelling to the older generation of ANC leaders.

Although at first hostile to white communists, the Youth Leaguers soon modified their attitude. The South African Communist Party, the only party with white members to associate itself unreservedly with black resistance in the preceding three decades, became a useful ally in the struggle against apartheid. By the late 1940s the ANC was committed to mass defiance of apartheid and had cemented an alliance with the communists. This bond was strengthened when that party was banned in 1950, and a Congress of Democrats formed largely by white communists forged an alliance with the ANC.

Even then prospects for accommodation did not seem irretrievably lost. Black mobilization in the 1950s was harassed but not banned. And, despite the ANC's new militancy, its Christian liberal tradition proved tenacious. The president of the ANC for much of the decade, Chief Albert Luthuli, was steeped in Christian social democracy. (He was awarded the Nobel Peace Prize in 1960.) Mandela, then head of the ANC in the Transvaal Province (the country's most populous province and its economic heartland), revealed later that he would have favored accepting limited African representation in Parliament as a stage on the route to universal franchise. The ANC mixed civil disobedience with calls on the government to negotiate. But whites' resistance to compromise stiffened, and the pleas were ignored.

By the late 1950s the contradiction between allowing blacks to mobilize and ignoring their demands ensured growing instability, culminating in the shooting deaths in March 1960 of nearly seventy Africans at the Sharpeville police station south of Johannesburg. The government reacted by banning the ANC and the more militant, black exclusivist Pan-Africanist Congress, which had broken away from the ANC the previous year under the leadership of Robert Sobukwe. In addition, the government implemented the first of a series of laws infringing on due process and individual liberties. Reestablished in exile, the ANC determined to destroy the white state by force.

If the ANC's response seemed to exclude the peaceful extension of democratic institutions, the strategy of the National Party, beginning in the 1960s, did so more forcefully. In its attempt to quell African resistance, the National Party enacted security laws that curbed the rights of individuals, freedom of expression, and political activity by the opposition. The state exercised unlimited power to detain individuals, to ban opponents from political and even social activity, and to outlaw publications that furthered communism, a term defined so widely that it sometimes encompassed liberal opinion. Opposition movements that did not participate in Parliament or in the separate institutions created for the majority were outlawed or subject to security action. The press, although it remained privately owned, was subject by the 1980s to more than a hundred laws restricting reportage and comment. Although the National Party was wedded to the form of parliamentary procedure, legislation increasingly transferred power from the judiciary and legislature to the "opinion" of the executive. Ironically, the British democratic tradition against which Afrikaner nationalists had fought helped them to secure political dominance: the Westminster doctrine of parliamentary supremacy prevented the judiciary from pronouncing on legislation. Only administrative acts could be challenged in the courts.

In its attempt to consolidate Afrikaner power, the National Party used ethnic patronage in the civil service, the judiciary, and parastatals (state-owned corporations). The Afrikaner Brotherhood, a secret society to which most cabinet ministers and National Party intellectuals belonged, was the prime vehicle; membership was essential for senior public appointments. Because a guaranteed Afrikaner majority ensured repeated reelection of the National Party, the response of English speakers was either to forgo politics for business and the professions or to regard parliamentary activity as a form of protest politics. The result was a "white

democracy" in which the same party was routinely returned to power for more than four decades. In this white political culture, politics became the route to advancement for Afrikaner nationalists and an object of indifference for the remaining 40 percent of the white population.

But it was above all the National Party's racial program that militated against a peaceful expansion of democracy. The election of Hendrik Verwoerd as prime minister in 1958 transformed the policy of white mastery into a rigid ideology—apartheid. Verwoerd and his successors ostensibly rejected white domination. They insisted that self-determination would be extended to black South Africa—but not in a single polity. Verwoerd made 87 percent of the country "white South Africa." In the remaining 13 percent of the country, black Africans were encouraged to develop their own representative institutions and to establish independent states. But Africans were not, in this view, a homogeneous group: the tribal units that existed before white conquest were the authentic instruments of black national identity. Ten black "homelands" were therefore established, and in 1971 each black South African was assigned to one.

The ideology, ostensibly more egalitarian than its predecessor, precluded an expanded democracy. Black exclusion from central government became an article of ideological faith. Because black people were now citizens of other "states," to which they would have to return to exercise their "citizenship," they were stripped of all rights and entitlements in the white 87 percent. Property ownership and the right to work in skilled positions and, in many cases, to live as a family were available in the ethnic homelands only; adequate education and health care were available nowhere. Urban black townships were starved of resources in order to induce their residents to return to their homelands. The government's policy not only radicalized blacks, the direct victims of apartheid prohibitions, but stunted their opportunities to participate in associations and democratic institutions.

The assignment of separate, ethnically based, political institutions to the majority, rationalized as a training in democracy, had precisely the reverse effect. These institutions—elected ethnic legislatures in the homelands and local (cross-ethnic) councils in the urban areas—were denied resources and effective powers and so were forced to act as agents of white rule. Black nationalists viewed them as a symbol of exclusion from the central polity and as major vehicles of white domination. To frustrate apartheid, black nationalists mobilized against its closest and most vulnerable manifestations—black elected councils and administrations. During the 1970s and 1980s the election boycott became a primary weapon of resistance. Persons who assumed elected office were vilified; in the 1980s they became victims of violence. Participation in representative institutions by blacks was transformed from a majority aspiration to an act of betrayal.

End of Oligarchy

From the late 1960s on, the unworkability of apartheid became increasingly evident. Economic and demographic pressures made it harder for the government to control the kind of work blacks did and where they lived. In 1973 industrial strikes in the port city of Durban signaled the end of workers' quiescence. Internal resistance was revived by the black consciousness movement. Its theorist, Stephen Biko (who died in police custody in 1977), stressed black assertiveness and self-sufficiency. In 1976 conflict in the Soweto township outside Johannesburg began a decade and a half of militant urban resistance. Almost imperceptibly at first, the National Party began to retreat from apartheid.

The ensuing reform period saw the increasing recognition of black urban permanence. As it became clear that people who were not leaving the white heartland would voice political demands within it, the government began a series of tortuous experiments in "broadening democracy" while maintaining white supremacy. Changes were made only when necessary and if white political dominance was not threatened. Prime Minister Pieter W. Botha introduced a constitution bill (approved in 1983) that extended the franchise to the colored and Asian minorities but in a form that assigned them a subordinate role and excluded the African majority; the Africans were to be content with municipal government in segregated townships (itself a concession). These actions sparked the most aggressive protests yet, and in 1985 Botha was forced to concede the principle of African citizenship in a common polity for the first time. Even then the constitutional changes proposed by his government envisaged separate and subordinate black representation.

Government attempts to strengthen black political participation in subordinate forums merely heightened mobilization against those forums and their incumbents. In the absence of legitimate political channels, the foes of apartheid sought to render the country ungovernable by withholding participation in local councils and by boycotting schools and white-owned stores. The resistance, led by students who rejected their elders' passive acceptance of

white domination, became increasingly coercive. The government responded with stringent security action, culminating in the 1986 declaration of a state of emergency, which was used to suppress domestic resistance movements in the hope that "moderate" black leaders would emerge to negotiate the political incorporation of blacks on white terms. The state of emergency stayed in effect until 1990.

A Fragile Settlement

Against this background, South Africa began to negotiate democracy. By 1990 apartheid, and economic sanctions imposed by most Western governments in reaction to it, had weakened South Africa's economy. Reform and repression had failed to produce a compliant majority leadership willing to negotiate on the government's terms. International developments (including the collapse of communist regimes) convinced the white government that a favorable settlement could be worked out. All these factors prompted de Klerk, who succeeded Botha in 1989, to lift the bans on the ANC, the Communist Party, and the Pan-Africanist Congress on February 2, 1990, and to invite them to negotiate a new order.

Thus began a process that, despite repeated setbacks, moved almost inevitably to a settlement. But it also triggered the bloodiest political violence in the country's history. The prospect of democracy was resisted by white right-wingers and by blacks who had controlled homeland governments and who feared that majority rule would reduce them to impotence.

For both the white elite and the black resistance, a negotiated compromise was a second-best option. Throughout the reform period the National Party's strategy had been to yield only as much as was necessary to remain in power. By the 1990s the parameters of the possible had shifted, but the goal remained almost unchanged: de Klerk and his party stressed that they must have a guaranteed share in government once the vote was extended to all. Not until three years into the transition would they concede that apartheid was morally untenable; at this point they acknowledged only that it had not worked. White South Africa's leadership was not embracing a competitive democracy in a reconciled nation but attempting to concede universal franchise on terms that would secure them a share of power almost regardless of election results.

By the early 1990s the ANC had become the most pragmatic champion of majority liberation. Willing to negotiate a compromise, it faced considerable opposition within its own constituency. Three decades of exile and guerrilla activity had built a revolutionary culture intent on destroying minority power, not compromising with it. The youth activists who had led the internal resistance of the 1980s were more impatient with compromise than were the exiles. Economic stagnation and vast inequalities in access to social goods ensured that opponents of compromise would enjoy an audience among key sections of the ANC constituency.

The fact that a settlement was being attempted at all, however, confirmed the lack of alternatives to a compromise between the country's major power blocs. The costs of white rule had become unsustainable, yet the white government retained enough military force to make revolution impossible. The white government and the ANC had little option but to continue to move toward the settlement they had reached in November 1993. A five-year interim constitution provided for the election of a government of national unity in which the larger minority parties would be represented in proportion to their support. It also specified that a bicameral national legislature would draft the final constitution. The shared cabinet reflected an acknowledgment by the ANC that democracy was likely to survive only if the country's white rulers, whom it expected to defeat in an election, retained a role in government. Agreement on the interim constitution opened the way for an election in April 1994.

The prospects for democratic compromise looked bleak during the period before the country's first nonracial election. The Inkatha Freedom Party formed an alliance with white right-wingers and rejected participation in the election until its demand for vastly increased powers for the region in which it was strongest was met. The Inkatha controlled the homeland assigned to Zulu-speaking blacks, and it alone among the homeland parties commanded significant support. The Inkatha also demanded a constitutional role for the Zulu king, with whom it cooperated in rallying opposition to a settlement among Zulu speakers who felt more comfortable with traditional institutions than with democracy. The Inkatha's demands heightened violence and raised the prospect that the new democracy would begin without the participation of a significant minority party that had shown its ability to threaten stability.

The strength of the pressures that forced the country's politicians to resign themselves to compromise became evident a week before the April 26–28 election. At this eleventh hour the Inkatha, in negotiation with the ANC and the government, agreed to participate in the election.

By then a significant section of the white right wing had already joined the democratic contest. Against all expectations, the country's first universal franchise election included the entire spectrum of opinion except for the most extreme elements of the white right wing.

The election was marred by significant administrative failures on the part of a newly created Independent Electoral Commission and by allegations of fraud by some competing parties. But flawed as the election clearly was, it vastly strengthened prospects for consolidating a fragile democracy. The country's new voters, despite being forced to wait as long as three days to cast their ballots in some cases, greeted the inconvenience with forbearance. Violence declined sharply during the election period. And the major competing parties, after loudly accusing each other of vote rigging, negotiated compromises that enabled a result to be declared with the support of all parties.

The outcome—whether serendipitously or as a result of interparty negotiation—was tailor-made for the power-sharing compromise that the election was meant to produce. As expected, the ANC won a comfortable majority (62 percent of the vote), but it failed to gain the two-thirds necessary to dominate drafting of the permanent constitution. The National Party achieved the 20 percent necessary, according to the agreed constitutional formula, for de Klerk to become one of two executive vice presidents; Thabo Mbeki of the ANC was the other. It also won control of one of the nine provinces created by the constitutional settlement. The Inkatha won control of the Kwazulu-Natal Province, where its support was concentrated, and 10 percent of the national vote, enough to appoint three cabinet ministers. In short, the main contenders won enough votes to ensure their commitment to the new order. On May 9 the National Assembly elected Nelson Mandela president unanimously.

In its first few years, the government of national unity negotiated the shoals of shared power without major difficulty despite the discomfit caused by unpleasant revelations about the liberation struggle era. The most serious rifts occurred between the government and the Inkatha Freedom Party, whose members walked out of Parliament—and thus out of the constituent assembly—in April 1995 reiterating their demands for greater autonomy for Kwazulu-Natal Province and a role for the Zulu king. Violence between ANC and Inkatha followers in August and December 1995 left nearly a score dead. By contrast, relations between the government and white factions, including Afrikaner, were characterized by accommodation.

The constituent assembly finished its work on the new constitution in late 1996, and President Mandela signed the document into law on December 10. The constitution, which became effective in February of the following year, provided for a continuation of the government of national unity until 1999. After that time, simple majority rule will prevail, and minority parties will no longer be guaranteed a voice in government.

Conclusion

South Africa's new democratic rulers assumed office against a background of conflict that served as a reminder of democracy's fragility. The fact that the protagonists now shared power in the same executive did not mean that the potential for conflict had ended. Rather, the potential for conflict had been imported into the heart of government.

Although corrupted by decades of apartheid, a constitutional tradition nevertheless existed. This, together with international pressure for democratization, held out some prospect for the emergence of a democratic center. And, despite the legacy of the past four decades, a diverse and often vigorous civil society sometimes showed greater propensity for pragmatism and accommodation than did the political elites. Economic interdependence between blacks and whites also weakened support on both sides for extreme solutions.

The next decade will determine whether South Africa can build a sufficient sense of common national purpose to sustain a democracy. But the post-1948 legacy of violence and racial polarization seems likely to ensure that a South African democracy will encounter rough periods. South Africa remains a divided society in which pluralism and compromise presented themselves to political leaders as an unavoidable necessity, not a preferred option. Its democratic experiment will demonstrate whether, for want of alternatives, its politicians will confound those who doubt the viability of democracy in divided societies.

BIBLIOGRAPHY

Adam, Heribert, and Kogila Moodley. *The Negotiated Revolution: Society and Politics in Post-Apartheid South Africa.* Johannesburg: Jonathan Ball, 1993.

Davenport, T. R. H. *South Africa: A Modern History.* Johannesburg: Macmillan, 1987; London: Macmillan, 1991.

Du Toit, André, and Hermann Giliomee. *Afrikaner Political Thought, 1780–1850.* Vol. 1 of *Afrikaner Political Thought.* Berkeley: University of California Press, 1983.

Friedman, Steven, ed. *The Long Journey: South Africa's Quest for a Negotiated Settlement.* Johannesburg: Ravan Press; Athens: Ohio University Press, 1993.

———, and Doreen Atkinson, eds. *The Small Miracle: South Africa's Negotiated Settlement.* Johannesburg: Ravan Press, 1994.

Giliomee, Hermann, and Lawrence Schlemmer. *From Apartheid to Nation-Building.* Cape Town: Oxford University Press, 1989.

Horowitz, Donald. *A Democratic South Africa? Constitutional Engineering in a Divided Society.* Cape Town: Oxford University Press, 1991.

Lodge, Tom. *Black Politics in South Africa Since 1945.* London: Longman, 1983.

Roux, Edward. *Time Longer Than Rope: A History of the Black Man's Struggle for Freedom in South Africa.* Madison: University of Wisconsin Press, 1964.

Slabbert, Frederick van Zyl. *The Quest for Democracy: South Africa in Transition.* Harmondsworth, England: Penguin Forum Series, 1992.

South Korea

Independent East Asian country that was established in 1948. South Korea, officially known as the Republic of Korea, is a model of an authoritarian system that sponsored economic growth and development, thereby setting the stage for a transition to democracy in the late 1980s.

Historical Background

The last native Korean dynasty, the Yi, was overthrown in 1910, after more than five centuries of authoritarian rule based on Confucianism. From 1910 to 1945 the Japanese ruled Korea as a colony. After World War II Korea was divided by the Allies into two zones of occupation, with Soviet troops in the north and U.S. forces in the south. In 1948 Korea was officially divided into two states: the Republic of Korea (South Korea) and the Democratic People's Republic (North Korea). Syngman Rhee was elected the first president of South Korea by its unicameral National Assembly. His government initially attempted to establish a constitutional democracy but soon became increasingly authoritarian.

The Korean War began in June 1950. North Korea, with Soviet support, attacked South Korea, which had United Nations forces under the leadership of the United States. The North Korean forces were soon augmented by Chinese communist troops. Negotiations for a cease-fire began as early as 1951 but dragged on for almost two years. The war officially ended in July 1953.

In 1960 Rhee and his followers rigged the presidential election for his third term. This act led to student demonstrations against the dictatorship, which brought down the government. The parliamentary government of Chang

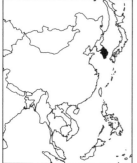

economic and social development while denying political competition, participation, and civil and political liberties for the people. In the presidential election of 1971 Park was almost defeated by the opposition leader Kim Dae Jung, who received 46 percent of the popular vote. The next year Park instituted the so-called Yushin (revitalizing reform) Constitution by which, in the name of national security, all opposition political parties and democracy movements were disbanded. In 1979 Park was assassinated by his own security chief over disagreements about how to cope with increasing disorder and demands for democracy in South Korea.

One of several causes of the democratic movement in the 1970s was social and economic change. The economy was then beginning a transformation from an agrarian to a manufacturing base. More than 65 percent of the work force was engaged in industry, while less than 15 percent worked in the agricultural sector. Thus the Republic of Korea achieved the status of a newly industrializing country as measured by the proportion of gross domestic product attributable to industry (more than 60 percent). Furthermore, the country was becoming urbanized: in the 1970s more than half the population lived in cities.

By the end of the 1970s the level of literacy in rural areas had reached 85 percent, and compulsory education had been extended to middle school. There was effective mass communication by means of radio, television, and newspapers. In addition, despite the creation of *chaebol* (conglomerates of capital industries), the Republic of Korea had a rather equitable distribution of wealth—a factor widely considered to be strongly conducive to democracy.

After the assassination of President Park, however, martial law was instituted and all political activity was barred. During the transition from Park's government to a democratic regime, social and economic disorder erupted. Maj. Gen. Chun Doo Hwan, security chief in the capital city of Seoul, carried out a coup in December 1979 that overthrew the caretaker government and established a military regime. Chun's regime became the most repressive in modern Korean history, in large part because of its ruthless suppression of the 1980 Kwangju uprising. Although there was widespread opposition to his regime, Chun's government lasted until 1987.

A New Movement for Democracy

In the late 1980s the Chun regime was finally forced to make concessions to a democratic movement led by students and intellectuals and including many members of the middle class. The movement's leaders demanded free

Myon (John M. Chang), which followed Rhee's regime, was considered the most democratic government in South Korea's history. That government was overthrown in 1961 by a military coup led by Maj. Gen. Park Chung Hee.

Park, who assumed the presidency, ruled South Korea with an iron fist, turning it into a garrison state. His rationale for such repressive rule was twofold: the need to counter the constant threat from the communist regime in North Korea and the argument that South Korea, with a per capita gross national product of $87, could not afford the luxury of democracy. By heavily promoting economic growth and development, Park attempted to win the support of students, intellectuals, and champions of human rights who strongly opposed his dictatorship. He believed that when the per capita GNP reached $2,000, a transition from authoritarianism to democracy would be possible.

But the Park regime sought legitimacy on the basis of

and direct election of the president and an end to Chun's regime. South Korea was scheduled to host the 1988 summer Olympic games, and worldwide attention was focused on the country. After many weeks of escalating tension and violent confrontations between tear gas–wielding police and protesters, Chun's government finally yielded, and elections were scheduled.

Roh Tae Woo was the leader and presidential nominee of the ruling Democratic Justice Party, whose election was virtually assured. Roh, who had participated in the coup that brought Chun to power, had held numerous posts in Chun's government. In June 1987, at the peak of the violence and disorder, he announced a campaign pledge: his successor would be elected by popular vote in a free election under a democratic constitution. Roh won the election. The consequent constitutional amendment, approved by the National Assembly on October 12, 1987, by a vote of 254 to 4, changed the method of election from indirect to popular vote, balanced the executive and legislative powers, and provided for decentralization of government. In the October 27 referendum the constitution won resounding approval. Voter turnout was also high: more than three-fourths of eligible voters went to the polls.

The parliamentary election of 1988 brought an unexpected setback to the ruling Democratic Justice Party, which failed to secure a majority in the National Assembly. The Party for Peace and Democracy, led by Kim Dae Jung, became the largest opposition party; two other opposition parties also won a significant number of seats. Together, the three opposition parties held a substantial majority of seats. If they cooperated, they could reject presidential nominations, stall budget deliberations, and control the legislative process. As a consequence, in 1990 the Democratic Justice Party merged with two of the opposition parties to create the Democratic Liberal Party. Kim Dae Jung's reorganized Democratic Party was left as the only opposition party. Even so, there were no strong differences between the parties: both were basically conservative entities organized by political personalities. In 1992 Kim Young Sam, the Democratic Liberal Party candidate, was elected president; he was inaugurated in early 1993 for a five-year term and was the first non–military officer to win the presidency since 1960.

The process of democratization that began in 1987 made South Korean society more open, diverse, and decentralized than it had ever been before. The mass media were freed from government restrictions, thousands of political prisoners were released from prison, and long-suppressed labor unions were permitted to organize for better wages and improved working conditions. But the process also triggered explosions of long-suppressed issues. Social order deteriorated and crime increased. Economic discipline was less rigorous. As a result the balance of payments began to shift from surplus to deficit, and the rate of economic growth and development slowed.

Impediments to Democracy

The process of democratization in South Korea, though steady, suffered from several weaknesses. One problem was the relative underdevelopment of the political parties. The parties were never institutionalized; instead, they were organized and operated around political personalities with similar political ideologies and little commitment to the programs and policies set forth by the parties themselves. Party organizations were dissolved when their leaders lost an election or resigned from politics, in part because campaign financing depended heavily on the party leader's ability to bring in money, rather than on contributions from party members. In addition, since the parties were organized on the basis of personalities and regional ties, they did not really represent the views of voters.

Other problems included the political factionalism that denied a stable majority in parliament and undercut the president's support base, as well as the regionalism that tended to fragment South Korean society. The most serious problem in South Korea's democratic transition was the political culture of its leaders, who continued to invoke authoritarian loyalties and to support hierarchical structures in political and social organizations.

The traditional political ideology of Confucianism could not easily be eradicated or transmuted into a civic culture. A public opinion survey conducted in 1992, after five years' experience with democracy, showed that a large percentage of the South Korean population still supported an authoritarian political culture. Only half believed that democratic reform might be achieved by the late 1990s. One-fourth of the people expressed support for dictatorial rule and believed that it was good for South Korea.

New Stage in the Transition

On the positive side, almost two-thirds of the South Korean population was born after the Korean War. These generations learned about democratic values and institutions in school and resisted the authoritarian political culture of the 1970s and 1980s. Better educated and more urban than the older generation, they were firmly committed to democratic values.

Moreover, at least one important element of democratization was being put in place: the decentralization of authority and greater local autonomy. Under the authoritarian military regimes of Park and Chun, local self-government was nonexistent and could not even be discussed. The leaders feared that local autonomy would mean the end of their regimes.

After 1987 the democratization process directed attention to the relationship between democracy and local autonomy. Local self-government became a hot issue in political debates. Discussions were held between the ruling and opposition parties on when and how to revive local government. After a long delay, elections for local assemblies were held in 1991, and legislative activities were inaugurated. The election of provincial, municipal, and local officials, however, was postponed until 1995.

Despite the encouraging expansion of local self-government, the weakness of the national party system continued to haunt the government. Between Kim's inauguration in February 1993 and December 1995, five different individuals served as prime minister. The quick turnover was attributable as much to shifting loyalties as to policy differences. The underlying party alignments also underwent reorganization prior to the April 1996 legislative elections, just as they had earlier in the decade.

Compounding the government instability, revelations began to surface of massive corruption. Former presidents Roh and Chun were indicted at the end of 1995 and early 1996 for taking bribes totaling hundreds of millions of dollars. President Kim and a close adviser were also implicated in an election financing scandal, but that was a side-show to the prosecution and conviction (in 1996) of Roh, Chun, and about two dozen of their associates.

All-in-all, President Kim has made little headway toward changing the political culture of government, the leadership, or the party system.

BIBLIOGRAPHY

Diamond, Larry, Juan J. Linz, and Seymour Martin Lipset, eds. *Democracy in Developing Countries: Asia.* Boulder, Colo.: Lynne Rienner; London: Adamantine Press, 1989.

Kim, Ilpyong J., and Young Whan Kihl, eds. *Political Change in South Korea.* New York: Paragon House, 1988.

Kim, Ilpyong J., and Jane Shapiro Zacek, eds. *Establishing Democratic Rule: The Emergence of Local Governments in Post-Authoritarian Systems.* Washington, D.C.: Washington Institute Press, 1993.

Linz, Juan J. *The Breakdown of Democratic Regimes: Crisis, Breakdown, and Reequilibration.* Baltimore: Johns Hopkins University Press, 1978.

———. "Transition to Democracy." *Washington Quarterly* 13 (summer 1990): 143–164.

Lipset, Seymour Martin. "Some Social Requisites of Democracy: Economic Development and Political Legitimacy." *American Political Science Review* 53 (1959): 75.

Macdonald, Donald S. "Korea's Transition to Democracy." In *Democracy in Korea: The Roh Tae Woo Years,* edited by Christopher J. Sigur. New York: Council on Ethics and International Affairs, 1992.

Sri Lanka

An island republic off the southern tip of India, once a British colony. Sri Lanka (formerly Ceylon) became independent in 1948, after more than 400 years under European colonial tutelage. The Portuguese first established themselves in the coastal areas in 1517. The Dutch displaced the Portuguese in 1655 and were ousted in 1795 by the British. In 1815 the British gained control of the whole island, including the Kandyan kingdom in the mountains.

From the 1930s on, Sri Lanka developed a strong tradition of constitutional, democratic practice. Between 1931 and 1993 eleven national elections were held. Two of these, based on a universal franchise, took place before independence. Between 1956 and 1977 governments changed hands peacefully in six successive elections. In every case, a government defeated at the polls relinquished power. There were no successful coups d'état; the military did not take control. Few countries have shown such a sustained high level of political participation as Sri Lanka. Until the 1980s electoral turnouts were often greater than 80 percent. In the 1980s and early 1990s, however, the Sri Lankan political system faced major challenges.

Sri Lanka's record of democratic practice is all the more remarkable because the country is a complex, multiethnic society. The Sinhala-speaking majority, mostly Buddhist, makes up more than 70 percent of the population. The principal minority is Sri Lankan Tamils; mostly Hindu and speaking Tamil, they represent 12 percent of the population. Although Sinhala is the official language, both Tamil and Sinhala are recognized as "national languages" in the constitution of 1978. Two-thirds of the Tamils have been concentrated in the Jaffna peninsula and northern and eastern provinces of the island. The Tamils played an important role in the country's growth; for example, in the 1950s more than 40 percent of clerical service recruits and more than 30 percent of university graduates were Sri Lankan Tamils. A smaller minority (5.5 percent) is the "estate Tamils," descendants of Tamil people brought from India in the nineteenth century to work British-owned tea estates in the central highlands. The rest of the population is Muslim and Christian (about 7 percent each). About 10 percent of the population speaks English. Within the principal communities caste distinctions are important and helped shape political identities.

The constitution introduced by the British in 1931 established universal adult franchise for the first time in a non-Western colony. There were no literacy requirements for voting, and Sri Lankan voters turned out in large numbers that year to elect members of the State Council, which had power and responsibility for all aspects of internal civil administration. Legislators used these powers to introduce far-reaching reforms in social welfare, education, health care, and land reform.

In 1947 the two principal communities were led by men of similar educational background, English speakers of anglicized culture, who were familiar with the restraints and conventions of contemporary British political practices. As spokesman for leading Sinhalese politicians, D. S. Senanayake negotiated the independence agreement with the British, which a number of Tamil leaders also agreed to. He became the country's first prime minister, and his party, the United National Party, formed the first independence government.

The 1948 independence constitution affirmed the principle of majority rule, but it also included protections for the minorities. For example, section 29(2) prohibited legislation discriminating against a community or followers of a religion. Moreover, areas in which minority groups were concentrated and less developed rural areas received more than their proportionate share of representatives in the new State Council, as a counterbalance to the power of the urban elite. Sinhalese and Tamil were both named national languages, although the language of government in effect remained English. The new state, called Ceylon, was secular; there was no official religion.

The Political Pendulum

Unlike many new democracies, where one-party rule quickly eliminated competition among parties, Sri Lanka retained political choice. Since 1948 the pendulum of politics has swung several times between the United National Party and the Sri Lanka Freedom Party (since 1993 the principal member of the People's Alliance coalition).

After the death of Senanayake in 1952, his son Dudley took his place. In 1952, in a massive 70 percent turnout, voters once again favored the United National Party. In

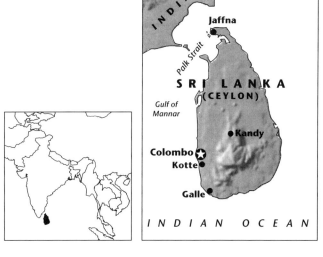

1951, however, the independence coalition had split when S. W. R. D. Bandaranaike organized the Sri Lanka Freedom Party. That party won by a landslide in 1956. Actively supported by Buddhist priests and the educated, Sinhala-speaking middle class, the party emphasized the politics of cultural nationalism and the special character of Ceylon as a Sinhala-speaking, Buddhist country. It promised to make Sinhala the sole official language. The United National Party won only eight seats in 1956, and all but one cabinet minister were voted out. The majority of the population identified with the government more than before. The Freedom Party government was "socialist"; it encouraged the organization of labor and advocated a larger role for the government in the economy.

Bandaranaike was assassinated in 1959. An election in early 1960 gave the United National Party the most seats but not a majority, and Dudley Senanayake preferred to call a new election. In July, Bandaranaike's widow, Sirimavo Bandaranaike, won a sufficient majority for the Freedom Party to govern for the next four years. She became the world's first woman prime minister.

In late 1964 the United National Party engineered a vote of no confidence, bringing the Freedom Party government to a premature end. In the 1965 election, the United National Party narrowly returned to power for another five years under Dudley Senanayake's leadership. This time, however, the party shared power with the Tamil Federal Party, founded in 1951 to promote Tamil interests. Departing from the socialist policies of the Freedom Party, the new government successfully increased rice production.

In 1970 the pendulum swung once more, and the Freedom Party formed a government in coalition with three Marxist parties. A new constitution was adopted in 1972. It addressed Sinhalese grievances by reviving the country's ancient, pre-European name *Lanka* and adding the honorific *Sri* and by designating Sinhala as the sole official language. It strengthened the executive by eliminating the Senate and ending the judicial review of legislation. The new government adopted an economic policy that favored government controls and import substitution (a collection of policies designed to promote a country's self-sufficiency). It nationalized many enterprises, implemented a major land reform, and expanded government-managed industries.

The government faced a major challenge in 1971, when thousands of unemployed rural Sinhalese youths, led by the People's Liberation Front, attempted a one-night seizure of power. The insurrection was put down vigorously, resulting in more than 1,000 deaths. Some 14,000 youths were held for a year in rehabilitation camps. At the same time, the international increase in the price of oil, along with further deterioration of Sri Lanka's terms of trade and strengthening of government controls on trade, contributed to economic stagnation and widespread frustration.

In 1977 the United National Party returned to power, gaining a four-fifths majority, the largest ever achieved by a single party. Except for a few dissenting ministers, the government under President J. R. Jayewardene supported ethnic and caste inclusion, reversed many of the previous government's economic policies, and opened the economy with the help of the World Bank. It undertook major hydroelectric projects and encouraged foreign investment in export industries. Ranasinghe Premadasa, the prime minister, promoted rural housing and urban development. For a time the economy registered growth rates of 5–6 percent, though inflation sharpened contrasts between rich and poor. The government established another new constitution, this one giving more powers to a directly elected executive president. Proponents claimed the change was essential to ensure the political stability necessary to promote economic development like that of Singapore. The constitution also introduced proportional representation for parliamentary elections.

In 1982 a presidential election returned Jayewardene for a second term. Instead of calling a parliamentary election as expected, he organized a controversial referendum that approved prolonging the life of the existing parliament for another five years. Although the 1978 constitution permitted such a referendum, many voters resented being deprived of the time-honored opportunity to vote in an election.

Characteristics of the System, 1931–1983

By most criteria for assessing newly independent regimes, Sri Lanka for many years seemed a model democracy. Electoral turnouts remained high, and politicization went unusually far. Based on universal franchise, the political system of Sri Lanka had become a multiparty system in which two major parties—the United National Party and the Freedom Party—replaced each other periodically. Meanwhile smaller Marxist parties organized and utilized trade unions, and parties of the ethnic minorities continued to voice their growing sense of grievance.

Parties competed by outbidding each other in offering benefits to the voters. For many years the bureaucracy was reasonably effective. As a result, the people of Sri Lanka were better served by health clinics, nutrition programs, and elementary and secondary education than any others in South Asia. On the other hand, competing politicians often raised expectations beyond what the political economy could deliver and intensified local rivalries. Competition for leadership within the major communities induced rivals to accentuate ethnic differences between the communities.

In spite of brief periods of constraint, there was considerable public debate, much of it appearing in newspapers in the three main languages. At independence, more than half the population of Sri Lanka could read and write; by the 1980s the literacy rate had climbed to more than 90 percent.

An electoral commission oversaw the orderliness, secrecy, and fairness of elections, and the police generally protected voters from overly zealous party workers—except in the violence associated with the 1983 referendum and the 1988 and 1989 elections.

Whenever a party enjoyed a landslide victory, as in 1956 and 1977, minority parties, such as the Tamil ethnic parties, had little parliamentary leverage. When the major parties were more evenly matched, however, as in the 1960s, the Tamil ethnic parties could offer their support to whichever major party was most responsive to their interests.

From 1948 to 1993 Sri Lanka had three different constitutions. Both the Freedom Party and the United National Party governments manipulated the constitutions to their short-run political advantage, but they remained fundamentally within constitutional bounds, except during times of crisis.

Critics argued that "the people" were not well represented by the major parties. For example, neither party was internally democratic; each was led by wealthy members of the elite or highly placed professionals. Leadership of both parties remained within the founding families. This situation was especially so with the Freedom Party. Structurally, each party was a loose coalition of patron-client relationships or caste followings. By the 1977 election, however, other political figures, people of humble beginnings, had become prominent.

Political Challenges to the Establishment

Two major movements challenged the political establishment. The most protracted was the Tamil secessionist movement, which emerged in the Jaffna region in the mid-1970s. For a long time some Tamils had wanted to replace the highly centralized, "colonial" structure of government in Sri Lanka with some form of autonomy. Their demands had been consistently rejected by the majority.

The Tamils worried about their political future when they heard majority leaders emphasize the Sinhala character of Sri Lanka. At the same time, Sinhala zealots among priests and teachers depicted Tamils as their historic enemies. The Freedom Party, hard pressed by the People's Liberation Front in 1971, increased the number of university openings for unemployed Sinhalese youths by reducing the disproportionate number of university places that historically had been filled by Tamils. It also virtually ceased the recruitment of Tamils into the national police and military services. Anti-Tamil riots took place after each election. The excesses committed by the police and army in efforts to repress disorders in the north often drew new members to the Tamil secessionist movement.

The accumulation of cultural and career grievances released unexpected political energies. Tamils became more militant, and Tamil members of the parliament, seeking reelection and unable to ignore the impatient youths, increasingly advocated independence. Their secessionist rhetoric in turn increased Sinhalese anxieties.

The Tamil sense of grievance was further intensified by anti-Tamil riots following the 1977 election, when the United National Party returned to power. The government attempted to satisfy Tamil grievances by constitutional changes, by administrative order, and by protracted negotiations and hesitant implementation of district development councils. The measures were not sufficient to calm the Tamils' anger and relieve their fear. Radical Tamil groups, including the Tamil Liberation Tigers, blocked government efforts to restore order and organized terrorist incidents.

In 1983 Sri Lanka experienced the worst anti-Tamil riots ever. The event radicalized many Tamils who had kept hoping for a negotiated resolution to the situation. Thousands of Tamils fled to Madras, India, where competing politicians dramatized their support for one or another faction of Tamil militants. Indira Gandhi, prime minister of India, actively involved her government in the issue, with offers of mediation between the Sri Lankan capital, Colombo, and Jaffna. She also offered direct assistance to the militants in the form of training camps, communications, money, and arms.

Following a dual policy, President Jayewardene negotiated with the more moderate Tamil leaders and also strengthened defenses. He gradually tripled the size of the armed forces, and by 1988 he had increased defense spending from 1 percent of the gross domestic product (GDP) to more than 5 percent.

The radical Tamils made repeated attacks on government facilities. They intimidated and even assassinated Tamils who cooperated with the government, and they staged terrorist attacks in the south. As the conflict continued, the extremist Tamil Liberation Tigers came to dominate the movement.

In 1987 Jayewardene and Rajiv Gandhi, who succeeded Indira Gandhi as prime minister of India, negotiated the Indo–Sri Lanka Accord. The Sri Lankan government acknowledged that Sri Lanka was a multiethnic state where language and other rights of minorities would be duly protected. The agreement defined a devolution of government powers to provincial councils. For its part, the government of India agreed to send a peacekeeping force to reassure the militants and guarantee implementation of the accord.

The Tamil Liberation Tigers turned on the Indian peacekeepers. The initial 3,000 Indian troops grew to 60,000. By the time the Indian army was asked to withdraw by Sri Lankan president Ranasinghe Premadasa in 1990, it had lost more 1,200 men, and more than twice as many were seriously wounded.

Jayewardene's "invitation" to the Indian peacekeepers profoundly affected Sri Lankan domestic politics, precipitating a second major challenge, the reemergence of the People's Liberation Front.

The presence of Indian troops touched a sensitive Sinhalese nerve, providing a near perfect justification for the rebirth of the People's Liberation Front and its campaign to destroy the Sri Lankan political establishment. In 1988–1989 the People's Liberation Front tried to disrupt elections by assassinating political candidates and known supporters of the major parties. During the summer of

1988 it virtually brought Colombo, Kandy, and other cities to a halt through strikes, work stoppages, and assassinations. In the end, by directly threatening the lives of the families of military and police officers, the People's Liberation Front roused the army to action. The army demolished party cadres, captured and killed Front leaders, and eliminated known and suspected followers. In this atmosphere of suspicion and deadly violence, innocent people undoubtedly also "disappeared."

In 1988, toward the end of his term, Jayewardene passed leadership of the United National Party to his prime minister, Premadasa. Despite violent efforts by the People's Liberation Front to prevent elections in December 1988, Premadasa was narrowly—and, the opposition claimed, dubiously—elected executive president. In the face of threats from the People's Liberation Front, only 55 percent of the electorate dared go to the polls. Parliamentary elections held in February 1989 under proportional representation confirmed the United National Party in power for five more years, but with a much narrower majority than before.

The years 1983–1989 were the worst ever for democracy in Sri Lanka, as the competitive ballot was replaced by violence. An estimated 30,000 people died; hundreds of thousands more became refugees, and thousands left the island permanently.

Return to Normalcy?

After the destruction of the People's Liberation Front in 1992, provincial council elections were held in 1993 under nearly normal conditions of public peace, except in the north and east, where the Tamil Liberation Tigers effectively blocked free elections. This time 77 percent of eligible voters cast ballots, suggesting that once again Sri Lanka was returning to orderly democratic processes. Indeed, in the next national election, in August 1994, the United National Party was replaced after seventeen years in power, when the Sri Lanka Freedom Party-dominated People's Alliance won a near majority on a platform of ending the war. Chandrika Bandaranaike Kumaratunga, the daughter of two former prime ministers, became prime minister. Her mother became president.

In spite of this positive sign, Sri Lanka had an army three times larger than before, weapons were readily available among the population, and communal differences remained acute. The Tamil Liberation Tigers, their membership concentrated largely in the Jaffna peninsula, remained intractable, unilaterally breaking a truce offered by the new government and rejecting a more generous offer of devolution of powers to Tamil areas.

See also *India.*

BIBLIOGRAPHY

Coomeraswamy, Radikha. *Sri Lanka: The Crisis of the Anglo-American Constitutional Traditions in a Developing Society.* New Delhi: Vikas, 1984.

deSilva, K. M. *A History of Ceylon.* London: C. Hurst, 1981.

———. *Managing Ethnic Tensions in Multi-Ethnic Societies: Sri Lanka 1880–1985.* Lanham, Md.: University Press of America, 1986.

Manor, James. *Sri Lanka in Change and Crisis.* London: Croom Helm, 1984.

Obeyesekere, Gananath. "Sinhalese-Buddhist Identity in Ceylon." In *Ethnic Identity: Cultural Continuities and Change,* edited by George deVos and Lola Romanucci-Ross. Palo Alto, Calif.: Mayfield Publishing, 1982.

Ratnatunga, Sinha. *Politics of Terrorism: The Sri Lanka Experience.* Balconnen, Australia: International Fellowship for Social and Economic Development, 1986.

Roberts, Michael, ed. *Collective Identities, Nationalisms and Protest in Modern Sri Lanka.* Colombo, Sri Lanka: Marga Institute, 1979.

Tambiah, S. J. *Ethnic Fratricide and the Dismantling of Democracy.* Chicago: University of Chicago Press, 1986.

Wilson, A. Jayeratnam. *Politics in Sri Lanka: 1947–1973.* London: Macmillan, 1974.

Wriggins, W. Howard. *Ceylon, Dilemmas of a New Nation.* Princeton: Princeton University Press, 1960.

Sudan

Independent country, located in Northeast Africa, that has had a troubled and violent political history since independence in 1956. The largest country in Africa, Sudan is split by severe social cleavages that have led to alternating periods of civilian and military rule. The most fundamental cleavage is that between the predominantly Islamic north and the culturally African south. Both regions also have ethnic and ideological divisions, and the north is divided along the lines of various Islamic sects.

Sudan's nearly 600 ethnic groups speak more than 400 languages and dialects, although Arabic and English are commonly spoken by the elite. People identifying themselves as Arabs are the largest single group, constituting nearly 40 percent of the total population and a majority in the north. Most of the residents of the south speak Nilotic languages; the Dinka, Nuer, and Shilluk are the major ethnic groups there.

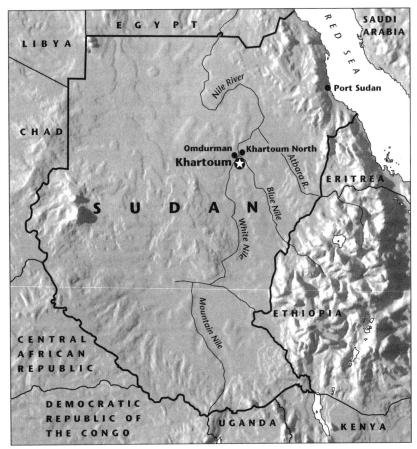

Colonial Legacy

From 1821 to 1885 Egypt governed Sudan but viewed the region predominantly as a source of slaves. In the early 1880s a Sudanese religious leader known as the Mahdi led a *jihad* to expel the Egyptians. From 1885 to 1898 the Mahdist regime (known as the Mahdiyah) ruled Sudan. British forces destroyed the Mahdiyah and established joint Anglo-Egyptian control in 1899. Egypt's role in this joint administration was limited, and the British governor general acted as a de facto colonial authority.

The British generated economic activity, such as the Gezira cotton scheme along the Nile, but generally they governed indirectly through local elites, many of them members of the Ansar, the followers of the Mahdi. London closed the south to outsiders, including northern Sudanese, leaving the region isolated and with only limited social services provided by Christian missionaries. The British granted Sudan independence in 1956, after settling issues with Egypt and determining that the south would be part of the new state. The legacy of colonialism, notably the favoritism toward certain northern groups and the differential economic development that favored the north,

widened the social cleavages that continue to plague independent Sudan.

Since independence a wide variety of leaders and regime types have sought the basis for stable power without enduring success. Sudan's society consists of a number of well-organized constituencies prone to factionalism. In the north many people have been divided into competing sects based on politically and economically powerful Islamic orders. The Ansar, led by the descendants of the Mahdi, are particularly strong in rural areas. They are organized politically in the Umma Party, led since the 1960s by Sadiq al-Mahdi. The Khatmiyah, a rival sect, is led by the Mirghani family. The Khatmiyah, along with other more secular and urbanized groups, form the core of the Democratic Unionist Party. The Sudanese Communist Party (based in the universities and labor unions) wielded significant political influence in the 1950s and 1960s. The Muslim Brotherhood, which developed in opposition to the communists and to the secularization of Sudanese society, began to cultivate important political support beginning in the mid-1970s and competed in the 1986 elections under the name of the National Islamic Front. The south has been united primarily by its shared apprehension of domination by northern Arabs. Armed insurgencies, led at first by the Anyanya (scorpion) guerrillas and since 1983 by the Sudanese People's Liberation Movement, have resisted the northern-based governments.

Sudan has had extensive if troubled experience with democratic politics. Relatively free multiparty elections were held in 1953 (under British rule), 1958, 1965, 1968, and 1986. Unfortunately, the highly divided nature of Sudanese society has prevented any party from winning a majority of seats. As a result, each parliamentary period has been marked by weak coalition governments, plagued by inter- and intraparty rivalries, corruption, and byzantine maneuvering for partisan or personal gain. The military intervened in 1958, 1969, 1985, and 1989—years when party defections and deadlock prevented effective action to manage Sudan's severe social and economic problems.

Early Years of Independence

The first postindependence government was formed on the basis of multiparty elections for a Constituent Assembly in 1953. These gave the National Unionist Party (the predecessor of the Democratic Unionist Party) the most seats, followed by Umma. Ismail al-Azhari, the first prime minister, lost his support in Parliament to Abdallah Khalil in July 1956. Khalil put together a coalition of Umma supporters and defectors from the National Unionist Party and won the next election in 1958. Southerners participated in the 1958 campaign in a loose association known as the southern liberal bloc. Khalil's governing coalition, however, suffered from factionalism and corruption. The weak regime drifted and threatened to splinter, while challenges mounted from the radical movement, trade unions, and general economic decline.

In November 1958 Khalil organized a "preemptive coup" in collaboration with the army's senior officers. The new regime, led by Maj. Gen. Ibrahim Abbud, banned all political parties but ruled for the next six years with the active support of significant parts of the old elite. In 1963 Abbud established locally elected councils that in turn selected delegates to provincial and central councils. Abbud succeeded in settling a longstanding dispute with Egypt over water rights, and he improved economic conditions. Over time, however, he became increasingly authoritarian and isolated. Opposition developed among radical dissidents in the armed forces and the Communist Party. Most important, Abbud's attempts to impose Arab and Islamic culture on the south escalated the armed resistance in that region.

A general strike and violent riots, known as the October Revolution, overthrew Abbud in November 1964. A transitional regime led by Sir al-Khatim Khalifa tried to create a government based on the new political forces involved in the demonstrations (professional groups and trade unions organized in the United National Front). Eventually, however, this regime proved unable to contain the power of the old establishment (religious leaders, large landowners, merchants). Elections in 1965 gave Umma and the National Unionist Party a majority of seats. No voting took place in the war-torn south until 1967.

The period from 1965 until 1969 saw a variety of weak governments in which leaders tried to build coalitions among the principal political parties. Divisions within Umma made the task of building a strong coalition extremely difficult. Throughout this period Sudan's problems, particularly the war in the south, resisted resolution.

Military Coup and Civil War

This chaotic democratic period ended on May 25, 1969, when a group of radical young officers led by Col. Jaafar Muhammed al-Numeiri seized power. Over the next sixteen years Numeiri experimented with a variety of political structures and made alliances with diverse social groups in an attempt to stabilize and institutionalize his power.

Immediately after the coup, Numeiri banned political parties and ruled through a Revolutionary Command Council. His first cabinet included a number of radical civilians with ties to the Sudanese Communist Party. Numeiri's first battles were against the Ansar sect, which fought government forces for control of Aba Island near Khartoum in March 1970. Next, Numeiri moved against the Communist Party, marginalizing its base until the Communists struck back, staging a nearly successful coup in July 1971. In an effort to establish a new basis for his power, Numeiri dissolved the Revolutionary Command Council and promulgated a new constitution that provided for a presidential form of government. A dubious October 1971 plebiscite endorsed Numeiri for a six-year term with 98.6 percent of the vote.

Following his move against the Communist Party, Numeiri looked to the south as a potential new base of support. In March 1972 Numeiri's government signed the Addis Ababa accords with the Anyanya guerrillas, ending the destructive civil war. This agreement provided the south autonomy with an appointed regional president and an elected Southern Regional Assembly. Elections for the assembly took place in 1973 and 1978. Widely hailed as an indication of Numeiri's leadership, the agreement gave him popular support both in the south and the north and won him international favor.

To further his hold on Sudanese politics, Numeiri organized the Sudan Socialist Union in January 1972 as an all-encompassing umbrella to channel political participation and penetrate the countryside. Numeiri constructed a variety of affiliated professional and mass organizations and a system of local councils that sent delegates to higher provincial councils. Elections in 1974 for a slate of candidates approved by the Sudan Socialist Union created a People's Assembly. The assembly had the authority to pass legislation, but the powerful presidency could veto and rule by decree.

After mending fences with the south, Numeiri's focus shifted to opposition from traditional Muslim groups in the north. The president survived a violent Ansar-inspired coup attempt in July 1976 and the following year opened talks with exiled Ansar leader Sadiq al-Mahdi (then heading the conservative National Front). Numeiri and al-Mahdi reached an agreement that allowed members of the traditional sectarian parties to participate as individuals in the 1978 People's Assembly elections. Although still technically a single-party system, the Sudan Socialist Union lost its coherence, and the People's Assembly broke down because of factionalism and corruption.

By 1983 Numeiri had become increasingly dependent on the traditional sectarian parties for support. As a result, he abandoned his greatest accomplishment, the peace agreement with the south. In June 1983 Numeiri unilaterally subdivided the south, effectively annulling the Addis Ababa agreements and unleashing renewed armed conflict. In September 1983, in an effort to undercut his fundamentalist opponents and consolidate his constituency in the north, Numeiri adopted *shari'a* (law based on the religious principles of Islam). In response, the Sudanese People's Liberation Movement began an insurgency in the south that quickly frustrated Khartoum's ability to govern.

Numeiri's political dominance withered in the face of a popular uprising (the *intifada)* provoked by spiraling inflation, corruption, and strikes that followed currency devaluations and removal of food subsidies. Pushed by mobilized urban groups of professionals, the military overthrew Numeiri on April 6, 1985, and formed a Transitional Military Council. Under the leadership of Lt. Gen. Abd al-Rahman Siwar al-Dahab, the military council dismantled the Sudan Socialist Union, legalized the old political parties, held elections, and turned over power after one year.

More than forty political parties competed in the generally free elections in April 1986. No voting took place in 37 of the 68 southern constituencies, however, because of continuing civil conflict. Southern insurgents in the Sudanese People's Liberation Movement under the leadership of John Garang demanded that the military give up power immediately and refused to participate in the elections.

Of the 264 constituencies where polling occurred in 1986, Umma won 99 seats, the Democratic Unionist Party won 63, the National Islamic Front (the political organization of the Muslim Brotherhood) won 51, and other regional parties (including several based among southerners) won the remainder. Umma leader Sadiq al-Mahdi formed a coalition government that included Umma, the Democratic Unionist Party, and several of the regional parties. It was opposed by the National Islamic Front and the Communist Party.

During the next three years, a continuous series of crises developed, leading to six successive coalition governments. Yet Prime Minister al-Mahdi and his coalition partners opened talks with Garang and the People's Liberation Movement and seemed to be near a peace agreement. The military stepped in again in June 1989, however, aborting both the peace process and the democratic experiment.

Gen. Umar Hassan Ahmad al-Bashir led the coup and established a Revolutionary Command Council of National Salvation. The military dissolved the elected legislature, arrested al-Mahdi and other leaders, and banned political parties again. Relying on the fundamentalist National Islamic Front for support, al-Bashir's government sharply limited political activity and pursued a brutal war against insurgents in the south. A constitutional conference in April 1991 failed to resolve the deep and bitter conflict between those who insisted on *shari'a* and those who demanded a secular constitution. Umma and the Democratic Unionist Party operated in exile and in 1990 formed an alliance with the People's Liberation Movement to create the National Democratic Alliance. The alliance stated its commitment to democracy and a secular constitution.

Between the coup of 1989 and 1997, al-Bashir introduced a number of cosmetic changes, but nothing substantive. In October 1993 the Revolutionary Command Council named al-Bashir president, then was dissolved. In 1996 elections, al-Bashir was reelected president, and a new National Assembly was convoked. All opposition parties boycotted the elections.

Through the mid–1990s Sudan suffered from an authoritarian form of government, extensive human rights violations, and a devastating civil war. The historical experience with democracy—most notably the parliamentary government established at independence in 1956 and the two parliamentary periods that followed military rule in 1964 and 1986—demonstrates the latent strength of the nation's democratic tradition. Elected government is a widely held aspiration of the Sudanese people. Despite its prevalence, military rule is regarded as an aberration, a temporary condition until new elections can be held. As its deeply rooted and powerful political movements indicate, the nation's civil society is well organized even if highly divided. Although elected governments have failed to endure in Sudan in the past, further efforts to build democracy are likely.

See also *Africa, Subsaharan.*

BIBLIOGRAPHY

Bechtold, Peter. "More Turbulence in Sudan: A New Politics This Time?" *Middle East Journal* 44 (autumn 1990): 579–595.

Deng, Francis. *War of Visions: Conflict of Identities in the Sudan.* Washington, D.C.: Brookings Institution, 1995.

Holt, P. M., and M. W. Daly. *A History of the Sudan: from the Coming of Islam to the Present Day.* 4th ed. London: Longman, 1986.

Medani, Khalid. "Sudan's Human and Political Crisis." *Current History* 92 (May 1993): 203–207.

Niblock, Tim. *Class and Power in Sudan: The Dynamics of Sudanese Politics, 1898–1985.* Albany: State University of New York Press; London: Macmillan, 1987.

Woodward, Peter. *Sudan, 1898–1989: The Unstable State.* Boulder, Colo.: Lynne Rienner, 1990.

T

Taiwan

A small, semitropical island about one hundred miles east of mainland China, the center of government of the Republic of China since 1949. The central government of the Republic of China and the Nationalist Party (the Kuomintang, or KMT) moved from the mainland to Taiwan in 1949, after being defeated in a civil war with the Communist Party and its armed forces. The Republic of China furnishes a rare example of an authoritarian state gradually letting go of power to promote a democratic political system.

Taiwan's population in the mid-1990s was about 21 million. About 85 percent of the population are native Taiwanese; the rest came from other provinces of mainland China.

Establishment of Authoritarian Rule

Imperial Japan occupied Taiwan between 1895 and the end of World War II. In 1943 the Cairo Conference mandated that Taiwan and other territories be restored to China, and on October 25, 1945, Japan formally returned Taiwan to the control of the central government of the Republic of China. The retreat of the government to Taiwan in 1949 divided China into two sovereign states: the People's Republic of China, which under Communist rule governed the mainland provinces, and the Republic of China, which governed Taiwan and its small offshore islands. The government of the Republic of China and the ruling Nationalist Party insisted that they represented the mainland provinces and that the regime of the Communist People's Republic was illegitimate.

To underscore that claim, the Republic of China in 1948 added to its 1947 constitution eleven amendments called the Temporary Provisions, which were to be effective during the period of Communist rebellion. The Temporary

Provisions nullified much of the constitution and granted the president's office great powers. On May 19, 1949, the Republic of China imposed martial law in Taiwan; this action allowed military courts to judge and sentence any individuals or groups threatening national security. It also guaranteed that no political party would organize to challenge the Nationalist Party.

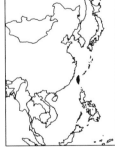

The government continued to rule by martial law until

July 15, 1987. The lifting of martial law permitted the rapid evolution of a political marketplace in which other parties competed with the Nationalist Party in elections to select leaders who represented the people of Taiwan rather than the mainland. This transition to democracy was not only permitted but encouraged by the government. The process of democratization in Taiwan was unique because the Nationalist-ruled authoritarian state initiated democratic reforms while still threatened by an external enemy, the People's Republic of China.

In addition, the state faced the threat of the Taiwanese nationalist movement, which sought to overthrow the government by peaceful or violent means. That nationalist movement began in February 1947 with an uprising in Taiwan; the government ruthlessly suppressed it. Many embittered Taiwanese fled to join opposition groups that were forming in Japan, the United States, and elsewhere.

The Nationalist Party and the government of the Republic of China controlled Taiwan's society rigidly and dealt harshly with individuals who threatened national security or undermined party and government rule. Security personnel, as well as the police, monitored the activities of intellectuals, journalists, educators, politicians, and professionals who were perceived as criticizing or opposing the regime. The government conducted a campaign of "white terror" in the 1950s, arresting anyone alleged to be a critic of or a threat to the government and the ruling party. It is estimated that tens of thousands of people were incarcerated for varying periods.

Unlike the communist parties and other despotic regimes that ruled many nations in the decades after World War II, the development-oriented, authoritarian Nationalist Party was committed to building a democracy. Its leadership adhered to the ideology of the political theorist and revolutionary Sun Yat-sen (1866–1925). Sun's doctrine encouraged a strong commitment to building a Chinese-style democracy in Taiwan—but only after the Nationalists decided when and under what conditions political reforms should be introduced. Because of the severity of external and internal threats, the Nationalist leadership waited until the spring of 1986 to decide to reform the polity.

Until then, Nationalist leaders and government officials had established a limited democracy by adhering to the 1947 constitution for governing Taiwan. That constitution provided for five branches, or Yuans: the Executive, Legislative, and Judicial Yuans; the Control Yuan, which monitored general administration; and the Examination Yuan, which oversaw civil service examinations. The constitution stipulated that elections must be held every six years to select a new National Assembly. This would have meant a new election in 1953 (the first election under the constitution had been held on the mainland in 1947), but an election was impossible in the divided nation. The Executive Yuan finally obtained a legal ruling in January 1954 allowing all first-term elected representatives of the central government to continue to serve and enjoy their rights beyond 1953. The National Assembly, made up of mainlanders elected in 1947, continued to elect a president and vice president every six years until March 1990, when this procedure was used for the last time. The Legislative Yuan, composed exclusively of mainlanders, rubber-stamped legislative bills submitted by the Nationalist Party and the Executive Yuan. In this way, the mainlander-dominated government and the Nationalists ruled the Republic of China.

Modernization and Reform

Between 1950 and 1955 the authoritarian government launched reforms to modernize and gradually democratize the economy and polity of the Republic of China. A land-reform program redistributed land to poor farmers and landless households by granting them low-interest loans to purchase land and compensating landowners with bonds. In 1950 regular elections began for town, city, and provincial councils, city mayors, and district chiefs. By 1952 primary school children received free education. These reforms set the stage for the people to prosper with equity, for more people to become educated, and for the people to participate in local government.

By 1970 about 70 percent of the people lived in towns and cities of more than 2,000 persons. Taiwan's citizens, though highly literate and reasonably well educated, still had an income of only $389 per capita. Local elections became a regular activity in people's lives. A new civil society took form, and more young people entered political life.

When mainlander representatives in the central government retired or died, resulting vacancies had to be filled. To that end the Nationalists and the government permitted supplementary national elections in 1969 in which competing candidates could be elected to fill vacancies in the Legislative Yuan, the Control Yuan, and the National Assembly. This reform allowed young politicians, especially those who opposed the Nationalist Party, to be elected to government positions. The ruling party, however, still held a majority and continued to control central government policies and to pass laws.

During the 1970s and early 1980s many politicians referred to themselves as "outside the Nationalist Party" and began to oppose the regime. They published magazines critical of the Nationalists and the government. Although the government banned these publications, others soon appeared. This upsurge of political discussion and election activity reflected a growing political opposition demanding greater democracy. As Taiwan's civil society grew, the nation also was becoming more isolated in the world. The People's Republic had replaced the Republic of China in the United Nations in 1972, and the United States broke diplomatic relations with the Republic of China in 1979.

In the midst of these events Chiang Ching-kuo, the son of Chiang Kai-shek (who was president of China from 1928 to 1949), came to power. Born in 1909, he had spent twelve years of his youth as a hostage in the Soviet Union. His father had groomed him to be his successor. Chiang Ching-kuo became the sixth president of the Republic of China in March 1978 and was reelected in 1984, after naming Lee Teng-hui, a brilliant economist, official, and native Taiwanese, to be his vice president. As early as the 1970s Chiang had recruited talented Taiwanese for party and government positions and considered how to expand democracy.

End of Martial Law

Preoccupied with Taiwan's increased international isolation, a growing political opposition, his own worsening health, and several major scandals within the KMT, Chiang did not undertake political reform until 1986. Like his father, he wanted to reestablish the 1947 constitution and the doctrine of Sun Yat-sen on the Chinese mainland. He finally believed that China could be unified only if a democracy was first built in Taiwan. No one but Chiang had the power to initiate political reform and make his party accept it.

Chiang decided that the Nationalist Party must lift martial law, allow a free press to develop and political parties to form, and amend the constitution to provide for election of all national officials and representatives. These political reforms were dangerous because the Taiwanese nationalist movement, the Communist People's Republic, and KMT conservatives could intervene and cause turmoil, but time was running out on the seventy-seven-year-old president.

In late March 1986 Chiang established a reform committee made up of twelve people to study how to replace martial law with a new security law, establish a law to allow political parties to compete, and amend the constitution to hold national elections.

Before the committee completed its work, some of the "outside" politicians illegally established the Democratic Progressive Party. Chiang refused to outlaw the party and jail its leaders, even though they had defied martial law. Instead, he urged his party to press forward with reform and use the law and the constitution to promote democracy.

In January 1987 the government allowed newspapers to expand their daily editions and ended censorship. By July 15 the government had enacted a new security law and lifted martial law. The Nationalist Party and government then passed a law giving political parties the right to register and compete in elections. These legal reforms transformed Taiwan's political life. In November 1987 Chiang obtained party and government agreement to allow citizens who were not officials to visit their relatives on the mainland. In campaigning for the December 19, 1989, election, people publicly debated for the first time whether Taiwan should become the Republic of Taiwan, and the Democratic Progressive Party won six of the twenty mayoral/county magistrate seats—a major setback for the Nationalists.

Chiang died on January 13, 1988. A few hours later, in a smooth leadership succession, his vice president, Lee Teng-hui, became the first Taiwanese to be elected president of the Republic of China. At the Seventh Nationalist Party Congress in July, party members approved President Lee as party chairman. He was the first person to serve concurrently as the nation's president and Nationalist Party chairman since 1949. A major transfer of political power took place over the next five years, first within the Nationalist Party and then in the new political marketplace. The speed of democratization between 1986 and 1994 was unprecedented in the history of Chinese civilization.

Democratic Transition

Between 1990 and 1994 several major events threatened the democratic transition. First, in the March 20, 1990, presidential election, Lee defeated a group of mainland Nationalist Party politicians in the National Assembly who tried to replace him. His triumph was marred by widespread public protests against the National Assembly and demands that the senior representatives retire. In order to resolve this crisis, Lee promised the nation that within three years he would complete constitutional reform, broadening elections and making democracy a reality in Taiwan.

Few people believed the new president could keep his word. Meanwhile, the People's Republic pressured Taiwan to become a special province with great autonomy and to expand its economic links with the mainland. The Democratic Progressive Party demanded the elimination of the National Assembly and a redraft of the 1947 constitution, hoping to create a Republic of Taiwan without any links to the mainland.

Lee dealt with the threat of Taiwanese nationalism by convening a conference on national affairs in June and July 1990, at which 225 public figures and scholars from across the political spectrum met to discuss political reform. Lee even invited Taiwanese dissidents from abroad and representatives of other parties. The conference was a turning point in the political life of Taiwan. The Democratic Progressive Party and Nationalists achieved a political reconciliation and agreed to exchange information.

Opposition politicians had always blamed the Nationalists for their repression of the February 1947 uprising. The Office of the President and the Executive Yuan set up a commission of experts to review that tragic affair. In the spring of 1992 the commission issued a report in part blaming the government and recommending that a memorial be established and compensation paid to the victims. In May 1993 the government approved the commission's recommendations, thus putting the issue to rest.

In October 1990 President Lee assembled private citizens and leading politicians, including K'ang Ning-hsiang of the Democratic Progressive Party, in a commission to study the unification of China and to formulate a policy toward the People's Republic. In February 1991 the commission presented a three-stage plan for the unification of the Republic of China and the People's Republic in the distant future, provided the people of both states agreed. This blueprint became the basis for a new, pragmatic foreign policy toward the People's Republic.

In mid-1990 the Judicial Yuan had ruled that all senior representatives of the central government must retire by December 31, 1991. The president convened the National Assembly in April 1991 to annul the Temporary Provisions, end the war with the communists, and pass additional articles stipulating elections for a new National Assembly and Legislative Yuan. The National Assembly elections, held in late 1991, were peaceful; the KMT won three-quarters of the seats—a majority vote to amend the constitution.

The new National Assembly represented only the voters of Taiwan and its offshore islands, rather than claiming to represent the mainland. It convened in spring 1992. By May it had passed eight new articles, which called for election of a president and vice president by 1996 and presidential nomination of members of the Judicial, Examination, and Control Yuans, subject to approval by the National Assembly. In December 1992 elections for the Legislative Yuan were held, and the Democratic Progressives won 50 of the 161 seats.

By May 1993 Lee had fulfilled his promise to reform the 1947 constitution; the Nationalist Party, in cooperation with other political parties, had expanded central government elections for Taiwan and its offshore islands. The Democratic Progressive Party complied with the rules and competed in those elections. It gradually expanded its political power in the new Legislative Yuan and won appointments to the Control Yuan in February 1993. By working within the framework of the constitution and seeking voter support in the political marketplace, the Democratic Progressive Party demonstrated that it was a responsible opposition party.

During 1993–1994 the party elders of Chiang Ching-kuo's generation voluntarily retired from the government and party without trying to undermine the political reforms. The Nationalist Party began splitting in 1993, and in 1994 a faction of mainlanders left the party to form the New Party. In mid-August 1994 the Nationalists held their Fourteenth Party Congress, which elected four vice chairs, cast secret ballots for the party chairman (reelecting Lee Teng-hui) for the first time in party history, and elected younger Taiwanese to the central and standing committees. Lee had now neutralized his opponents in the KMT.

In the summer of 1994 the National Assembly again amended the constitution, to include rules for popular election of the president and vice president. In late November 1994 the nation held the first election for a provincial governor and for mayors of Kaohsiung and Taipei. The Nationalist Party candidates easily won the provincial governorship and Kaohsiung mayoral election, but the party lost the Taipei mayoral race to the Democratic Progressive candidate.

In the regularly scheduled Legislative Yuan elections of December 2, 1995, the KMT suffered a setback, but with 85 seats it still maintained a slim majority in the 164-seat body. The KMT won a more comfortable majority in the National Assembly balloting of March 1996, in which it claimed 183 of 334 seats. Also in March 1996, direct democracy was extended by the first ever popular election of a Chinese leader. President Lee won 54 percent of the vote to defeat three other candidates, securing for himself a second six-year term.

Chiang's decision in 1986 to end martial law, end censorship of the press, and allow political parties to form and compete were given full effect after his death by the 1991,

1992, and 1994 amendments to the 1947 constitution, engineered by Lee Teng-hui. The rapid transition from a limited democracy to a full democracy in Taiwan between 1986 and 1996 was a political miracle in twentieth-century Chinese politics, making Taiwan the first Chinese democracy.

See also *China*.

BIBLIOGRAPHY

Chao, Linda, and Ramon H. Myers. "The First Chinese Democracy of the Republic of China on Taiwan, 1986–1994." *Asian Survey* 34 (March 1994): 213–230.

Cheng, Tun-jen, and Stephen Haggard, eds. *Political Change in Taiwan*. Boulder, Colo.: Lynne Rienner, 1992.

Chiu, Hungdah. *China and the Taiwan Issue*. New York: Praeger, 1979.

———. *Constitutional Development and Reform in the Republic of China on Taiwan (with Documents)*. Occasional Papers/Reprints Series in Contemporary Asian Studies 2:61. College Park: University of Maryland, School of Law, 1993.

———, ed. *China and the Question of Taiwan: Documents and Analysis*. New York: Praeger, 1973.

Leng, Shao-chuan, ed. *Chiang Ching-kuo's Leadership in the Development of the Republic of China on Taiwan*. Lanham, Md.: University Press of America, 1993.

Tien, Hung-mao. *The Great Transition: Political and Social Change in the Republic of China*. Stanford: Hoover Institution Press, 1989.

Tsang, Steve, ed. *In the Shadow of China: Political Developments in Taiwan since 1948*. London: Hurst; Honolulu: University of Hawaii Press, 1993.

Thailand

A constitutional monarchy of Southeast Asia and the only nation of that region never colonized by Western powers. The history of politics in Thailand (formerly known as Siam) is a history of authoritarian rule. From its earliest kingdom in Sukhothai (c.1238–1350), Thailand was led by paternalistic kings whose duty it was to solve all the problems of their subjects. In the Ayuthaya period (1350–1767) these rulers were transformed into autocratic god-kings. Even today that perception remains an important element of the veneration shown to the king. The king was Lord of Life, with total power over every aspect of society.

The destruction of the city of Ayuthaya by invading Burmese in 1767 was a traumatic event in Thai history. The kingdom was nearly destroyed, but the Thais soon recovered and established life under a new centralized government in Bangkok. Once again a dynasty was established. The ninth monarch of the Chakri dynasty, King Bhumibol Adulyadej, was Thailand's reigning monarch in the mid–1990s.

The Chakri kings strengthened their position by creating a more "modern" and efficient governmental system led by Western-trained bureaucrats. Several of the Chakris were reformers who unintentionally brought about their own demise as they opened the kingdom to Western ideas of limited government. In 1932 the absolute monarchy was overthrown and replaced by a new oligarchy consisting of Western-trained bureaucrats and members of the military. These new forces promulgated constitutions, making the nation a constitutional monarchy. They continued to dominate Thai politics in the mid–1990s. The kingdom was renamed Thailand in 1939.

Fashioning a Semidemocracy

The political culture of Thailand, with its emphasis on deference to authority and hierarchical social relations, is not conducive to democratic rule. Nevertheless, in the 1980s Thailand fashioned a semidemocracy that defied the expectations of most observers of Thai politics. *Semidemocracy* refers to the balance between Western-style democracy and the authoritarian values that favor and buttress military involvement in governmental affairs. The balance is uniquely Thai, a blend that has been legitimated in the minds of both the rulers and the ruled.

The success of Thailand's semidemocracy was partly a result of the economic boom of the 1980s, which allowed the government to meet the needs of the citizenry. This remarkable period of economic development brought high levels of education, literacy, access to the media, and travel—all of which heightened Thais' awareness of democratic values and expanded their horizons.

The Thai people approved of the semidemocracy because of the orderly society and economic growth that accompanied it. In the past, the democratic orientations of the Thais had been a matter of form rather than substance. Other values—security, development, deference, personalism, and economic stability—took precedence over those more directly related to citizen participation in governmental affairs. The economic achievements of the 1980s helped the Thais appreciate democratic values as much as other cherished values. The semidemocracy also provided the Thai people with an example of successful democratic government. Most viewed the earlier period of democracy, from 1973 to 1976, as a time of chaos, disorder, and economic travail.

In the 1980s and early 1990s the Thai political system

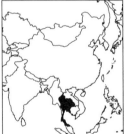

received the largest plurality of votes. Chatchai's predecessor, Gen. Prem Tinsulanond, had led Thailand during a period of economic growth. His administration had been deemed acceptable to both civilians and the military, and he had been expected to continue in office. His refusal to be a candidate opened the way for civilian leadership under Chatchai.

The smooth transition reflected the new optimism about Thailand's evolution toward democracy. Chatchai was able to assume power without relying on the support of the army, and the constitutional provisions for elections worked well in the transfer of political power. Thus it was all the more shocking when a military coup d'état took place in February 1991. The coup was an assault on the notion that Thailand had successfully institutionalized democratic and civilian government.

The 1991 Coup and Its Aftermath

The last successful coup had taken place in 1977. The peaceful interval of more than a decade lulled the Chatchai administration into believing that the days of coups were over. Furthermore, the communist insurgency that had plagued Thailand in the 1960s and 1970s had been quelled, and there was no external threat to Thai security. There seemed to be no compelling motive for military intervention in governmental affairs. The stronger role of political parties and the parliament, as well as a general attitude favorable to democratic civilian rule, also seemed to have reduced the influence of the military. The determination of King Bhumibol Adulyadej to oppose a military coup was believed to lessen the chance that such a coup would succeed. Moreover, Thailand's remarkable economic growth of 11 percent per year (the highest in the world for three years) seemed to provide a bulwark against intervention by the military. Military leaders had a stake in the status quo because they benefited from the enormous profits generated by the booming Thai economy. Finally, the Thai military was thought to have accepted Chatchai, himself a former army general, because of the generous budget he allotted to the military.

But counter to this analysis, and against all expectations, Sunthorn Kongsompong, who was supreme commander, and Suchinda Kraprayoon, the army commander in chief, abrogated the constitution on February 23, 1991, and dismissed the elected government. In its place they set up a temporary National Peacekeeping Council, with powers of martial law, and established themselves as the ultimate arbiters of public policy. Initially the Thai people

seemed well able to cope with the changing needs and demands of the people. This ability was due in part to the strengthening of political institutions and in part to the rise of pressure groups representing the interests of an increasingly pluralistic society. These changes accompanied the process of democratization, which drew more citizens to become involved in the political sphere. Democratization also reduced the importance of personalism as it increased the observance of laws and the recognition of governmental institutions in public-policy decision making.

The clearest sign of change in contemporary Thai politics was the rise to power in 1988 of Chatchai Choonhavan, the first elected member of parliament to become prime minister since 1976. Chatchai became prime minister following the 1988 elections, when the political party he led made no resistance to the coup, though they did not enthusiastically support it; there were no public protests or demonstrations.

The 1991 coup demonstrated that democratization had not ended the personalism and factionalism of traditional Thai politics. Even among the partners in the ruling coalition that was in power when the coup occurred, factional conflict remained the norm as party leaders vied for the most influential cabinet positions.

A problem related to personalism was corruption, which also continued to be an important part of the political scene. The phenomenal economic growth of the 1980s had brought large amounts of capital into the financial system, and these new resources were the target of public officials out for private gain. Thai citizens were skeptical about the Chatchai administration's professed concern for the majority, which did not benefit from the growth of the economy.

The National Peacekeeping Council claimed that corruption, factionalism, and the rise of a "parliamentary dictatorship" were the main reasons for the coup. In particular, the military complained of rampant vote buying, leading to the election of the rich rather than the most qualified. In fact, the number of wealthy capitalists elected to parliament and chosen for the cabinet had risen steadily in the past decades, but the increase was especially clear in the Chatchai administration.

The complaint of corruption was an important legitimizing rationale for the coup. The more direct cause, however, was a pattern of slights inflicted by Chatchai, which the military perceived as threats to its traditional prerogatives. Chatchai set forth the principle that the military must be subordinate to a civilian prime minister. This principle was intolerable to the military rulers, who had enjoyed greater influence in past military and civilian administrations.

The coup temporarily ended Thailand's steady progress toward democratization and embarrassed the nation in its expanding international affairs. The conventional wisdom was not completely wrong in holding that coups were a thing of the past, however. Realizing that times had indeed changed, the National Peacekeeping Council moved quickly to establish an interim constitution and name a prime minister. The council chose Anand Panyarachun, a distinguished civilian diplomat, administrator, and businessman, to serve as prime minister. His appointment was a sign that the military believed the people would not long tolerate direct military rule.

Anand scheduled a nationwide parliamentary election for March 1992. Corruption was widespread. Political parties sold their names and vote-mobilizing organizations to candidates. Candidates received up to several hundred thousand dollars each for campaign purposes. These funds were often given in cash, so they could not be accounted for. Candidates used the money they received from political parties to pay potential voters for their support. Corruption became the centerpiece of the Thai electoral system.

The elections on March 22 resulted in a narrow victory for parties aligned with the military. Eventually the coalition named General Suchinda as prime minister despite his unequivocal declaration that he would not accept the office. His nomination was approved by the king and the parliament with the concurrence of the speaker of the parliament, and Suchinda took office. In what Thais referred to as "the second coup" or "the silent coup," General Suchinda had engineered military control over the position of prime minister. In so doing he reversed the steps Thailand had taken toward democratic government. To express their dismay, some 50,000 protesters demonstrated against the new government following the announcement of Suchinda's appointment.

Suchinda's time in office was brief: he was driven from office after only forty-eight days. Massive anti-Suchinda demonstrations by hundreds of thousands of Thais took place in May, and hundreds died when the military tried to stop the protests. The conflict between Thailand's reverence for tradition and its headlong plunge into modernity was the major factor in these events. Suchinda mistakenly bet that the forces of tradition as exemplified by the military would prevail. He underestimated the power of the ideal of democracy among the country's increasingly educated and sophisticated citizens.

Suchinda misunderstood the reaction he would generate by approving a violent response to the antigovernment demonstrations. He declared a state of emergency, which effectively took away citizens' civil liberties. At the same time, censorship of the media and the sight of police officers and troops bludgeoning demonstrators wiped out any appearance of legitimacy Suchinda might have had. His claim that the demonstrators and their leaders were pawns of "communist" elements who desired the end of the monarchy was vintage rhetoric from the 1960s, irrelevant to the realities of the 1990s.

Return to Civilian Government

When the crisis of May 1992 turned into chaos and potential civil war, King Bhumibol Adulyadej stepped in to play a crucial role in determining political succession. His extraordinary intervention on May 20 forced the resignation of Suchinda and placed the immense prestige of the monarch on the side of democratic rule. Suchinda had no choice but to resign.

The establishment of a civilian administration was more difficult than the removal of Suchinda, who went into hiding, protected by troops loyal to him. In a second extraordinary intervention, the king approved the return of Anand Panyarachun as prime minister. The appointment was enthusiastically received by most Thais, who recalled that Anand had won international praise for running an honest and efficient government following the 1991 coup.

The election that took place September 13, 1992, was considered one of the fairest in Thai history because of the oversight of "watchdog" groups. A coalition of pro-democracy parties, plus one party that had supported the military in the previous administration, formed a government under the leadership of a civilian politician. Chuan Leekpai, the soft-spoken, fair-minded, moderate leader of the Democrat Party from Trang Province, became prime minister—the first prime minister since the mid–1970s to lack a military background. He led a 207-seat coalition in the 360-member House of Representatives. Prime Minister Chuan's challenge was to find a balance between democratic rule and sensitivity to the traditional prerogatives of the Thai military.

The Chuan government was unstable almost from the start, with parties leaving and entering the coalition over various issues. Finally, the government collapsed in May 1995. After the early elections of July 2, an equally unstable right-wing coalition of seven parties came to power. That government fell in September 1996, and a six-member coalition government took office following November 17 elections. The new prime minister, retired general Chaovalit Yongchaiyut of the New Aspiration Party, retained close ties to the military and as such represented a return to traditional, military-dominated politics.

But just as economic achievements had buttressed the government in the 1980s and early 1990s, an economic downturn in the middle of the 1990s rocked the government. The long-quiescent but growing middle class began to rumble when in 1997 the local currency lost nearly a third of its value and the stock market lost more than a third. The economic crisis begot a political crisis almost overnight. In response, the parliament and government grudgingly adopted a new constitution in September 1997 that many hoped would lead to less corruption, greater accountability, a more professional and responsive parliament, and, indirectly, economic improvement. Whether the document would affect these changes was an open question.

Conclusion

The struggle between state officials led by the military, on the one hand, and politicians and business elites, on the other, continues to be at the center stage of Thai political activity. The 1991 military coup and the subsequent debate on how to fashion a new government exemplified both the attempt and the failure to resolve this struggle. The public explanations for the coup—corruption and parliamentary dictatorship—were rationalizations by military leaders who moved to secure prerogatives they thought were threatened by civilian leadership.

Despite the difficulties encountered between 1991 and 1997 in removing the military from politics, there are reasons to be optimistic about the long-term prospects for democratic rule and a move away from military-dominated, authoritarian, self-serving centralized government. First, Thailand has successfully ended internal insurgency. Second, there are no serious outside threats to the kingdom's security. Third, despite recent economic setbacks, Thailand has excellent prospects for development. Fourth, there has been increasing professionalization of the armed forces. Finally, the international movement toward democratization has penetrated most of the major groups in Thai society, including the military.

The rise of an educated, cosmopolitan middle class is often viewed as essential to stable government. In Thailand the middle class has increasingly become a focal point of economic and political decision making. Supporting the middle class are new interest groups that are demanding rights and resources formerly thought to be reserved for the elites. Along with political parties and parliament, these new organizations are taking on the functions once served by patron-client networks.

See also *Asia, Southeast.*

BIBLIOGRAPHY

Girling, John L. S. *Thailand: Society and Politics.* Ithaca, N.Y.: Cornell University Press, 1981.

Laothamatas, Anek. *From Bureaucratic Polity to Liberal Corporatism:*

Business Associations and the New Political Economy of Thailand. Boulder, Colo.: Westview Press, 1991.

Likhit, Dhiravegin. *The Bureaucratic Elite of Thailand.* Bangkok: Thai Khadi Research Institute, Thammasat University, 1978.

Morell, David, and Chai-Anan Samudavanija. *Political Conflict in Thailand: Reform, Reaction, Revolution.* Cambridge, Mass.: Oelgesclager, Gunn, and Hain, 1981.

Neher, Clark D. *Modern Thai Politics, from Village to Nation.* 2d ed. Cambridge, Mass.: Schenkman, 1979.

———, and Mungkandi Wiwat, eds. *U.S.–Thailand Relations in a New International Era.* Berkeley: Institute of East Asian Studies, University of California, 1990.

Somsakdi, Xuto, ed. *Government and Politics of Thailand.* Oxford: Oxford University Press, 1987.

Wilson, David A. *Politics in Thailand.* Ithaca, N.Y.: Cornell University Press, 1962.

Theory, African

African democratic theory is an aspect of African political thought that shows ambivalence toward the role of democracy in the management of African public affairs. The attention of theorists to democratic modes in Africa has sometimes been indirect, as it was in the political arrangements of precolonial Africa. In many other instances, democratic issues have been addressed more directly, as has been the case during the colonial and postcolonial periods.

Precolonial Indigenous Societies

The parentage of modern African studies can be traced to colonial social anthropology. Scholars in that field studied the principles of government in Africa's indigenous societies in order to facilitate the administration of European colonies established in the last quarter of the nineteenth century. The most famous formulation of these principles was provided by Meyer Fortes and E. E. Evans-Pritchard in their distinction between hierarchically organized societies, which were ruled by chiefly aristocratic orders, and egalitarian societies, which were governed by more democratic processes (*African Political Systems,* 1940).

The more egalitarian societies were based on kinship lineages that organized their fluid politics on the basis of situational alliances. The modern construction of democratic thought in Africa has grown largely from this egalitarian version of indigenous politics—a kind of precursor of democracy, or protodemocracy, which respected and protected the role of individuals in traditional politics—and has been opposed to the principle of aristocratic governance.

The most illustrous example of protodemocratic governance in indigenous Africa is the Igbo political system in southeastern Nigeria. Igbo public affairs were managed on the basis of open discussions involving all adult male members of the community in a democratic forum. Social anthropologists paid considerable attention to the politics of egalitarian and protodemocratic societies exemplified by the Igbo system. Such other indigenous groups as the Tiv in northern Nigeria, the Nuer in Sudan, and the Tallensi in Ghana provided the model of what social anthropologists labeled *segmentary lineage systems;* in these groups, politics was organized on the basis of varying kinship alliances. Although these stateless societies lacked the aristocratic hierarchies of kingdoms, they were able to govern themselves effectively. Their unit of political action was the kin group to which the individual was firmly tied—in place of a formal state.

Although the egalitarian systems had an apparent relationship to democratic means of governance, some traditional aristocratic societies also had features that could foster democratic behaviors. For instance, many traditional states in Africa excelled in creating the kinds of constitutional formations on which liberal democracy thrives. Succession in most indigenous states was regulated by custom and constitutional usage. Furthermore, many traditional states practiced constitutional restraint. For example, the Fanti confederacy, a collection of traditional Akan states situated in modern Ghana, was formed in 1867 as a constitutional arrangement to stop warfare among neighboring states and to promote cohesion.

Unfortunately, in the wider sphere of precolonial African geopolitics, the simpler stateless societies fell victims to the ambitions of more powerful neighboring kingdoms. This was especially the case during the era of the slave trade in Africa, when aristocratic societies exploited weaker ones that were based on popular and democratic modes of governance.

The Slave Trade

The slave trade sharpened the distinction between aristocratic societies and stateless societies in Africa. The democratic principle was threatened by the Arab slave trade (c. 950–1850) and the European slave trade (1480–1850). These were enforced by state organizations, and most kin-based stateless societies in Africa suffered disproportionately. There is ample evidence that the internal protodemocratic organization of stateless societies deteriorated during the slave trade. For example, the Igbo institution of *osu* forbade the bestowal of citizenship status and privileges on kinless persons. That principle led to the utter degradation of kinless persons in a society suffused with kinship, and it palpably diminished the potential for the development of democratic processes in Igboland.

The problems of the slave trade brought to the fore of African politics the antagonism between democratic advocacy and practice and aristocratic privilege. The community of ex-slave "recaptives" of Sierra Leone advocated and practiced democratic self-governance for a short while in the latter half of the nineteenth century. The organization of this community was conceived by the leadership of the descendants of those whom British abolitionist expeditions had recaptured from slave-running ships in the Atlantic and resettled in Sierra Leone. The community's leader, James Africanus Horton, a direct descendant of an Igbo recaptive, designed a mode of self-government that was based on British democratic institutions but fully run by Africans. This system of self-government was practiced briefly in Horton's own political base on McCarthy Island in Sierra Leone. In contrast, native African aristocrats preferred to retain traditional African aristocratic institutions as a definition of African independence.

Democracy's Misfortunes in Africa

European contact with Africa from the end of the eighteenth century onward coincided with the growth and expansion of democratic institutions and traditions in Western Europe. Indeed, the four French communes of Saint-Louis in Senegal, including its African residents, were part of the original experimentation with democracy following the French Revolution (1789) and the revolution of 1848. By 1848 the residents of Saint-Louis were holding local elections, involving both the French and the Africans, to run their own affairs. At one point a Creole Senegalese was elected mayor of Saint-Louis. African leaders in this era—including especially the influential Edward Wilmot Blyden, a statesman based in Liberia who was of Caribbean origin and descended from former Igbo slaves—encouraged the expansion of European contact with Africa because they were convinced that Africa would benefit from the burgeoning democratic impulse in Europe.

Subsequent European expansion and imperialism in Africa actually had the opposite result. The colonizers nullified democratic self-rule among the Sierra Leonean recaptives; they severely limited, for Senegalese, the democratic benefits from the republicanism of the revolution of 1848; and they disenfranchised Africans in the Cape Colony of South Africa. Indeed, European imperialism not only limited the democratic potential inherent in indigenous African institutions but also denied Europe's African colonies any potential benefits from the growing democratic movement inside imperial European nations.

The three dominant models of European colonial rule in Africa were intrinsically antidemocratic. These were indirect rule, assimilation, and separatist doctrine. The British doctrine of indirect rule grew out of negotiations in the early part of the twentieth century between the Fulani aristocracy, the old conquerors of Hausaland in modern northern Nigeria, and the British, the region's new conquerors. Forerunners of the practice can be traced to English rule in Ireland and British rule in India.

From its outset indirect rule involved layers of hierarchy based on chiefs and discouraged democratic practices, even those inherent in traditional rulership. Indirect rule imposed new aristocratic orders on egalitarian societies. For example, British colonial rulers created a new rank of warrant chiefs among the egalitarian Igbo by issuing warrants or certificates of authority to men who previously exercised no special political powers. Indirect rule also curtailed the traditional checks and balances that had restrained rulers from arbitrary and despotic rule in traditional states.

In French colonies the doctrine and practice of assimilation set criteria for Africans to become French citizens, thus devaluing the political worth of ordinary individuals, the overwhelming majority, in the colonies. This practice was a major breach and reversal of the democratic principles of the French Revolution.

Various separatist doctrines and devices informed colonial rule in European settler colonies—ranging from Kenya, Rhodesia, and the Portuguese colonies to South Africa with its system of apartheid. These practices represented open denials of democratic self-rule for Africans.

Colonialism's attack on democratic prospects in Africa had two devastating results. First, colonialism devalued Africa's political cultures, placing them beneath Europe's and implying that they were not capable of organizing democratic self-government. Second, the colonial state treated the individual as a subject rather than as a citizen. Consequently, Africans were alienated from the colonial state and found their political forums in kinship enclaves, which thus became politicized. Kinship systems expanded enormously under colonialism, and the public realm became fragmented. Such fragmentation is hardly hospitable to democracy, which thrives best when citizens operate within a single public realm that they value and nourish.

Anticolonialism

Anticolonialism arose from the ranks and works of pan-Africanism, the movement begun by Africans residing in the United States and the Caribbean at the beginning of the twentieth century. Its primary purpose was to improve the political and social situation of Africa and Africans. Pan-African advocates of the nineteenth and early twentieth centuries were confident that European colonialism would be beneficial for Africans largely because they believed that the introduction of European political institutions would lead to liberal democratic rule in Africa. This was clearly their expectation at the time of the First Pan-African Congress, which was held in London in 1900 and was largely organized and directed by W. E. B. Du Bois, the African American intellectual. Du Bois and the congress wanted European colonialism to prepare Africans for democratic rule, primarily through education.

Pan-African nationalism quickly turned against colonialism when these expectations foundered, leading Du Bois, forty-five years after the First Pan-African Congress, to characterize colonialism as the antithesis of democracy and freedom. Anticolonialism turned European imperialism on its head, charging it with tyranny and subversion of democracy. A series of native African nationalists—beginning with Nnamdi Azikiwe from Nigeria and including Kwame Nkrumah (Ghana), Mbonu Ojike (Nigeria), and many others, who were educated in the United States and Europe—challenged European imperialism for its antidemocratic character.

Anticolonialism's conception of democracy was, however, remarkably different from contemporary European usage. Whereas European democracy emphasized the unique individual's rights, democracy-professing anticolonialism attacked imperialism for devaluing African cultures and for allowing aliens to rule indigenous African peoples. While democratic freedom meant the achievement of positive rights for the ordinary European, for the African nationalist democracy had a negative meaning of gaining the right not to be ruled by foreigners. Accordingly, individuals never much mattered in the anticolonialist concept of democracy. Whereas domestic tyranny was the enemy of democracy in European politics, Pan-African anticolonialists preached that democracy would be achieved if Africans rid themselves of foreign tyranny. This lack of attention to the needs of the individual, and the emphasis on collective rights of Africans, colored the meaning of democracy in colonial Africa. That limited concept now haunts African politics, for foreign tyrannies have departed and internal tyrants have replaced alien colonial rulers.

Evolution of Democratic Institutions

African independence movements had two parts whose distinction from each other will help to clarify the construction of democratic institutions in Africa. There was, first, a period of anticolonialism marked by unmitigated antagonism between the European imperialists and their main critics, African nationalists. This period was followed in some countries by decolonization, a period of negotiation and cooperation between the colonizers and their African challengers in arrangements for terminating colonial rule. The relationship between anticolonialism and decolonization is paramount in assessing the potential for democracy in any African nation.

Anticolonialism was widespread in twentieth-century Africa and can be identified in every region of Subsaharan Africa. In West Africa it took the form of elitist confrontation with colonialism, sometimes in fierce rhetoric, for which Azikiwe and Nkrumah were particularly famous. It also involved civil disobedience by trade unions and student organizations. In West Africa such actions were punished by the colonizers and resulted in court trials for many nationalists, earning jail terms for some, like Nkrumah in Ghana and Anthony Enahoro in Nigeria.

In East Africa in the 1950s the Mau Mau war was waged against white settlers in the Kenyan highlands. The British countered in heavy reprisals, court trials, and imprisonment of many nationalists, including Jomo Kenyatta, who eventually became Kenya's first prime minister. The Kenyan experience was to be repeated in other British settler territories in Rhodesia and South Africa. Anticolonialism was particularly bloody in the Portuguese colonies because of Portugal's absolutist definition of its colonies as Outer Portugal. Varying degrees of anticolonialism can be traced in other colonial experiences—in the Belgian Congo and in the French colonies in West and Central Africa.

Although all colonial regimes and regions experienced anticolonialism, not all of them had organized programs of decolonization. The need to grant independence to its African colonies was first recognized by Great Britain following World War II. The pattern of negotiations with British colonies had been established in India, which was granted independence in 1947.

In general, British colonies went through the routine of decolonization in two stages. First, there was an attempt in each case to reconcile the aspirations and claims of the nationalists with the objectives of the British government in granting self-rule. The nationalists who fostered anticolonialism had demonized the imperialists as enemies; conversely, the colonizers had portrayed nationalists as dangerous and irresponsible. Decolonization afforded each side the opportunity to reevaluate the opponent's positions.

Second, decolonization included various attempts to reconcile competing proposals for governmental arrangements by vested interests in the colonies. This reconciliation process was particularly important in dealing with the rift between anticolonial nationalists and the chieftains who collaborated with colonial rulers and who tended to reject the call by the anticolonial nationalists for full-blown democracy.

In Ghana, there were attempts to reconcile Nkrumah's expansive political ambitions with the more conservative opposition to his call for wholesale democracy involving all regions of Ghana in one undifferentiated forum. In Nigeria, Azikiwe's notion of a common platform for all voters had to be reconciled with the views of Obafemi Awolowo and Ahmadu Bello. Awolowo was the leader of the powerful Yoruba, whose idea of a "people's republic" was a confederation of small ethnic states (the "people" in Awolowo's people's republic referred to cultural groupings, not to individuals). Bello represented the Fulani aristocracy, which was fighting for a restoration of its nineteenth-century empire in northern Nigeria. In Zimbabwe, compromises had to be forged not only between the African nationalists and the white settlers but also between two major factions among the nationalists.

Above all else, decolonization was a period of constitution making, embodying compromises between competing viewpoints. Under the British sphere, decolonization was partially a process of building governmental structures that were for the most part patterned on British parliamentary democracy.

Other European colonial powers did not fare as well as the British in negotiating decolonization for their African colonies. After a period of denying the need to do so, the French began a regime of decolonization following the general referendum in France's African colonies in 1958. Guinea, under Ahmed Sékou Touré's guidance, was allowed to opt for immediate independence, while all other French colonies chose gradual weaning toward independence in 1960. Decolonization in the French colonies included copying French ideals of democracy.

In contrast, there was little opportunity for decolonization in colonies ruled by Belgium and Portugal. The Democratic Republic of the Congo (formerly Zaire), Rwanda, and Burundi were plunged into immediate independence from Belgium, without any period of measured decolo-

nization. The Portuguese colonies of Angola, Mozambique, and Guinea-Bissau went through treacherous wars of liberation in order to gain their independence from Portugal, without the opportunity of negotiation under the aegis of decolonization.

In general, African nations that had marked transitions from periods of anticolonialism to regimes of decolonization have had fewer problems with the management of the institutions of parliamentary democracy than have those nations that never experienced a weaning transition from anticolonialism to decolonization. The political disasters in all the former Belgian and Portuguese colonies may well have multiple causes—but the inability of opponents in these nations to compromise may ultimately be traced to their lack of preparation under a regime of decolonization. Democracy thrives in a political culture of tolerance such as was cultivated by regimes of decolonization. On the other hand, democracy does poorly in circumstances of intolerance such as the absolutism that anticolonialism fomented. The weaning from anticolonialism to decolonization was an act of institutional political socialization that may have fostered the ability to run democratic regimes and to revive them when they are imperiled.

The Cold War Period

Whatever its inherent benefits, decolonization was of short duration and in most instances represented a hurried attempt to reverse the dictatorship of imperialism by replacing the institutions of colonial rule with new democratic structures. The democracies that followed colonialism faltered badly, in most instances yielding to military dictatorships, personal rule, or one-party state dictatorships. It is entirely possible that the failures of these democracies were the natural consequence of Africa's harsh history of tyranny under colonial rule and that the democratic pretensions of decolonization could not overtake an entrenched political culture of dictatorship.

Even so, the international environment of the 1960s through the mid-1980s was inhospitable for emerging democracies. During this cold war era the Western democracies were willing to support dictatorships in African countries in exchange for their promise to take sides with the West against the menace of Soviet communism. As a consequence, democratic stirrings in Africa did not receive wholesale support from established Western democracies, and, more remarkably, dictatorship gained specious respectability as an acceptable alternative to democracy.

Aristide Zolberg's *Creating Political Order* (1966) captures the views of postcolonial African leaders who monopolized power on the claim that their first responsibility was to create political order and improve the prestige and economic health of their nations. Touré of Guinea, Nkrumah of Ghana, Kenneth Kaunda of Zambia, and many other monopolizers of power in African nations were sophisticated men of letters, who read what Western social scientists wrote about them. They followed and encouraged "charismatic legitimation theory," which argued that the apparent dictatorship of charismatic rulers would eventually pay dividends for their nations. Various dictators embraced this version of the principle of developmental dictatorship, which contended that rapid escape from economic backwardness required a period of dictatorship.

The rationalization of dictatorship attained its intellectual peak in the theory of one-party state democracy in Tanzania under the benign guidance of Julius Nyerere, Tanzania's first president. The goal of one-party state democracy was the people's sovereignty and strong government. Missing from this ideology was any reference to the needs of the unique individual, the concern of liberal democracy. Clearly, the theory of one-party state democracy inherited the collectivistic strands of anticolonial nationalist thought.

One-party state democracy sought to enforce communal consensus and to avoid the dissension that seemed to be the nemesis of liberal democracy. In pursuing these goals, its protagonists have frequently misstated and exaggerated the degree of consensus in the traditional African societies they sometimes claimed as their model. In reality, one-party state democracy—as much in capitalist Kenya as in socialist Tanzania—was closer to the command politics in the Soviet Union than to traditional African politics. Not unexpectedly, the appeal and legitimacy of this form of government waned with the end of the cold war.

Prospects in the Multiethnic States

Despite the barriers to democracy in postcolonial Africa, especially during the cold war, the basis for democratic governance has not been eradicated. Richard Sklar, who has provided a major analysis of democracy in Africa, maintains that democracy's infrastructure is not absent from Africa's social and cultural institutions. Although three of Africa's smallest and relatively uncomplicated nations—Mauritania, Gambia, and Botswana—have usually provided examples of surviving democracies, the lasting elements of democracy are more apparent in less homogeneous countries. The cost of managing dictatorship in

multiethnic nations is very high, and trends toward the compromises of democracies may be encouraged by these nations' own political momentum. That is why Nigeria's and South Africa's political experiences may contain seeds of democracy that will survive as lasting examples for other African nations.

From 1976 to 1979 Nigerians sought to overcome their political divisions through constitutional engineering. The principal problems that faced Nigeria's constitution makers were two. First, Nigerians owed their loyalties primarily to their ethnic groups, starving the greater nation of badly needed support. Second, ethnic groups competed to obtain common public goods for their own exclusive benefit; stronger groups were able to monopolize power. The solution was to organize a constitution in which access to power required winning support from more than one's own ethnic or subethnic constituency and in which common benefits and public goods had to be distributed on the basis of the federal attributes of the nation or its subunits. This was what the constitution makers branded *federal character*. Its inept administration by a corrupt regime turned out to be unsatisfactory, but most Nigerians believe the principle of federal character was sound.

Although establishing democracy was not the announced purpose of Nigeria's 1979 constitution, the consequences of the constitution were clearly democratic. As a democratic document, however, it was marked by a characteristic endemic to African democratic thought. It made individuals, and their needs, the instrument of public policy rather than its goal. The aim of the constitution was to strengthen the state by redirecting individuals' loyalties and also to protect all ethnic groups. Western liberal democracy sees the individual as the end of politics, whereas African political thought since the era of the slave trade has consistently belittled the worth of the individual, subsuming the person's essence under some kinship grouping. Although individuals do have value within their own ethnic groups, they count for little in the wider national arena. The worth of the individual is a strand of liberal democratic thought that has not taken root in Africa.

Ironically, in light of the country's dismal record, South Africa's political experience may supply such liberal elements to African political thought. David Horowitz, in *A Democratic South Africa?* (1991), has suggested that the Nigerian constitutional experience could be helpful to South Africa by leading it to design a constitutional system that compels contestants for power to look beyond their ethnic base. But South Africa has a different political tradition from Nigeria's, one that is liable to enrich Africa's political thought further. The liberal tradition of respecting the individual's worth and dignity is strong in those fragments of South Africa (Afrikaners, the English, and the Jews) that have been included in the state—although the same regard has not been extended to the African masses who were until recently outside the South African apartheid state. In neighboring Zimbabwe the settlers' political culture is being blended with that of the indigenous people. Similarly, one imagines that the South African state will accord the same respect to its indigenous African citizens as to those already privileged to be South African citizens; in so doing, it will increase the notional worth of the ideal citizen by focusing on the unique individual's needs and on individual human dignity as the goal of public policy.

Prospects for the Second Liberation

Democracy has fared poorly in Africa since colonial times. The hopes for a democratic order in postcolonial Africa have largely been unfulfilled. However, given favorable new international circumstances since the end of the cold war, and disgust with dictatorship in domestic affairs, prospects for renewed engagement with democracy in African nations appear good. Unfortunately, Samuel Huntington's conclusions in *The Third Wave* (1991), which accords economic prosperity a large share in the emergence of democracy, are not wholly encouraging with respect to Africa's chances. There is clamor among informed Africans, scholars, and politicians, as well as foreign scholars of African politics, for renewed commitment to democracy, a call labeled in the late 1980s and 1990s the *second liberation*. The diagnosis of democracy's ills—and hopes for cure through the second liberation—varies widely.

The first credible African voices calling for second liberation democracy tied it to popular struggles. In *Popular Struggles for Democracy in Africa* (1987), the Kenyan political scientist Peter Anyang' Nyong'o and his African coauthors saw popular struggles against dictatorship as the means to democracy. The control of the state is at issue here, and this view permits the establishment of participatory one-party state democracy. Indeed, much of the blame for Africa's undemocratic circumstances has been laid to states' inefficiency in the hands of corrupt and inept tyrants.

Other scholars, such as Michael Bratton, see the absence of the institutions of civil society as the cause of Africa's problems with democracy, sometimes implying that such institutions could be alternatives to the state. The ultimate quest of the second liberation movement is to "liberate" the African masses. Questions remain about what structures and processes the masses should be liberated from. The diversity of viewpoints on the second liberation is troubling to African democratic theory and suggests the need to specify the elements of that theory, since in this area familiarity with Western notions of democracy often imposes false categories on African political thought.

There are three constructs whose interrelationship provides the context for African democratic theory. These are the state, kinship, and the individual.

Derived from the colonial state, the modern African state is the civil arm of African nations. Although the African state may look like the Western state, on which it was originally modeled, its functions and its relationships with society and the individual are radically different from the familiar pattern of the Western state. The elements of the state have not been fully aligned with those of society because the African state's origins are outside indigenous African societies. Moreover, the individual has largely been alienated from the state—a relationship that persists from colonialism and one that postcolonial states have not corrected.

Kinship, broadly conceived to include ethnic groups and other categories of assumed blood relationships, is the most potent representation of society in Africa. From the slave trade era through colonialism and into our times, kinship has acquired an extraordinary significance in African public affairs. It provides an alternative public forum to the state's civic public. For their political actions, many Africans have come to rely on kinship's primordial publics, political forums limited to those bonded by the same moral ties of assumed blood relationships. Whereas the state has largely had difficult relationships with the individual, primordial publics have managed individuals' welfare. Many Africans live outside the purview of the state and rely on kinship groupings for their security. But the price that Africa pays for this arrangement is that the public realm is severely fragmented along the fault lines of kinship groupings.

For the individual, the second liberation can mean only two types of freedom. First, individuals need negative freedom from kinship groupings. But that freedom will become a possibility only if the state provides the essential personal security for which individuals now rely on their kinship networks. Second, the individual can enjoy positive freedom only by gaining legal, political, and social rights in the state's civic public realm. Only when individuals gain the freedom to exercise their rights in the civic public domain can Africans expect to participate fully in democratic freedoms. The romantic views of those advocating civil society as a replacement for the state to the contrary, the second liberation calls for the state's strengthening into a responsible organization, not its weakening.

See also *Africa, Horn of; Africa, Lusophone; Africa, Subsaharan; African independence movements.*

BIBLIOGRAPHY

Diamond, Larry, Juan J. Linz, and Seymour Lipset, eds. *Democracy in Developing Countries: Africa.* Boulder, Colo.: Lynne Rienner; London: Adamantine Press, 1988.

Du Bois, W. E. B. *Color and Democracy: Colonies and Peace.* Millwood, N.Y.: Kraus-Thomson, 1945.

Ekeh, Peter P. "Colonialism and the Two Publics in Africa: A Theoretical Statement." *Comparative Studies in Society and History* 17 (1975): 91–112.

————, and Eghosa E. Osaghae, eds. *Federal Character and Federalism in Nigeria.* Ibadan, Nigeria: Heinemann, 1989.

Eribor, Festus, Oyeleye Oyediran, Mulatu Wubneh, and Leo Zonn, eds. *Window on Africa: Democratization and Media Exposure.* Greenville, N.C.: Center for International Programs, East Carolina University, 1993.

Jennings, Ivor. *Democracy in Africa.* Cambridge: Cambridge University Press, 1963.

Nyong'o, Peter Anyang', ed. *Popular Struggles for Democracy in Africa.* Atlantic Highlands, N.J., and London: Zed Books, 1987.

Padmore, George, ed. *History of the Pan-African Congress.* London: Hammersmith Bookshop, 1963.

Sklar, Richard L. "Democracy in Africa." In *Political Domination in Africa,* edited by Patrick Chabal. Cambridge: Cambridge University Press, 1986.

Wiseman, John A. *Democracy in Black Africa: Survival and Revival.* New York: Paragon House, 1990.

Tunisia

A presidential republic located between Algeria and Libya on the northern coast of Africa. Inhabited by descendants of its original Berber-speaking inhabitants, Tunisia has a distinctively Mediterranean culture and reflects the influences of successive waves of invaders, including the Phoenicians, Romans, Arabs, Turks, and French. Tunisia is the most arabized country of North Africa, although to continue its economic development, the country remains dependent on Western investment, capital, trade, and tourism.

The Arabic influence stems from a succession of Islamic monarchies dating back to the seventh century. The traditional ruler, the bey, strengthened the authority of the central state by creating a bureaucratic elite and initiating po-

litical reforms along European lines. Before the colonial era, Tunisia adopted—in response to growing Western encroachments—a constitution promoting Western values: fair taxation, property rights, religious freedom, and centralized administration. After France declared Tunisia a formal protectorate in 1883, the country continued to absorb Western ideas and practices in spite of their limited popularity. While the country remained under French control, the traditional leaders served as nominal rulers and exercised influence as the religious and political elite.

Early in the twentieth century a group called the Young Tunisians demanded an updated Islamic legal system, a renewal of Arabic culture, Western education, and democratic reforms. Nationalistic demands resurfaced in the 1920s and again in the 1930s when a new generation of leaders founded the Neo-Destour (New Constitution) Party. The French granted Tunisia full independence in 1956. Habib Bourguiba, the leader of the modern nationalist movement, became the country's first president. During his first years in office he used his image as father of the nation to consolidate power, maintain legitimacy, and gain popular support.

Habib Bourguiba, Father of the Nation

Bourguiba's New Constitution Party supporters won all the seats in the first Constitutional Assembly elections held in 1956 and quickly consolidated their power. In 1957 the new government abolished the monarchy, proclaimed Tunisia a republic, and elected Bourguiba to the new office of president. A 1959 constitution codified the existing presidential system. The president was assigned broad discretionary powers, including the authority to legislate by decree and to appoint all civil and military officials, including the prime minister, the cabinet, and the governors of the country's twenty-three provinces. In fact, the president became head of state and government and supreme commander of the armed forces.

President Bourguiba dominated all aspects of political life in Tunisia during the postindependence era. He ran unopposed in presidential elections and was declared "president for life" by the National Assembly in 1975. His supporters in the New Constitution Party, renamed the Destourien Socialist Party in the 1960s and the Democratic Constitutional Assembly in 1988, continued to win all the seats in the National Assembly in spite of a declaration proclaiming Tunisia a multiparty system.

This fusion of state and party was reinforced over the years through the use of patronage and other privileges for the urban, Western-oriented elite. Bourguiba maintained a

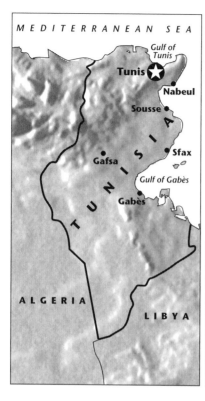

highly personalized system of patronage networks centered on himself. He prevented his ministers from forming coalitions and limited the participation of military leaders in politics. Leaders of organized centers of opposition were neutralized through co-optation and repression. The General Union of Tunisian Workers, which had been a powerful ally in the independence struggle, was quickly made a junior partner in the first government, and opposition political parties were banned until 1981. The party-government apparatus founded a host of affiliated organizations, allegedly to represent all segments of society.

Bourguiba's early popularity permitted his government to implement far-reaching political, social, and religious reforms, including universal suffrage and a uniform code of justice that abolished many common Islamic practices. Among Bourguiba's most enduring legacies are the substantial legal, political, and social rights enjoyed by women in modern Tunisia. Western aid assisted Bourguiba's implementation of reforms throughout the cold war era. After his government abandoned socialist reforms in 1969, Bourguiba cultivated an international image as a pro-Western, moderate leader pursuing a modernization strategy based on a pragmatic mixture of socialism and capitalism. Even as Bourguiba's popularity waned and he increasingly relied on authoritarian measures and repression to

quiet opponents, Western governments continued to support him as an important cold war ally and a moderate leader who was opposed to Islamic fundamentalism. Western financial support became increasingly important by the mid-1980s, as the regime faced critical fiscal and debt crises.

These crises had their roots in the widespread discontent produced by governmental efforts to collectivize agriculture in the 1960s. Although abandoned in 1969, the program dislocated large numbers of peasants, alienated much of the Sahelian landed bourgeoisie, and was partially responsible for the governmental policy of holding the wages of organized labor constant for several years. Political alienation continued through the 1970s after the government switched to a Western-type economic liberalization program. A small Western-oriented elite was the main beneficiary of economic growth. During the 1970s the living standards of the workers, peasants, students, and youth deteriorated. But unauthorized strikes halted once the government arrested labor union leaders and, in 1978, declared a general state of emergency. Economic and social unrest resurfaced in the mid-1980s, when the government lifted price subsidies on food as part of an economic austerity program. Urban riots and street violence were stopped only after Bourguiba personally intervened to reverse food price increases, the government postponed implementation of several features of the structural adjustment program, and another state of emergency was imposed.

By the 1980s the government also faced increased challenges by Islamic fundamentalists. In 1980 a group calling itself the Tunisian Armed Resistance caught the government off guard by attacking the mining town of Gafsa. Although the army recaptured Gafsa, throughout the 1980s the government viewed Islamic opponents as a serious threat to political order.

In 1981, to cope with a growing crisis of legitimacy, the government engaged some of the weaker non-Islamic political parties in the legislative elections. In response to this political opening, a new organization, the Islamic Tendency Movement, was established. It claimed to offer a religious-political alternative to official Tunisian Islam at the ballot box. The movement's leader, Rachid Ghanouchi, denounced violence and urged religious opponents to participate in the electoral process. But Bourguiba undermined the credibility of this political opening by rigging the elections and eliminating the Islamic Tendency Movement as a political force. In fact, he imprisoned or forced into exile the group's entire leadership. As a result, popular support for political Islamicists increased markedly, and the movement splintered into factions, including several factions espousing violence.

When thirteen foreign tourists were injured by bomb explosions at resort hotels in 1987, Bourguiba used the pretext of foreign involvement to arrest at least 3,000 Islamic fundamentalists. In September 1987 the highly publicized trial of 90 Islamic fundamentalists accused of plotting against the government resulted in the acquittal of 14 defendants; 7, however, received the death penalty. Bourguiba was rumored to have been infuriated by the outcomes, but before he could order new trials, he was removed from power in a palace coup.

Ben Ali and a New Political Consensus

Bourguiba's prime minister, Zine el-Abidine Ben Ali, with the support of other cabinet ministers, forced Bourguiba to retire in November 1987, after Bourguiba exhibited increasingly erratic behavior. Once in power, Ben Ali, a former minister of the interior and army general, promised to initiate reforms designed to ensure greater political freedom and popular participation. And, indeed, in its first few years his regime implemented several actions that were widely supported and suggested that the government was sincere about its commitment to forge a new political consensus. Opposition newspapers were permitted to publish; the National Assembly approved legislation limiting the period a person could be held in police custody without charge; the State Security Court and prosecutor-general post were abolished; and thousands of political and nonpolitical detainees were freed. Tunisia also became the first Arab nation to ratify the United Nations convention against torture.

The government implemented a number of political reforms designed to widen participation in government. In 1988 the presidency-for-life was abolished, new guidelines for presidential succession were established, and legislation establishing a multiparty system was passed. Although this legislation legalized political parties, any groups organized along religious, racial, regional, or linguistic lines were prohibited from operating as political parties. In a national pact proposal in 1989, the government invited non-Islamic party leaders to stand for national election in a coalition with the Democratic Constitutional Assembly. Although this offer was rejected, all of the non-Islamic opposition parties, except the Communist Party, participated in the 1989 elections. Moreover, supporters of the Islamic Tendency Movement organized as a newly formed political party, the Renaissance Movement (known as Nahda), and

ran as "independent" candidates in nineteen of the twenty-five voting districts. But none of the legally recognized opposition parties won any seats in this election, and the Democratic Constitutional Assembly retained all the National Assembly seats. Although Ben Ali was said to have received 99 percent of the vote in the presidential election, various Islamic "independents" received between 13 and 25 percent of the vote among Assembly constituencies. The aggregate vote indicated that the government's main opponents would continue to be political Islamicists.

After the election, in an effort to find an alternative to legalizing political Islamicists, the government instituted additional reforms designed to increase participation by the six legal non-Islamic political parties and other groups in government. In 1991 President Ben Ali permitted increased media coverage of the activities of the legal opposition parties, promised financial aid for the electoral campaigns and party activities of these parties, and invited opposition leaders to participate in discussions of the five-year development plan. In 1992 he announced that presidential and parliamentary elections would be held in March 1994. Throughout 1993 the government and opposition parties held talks designed to ensure some non-Democratic Constitutional Assembly representation in the National Assembly after the elections. The government agreed to allow 19 of the 163 seats in the chamber to be filled through proportional representation, whereby representatives of a given party are elected according to the proportion of the popular vote that party receives. Despite these concessions, the Democratic Constitutional Assembly, thanks in large part to stilted candidacy requirements, won 144 seats in the March 20, 1994, balloting. Ben Ali was reelected president without challenge on the same day.

In the early 1990s the government also took steps to eliminate the Islamic opposition. In 1991 the newly legalized arms of Nahda, the newspaper *Al Fajr* and the Tunisian General Union of Students, were crushed. Demonstrations by Islamic militants were violently suppressed, and Nahda was blamed for student protests and worker unrest. In May 1991 the government, claiming to have discovered a plot, detained thousands of Nahda activists.

Increased security crackdowns and the conviction of Nahda leaders and activists for subversive activities in a series of highly publicized trials during September 1992 effectively marginalized political opponents. Most of Nahda's leadership and a high proportion of its members were imprisoned or forced to live abroad. The government, however, had to counteract negative publicity at home and abroad, including allegations of torture of political detainees. While Ben Ali continued to stress the need for strong-arm tactics to prevent chaos in Algeria from spilling over into Tunisia, he also emphasized Tunisia's commitment to economic and political liberalization.

Most observers do not believe that the parliamentary reforms will lead to a representative opposition bloc in the National Assembly or will meet the expectations of an increasingly sophisticated and educated electorate for meaningful political reforms. It now appears that Ben Ali attempted to maintain his reputation abroad as a champion of human rights and political change, while using the party-state apparatus and the military to strengthen his power base, to stop political protests, and to crush Islamic opponents at home. After assuming the presidency, Ben Ali replaced Bourguiba's relatives and close associates in the cabinet with military officers, but he retained many of the practices introduced by Bourguiba to control the party. To manage internal security, Ben Ali formed a new National Security Council (consisting of himself, the prime minister, the minister of state for defense, the minister of foreign affairs, and the minister of the interior). Although a larger role for the military in government has prevented overt Islamic political activities, the political elite and growing numbers of the middle class remain concerned about future political stability as they witness a resurgence in support for Islamic fundamentalism. The battle between the government and Islamic militants is likely to continue. The outcome may depend on the success of economic and political reforms.

BIBLIOGRAPHY

Entelis, John P. *Comparative Politics of North Africa: Algeria, Morocco, and Tunisia.* Syracuse: Syracuse University Press, 1980.

Moore, Clement Henry. *Politics in North Africa.* Boston: Little, Brown, 1970.

Nelson, Harold D., ed. *Tunisia: A Country Study.* 3d ed. Washington, D.C.: Library of Congress, Government Printing Office, 1988.

Parker, Richard B. *North Africa: Regional Tensions and Strategic Concerns.* New York: Praeger, 1987.

"Tunisia." In *The Middle East and North Africa, 1993.* 39th ed. London: Europa Publications, 1993.

Vandewalle, Dirk. "From the New State to the New Era: Toward a Second Republic in Tunisia." *Middle East Journal* 42 (autumn 1988): 602–620.

Ware, L. B. "Ben Ali's Constitutional Coup in Tunisia." *Middle East Journal* 42 (autumn 1988): 587–601.

Zartman, I. William, and William Mark Habeeb, eds. *Polity and Society in Contemporary North Africa.* Boulder, Colo.: Westview Press, 1993.

Turkey

A predominantly Islamic nation in Asia and Europe that began its transition to democracy in the late 1940s. After the final defeat of the Ottoman Empire in World War I, Turkey emerged, under the leadership of Kemal Atatürk, as the only sovereign successor state.

Between the fourteenth and seventeenth centuries the realm of the Ottoman sultans had expanded into a large empire that extended from Hungary to Yemen and from Algeria to the Caucasus. Its military and administrative hierarchies and much of its agricultural population were Islamic. Yet Christians (in the Balkans, in Lebanon and Egypt, and in the capital of Istanbul) and Jews (in Istanbul, Salonika, and other major cities) lived by their own traditional laws and dominated much of the empire's economy. From 1683 to 1913 the Ottoman Empire lost its Balkan and African territories in military defeats. As a result of the final defeat of 1918, most of the remaining empire (including its capital of Istanbul and its Arab-speaking territories of Syria, Lebanon, Palestine, and Iraq) was occupied by the victorious powers of Britain, France, and Italy, and its Anatolian heartland was invaded by Greek military forces.

National Identity and Political Institutions

From 1919 to 1923 a Turkish war of independence, organized under Atatürk's leadership, defeated the Greek invasion and other attempts at partition. After the Treaty of Lausanne in 1923 provided international recognition for the new state, the Republic of Turkey, with its capital in Ankara, was officially proclaimed. Whereas Ottoman leaders had felt ambivalent about their commitment to the Ottoman tradition, Islam, or Turkish nationhood, the defeat of 1918 and the victory of 1923 firmly established Turkey's national identity.

The country's commitment to Westernization, initiated by the Ottoman upper class in the nineteenth century, soon turned, under Atatürk's presidency (1923–1938), into a peaceful cultural revolution that included secular laws and education, religious freedom, adoption of the Roman alphabet, and equality of men and women. Yet, except for two brief experiments with legal opposition—in 1924–1925 and again in 1930—Turkey remained a single-party authoritarian system based on Atatürk's Republican People's Party.

Ismet Inönü, the military commander in the war of independence and prime minister under Atatürk (1923–1924,

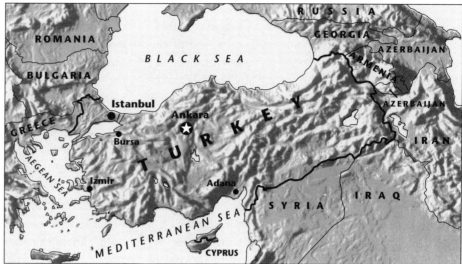

1925–1937), succeeded Atatürk as president (1938–1950). In the early years of the cold war after 1945, Inönü launched what soon became a second peaceful revolution: the country's transition from single-party dictatorship to multiparty competition. Although the movement toward democracy suffered major setbacks in the military interventions of 1960–1961, 1971–1973, and 1980–1983, each time the military reproclaimed democracy. Since the mid-1980s public opinion has been firmly on the side of democracy. The landmarks in this final transition were the 1983 parliamentary elections, in which an opposition party decisively defeated the artificial parties sponsored by the 1980 junta, and the 1987 national referendum, which by a close but clear majority amended the provisions of the 1982 constitution that had banned the party leaders of the 1970s from political participation.

Turkey's constitutional system has been strongly parliamentary, with a unicameral legislature in the First Republic (1923–1960) and Third Republic (1983–   ) and a bicameral legislature in the Second Republic (1961–1980). Throughout, presidents of the republic have been elected by the legislature (Grand National Assembly), although those of 1961–1980 and 1982–1989 were military figures selected in the wake of coups.

Some significant shifts in Turkey's pattern of political parties have stemmed from changes in its election laws. The voting system inherited from Atatürk's single-party days was a multiple-member plurality system (similar to that used by the U.S. electoral college), which guaranteed the concentration of voters within two parties and heavy majorities for the winning party. Because the government

of Adnan Menderes (1950–1960) had relied on those heavy majorities (86 percent in 1950, 93 percent in 1954, and 70 percent in 1957) in setting its increasingly authoritarian course, the 1961 constitution shifted to the opposite extreme: a system of proportional representation that allocates seats among party lists in multiple-member districts, much as in Germany's Weimar Republic or in Israel.

Under this system the Justice Party won parliamentary majorities in 1965 and 1969, yet by the 1970s the result was a fragmentation of parties and recurrent deadlocks before coalition governments could be formed or a new president elected. This governmental paralysis encouraged the mounting wave of terrorism of the late 1970s and the military intervention of 1980. Under the 1982 constitution Turkey has proceeded to a more balanced electoral system that guarantees some proportionality without encouraging party splintering or deadlocks in forming governments.

Meanwhile, the social base of Turkish politics has expanded substantially. The party leaders of the 1960s and 1970s had been drawn from the urban upper class, much like those of the single-party regime under Atatürk and Inönü. By contrast, the ban imposed from 1982 to 1987 on party leaders and members of parliament of the 1970s encouraged the emergence of new leaders, including many successful businesspeople attracted to the Motherland Party. Tansu Çiller's accession to the premiership in 1993 appeared to mark the coming of a new generation, which, amid the intense party realignments of the early 1990s, might overcome the splits and rivalries resulting from the military coup in 1980 and the ban on former politicians in 1982.

Democratic Transition and Military Intervention

Turkey's transition toward democracy began in mid-1945 as President Inönü announced that, in view of the democracies' victory in World War II, Turkey must take seriously Atatürk's populist principles. Thus Inönü lifted restrictions on freedom of the press and on the formation of opposition parties. Turkey had remained neutral in World War II, except for making a last-minute declaration of war on the Axis powers in February 1945 in order to join the San Francisco conference that was to establish the United Nations. Nonetheless, years of maximum military mobilization and isolation from foreign trade had produced economic hardship and much political dissatisfaction.

Above all, Turkey was facing Soviet demands for the cession of three northeastern provinces and joint control of the Turkish straits (Bosphorus and Dardanelles): this was Moscow's opening move in what soon became the cold war. Thus Inönü was eager both to relieve domestic pressures and to secure the support of the United States, as later provided through the Truman Doctrine of aid to Greece and Turkey in 1947 and Turkey's entry into the North Atlantic Treaty Organization in 1952.

Inönü envisaged his own role in the new democratic system as that of a politically neutral president. Yet his withdrawal from day-to-day political leadership prompted the authoritarian elements in his governing Republican People's Party to prolong their grip on power by calling early elections in July 1946. The elections were fraught with dishonest counts. But, as public indignation mounted and was reported in the newly freed press, Inönü installed a more liberal party leadership and informed the citizenry that both the government and the opposition were legitimate contenders for power. When an honest election in 1950 gave a large majority to the opposition Democratic Party under Adnan Menderes, Inönü refused military advice that the problem could be solved by a coup, yielded his presidential office to the Democratic chair, Celal Bayar, and assumed the new role of opposition leader in parliament.

Nonetheless, the political role of the military was to remain ambiguous for several decades. By the late 1950s growing economic dissatisfaction led Menderes's government to drift toward authoritarianism by harassing newspapers; closing down the Nation Party, an opposition group with an Islamic base; and having the police disrupt other opposition meetings.

Amid mounting unrest the military refused to let themselves be used for Menderes's plans of restoring order by martial law. Instead, they formed a National Unity Committee of leading officers, who in their May 1960 coup proclaimed the need to restore democracy. Democratic Party leaders were tried for violating the constitution, and Menderes himself was sentenced to death by hanging. Yet the junta under Gen. Cemal Gürsel rejected plans of its own right-wing members to impose a permanent authoritarian regime. Instead, a new constitution was formulated by a civilian assembly, and, after free elections in October 1961, full civilian rule was restored, except for the continuing service of military presidents from 1961 to 1989.

By 1971, as cabinet crises and parliamentary deadlocks paralyzed Turkey's Second Republic, the military intervened in what became known as the "coup by memorandum," forcing the parliament to accept a cabinet of bureaucrats endorsed by the military. Following the 1973 elections the initiative shifted back to the civilians. A cabinet was formed early in 1974 by the center-left Republican People's Party, now led by Inönü's successor Bülent Ecevit, and by the Islamic National Salvation Party.

In July 1974 this unlikely coalition, which agreed on few domestic issues, eagerly ordered the Turkish invasion of northern Cyprus in response to a Greek nationalist coup in Nicosia instigated by the right-wing military government in Athens. Soon Turkey faced more parliamentary crises and a surge of partisan gun battles in city streets, with the Marxist Turkish Labor Party acquiring its weapons from Syria and the Soviet bloc and the rightist Nationalist Action Party acquiring its weapons from the illegal drug trade and secret connections in the Turkish military.

In 1980, in response to the mounting terrorism on the streets and an endless deadlock in parliamentary elections for the next president, the military once again intervened, initially with much public approval. Later the junta convened a civilian constitutional assembly and imposed a ban on all the parties and leaders of the 1970s. It then organized a Nationalist Democracy Party under a retired officer and a Populist Party under a bureaucrat, which it expected to see elected as the government and the opposition. The junta's scheme of pseudo-democracy was foiled, however, by a clever maneuver of Turgut Özal, who had been the government's expert on foreign debt and who in 1980–1982 was the junta's chief economist. Registering his Motherland Party just before the deadline, Özal launched a folksy, populist campaign at public meetings and on television and secured a decisive Motherland Party victory in November 1983.

Liberalization and the Consolidation of Democracy

The following years brought a period of informal collaboration, with Gen. Kenan Evren in the presidency making major foreign policy decisions and Özal and his Motherland Party majority developing their neoliberal economic policies. Within a few years the military-sponsored parties disappeared, and the political parties of the 1970s reappeared under new names. Turkey now enjoyed full freedom of expression, and the continuing ban on the politicians of the 1970s became highly controversial. In 1987 a referendum restored those former leaders to full participation.

The neoliberal economic policies of the Özal government had mixed effects: they stimulated private business, but they also contributed to mounting inflation and unemployment. When Evren's presidential term expired in 1989, Özal used his heavy parliamentary majority to have himself elected president, even though opinion polls showed his Motherland Party at an all-time low. Although he had previously criticized Evren for playing too political a role in the presidency, Özal himself made extensive and controversial use of his own presidential powers in the Persian Gulf war of 1991. For instance, he authorized the use of Turkey's Incirlik air base against Iraq without legislative approval or consultation, thereby prompting high-level military resignations.

In the October 1991 elections the Motherland Party lost its parliamentary majority, and the next government was formed by a coalition of Süleyman Demirel's leading True Path Party and Erdal İnönü's Social Democratic People's Party. Several months after Özal's death in April 1993, Demirel was elected president. He was succeeded as True Path Party leader and prime minister by Tansu Çiller, the first woman to head Turkey's government.

Just over two years into her term as prime minister, Çiller was defeated on a no-confidence vote and resigned in October 1995. Premature elections were held on December 24, and the Welfare Party emerged with 158 seats, the most of any party, in the 550-seat Grand National Assembly. After the collapse of one coalition arrangement, Necmettin Erbakan of the Welfare Party became prime minister on June 28, 1996.

Erbakan was soon on a collision course with the military over the secular nature of the state. He was Turkey's first pro-Islamic head of government since 1923, and his party had long advocated a return to Islamic government. On June 18, 1997, Erbakan resigned under pressure from the military and was replaced as prime minister by Mesut Yilmaz of the center-right Motherland Party.

Political Parties and Policy Issues

The pattern of political parties in Turkey since the late 1940s has been remarkably consistent, despite reorganizations and name changes imposed by the coups of 1960 and 1980. Electoral competition has focused mostly on two major parties.

On the center-left, Ismet İnönü's Republican People's Party at first appealed mainly to the urban middle class, but by the 1970s, under Bülent Ecevit's leadership, it had moved in a democratic-socialist direction with strong support from labor unions. By the 1980s its successor was called the Social Democratic (or later Social Democratic People's) Party.

On the center-right, the Democratic Party under Bayar and Menderes built up a network of support in the country's agricultural districts and small towns and, with U.S. aid in the 1950s, initiated such major changes as rural road networks and improved irrigation. The same line was continued by the Justice Party (so named in obvious protest against the hanging of Menderes by the 1960 junta) and the True Path Party, both led by Süleyman Demirel. In the vacuum produced by the military's ban on former parties, Turgut Özal's Motherland Party emerged in 1983 as another center-right party, with its main support from business circles.

On the far left the Turkish Labor Party emerged in the mid-1960s. Severe restrictions on organizations with (or suspected of) communist connections reduced its effectiveness, however.

Toward the right of the spectrum, there always has been a party advocating a return from secularism toward Islam, such as the (Republican) Nation Party of the 1950s and, since the 1970s, the National Salvation and Welfare Parties led by Erbakan. Their appeal had been blunted by government concessions from Atatürk's rigid secularism. For example, the Islamic prayer call in Arabic was restored in 1950—it had been pure Turkish since Atatürk's days—and theological faculties at universities and optional religious classes were reinstated in public schools.

Interestingly, secularism has given more freedom to Turkey's Alevi Muslims, a dissident group related to but not identical to the Shiʻites and variously estimated at 10–20 percent of Turkey's total population. Most of the Alevis are concentrated in central Anatolia, and they strongly endorse such secularist parties as the Republican People's or Democratic Left, which they consider to be the best guarantee against oppression by the Sunni Muslim majority.

All in all, Turkey has become a society in which citizens may be as religious or as nonobservant as they choose. And, although observance is predominant in villages and small towns (where shopkeepers do not dare to open their stores during the Muslim holy month of Ramadan), the steady stream of migration allows anyone to move to medium-sized and large cities, where secularism and religious choice set the tone. It also is symbolic of Turkey's full commitment to Western values that its 1987 application for membership in the European Community (now the European Union) was sponsored by Prime Minister Özal, a former pilgrim to Mecca who kept his religious beliefs strictly private.

On the far right, there has usually been an ultranationalist party, notably the Nationalist Action and Nationalist Labor Parties, both founded by Col. Alpaslan Türkeş, who had been the leader of the authoritarian minority of the 1960 junta. The main tenet of these groups was Panturkism—that is, political unity between Turkey and the Turkic-speaking Central Asian republics. Its followers were closely involved in the terrorist battles of the 1970s between the left and the right. The Islamic and Panturkish right were briefly united in the early 1960s, and typically their joint or separate support since the 1970s has ranged from 9 to 17 percent of the popular vote. It also should be noted that, whereas Panturkism remained a utopian dream throughout the Soviet period, Ankara governments have cultivated close economic and cultural relations with the postcommunist countries from Romania to Kyrgyzstan (for example, by establishing the Black Sea Economic Cooperation Zone in 1992 and encouraging frequent visits between Turkish and Central Asian governments).

The Unresolved Kurdish Problem

One significant development of the early 1990s was the increasing acceptance of Turkey's substantial Kurdish minority as equal citizens. In 1925 a major rebellion broke out against the newly proclaimed Republic of Turkey, led by Islamic religious groups and centered on the Kurdish-speaking areas in the southeast. From that time on, it was illegal to speak Kurdish in public, and much of the Kurdish-populated southeast remained under martial law for many decades. As a result of this suppression (and also because many ethnic Kurds now speak Turkish as their mother tongue), no reliable figures on Turkey's Kurdish population are available, although their number has been variously estimated at 4 to 11 million (or 7 to 20 percent of the total population).

In February 1991 the ban on speaking Kurdish in public was lifted, and Kurdish-language publications began to appear. In the October 1991 elections a party allied with the Social Democratic People's Party openly appealed to Kurdish support in the southeast, and in the 1991–1993 Demirel cabinet both the foreign minister and the head of the newly established Human Rights Ministry were known to be of Kurdish background. Indeed, the Ankara government took care to establish friendly relations with the leadership of the Kurdish autonomous region in northern Iraq. Nonetheless, in the early 1990s the Kurdish terrorist activities intensified throughout Turkey's southeast, as the Kurdish Workers' Party moved its headquarters from Syrian-controlled Lebanon to semi-independent northern Iraq. The Turkish military escalated its repressive actions against those terrorist inroads.

Consolidation of Democracy

Clearly in the past half-century Turkish democracy has gone through serious crises and temporary setbacks. Yet the remarkable outcome is that democratic institutions and attitudes have been progressively consolidated and Turkey has become the only fully established democracy in the Muslim Middle East—and, indeed, one of the few throughout Asia or Africa. Three factors have contributed crucially to this result.

First, Turkey's secular national identity has been firmly established since the 1920s, in contrast to those of the Arab peoples, many of whom still are insecure in their national identities based on their present borders (Algeria, Egypt, Iraq, and Kuwait, among others), or on a common Arab language (from Morocco to Oman), or on Islam. Second, Turkey, unlike many developing countries, has an effective and impartial government because the new republic inherited most of the Ottoman Empire's bureaucratic and educational institutions. And, third, the organizational links between Ankara and the provinces developed in Atatürk's days of benevolent authoritarianism have been vastly expanded since the 1950s through party competition, internal migration, and the development of economic enterprises.

As in other Middle Eastern or developing countries, the major alternative to democracy has remained military-authoritarian rule, but here too Turkey differs significantly from its neighbors. Its military, from late Ottoman days and victory in Turkey's war of independence (1919–1923) to the cold war alliance with the United States, has been oriented toward the West and has maintained the highest professional standards. Thus military interventions have remained of short duration. Above all, the increasingly strong commitment of the population to democracy ultimately has given military leaders a choice only between accepting democracy or imposing a degree of military tyranny that they could not square with their own principles.

In summary, Turkey, aside from its unresolved Kurdish problem, has a well-structured political and social framework for democracy. Half a century after Ismet Inönü's first democratic moves in 1945, the country's commitment to an open political process seems beyond question, the crucial turning points being the outcomes of the 1983 election in favor of the nonmilitarily sponsored Motherland Party and of the 1987 referendum on the reentry of former politicians into the political arena.

BIBLIOGRAPHY

Ahmad, Feroz. *The Turkish Experiment in Democracy, 1950–1975.* Boulder, Colo.: Westview Press; London: C. Hurst, 1977.

Bianchi, Robert B. *Interest Groups and Political Development in Turkey.* Princeton: Princeton University Press, 1984.

Hale, William M. *The Political and Economic Development of Modern Turkey.* New York: St. Martin's, 1981.

Harris, George S. *Turkey: Coping with Crisis.* Boulder, Colo.: Westview Press, 1985.

Heper, Metin, and Jacob M. Landau, eds. *Political Parties and Democracy in Turkey.* London: I. B. Tauris, 1991.

Lewis, Bernard. *The Emergence of Modern Turkey.* 2d ed. London and New York: Oxford University Press, 1968.

Rustow, Dankwart A. "A Democratic Turkey Faces New Challenges." *Global Affairs* 8 (spring 1993): 58–70.

———. *Turkey: America's Forgotten Ally.* New York: Council on Foreign Relations, 1987.

Tachau, Frank. *Turkey: The Politics of Authority, Democracy, and Development.* New York: Praeger, 1984.

Weiker, Walter F. *The Modernization of Turkey: From Atatürk to the Present Day.* New York: Holmes and Meier, 1981.

U

Uganda

A landlocked country in East Central Africa where attempts at multiparty democracy have not precluded state-sponsored violence. Today Uganda is experimenting with novel forms of political participation.

Since gaining independence from Great Britain in 1962, Uganda has experienced many types of political structures, veering from civilian to military regimes to near anarchy. Not only were Uganda's episodes with formally democratic institutions under civilian rule highly unstable; they often provided a context for heavily repressive government policies.

Ugandans brought a maturity, and a cynicism hardened by years of political violence and economic decline, to discussions of democracy—in particular, the form democracy should take in their country and the way it should be expressed in the new constitution adopted in September 1995. One source of popular cynicism toward democracy in Uganda has been the performance of its political parties—especially the Uganda People's Congress (UPC) and the Democratic Party. All parties, but particularly the UPC, have practiced extraconstitutional and nondemocratic behavior.

From Independence to Idi Amin

In many ways Uganda's political parties have embodied the contradictions of a British colonial legacy, beginning in 1894. In constructing a protectorate in Uganda, the British both entered into treaties with collaborating precolonial polities and defeated recalcitrant groups in warfare. The final boundaries of the protectorate combined into a single administrative unit centralized kingdoms, the remnants of precolonial empires, and decentralized political groupings.

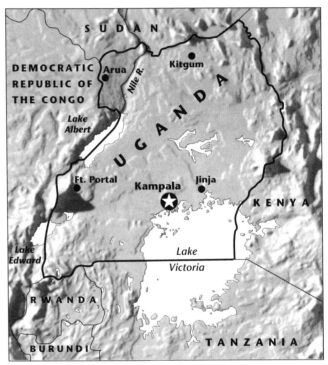

The British developed the south and left the north as a reserve for labor and military recruitment. They left the central government weak while strengthening the ethnic consciousness of subunits through policies of "indirect rule." The most significant result of these policies was the quasi-autonomous status of the southern kingdom of Buganda, led by its *kabaka* (king) and his chiefs. Buganda had the largest ethnic grouping in the protectorate (the Baganda tribal group represented 20 percent of the population), and it also was the most economically vibrant region. During this period,

Buganda alternated between threats to become a separate state and efforts to secure dominance in an independent Uganda. Northern ethnic groups—particularly the Langi and Acholi—perceived their interests as circumscribed by Buganda's privileged position.

The UPC, led by Milton Obote, was the party of government for two periods of Uganda's postindependence history (1962–1971 and 1980–1985). It emerged before independence as a loose coalition of local elites with followings in various ethnic communities. What bound the UPC together was a desire to share in the spoils of political control, a vision of a strong central state that would supersede the federal tendencies fostered by colonial policies, and the Anglican faith of most of its leaders. By 1961 it controlled most district councils, with the key exception of Buganda, where its antifederal stance was deeply resented.

Ironically, the UPC entered into an alliance with the subnationalist party of Buganda—Kabaka Yekka, meaning "the king alone"—and defeated the Democratic Party in Uganda's independence elections in 1962. Obote became prime minister. This marriage of convenience proved to be short lived: members from other parties crossed the floor to join the UPC, giving it an absolute majority in the parliament. Freed from dependence on Buganda, Obote moved toward disassembling Uganda's federal structure by repressing opposition and abolishing all four of Uganda's kingdoms, including Buganda. (Several of these kingdoms were restored in 1993.) In addition, he imposed a new constitution that established a highly centralized state apparatus, giving direct control over local governments to the national executive. Obote declared himself president within this new structure. Ideologically, he labeled this shift a "move to the left," which was formalized in his Common Man's Charter. But more important in the long run was the domination of the UPC by the interests of political elites from the north of Uganda—the home region of both Obote and the bulk of the Ugandan army, upon which he was becoming increasingly dependent.

The origins of the Democratic Party lay in the mobilization of educated Catholics, at first in Buganda and later throughout the country. The party's most important leader, Benedicto Kiwanuka, served briefly as prime minister after a Democratic Party victory in the pre-independence elections of 1961. Buganda's Anglican political elite greatly resented this outcome, leading to its ill-fated alliance with the UPC.

After the Democratic Party's defeat in the 1962 elections, it took on the role of parliamentary opposition. Within the next few years many parliamentarians in the party, who were enticed by promises of patronage and ministerial posts, joined the UPC rather than remain in opposition. The Democratic Party became virtually moribund in the late 1960s as the UPC moved toward one-party rule.

By 1969 Uganda had become a one-party state. Elections within a one-party framework were planned for 1971, the first since independence. But the coup led by Maj. Gen. Idi Amin in that year preempted the elections. Amin banned all political parties, and many UPC leaders went into exile. A notorious military dictatorship was established, with Amin declaring himself "life president." He quickly expelled Uganda's Asian population, the backbone of the commercial sector of the economy, and embarked on a reign of terror against intellectuals, members of the armed forces from supposedly disloyal ethnic groups, and all critics and opponents of the regime. Human rights violations occurred on a massive scale, with estimates of 100,000–250,000 deaths.

More Years of Turmoil

Obote returned to the political scene after the 1979 defeat of Amin's army by Tanzanian troops and a broad dissident force, the Uganda National Liberation Army (UNLA) and the Uganda National Liberation Front. The National Liberation Front, the political wing, appointed and then deposed several heads of state within a brief period before calling elections in 1980. These elections, organized by an electoral commission largely sympathetic to the UPC, resulted in a victory for the UPC and for Obote—a victory that many observers and most Ugandans regarded as rigged.

The Democratic Party had reconstituted itself for the 1980 elections under the leadership of Paul Ssemogerere, who, according to most accounts, would have become president if not for the rigged results. Once again it became a parliamentary opposition party and through its newspaper strongly denounced the army's human rights record. After the election it was evident that the social base of the Democratic Party had been transformed. In addition to retaining some support among Catholics, the Democratic Party swept Buganda, where it had made common cause with those who hated Obote and the UPC.

Among the prominent Ugandans rejecting the election results was Yoweri Kaguta Museveni, who formed the National Resistance Army (NRA) and began a guerrilla struggle. The north-south divide in Uganda was starkly revealed in the course of the guerrilla war, which was fought entirely in the south, particularly the region of Buganda known as the Luwero Triangle. The UNLA's counterinsurgency killed hundreds of thousands of civilians, even surpassing the excesses of Amin's regime. In addition, the UPC cadre and its youth wing ran roughshod over the population, persecuting Democratic Party and suspected NRA supporters. That such events could occur in a nominally democratic, multiparty regime was a lesson not lost on most Ugandans, and it is a source of their cynicism today.

In 1985, with the NRA capturing portions of western Uganda, a factional squabble within the military led to a successful coup, removing Obote once again. The Democratic Party declared its support for the leader of the coup, Tito Okello Lutwa, and his followers despite their involvement in the army's atrocities. This declaration of support was regarded as opportunistic by many Ugandans. Like the floor crossings of the mid-1960s, it compromised the Democratic Party's image as a party committed to democratic rule. When Museveni and the NRA captured Kampala, the capital, in January 1986, the Democratic Party reversed itself and entered into a fragile grand coalition with the new National Resistance Movement government.

Government Under the National Resistance Movement

By the time the NRM captured state power, the polarization between north and south in Uganda was at its peak. The NRM has its base of support in the south, and various rebel movements in the north have resisted its rule. In combating these groups, the NRM has tarnished its reputation for discipline and observance of human rights, upon which its legitimacy is largely based.

Although the NRM has roots in the Uganda Patriotic Movement, a small party once headed by Museveni, it is generally hostile to multiparty competition and blames the behavior of parties for much of Uganda's political troubles. At the same time the NRM experimented with novel forms of popular participation that were embraced with guarded optimism by Uganda's weary population.

The NRM instituted a nationwide system of popular councils from the village to the district level. These "resistance councils" mandated direct elections to village committees and indirect elections to councils at each higher level of administration. While the indirect feature came under criticism, the resistance council system allowed Ugandans to participate more fully in politics than they had before. The councils were also used to elect members of the parliament indirectly, although some seats were re-

served for the army (NRA) and presidential appointments.

In addition to the council system, the NRM appointed a commission to write a new constitution for Uganda. Commissioners encouraged input from all sectors of Ugandan society and traveled to remote rural areas to solicit opinions. The commission submitted a draft constitution in December 1992, and a Constituent Assembly was elected on March 28, 1994.

The new constitution, adopted by the Constituent Assembly in September 1995 and never submitted to referendum, created a 279-member Parliament: 214 seats were to be filled through direct election from single-member districts; 62 seats were to be filled through indirect elections to ensure the representation of women (39 seats), the army (10 seats), the disabled (5 seats), youth (5 seats), and trade unions (3 seats); and 3 seats were to be held ex officio. Most important, the constitution banned public political party activity until 2001. The NRM considers itself an inclusive, populist movement, and it sees the resistance council system as the foundation of a "no-party" democracy. Party politics, the NRM believes, would only exacerbate regional, ethnic, and religious tensions. Elections to the new Parliament were held in June 1996 on a nonparty basis.

Overall, the NRM has demonstrated an ambiguous stance toward democratic politics. While occasionally showing authoritarian tendencies and limiting alternative political organization, it has encouraged popular participation in governance, especially at the local level. Most promising is the openness and engagement with which Ugandans are debating such issues given their skepticism toward political formulas of any kind. In the north, skepticism may still outweigh engagement, and the most difficult challenge for the NRM may be to ensure that whatever political arrangement is decided, it will reflect the genuine participation of all Ugandans.

See also *Africa, Subsaharan.*

BIBLIOGRAPHY

Apter, David E. *The Political Kingdom in Uganda: A Study of Bureaucratic Nationalism.* 2d ed. Princeton: Princeton University Press, 1967.

Hansen, Holger Bernt, and Michael Twaddle, eds. *Changing Uganda: The Dilemmas of Structural Adjustment and Revolutionary Change.* London: James Currey, 1991.

———. *Uganda Now: Between Decay and Development.* London: James Currey, 1988.

Kasfir, Nelson. *The Shrinking Political Arena: Participation and Ethnicity in African Politics, with a Case Study of Uganda.* Berkeley: University of California Press, 1976.

Kokole, Omari H., and Ali A. Mazrui. "Uganda: The Dual Polity and the Plural Society." In *Democracy in Developing Countries: Africa,* edited by Larry Diamond, Juan J. Linz, and Seymour Martin Lipset. Boulder, Colo.: Lynne Rienner; London: Adamantine Press, 1988.

Mamdani, Mahmood. "Contradictory Class Perspectives on the Question of Democracy: The Case of Uganda." In *Popular Struggles for Democracy in Africa,* edited by Peter Anyang' Nyong'o. London: United Nations University and Zed Books, 1987.

Mutibwa, Phares. *Uganda since Independence: A Story of Unfulfilled Hopes.* Trenton, N.J.: Africa World Press; London: Hurst, 1992.

Oloka-Onyango, Joe. "The National Resistance Movement, 'Grass-roots Democracy,' and Dictatorship in Uganda." In *Democracy and Socialism in Africa,* edited by Robin Cohen and Harry Goulbourne. Boulder, Colo.: Westview Press, 1991.

Z

Zambia

A land-locked, low-income country in Africa bordered by the Democratic Republic of the Congo (formerly Zaire) on the north and Zimbabwe on the south. Zambia was the first English-speaking state in Africa to make an electoral leadership transition in the post–cold war period. In October 1991 voters rejected a seventeen-year experiment with single-party rule by the United National Independence Party (UNIP) in favor of a broad-based opposition movement that promised a return to pluralistic and competitive politics. By electing trade unionist Frederick Chiluba as their new president, Zambians disavowed Kenneth Kaunda, a founder of the Zambian independence movement and a prominent African nationalist.

The case of Zambia illustrates three truths about poor countries that attempt to reject authoritarianism. First, mass demands for democratization often originate in popular resentment of declining economic opportunities and living standards. Second, an economic crisis alone is insufficient to propel a successful transition to democracy: other political-institutional conditions must be in place, including a unified opposition and a relatively neutral bureaucracy and judiciary. Third, the resultant political regimes are extremely fragile, and democratic institutions prove difficult to consolidate.

From Traditional to One-Party Rule

The colony of Northern Rhodesia was created in the late nineteenth century to protect mineral concessions extracted from indigenous chiefs by the British South Africa Company, founded by Cecil Rhodes. The British Colonial Office, which ruled from 1924 to 1953, amalgamated many indigenous polities—each with its own language, culture, and institutions—into a hybrid political system in which central colonial authority was exercised and, to a degree,

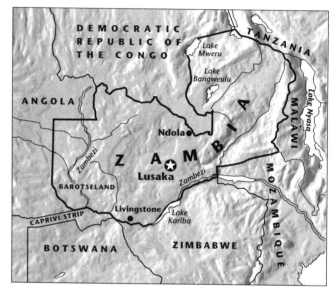

shared with local leaders. Although some traditional polities, such as the Lozi chiefdom, were highly centralized, others, such as the Tonga village, dispersed authority to headmen. Neither traditional nor colonial rule encouraged a democratic political culture since these regimes vested authority in appointed male elders and allowed few opportunities for political participation or competition.

Africans resisted colonial rule, initially by joining messianic religious sects and later through industrial strikes in the mining region, known as the Copper Belt. In response to the incorporation of Northern Rhodesia into the white settler–dominated Central African Federation in 1953, a new class of Western-educated leaders, including schoolteachers such as Kaunda, were able to build an anticolonial nationalist movement. Combining protest action with demands to broaden the electoral rolls, they pressured Great

Britain into permitting the first African government in 1962 and granting full political independence within the British Commonwealth in 1964. In that year Kaunda became the first president of Zambia under a republican constitution that affirmed freedom of political expression and association.

The First Republic (1964–1973) was marked by lively multiparty competition in which the United National Independence Party's electoral dominance was gradually eroded by regional opposition parties. To promote national unity, Kaunda skillfully balanced competing ethnic interests by distributing political appointments among the country's main ethnic groups. He avowed a preference for single-party rule but promised that UNIP could win its desired monopoly through the ballot box. As it happened, however, Kaunda ultimately resorted to coercion. Faced with possible defeat for UNIP in the 1973 parliamentary elections, he detained or co-opted opposition leaders and declared a single-party state on December 13, 1973.

The revised constitution for Zambia's Second Republic (1973–1991) enshrined the principle of party supremacy and empowered the president to appoint all senior party and government officials. The National Assembly was reduced to a "rubber stamp" that endorsed decisions taken in the UNIP Central Committee. Inspired by the ideas of Tanzania's president, Julius Nyerere, Zambian "one-party participatory democracy" at first permitted a measure of political competition within the ruling party. Over time, however, Kaunda manipulated electoral rules to consolidate UNIP control over the recruitment of parliamentary candidates and to eliminate challenges to his presidency. Under the banner of a socialistic ideology of "humanism," he also appointed party loyalists to patronage posts in the network of public corporations that dominated the Zambian economy. Voters showed their dissatisfaction with these policies by staying away from the polls and casting growing numbers of "no" votes in presidential elections.

Democratic Transition

Popular disenchantment deepened in the 1980s as Zambia's economy entered a prolonged downturn because of falling international copper prices and economic mismanagement at home. Lacking opportunities for political participation within the ruling party or outside it, the people shifted the locus of their opposition to civil society. Church, student, and business associations became havens for liberal political views and vehicles for the expression of dissent. At the core of Zambian civil society was the labor movement organized under the umbrella of the Zambia Congress of Trade Unions. Its membership comprised more than 80 percent of formal employees, and by the mid-1980s it was twice the size of UNIP. Under the leadership of Chairman Frederick Chiluba, who was imprisoned briefly by Kaunda in 1981, it resisted UNIP's efforts to incorporate workers into the ruling party.

Frustrated by the reluctance of the government, Zambia's main employer, to engage in collective bargaining or take adequate steps to reverse the country's economic decline, the Congress demanded greater governmental accountability. By late 1989 Chiluba began to call openly for the restoration of multiparty politics. In defense of this view, he pointed to the collapse of communist regimes in Eastern Europe. Africans, he argued, also should forsake the one-party system.

Such demands for political pluralism were backed by massive street demonstrations in Zambia's populous urban areas. The political crisis was exacerbated by food riots, the worst political violence since independence, and an attempted military coup in June 1990. In response, Kaunda made a series of historic political concessions. First, he permitted a referendum on a multiparty system. Second, he called for competitive elections monitored by international observers. Finally, he allowed constitutional revisions to reduce the executive powers of the presidency. To take advantage of these political openings, labor and business leaders convened a loose opposition alliance, which was hastily converted into a political party. Chiluba was elected to lead this Movement for Multiparty Democracy (MMD) and to be the party's candidate for the nation's presidency in the October 1991 elections.

The 1991 election campaign pitted MMD's critique of economic mismanagement and political repression against UNIP warnings that competitive politics would foster ethnic violence. In the end Zambia's first democratic election in more than two decades hinged on personalities, with voters expressing a clear determination to rid themselves of Kaunda. Chiluba won 76 percent of the presidential vote, and MMD candidates captured 125 out of 150 National Assembly seats. Zambia's Third Republic was born on November 1, 1991, as Chiluba took office with a strong electoral mandate to restore both political rights and economic well-being.

Features of the Transition

Why was Zambia able to exit from authoritarian rule through a peaceful election, a landmark event on a continent where such transfers of power are rare? Several factors help explain the Zambian exception.

First is the quality of leadership. Kaunda's instinct for political compromise led him to concede to demands other African rulers had stubbornly resisted. Kaunda was generous even in defeat, stepping aside promptly once it became apparent that the opposition had won. Second, compared with other African countries, Zambia has an unusually urbanized and well-educated population. This social structure laid the foundation for independent associational life, particularly among organized labor, and for energetic protest against elite corruption and declining living standards.

Third, the opposition in Zambia coalesced into a coherent political force. Although never a well-organized political party, the MMD did bring labor, business, professional, and religious interests together into a united social movement, unlike the fragmented opposition that characterized other regimes in Africa attempting transitions in the early 1990s. Finally, governmental institutions played vital independent roles. The courts, for example, ruled against UNIP in key court cases concerning the use of public resources for partisan political purposes. And the electoral commission displayed commendable impartiality in adjusting and enforcing electoral rules to ensure free and fair elections. Uncommonly for contemporary Africa, even the police and the military performed their roles neutrally.

All its institutional assets—reflective leaders, modern social classes, active voluntary associations, a professional bureaucracy—will be needed to consolidate democracy in Zambia. There is no going back from certain aspects of pluralism: the press, civic groups, and political parties have vigorously defended newly won freedoms of expression and association, and judges and civil servants have resisted politicians who sought to reassert supremacy over decision making. Nevertheless, certain generic problems of consolidating democracy in a poor country have become evident.

Problems of Democratic Consolidation

The political transition occurred rapidly in two short years between late 1989 and late 1991, allowing little time for the emergence of firm democratic institutions. Most notably, Zambia lacked a complement of effective political parties that could instill practices of popular participation and open competition: the MMD party organization began to fragment with the disappearance of the unifying goal of ousting Kaunda, and UNIP was reduced by its poor showing at the polls to a regional party with a base only in the Eastern Province. Indeed, MMD's lopsided electoral victory raised anew the prospect of one-party dominance of elections and the legislature.

Moreover, economic conditions in Zambia in the early 1990s hampered the consolidation of democratic gains. The MMD inherited a monumental national debt, a deteriorated physical infrastructure, a reputation for high risk among investors, and an accelerating rate of inflation. The government thus embarked on a radical economic reform program to reduce state employment, restore private ownership, and introduce free markets. In the short run this program deepened hardship for urban dwellers and increased opportunities for conspicuous consumption by economic elites. As strikes proliferated, especially in the public sector, former supporters turned against the MMD. The Zambian case supports the notion that democratic consolidation is not purely a political process but also demands social and economic change.

The elections of 1996 offered evidence of the fragile nature of Zambian democracy. UNIP, which had been the largest opposition group in the National Assembly, with twenty-five seats, boycotted the November elections. The party refused to participate after Kaunda was declared ineligible to run in the concurrent presidential election. With UNIP on the sidelines, MMD won 131 of 150 elective Assembly seats, and Chiluba was reelected president with almost 70 percent of the vote.

Fundamentally, the consolidation of democracy requires a political culture in which elites and masses alike value democratic practices as part of the natural order of things. Such values are not widespread in Zambia. At the mass level, voter turnout remains low, registering just 45 percent in the historic transition elections of 1991, below 14 percent in the local government elections of the following year, and only about 40 percent in the 1996 elections. The mass celebrations in response to the erroneous news of Kaunda's ouster during the aborted coup attempt of June 1990 indicate that many Zambians were willing to accept any form of political change—democratic or not—as long as it removed an unpopular leader. Moreover, the habits of one-party rule have proved to be resilient among political elites. A hard-line faction of MMD cabinet ministers has displayed a predilection for arbitrariness (for example, by convincing Chiluba temporarily to declare a state of emergency in 1993). Elements within UNIP, for their part, have tended to resort to plots and intrigue and have failed to develop an ethic of loyal opposition. For all these reasons, the young democracy in Zambia remains fragile and unconsolidated.

BIBLIOGRAPHY

Bratton, Michael. "Zambia Starts Over." *Journal of Democracy* 3 (April 1992): 81–94.

Chanda, Donald. *Democracy in Zambia: Key Speeches of President Chiluba, 1991–92.* Lusaka: Africa Press Trust, 1993.

Gann, L. H. *A History of Northern Rhodesia: Early Days to 1953.* London: Chatto and Windus, 1964.

Gertzel, Cherry, Carolyn Baylies, and Morris Szeftel. *The Dynamics of the One-Party State in Zambia.* Manchester: Manchester University Press, 1984.

Kaunda, Kenneth. *Zambia Shall Be Free: An Autobiography.* London: Heinemann, 1962.

Tordoff, William, ed. *Politics in Zambia.* Manchester: Manchester University Press, 1974.

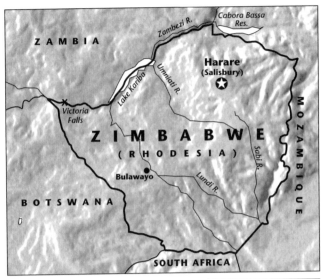

Zimbabwe

A landlocked country in southeastern Africa, which has had the constitutional form of democracy since 1980 but lacks electoral competition and free expression of ideas. The boundaries of Zimbabwe, originally called Southern Rhodesia, were drawn by the British South Africa Company in the 1890s. Before then the African population in the region consisted primarily of small-scale political organizations centered on villages, although the Ndebele in the Southwest had a hierarchical political structure centered on a king.

Historical Background

Led by Cecil Rhodes, the British South Africa Company searched the area for mineral wealth comparable to the rich deposits found in South Africa. The expected mineral bonanza never materialized, however. Faced with the company's virtual bankruptcy, the white settlers voted to become a self-governing colony of the United Kingdom in a 1922 referendum that excluded the participation of blacks. Although whites made up only a minuscule portion of the population, they took control of the region's internal affairs.

The whites were few in number, but there were still too many whites with a vested interest in controlling government to allow for the kind of easy decolonization that occurred in much of Africa. Rhodesian whites possessed a political voice and an ability to organize that made the colony fundamentally different from other African territories. On the other hand, there were not enough whites to institute a full-fledged program of apartheid as was being done in South Africa. Indeed, whites in what became Zim-

babwe never represented more than 2 percent of the population, compared with a peak population share of almost 20 percent for whites in South Africa. Only after a long and bloody war of national liberation did Zimbabwe achieve independence through formal decolonization.

In the decades after the 1922 referendum, whites slowly consolidated their power. Africans were forced off their land and herded into Tribal Trust Territories. The Rhodesian state expanded and created a large number of state-owned corporations (parastatals) to foster infrastructure, agriculture, and an iron and steel industry. Especially after World War II, with a significant influx of whites fleeing the gloom of postwar England, the economy boomed. Oppressive laws ensured white supremacy and prevented protest by the black majority.

Yet, alongside this complex system of economic and legal controls to repress Africans, a tradition of democratic politics developed among white Rhodesians. Elections occurred routinely, and occasionally the incumbents lost. But there was never a tradition of competition among parties representing different political ideals. Always aware that they were a tiny minority, the whites were never as divided by issues as they were united by fear of the Africans coming to power.

End of Colonial Rule

In 1964, faced with demands from Great Britain that Southern Rhodesia follow the continental trend and grant political power to the African majority, Ian Smith, the prime minister, promulgated a Unilateral Declaration of Independence. The declaration was declared illegal by the United Nations, which then imposed mandatory comprehensive sanctions against the renegade regime. These sanctions, however, had little effect. By enacting even more repressive legislation and exploiting the many loopholes in the global embargo, white Rhodesians managed to prosper.

Soon after the declaration a war of national liberation began, but the military threat against the settler regime was very limited because of the disorganization of the guerrilla armies, the effectiveness of the Rhodesian counterinsurgency effort, and support from the South African military. The Zimbabwe African People's Union (ZAPU), led by Joshua Nkomo and supported by the minority Ndebele, continued to fight from its bases in Zambia, but it was never a very effective organization. The party of the majority Shona was the Zimbabwe African National Union (ZANU), led by Robert Mugabe. Only in 1975, when Mugabe was able to open bases in newly independent Mozambique, did hostilities against the regime, based in Salisbury (now Harare), increase dramatically.

In 1979 Bishop Abel Muzorewa created a transitional regime. It was never acknowledged as legitimate by other countries, however, and it was clear to all inside the country that Smith was the power behind the throne. Demonstrating the oddity of that regime, the country was briefly known as Zimbabwe-Rhodesia. Its economy gradually deteriorated as a result of years of warfare, political uncertainty, sanctions, and white emigration.

Finally, the government regime was forced to negotiate with the Africans. The site of these negotiations, mediated by Lord Carrington, was Lancaster House in London. The elections held the following year were widely considered to be free and fair. Mugabe's Zimbabwe African National Union won a significant electoral victory: 63 percent of the vote and 57 of the 100 seats in Parliament. Most of Mugabe's support came from the Shona-dominated areas; he garnered less than 10 percent of the vote in the Ndebele-dominated areas of Matabeleland North and Matabeleland South. Muzorewa's party received almost no popular support.

The constitution drawn up at Lancaster House made numerous concessions to the whites. Most dramatically, a separate voting roll allowed whites to have a disproportionate number of seats in Parliament (20). To placate the politically important white farmers, seizure of land by the state was forbidden unless compensation was paid in for-

eign currency. These provisions could not be amended for seven years unless the white members of Parliament agreed.

The Government Since 1980

Zimbabwe's democratic experience since 1980 has been mixed. On a continent where many constitutions are irrelevant almost as soon as they are printed, the Mugabe regime has strictly adhered to the constitution, at least on a procedural level. Although the guaranteed white veto in Parliament was widely viewed as insulting, the constitution stood unchanged for the agreed seven years. Mugabe's government did not seize any land or nationalize any enterprises (unless market compensation was set). Only in 1987, at the end of the seven-year period specified in the Lancaster House constitution, did the government eliminate white seats in Parliament and enact legislation that permitted it to seize some land from white farmers. Within the parameters of the constitution, the courts in particular have been independent and energetic in defending individual rights, sometimes to the dismay of the government. There has been no retribution against the whites. Indeed, Ian Smith was allowed to participate fully in politics even though many in the country believe that he is a war criminal.

Beyond strict procedural adherence, Zimbabwe's democratic performance has been poor. Most dramatically, the regime probably killed between 1,000 and 2,000 people in Matabeleland in the mid-1980s, when Mugabe accused elements of the Zimbabwe African People's Union of collaborating with South Africa. Partially for ethnic reasons, the army of Zimbabwe went amok in this region, inflicting countless injuries and causing numerous people to flee their lands. Nearly a decade later the country still had not come to grips with this massacre. Ethnic conflict did lessen, however, in 1987 with the merger of ZANU and ZAPU to form the Zimbabwe African National Union–Patriotic Front (ZANU–PF).

Majority rule in Zimbabwe has been characterized by repression of ideas as well as violence. Because the government directly controls the electronic media, open debate and discussion are stymied. Especially during the 1980s, information on what was happening in the country was difficult to obtain. The state of emergency imposed by the minority white regime as well as other repressive laws were retained by the Mugabe regime during the 1980s, further inhibiting free political discussion.

The country did not experience a full-fledged national

debate about its political system until 1989, when ZANU–PF was about to create a de jure one-party state (as opposed to the de facto one-party state that had existed since 1980). A series of events, including the collapse of communism in central Europe, the release of Nelson Mandela in South Africa, and the end of the state of emergency in South Africa (particularly important given the stridency of Zimbabwe's criticism of apartheid), as well as the global trend toward democracy, demonstrated just how anachronistic the Mugabe government's political project had become. Indeed, Western donors warned that Zimbabwe would appear badly out of step with the rest of the world if it outlawed political competition just when so many other countries were overthrowing dictatorships. At the same time domestic opposition to the creation of a political monopoly for ZANU–PF increased. This opposition was sparked not only by the wave of democratic transitions in the late 1980s but also by the genuine desire of many Zimbabweans for a pluralistic order and an end to the corruption and authoritarianism of Mugabe's regime.

The elections in 1990 were open to other parties, although only one, the Zimbabwe Unity Movement, emerged as significant. While ZANU–PF won the vote count handily, only 54 percent of the eligible population voted. This low turnout indicated that many people were displeased with the political and economic performance of the regime, although they did not find the opposition compelling.

By the mid-1990s little had changed. Although Zimbabwe remained a multiparty system de jure, ZANU-PF dominated the government, legislature, and, most important, the electoral process. Ten parties registered to participate in the April 1995 legislative balloting, but four decided on the eve of the elections to boycott in protest of a stilted electoral system. ZANU-PF won 118 of the 120 elective legislative seats—55 of them unopposed. Again, turnout was low, at 57 percent. Mugabe was elected to a third term as president in March 1996 in balloting marred by even lower turnout and by the boycotts of his opponents, who withdrew citing harassment by government security personnel.

Although the de facto one-party state clearly lacks support in Zimbabwe, many questions remain about the country's political future. Political competition based on ideology has yet to emerge, and ZANU–PF continues to reserve for itself special access to the media. Like most African countries, Zimbabwe must develop innovative democratic institutions and procedures if its rural majority is to have political power commensurate with its interests. So far no democratic vision that would ensure full political participation has become generally accepted. The great democratic task ahead is for Zimbabweans to develop an indigenous democratic theory appropriate to their circumstances.

BIBLIOGRAPHY

Baynham, Simon, ed. *Zimbabwe in Transition.* Stockholm: Almqvist and Wiksell, 1992.

Herbst, Jeffrey. *State Politics in Zimbabwe.* Berkeley: University of California Press, 1990.

Mandaza, Ibbo, ed. *Zimbabwe: The Political Economy of Transition, 1980–1986.* Dakar: Council for the Development of Economic and Social Research in Africa, 1986.

———, and Lloyd Sachikonye, eds. *The One-Party State and Democracy.* Harare: Southern Africa Political Economy Series Trust, 1991.

Moyo, Jonathan N. *Voting for Democracy: Electoral Politics in Zimbabwe.* Harare: University of Zimbabwe Publications Office, 1992.

Sithole, Masipula. "Zimbabwe: In Search of Democracy." In *Democracy in Developing Countries: Africa,* edited by Larry Diamond, Juan J. Linz, and Seymour Martin Lipset. Boulder, Colo.: Lynne Rienner; London: Adamantine Press, 1988.

REFERENCE MATERIAL

CONSTITUTION OF JAPAN (1947)

Constitutions generally, as bedrock documents of a political culture, are more than a dispassionate list of individual rights and governing bodies, relationships, and procedures; they are an expression of deeply felt principles derived gradually over centuries concerning the proper organization of society. It is remarkable, then, that the postwar Japanese constitution has proved so durable—having stood almost unchanged for nearly five decades—given that it was imposed by a victorious enemy and that its terms were somewhat foreign to Japanese society and culture.

In the aftermath of World War II, the victorious Allied powers, led principally by the United States, resolved that Japan should become a constitutional democracy. In October 1945 the supreme commander for the Allied powers, Gen. Douglas MacArthur, instructed the Japanese government to draft a new constitution to replace the Meiji Constitution of 1889, under which the emperor had been all-powerful. When the Japanese submitted a draft that was deemed unacceptable by the Far Eastern Commission—the eleven Allied powers' forum for supervising the occupation of Japan—MacArthur had his staff write a constitution. After review by the Far Eastern Commission, the "MacArthur constitution" was submitted to the Japanese emperor and government, who accepted it with only minor modifications. Nominally, the new constitution was promulgated November 3, 1946, as an imperial amendment to the Meiji Constitution and took effect May 3, 1947.

The postwar document was drafted largely on the lines of the British parliamentary system, toward which the Japanese had been gravitating since the 1890s. In fact, many of its features had been present superficially in the Meiji Constitution: both documents made provision for a bicameral legislature, a cabinet, national elections, and the emperor. But the power relationships among them were to change dramatically. The postwar cabinet would answer to the legislature (the Diet), rather than to the emperor; both houses of the legislature (the House of Representatives and the House of Councillors) would be popularly elected, whereas only the lower house had been under Meiji; all national elections would be based on the principle of universal suffrage, whereas prewar suffrage had been severely limited; and, most important, all sovereignty would reside in the people, and the emperor would be no more than a figurehead. Whereas the Meiji Constitution had been a grant from the emperor to the people, the postwar constitution adopted the Western notion of government by consent of the governed. Its specific terms were solidly grounded in the Western notions of democratic, representative government: separation of powers, representation, accountability, procedural stability, and openness.

We, the Japanese people, acting through our duly elected representatives in the National Diet, determined that we shall secure for ourselves and our posterity the fruits of peaceful cooperation with all nations and the blessings of liberty throughout this land, and resolved that never again shall we be visited with the horrors of war through the action of government, do proclaim that sovereign power resides with the people and do firmly establish this Constitution. Government is a sacred trust of the people, the authority for which is derived from the people, the powers of which are exercised by the representatives of the people, and the benefits of which are enjoyed by the people. This is a universal principle of mankind upon which this constitution is founded. We reject and revoke all constitutions, laws, ordinances, and rescripts in conflict herewith.

We, the Japanese people, desire peace for all time and are deeply conscious of the high ideals controlling human relationship, and we have determined to preserve our security and existence, trusting in the justice and faith of the peace-loving peoples of the world. We desire to occupy an honored place in an international society striving for the preservation of peace, and the banishment of tyranny and slavery, oppression and intolerance for all time from the earth. We recognize that all peoples of the world have the right to live in peace, free from fear and want.

We believe that no nation is responsible to itself alone, but that laws of political morality are universal; and that obedience to such laws is incumbent upon all nations who would sustain their own sovereignty and justify their sovereign relationship with other nations.

We, the Japanese people, pledge our national honor to accomplish these high ideals and purposes with all our resources.

Chapter I
THE EMPEROR

ARTICLE 1. The Emperor shall be the symbol of the State and of the unity of the people, deriving his position from the will of the people with whom resides sovereign power.

ARTICLE 2. The Imperial Throne shall be dynastic and succeeded to in accordance with the Imperial House Law passed by the Diet.

ARTICLE 3. The advice and approval of the Cabinet shall be required for all acts of the Emperor in matters of state, and the Cabinet shall be responsible therefor.

ARTICLE 4. The Emperor shall perform only such acts in matters of state as are provided for in this Constitution and he shall not have powers related to government.

The Emperor may delegate the performance of his acts in matters of state as may be provided by law.

ARTICLE 5. When, in accordance with the Imperial House Law, a Regency is established, the Regent shall perform his acts in matters of state in the Emperor's name. In this case, paragraph one of the preceding article will be applicable.

ARTICLE 6. The Emperor shall appoint the Prime Minister as designated by the Diet.

The Emperor shall appoint the Chief Judge of the Supreme Court as designated by the Cabinet.

ARTICLE 7. The Emperor, with the advice and approval of the Cabinet, shall perform the following acts in matters of state on behalf of the people:

Promulgation of amendments of the constitution, laws, cabinet orders and treaties.

Convocation of the Diet.

Dissolution of the House of Representatives.

Proclamation of general election of members of the Diet.

Attestation of the appointment and dismissal of Ministers of State and other officials as provided for by law, and of full powers and credentials of Ambassadors and Ministers.

Attestation of general and special amnesty, commutation of punishment, reprieve, and restoration of rights.

Awarding of honors.

Attestation of instruments of ratification and other diplomatic documents as provided for by law.

Receiving foreign ambassadors and ministers.

Performance of ceremonial functions.

ARTICLE 8. No property can be given to, or received by, the Imperial House, nor can any gifts be made therefrom, without the authorization of the Diet.

Chapter II
RENUNCIATION OF WAR

ARTICLE 9. Aspiring sincerely to an international peace based on justice and order, the Japanese people forever renounce war as a sovereign right of the nation and the threat or use of force as means of settling international disputes.

In order to accomplish the aim of the preceding paragraph, land, sea, and air forces, as well as other war potential, will never be maintained. The right of belligerency of the state will not be recognized.

Chapter III
RIGHTS AND DUTIES OF THE PEOPLE

ARTICLE 10. The conditions necessary for being a Japanese national shall be determined by law.

ARTICLE 11. The people shall not be prevented from enjoying any of the fundamental human rights. These fundamental human rights guaranteed to the people by this Constitution shall be conferred upon the people of this and future generations as eternal and inviolate rights.

ARTICLE 12. The freedoms and rights guaranteed to the people by this Constitution shall be maintained by the constant endeavor of the people, who shall refrain from any abuse of these freedoms and rights and shall always be responsible for utilizing them for the public welfare.

ARTICLE 13. All of the people shall be respected as individuals. Their right to life, liberty, and the pursuit of happiness shall, to the extent that it does not interfere with the public welfare, be the supreme consideration in legislation and in other governmental affairs.

ARTICLE 14. All of the people are equal under the law and there shall be no discrimination in political, economic or social relations because of race, creed, sex, social status or family origin.

Peers and peerage shall not be recognized.

No privilege shall accompany any award of honor, decoration or any distinction, nor shall any such award be valid beyond the lifetime of the individual who now holds or hereafter may receive it.

ARTICLE 15. The people have the inalienable right to choose their public officials and to dismiss them.

All public officials are servants of the whole community and not of any group thereof.

Universal adult suffrage is guaranteed with regard to the election of public officials.

In all elections, secrecy of the ballot shall not be violated. A voter shall not be answerable, publicly or privately, for the choice he has made.

ARTICLE 16. Every person shall have the right of peaceful petition for the redress of damage, for the removal of public officials, for the enactment, repeal or amendment of laws, ordinances or regulations and for other matters; nor shall any person be in any way discriminated against for sponsoring such a petition.

ARTICLE 17. Every person may sue for redress as provided by law from the State or a public entity, in case he has suffered damage through illegal act of any public official.

ARTICLE 18. No person shall be held in bondage of any kind. Involuntary servitude, except as punishment for crime, is prohibited.

ARTICLE 19. Freedom of thought and conscience shall not be violated.

ARTICLE 20. Freedom of religion is guaranteed to all. No religious organization shall receive any privileges from the State, nor exercise any political authority.

No person shall be compelled to take part in any religious act, celebration, rite or practice.

The State and its organs shall refrain from religious education or any other religious activity.

ARTICLE 21. Freedom of assembly and association as well as speech, press and all other forms of expression are guaranteed.

No censorship shall be maintained, nor shall the secrecy of any means of communication be violated.

ARTICLE 22. Every person shall have freedom to choose and change his residence and to choose his occupation to the extent that it does not interfere with the public welfare.

Freedom of all persons to move to a foreign country and to divest themselves of their nationality shall be inviolate.

ARTICLE 23. Academic freedom is guaranteed.

ARTICLE 24. Marriage shall be based only on the mutual consent of both sexes and it shall be maintained through mutual cooperation with the equal rights of husband and wife as a basis.

With regard to choice of spouse, property rights, inheritance, choice of domicile, divorce and other matters pertaining to marriage and the family, laws shall be enacted from the standpoint of individual dignity and the essential equality of the sexes.

ARTICLE 25. All people shall have the right to maintain the minimum standards of wholesome and cultured living.

In all spheres of life, the State shall use its endeavors for the promotion and extension of social welfare and security, and of public health.

ARTICLE 26. All people shall have the right to receive an equal education correspondent to their ability, as provided by law.

All people shall be obligated to have all boys and girls under their protection receive ordinary education as provided for by law. Such compulsory education shall be free.

ARTICLE 27. All people shall have the right and the obligation to work.

Standards for wages, hours, rest and other working conditions shall be fixed by law.

Children shall not be exploited.

ARTICLE 28. The right of workers to organize and to bargain and act collectively is guaranteed.

ARTICLE 29 The right to own or to hold property is inviolable.

Property rights shall be defined by law, in conformity with the public welfare.

Private property may be taken for public use upon just compensation therefor.

ARTICLE 30. The people shall be liable to taxation as provided by law.

ARTICLE 31. No person shall be deprived of life or liberty, nor shall any other criminal penalty be imposed, except according to procedure established by law.

ARTICLE 32. No person shall be denied the right of access to the courts.

ARTICLE 33. No person shall be apprehended except upon warrant issued by a competent judicial officer which specifies the offense with which the person is charged, unless he is apprehended, the offense being committed.

ARTICLE 34. No person shall be arrested or detained without being at once informed of the charges against him or without the immediate privilege of counsel; nor shall he be detained without adequate cause; and upon demand of any person such cause must be immediately shown in open court in his presence and the presence of his counsel.

ARTICLE 35. The right of all persons to be secure in their homes, papers and effects against entries, searches and seizures shall not be impaired except upon warrant issued for adequate cause and particularly describing the place to be searched and things to be seized, or except as provided by Article 33.

Each search or seizure shall be made upon separate warrant issued by a competent judicial officer.

ARTICLE 36. The infliction of torture by any public officer and cruel punishments are absolutely forbidden.

ARTICLE 37. In all criminal cases the accused shall enjoy the right to a speedy and public trial by an impartial tribunal.

He shall be permitted full opportunity to examine all witnesses, and he shall have the right of compulsory process for obtaining witnesses on his behalf at public expense.

At all times the accused shall have the assistance of competent counsel who shall, if the accused is unable to secure the same by his own efforts, be assigned to his use by the State.

ARTICLE 38. No person shall be compelled to testify against himself.

Confession made under compulsion, torture or threat, or after prolonged arrest or detention shall not be admitted in evidence.

No person shall be convicted or punished in cases where the only proof against him is his own confession.

ARTICLE 39. No person shall be held criminally liable for an act which was lawful at the time it was committed, or of which he has been acquitted, nor shall he be placed in double jeopardy.

ARTICLE 40. Any person, in case he is acquitted after he has been arrested or detained, may sue the State for redress as provided by law.

Chapter IV
THE DIET

ARTICLE 41. The Diet shall be the highest organ of state power, and shall be the sole law-making organ of the State.

ARTICLE 42. The Diet shall consist of two Houses, namely the House of Representatives and the House of Councillors.

ARTICLE 43. Both Houses shall consist of elected members, representative of all the people.

The number of the members of each House shall be fixed by law.

ARTICLE 44. The qualifications of members of both Houses and their electors shall be fixed by law. However, there shall be no discrimination because of race, creed, sex, social status, family origin, education, property or income.

ARTICLE 45. The term of office of members of the House of Representatives shall be four years. However, the term shall be terminated before the full term is up in case the House of Representatives is dissolved.

ARTICLE 46. The term of office of members of the House of Councillors shall be six years, and election for half the members shall take place every three years.

ARTICLE 47. Electoral districts, method of voting and other matters pertaining to the method of election of members of both Houses shall be fixed by law.

ARTICLE 48. No person shall be permitted to be a member of both Houses simultaneously.

ARTICLE 49. Members of both Houses shall receive appropriate annual payment from the national treasury in accordance with law.

ARTICLE 50. Except in cases provided by law, members of both Houses shall be exempt from apprehension while the Diet is in session, and any members apprehended before the opening of the session shall be freed during the term of the session upon demand of the House.

ARTICLE 51. Members of both Houses shall not be held liable outside the House for speeches, debates or votes cast inside the House.

ARTICLE 52. An ordinary session of the Diet shall be convoked once per year.

ARTICLE 53. The Cabinet may determine to convoke extraordinary sessions of the Diet. When a quarter or more of the total members of either House makes the demand, the Cabinet must determine on such convocation.

ARTICLE 54. When the House of Representatives is dissolved, there must be a general election of members of the House of Representatives within forty (40) days from the date of dissolution, and the Diet must be convoked within thirty (30) days from the date of the election.

When the House of Representatives is dissolved, the House of Councillors is closed at the same time. However, the Cabinet may in time of national emergency convoke the House of Councillors in emergency session.

Measures taken at such session as mentioned in the proviso of the preceding paragraph shall be provisional and shall become null and void unless agreed to by the House of Representatives within a period of ten (10) days after the opening of the next session of the Diet.

ARTICLE 55. Each House shall judge disputes related to qualifications of its members. However, in order to deny a seat to any member, it is necessary to pass a resolution by a majority of two-thirds or more of the members present.

ARTICLE 56. Business cannot be transacted in either House unless one-third or more of total membership is present.

All matters shall be decided, in each House, by a majority of those present, except as elsewhere provided in the Constitution, and in case of a tie, the presiding officer shall decide the issue.

ARTICLE 57. Deliberation in each House shall be public. However, a secret meeting may be held where a majority of two-thirds or more of those members present passes a resolution therefor.

Each House shall keep a record of proceedings. This record shall be published and given general circulation, excepting such parts of proceedings of secret session as may be deemed to require secrecy.

Upon demand of one-fifth or more of the members present, votes of the members on any matter shall be recorded in the minutes.

ARTICLE 58. Each House shall select its own president and other officials.

Each House shall establish its rules pertaining to meetings, proceedings and internal discipline, and may punish members for disorderly conduct. However, in order to expel a member, a majority of two-thirds or more of those members present must pass a resolution thereon.

ARTICLE 59. A bill becomes a law on passage by both Houses, except as otherwise provided by the Constitution.

A bill which is passed by the House of Representatives, and upon which the House of Councillors makes a decision different from that of the House of Representatives, becomes a law when passed a second time by the House of Representatives by a majority of two-thirds or more of the members present.

The provision of the preceding paragraph does not preclude the House of Representatives from calling for the meeting of a joint committee of both Houses, provided for by law.

Failure by the House of Councillors to take final action within sixty (60) days after receipt of a bill passed by the House of Representatives, time in recess excepted, may be determined by the House of Representatives to constitute a rejection of the said bill by the House of Councillors.

ARTICLE 60. The budget must first be submitted to the House of Representatives.

Upon consideration of the budget, when the House of Councillors makes a decision different from that of the House of Representatives, and when no agreement can be reached even through a joint committee of both Houses, provided for by law, or in the case of failure by the House of Councillors to take final action within thirty (30) days, the period of recess excluded, after the receipt of the budget passed by the House of Representatives, the decision of the House of Representatives shall be the decision of the Diet.

ARTICLE 61. The second paragraph of the preceding article applies also to the Diet approval required for the conclusion of treaties.

ARTICLE 62. Each House may conduct investigations in relation to government, and may demand the presence and testimony of witnesses, and the production of records.

ARTICLE 63. The Prime Minister and other Ministers of State may, at any time, appear in either House for the purpose of speaking on bills, regardless of whether they are members of the House or not. They must appear when their presence is required in order to give answers or explanations.

ARTICLE 64. The Diet shall set up an impeachment court from among the members of both Houses for the purpose of trying those judges against whom removal proceedings have been instituted.

Matters relating to impeachment shall be provided by law.

Chapter V
THE CABINET

ARTICLE 65. Executive power shall be vested in the Cabinet.

ARTICLE 66. The Cabinet shall consist of the Prime Minister, who shall be its head, and other Ministers of State, as provided for by law.

The Prime Minister and other Ministers of State must be civilians.

The Cabinet, in the exercise of executive power, shall be collectively responsible to the Diet.

ARTICLE 67. The Prime Minister shall be designated from among the members of the Diet by a resolution of the Diet. This designation shall precede all other business.

If the House of Representatives and the House of Councillors disagree and if no agreement can be reached even through a joint committee of both Houses, provided for by law, or the House of Councillors fails to make designation within ten (10) days, exclusive of the period of recess, after the House of Representatives has made designation, the decision of the House of Representatives shall be the decision of the Diet.

ARTICLE 68. The Prime Minister shall appoint the Ministers of State. However, a majority of their number must be chosen from among the members of the Diet.

The Prime Minister may remove the Ministers of State as he chooses.

ARTICLE 69. If the House of Representatives passes a non-confidence resolution, or rejects a confidence resolution, the Cabinet shall resign en masse, unless the House of Representatives is dissolved within ten (10) days.

ARTICLE 70. When there is a vacancy in the post of Prime Minister, or upon the first convocation of the Diet after a general election of members of the House of Representatives, the Cabinet shall resign en masse.

ARTICLE 71. In the cases mentioned in the two preceding articles, the Cabinet shall continue its functions until the time when a new Prime Minister is appointed.

ARTICLE 72. The Prime Minister, representing the Cabinet, submits bills, reports on general national affairs and foreign relations to the Diet and exercises control and supervision over various administrative branches.

ARTICLE 73. The Cabinet, in addition to other general administrative functions, shall perform the following functions:

Administer the law faithfully; conduct affairs of state.

Manage foreign affairs.

Conclude treaties. However, it shall obtain prior or, depending on circumstances, subsequent approval of the Diet.

Administer the civil service, in accordance with standards established by law.

Prepare the budget, and present it to the Diet.

Enact cabinet orders in order to execute the provisions of this Constitution and of the law. However, it cannot include penal provisions in such cabinet orders unless authorized by such law.

Decide on general amnesty, special amnesty, commutation of punishment, reprieve, and restoration of rights.

ARTICLE 74. All laws and cabinet orders shall be signed by the competent Minister of State and countersigned by the Prime Minister.

ARTICLE 75. The Ministers of State, during their tenure of office, shall not be subject to legal action without the consent of the Prime Minister. However, the right to take that action is not impaired hereby.

Chapter VI
JUDICIARY

ARTICLE 76. The whole judicial power is vested in a Supreme Court and in such inferior courts as are established by law.

No extraordinary tribunal shall be established, nor shall any organ or agency of the Executive be given final judicial power.

All judges shall be independent in the exercise of their conscience and shall be bound only by this Constitution and the laws.

ARTICLE 77. The Supreme Court is vested with the rule-making power under which it determines the rules of procedure and of practice, and of matters relating to attorneys, the internal discipline of the courts and the administration of judicial affairs.

Public procurators shall be subject to the rule-making power of the Supreme Court.

The Supreme Court may delegate the power to make rules for inferior courts to such courts.

ARTICLE 78. Judges shall not be removed except by public impeachment unless judicially declared mentally or physically incompetent to perform official duties. No disciplinary action against judges shall be administered by any executive organ or agency.

ARTICLE 79. The Supreme Court shall consist of a Chief Judge and such number of judges as may be determined by law; all such judges excepting the Chief Judge shall be appointed by the Cabinet.

The appointment of the judges of the Supreme Court shall be reviewed by the people at the first general election of members of the House of Representatives following their appointment, and shall be reviewed again at the first general election of members of the House of Representatives after a lapse of ten (10) years, and in the same manner thereafter.

In cases mentioned in the foregoing paragraph, when the majority of the voters favors the dismissal of a judge, he shall be dismissed.

Matters pertaining to review shall be prescribed by law.

The judges of the Supreme Court shall be retired upon the attainment of the age as fixed by law.

All such judges shall receive, at regular stated intervals, adequate compensation which shall not be decreased during their terms of office.

ARTICLE 80. The judges of the inferior courts shall be appointed by the Cabinet from a list of persons nominated by the Supreme Court. All such judges shall hold office for a term of ten (10) years with privilege of reappointment, provided that they shall be retired upon the attainment of the age as fixed by law.

The judges of the inferior courts shall receive, at regular stated intervals, adequate compensation which shall not be decreased during their terms of office.

ARTICLE 81. The Supreme Court is the court of last resort with power to determine the constitutionality of any law, order, regulation or official act.

ARTICLE 82. Trials shall be conducted and judgment declared publicly.

Where a court unanimously determines publicity to be dangerous to public order or morals, a trial may be conducted privately, but trials of political offenses, offenses involving the press or cases wherein the rights of people as guaranteed in Chapter III of this Constitution are in question shall always be conducted publicly.

Chapter VII
FINANCE

ARTICLE 83. The power to administer national finances shall be exercised as the Diet shall determine.

ARTICLE 84. No new taxes shall be imposed or existing ones modified except by law or under such conditions as law may prescribe.

ARTICLE 85. No money shall be expended, nor shall the State obligate itself, except as authorized by the Diet.

ARTICLE 86. The Cabinet shall prepare and submit to the Diet for its consideration and decision a budget for each fiscal year.

ARTICLE 87. In order to provide for unforeseen deficiencies in the budget, a reserve fund may be authorized by the Diet to be expended upon the responsibility of the Cabinet.

The Cabinet must get subsequent approval of the Diet for all payments from the reserve fund.

ARTICLE 88. All property of the Imperial Household shall belong to the State. All expenses of the Imperial Household shall be appropriated by the Diet in the budget.

ARTICLE 89. No public money or other property shall be expended or appropriated for the use, benefit, or maintenance of any religious institution or association, or for any charitable, educational or benevolent enterprises not under the control of public authority.

ARTICLE 90. Final accounts of the expenditures and revenues of the State shall be audited annually by a Board of Audit and submitted by the Cabinet to the Diet, together with the statement of audit, during the fiscal year immediately following the period covered.

The organization and competency of the Board of Audit shall be determined by law.

ARTICLE 91. At regular intervals and at least annually the Cabinet shall report to the Diet and the people on the state of national finances.

Chapter VIII
LOCAL SELF-GOVERNMENT

ARTICLE 92. Regulations concerning organization and operations of local public entities shall be fixed by law in accordance with the principle of local autonomy.

ARTICLE 93. The local public entities shall establish assemblies as their deliberative organs, in accordance with law.

The chief executive officers of all local public entities, the members of their assemblies, and such other local officials as may be determined by law shall be elected by direct popular vote within their several communities.

ARTICLE 94. Local public entities shall have the right to manage their property, affairs and administration and to enact their own regulations within law.

ARTICLE 95. A special law, applicable only to one local public entity, cannot be enacted by the Diet without the consent of the majority of the voters of the local public entity concerned, obtained in accordance with law.

Chapter IX
AMENDMENTS

ARTICLE 96. Amendments to this Constitution shall be initiated by the Diet, through a concurring vote of two-thirds or more of all the members of each House and shall thereupon be submitted to the people for ratification, which shall require the affirmative vote of a majority of all votes cast thereon, at a special referendum or at such election as the Diet shall specify.

Amendments when so ratified shall immediately be promulgated by the Emperor in the name of the people, as an integral part of this Constitution.

Chapter X
SUPREME LAW

ARTICLE 97. The fundamental human rights by this Constitution guaranteed to the people of Japan are fruits of the age-old struggle of man to be free; they have survived the many exacting tests for durability and are conferred upon this and future generations in trust, to be held for all time inviolate.

ARTICLE 98. This Constitution shall be the supreme law of the nation and no law, ordinance, imperial rescript or other act of government, or part thereof, contrary to the provisions hereof, shall have legal force or validity.

The treaties concluded by Japan and established laws of nations shall be faithfully observed.

ARTICLE 99. The Emperor or the Regent as well as Ministers of State, members of the Diet, judges, and all other public officials have the obligation to respect and uphold this Constitution.

Chapter XI
SUPPLEMENTARY PROVISIONS

ARTICLE 100. This Constitution shall be enforced as from the day when the period of six months will have elapsed counting from the day of its promulgation.

The enactment of laws necessary for the enforcement of this Constitution, the election of members of the House of Councillors and the procedure for the convocation of the Diet and other preparatory procedures necessary for the enforcement of this Constitution may be executed before the day prescribed in the preceding paragraph.

ARTICLE 101. If the House of Councillors is not constituted before the effective date of this Constitution, the House of Representatives shall function as the Diet until such time as the House of Councillors shall be constituted.

ARTICLE 102. The term of office for half the members of the House of Councillors serving in the first term under this Constitution shall be three years. Members falling under this category shall be determined in accordance with law.

ARTICLE 103. The Ministers of State, members of the House of Representatives and judges in office on the effective date of this Constitution, and all other public officials who occupy positions corresponding to such positions as are recognized by this Constitution shall not forfeit their positions automatically on account of the enforcement of this Constitution unless otherwise specified by law. When, however, successors are elected or appointed under the provisions of this Constitution, they shall forfeit their positions as a matter of course.

ISRAELI DECLARATION OF INDEPENDENCE (1948)

Modern nationalism—fealty to the common purpose of one's nation—emerged along with the eighteenth-century Enlightenment notion of representative democracy. Both concepts sprang from the decline of feudal loyalty to a local noble and the decline of provincial attitudes in the face of expanded commerce. But because the Jews were so widely dispersed, Zionism, the Jewish nationalist movement, was slow to develop.

For almost 2,000 years, since the temple in Jerusalem was destroyed in A.D. 70 and the Jewish people were exiled from Palestine, the Jews were a nation without a state. They shared a common language and literature, lore and history, and customs and culture. Those shared characteristics, which are the essence of nationhood, were grounded in the Jewish religion. Yet it was the development of the secular concept of nationalism, which gained momentum in the nineteenth and twentieth centuries, that led to the declaration of an independent Jewish nation-state.

The success of the Zionist movement, revived and inspired in the late nineteenth century by Hungarian-born Theodor Herzl, owed much to the cataclysms of World War I (1914–1918) and World War II (1939–1945). In 1917 Great Britain seized control of Palestine from the Ottoman Empire, ending four hundred years of Turkish rule, and issued the Balfour Declaration, which expressed support for the establishment of a Jewish "national home" in Palestine while si-multaneously expressing support for the civil and religious rights of the non-Jewish population. The incompatibility of those two goals would vex British and international policy for thirty years.

British administration of Palestine, which was sanctioned by a 1922 mandate from the League of Nations, satisfied neither the Arabs nor the Jews. When Adolf Hitler came to power in Germany in 1933 and Jewish emigration from Europe to Palestine rose dramatically, tensions between Jews and non-Jews in Palestine escalated. The British could gain support neither for a unified Palestinian state to be run jointly by Jews and Arabs nor for a partition plan that would create two states. With no solution in sight, and with its occupation army taking casualties from both Jewish and Arab guerrilla movements, the British government turned the issue over to the United Nations and announced that it would relinquish its mandate.

After studying the issue, the United Nations voted on November 29, 1947, to partition Palestine. The Jews accepted the outcome, though they were unhappy with the borders; the Arab leaders of Egypt, Syria, Transjordan, Iraq, and Lebanon rejected the settlement. When the British mandate expired on May 14, 1948, and the last British troops left Palestine, the Jewish National Council proclaimed Israeli independence and open war broke out. Israel won the war a year later.

Issued at Tel Aviv on May 14, 1948 (5th of Iyar, 5708)

The Land of Israel was the birthplace of the Jewish people. Here their spiritual, religious and national identity was formed. Here they achieved independence and created a culture of national and universal significance. Here they wrote and gave the Bible to the world.

Exiled from Palestine, the Jewish people remained faithful to it in all the countries of their dispersion, never ceasing to pray and hope for their return and the restoration of their national freedom.

Impelled by this historic association, Jews strove throughout the centuries to go back to the land of their fathers and regain their statehood. In recent decades they returned in masses. They reclaimed the wilderness, revived their language, built cities and villages and established a vigorous and ever-growing community, with its own economic and cultural life. They sought peace yet were ever prepared to defend themselves. They brought the blessing of progress to all inhabitants of the country.

In the year 1897 the First Zionist Congress, inspired by Theodor Herzl's vision of the Jewish State, proclaimed the right of the Jewish people to national revival in their own country.

This right was acknowledged by the Balfour Declaration of November 2, 1917, and reaffirmed by the Mandate of the League of Nations, which gave explicit international recognition to the historic connection of the Jewish people with Palestine and their right to reconstitute their National Home.

The Nazi holocaust, which engulfed millions of Jews in Europe, proved anew the urgency of the re-establishment of the Jewish State, which would solve the problem of Jewish homelessness by opening the gates to all Jews and lifting the Jewish people to equality in the family of nations.

The survivors of the European catastrophe, as well as Jews from other lands, proclaiming their right to a life of dignity, freedom and labor, and undeterred by hazards, hardships and obstacles, have tried unceasingly to enter Palestine.

In the Second World War the Jewish people in Palestine made a full contribution in the struggle of the freedom-loving nations against the Nazi evil. The sacrifices of their soldiers and the efforts of their workers gained them title to rank with the peoples who founded the United Nations.

On November 29, 1947, the General Assembly of the United Nations adopted a Resolution for the establishment of an independent Jewish State in Palestine, and called upon the inhabitants of the country to take such steps as may be necessary on their part to put the plan into effect.

This recognition by the United Nations of the right of the Jewish people to establish their independent State may not be revoked. It is, moreover, the self-evident right of the Jewish people to be a nation, as all other nations, in its own sovereign State.

Accordingly, we, the members of the National Council, representing the Jewish people in Palestine and the Zionist movement of the world, met together in solemn assembly today, the day of termination of the British Mandate for Palestine, by virtue of the natural and historic right of the Jewish people and of the Resolution of the General Assembly of the United Nations.

Hereby proclaim the establishment of the Jewish State in Palestine, to be called *Israel.*

We hereby declare that as from the termination of the Mandate at midnight, this night of the 14th to 15th May, 1948, and until the setting up of the duly elected bodies of the State in accordance with a Constitution, to be drawn up by a Constituent Assembly not later than the first day of October, 1948, the present National Council shall act as the provisional administration, shall constitute the Provisional Government of the State of Israel.

The State of Israel will be open to the immigration of Jews from all countries of their dispersion; will promote the development of the country for the benefit of all its inhabitants; will be based on the precepts of liberty, justice and peace taught by the Hebrew Prophets; will uphold the full social and political equality of all its citizens, without distinction of race, creed or sex; will guarantee full freedom of conscience, worship, education and culture; will safeguard the sanctity and inviolability of the shrines and Holy Places of all religions; and will dedicate itself to the principles of the Charter of the United Nations.

The State of Israel will be ready to cooperate with the organs and representatives of the United Nations in the implementation of the Resolution of the Assembly of November 29, 1947, and will take steps to bring about the Economic Union over the whole of Palestine.

We appeal to the United Nations to assist the Jewish people in the building of its State and to admit Israel into the family of nations.

In the midst of wanton aggression, we yet call upon the Arab inhabitants of the State of Israel to return to the ways of peace and play their part in the development of the State, with full and equal citizenship and due representation in all its bodies and institutions—provisional or permanent.

We offer peace and unity to all the neighboring states and their peoples, and invite them to cooperate with the independent Jewish nation for the common good of all.

Our call goes out to the Jewish people all over the world to rally to our side in the task of immigration and development and to stand by us in the great struggle for the fulfillment of the dream of generations—the redemption of Israel.

With trust in Almighty God, we set our hand to this Declaration, at this Session of the Provisional State Council, in the city of Tel Aviv, on this Sabbath eve, the fifth of Iyar, 5708, the fourteenth day of May, 1948.

AFRICAN NATIONAL CONGRESS FREEDOM CHARTER (1955)

As late as the 1930s, European domination of Africa was virtually unchallenged across the continent. The African National Congress (ANC), which had been founded in 1912 under the name South African Native National Congress, had few members and sought only to improve some of the more odious aspects of colonial administration.

World War II (1939–1945) dramatically accelerated the urbanization and industrialization of South Africa, which had been developing slowly for several decades. As a result, the increasingly urbanized, educated, and sophisticated blacks of South Africa began to develop a sense of nationhood and nationalism and began to chafe under colonial rule.

Tensions between whites and blacks rose in the years following the war, and in 1948 the Afrikaner Nationalist Party was elected to power on a platform calling for rigid apartheid, or racial segregation, to guarantee white supremacy. The Nationalists immediately set about codifying the policy; they passed the Population Registration Act, the Group Areas Act, the Separate Representation of Voters Act, the Immorality of Mixed Marriages Act, and other discriminatory legislation.

The African National Congress, in turn, became more militant and began using boycotts, strikes, civil disobedience, and nationwide work stoppages, but it rigorously avoided violence. The ANC, in cooperation with other organizations representing Indians, coloreds, and liberal whites, called for a Congress of the People to draft a charter outlining a vision for the future of South Africa. Three thousand delegates to the congress met June 25–26, 1955, at Kliptown, near Johannesburg, and ratified the Freedom Charter, which subsequently was adopted as the official program of the ANC.

The charter expressed the liberal democratic ideals of political freedom and equality for all that had been resonating in Western political philosophy for two hundred years. It also encompassed the social and economic "rights" that had become common in post–World War II discourse. The charter's terms were moderate, and the ANC advocated a peaceful evolution. But to the Nationalist Party the document was radical because its goals could not be achieved without destroying the privileged economic and political status of whites.

The Freedom Charter evoked yet more government repression and, ironically, also fomented a schism within the black movement. In 1959 a faction withdrew from the ANC to form the Pan-Africanist Congress, a more militant organization that rejected the ANC's and the Freedom Charter's belief in cooperation with nonblack organizations. After being outlawed in 1961, the ANC, too, became more radical and began to advocate violence. But the ANC did not renounce its vision, as expressed in the Freedom Charter, of a democratic, nonracial South Africa.

Preamble

We, the people of South Africa, declare for all our country and the world to know:

That South Africa belongs to all who live in it, black and white, and that no government can justly claim authority unless it is based on the will of the people;

That our people have been robbed of their birthright to land, liberty and peace by a form of government founded on injustice and inequality;

That our country will never be prosperous or free until all our people live in brotherhood, enjoying equal rights and opportunities;

That only a democratic state, based on the will of the people, can secure to all their birthright without distinction of colour, race, sex or belief;

And therefore, we, the people of South Africa, black and white, together—equals, countrymen and brothers—adopt this Freedom Charter. And we pledge ourselves to strive together, sparing nothing of our strength and courage, until the democratic changes here set out have been won.

The people shall govern

Every man and woman shall have the right to vote for and stand as a candidate for all bodies which make laws;

All the people shall be entitled to take part in the administration of the country;

The rights of the people shall be the same regardless of race, colour or sex;

All bodies of minority rule, advisory boards, councils and authorities shall be replaced by democratic organs of self-government.

All national groups shall have equal rights

There shall be equal status in the bodies of state, in the courts and in the schools for all national groups and races;

All national groups shall be protected by law against insults to their race and national pride;

All people shall have equal rights to use their own language and to develop their own folk culture and customs;

All apartheid laws and practices shall be set aside.

The people shall share in the country's wealth

The national wealth of our country, the heritage of all South Africans, shall be restored to the people;

The mineral wealth beneath the soil, the banks and monopoly industry shall be transferred to the ownership of the people as a whole;

All other industries and trade shall be controlled to assist the well-being of the people;

All people shall have equal rights to trade where they choose, to manufacture and to enter all trades, crafts and professions.

The land shall be shared amongst those who work it

Restriction of land ownership on a racial basis shall be ended, and all the land redivided amongst those who work it, to banish famine and land hunger;

The state shall help the peasants with implements, seed, tractors and dams to save the soil and assist the tillers;

Freedom of movement shall be guaranteed to all who work on the land;

All shall have the right to occupy land wherever they choose;

People shall not be robbed of their cattle; forced labour and farm prisons shall be abolished.

All people shall be equal before the law

No one shall be imprisoned, deported or restricted without a fair trial;

No one shall be condemned by the order of any Government official;

The courts shall be representative of all the people;

Imprisonment shall be only for serious crimes against the people, and shall aim at re-education, not vengeance;

The police force and army shall be open to all on an equal basis and shall be the helpers and protectors of the people;

All laws which discriminate on grounds of race, colour or belief shall be repealed;

The preaching and practice of national, race or colour discrimination and contempt shall be a punishable crime.

All shall enjoy equal human rights

The law shall guarantee to all their right to speak, to organise, to meet together, to publish, to preach, to worship and to educate their children;

The privacy of the house from police raids shall be protected by law;

All shall be free to travel without restriction from countryside to town, from province to province, and from South Africa abroad;

Pass laws, permits and all other laws restricting these freedoms shall be abolished.

There shall be work and security

All who work shall be free to form trade unions, to elect their officers and to make wage agreements with their employers;

The state shall recognise the right and duty of all to work, and to draw full unemployment benefits;

Men and women of all races shall receive equal pay for equal work;

There shall be a forty-hour working week, a national minimum wage, paid annual leave, and sick leave for all workers, and maternity leave on full pay for all working mothers;

Miners, domestic workers, farm workers and civil servants shall have the same rights as all others who work;

Child labour, compound labour, the tot system and contract labour shall be abolished.

The doors of learning and of culture shall be opened

The government shall discover, develop and encourage national talent for the enhancement of our cultural life;

All the cultural treasures of mankind shall be open to all, by free exchange of books, ideas and contacts with other lands;

The aim of education shall be to teach the youth to love their people and their culture, to honour human brotherhood, liberty and peace;

Education shall be free, compulsory, universal and equal for all children;

Higher education and technical training shall be opened to all by means of state allowances and scholarships awarded on the basis of merit;

Adult illiteracy shall be ended by a mass state education plan;

Teachers shall have all the rights of other citizens;

The colour bar in cultural life, in sport and in education shall be abolished.

There shall be houses, security and comfort

All people shall have the right to live where they choose, to be decently housed, and to bring up their families in comfort and security;

Unused housing space shall be made available to the people;

Rent and prices shall be lowered, food plentiful and no one shall go hungry;

A preventive health scheme shall be run by the state;

Free medical care and hospitalisation shall be provided for all, with special care for mothers and young children;

Slums shall be demolished and new suburbs built where all have transport, roads, lighting, playing fields, creches and social centres;

The aged, the orphans, the disabled and the sick shall be cared for by the state;

Rest, leisure and recreation shall be the right of all;

Fenced locations and ghettoes shall be abolished, and laws which break up families shall be repealed.

There shall be peace and friendship

South Africa shall be a fully independent state, which respects the rights and sovereignty of all nations;

South Africa shall strive to maintain world peace and the settlement of all international disputes by negotiation—not war;

Peace and friendship amongst all our people shall be secured by upholding the equal rights, opportunities and status of all;

The people of the protectorates—Basutoland, Bechuanaland and Swaziland—shall be free to decide for themselves their own future;

The right of all the peoples of Africa to independence and self-government shall be recognised, and shall be the basis of close co-operation.

Let all who love their people and their country now say, as we say here; "These freedoms we will fight for, side by side, throughout our lives, until we have won our liberty.'

AFRICAN CHARTER ON HUMAN AND PEOPLES' RIGHTS (1981)

Despite tremendous strides that had taken place since the end of World War II in 1945, the African continent was still wrestling in 1981 with the legacies of European colonialism and other difficulties of external and indigenous origin. The African Charter on Human and Peoples' Rights, adopted at the eighteenth meeting of the heads of state and government of the Organization of African Unity (OAU), was both a reaction to the continent's difficulties and a statement of hope for the future.

As the colonial powers withdrew from Africa they left behind independent states but few nations and even fewer functioning democracies. The populations, living within state boundaries that bore little relation to the ethnic, cultural, historical, or linguistic map of Africa, had by and large not been prepared by the colonial powers to function as political democracies. In many cases the populations lacked a sense of nationhood or nationalism, adequate educational institutions, experience in politics and administration, and industrial development, with its attendant social transformations.

By 1981 great progress had been made in ameliorating the colonial legacy, but old problems persisted and new ones had developed. In the 1970s Africa had become a cold war battleground; Soviet and U.S. proxies fought civil wars in a number of states, including Angola, Mozambique, and Ethiopia, which served to destabilize much of the continent. White-ruled South Africa remained a thorn in the side of its neighbors, and Libya under Muammar al-Qaddafi fomented instability in Chad and Western Sahara. Domestic

political instability remained the norm. In 1980 roughly a dozen coups were attempted across the continent; five of them were successful, including one in Liberia that destroyed the continent's oldest republic. And periodic famine and refugee migrations further eroded political and economic stability.

Against this backdrop the OAU met in Nairobi, Kenya, June 24–28, 1981, to adopt the African Charter on Human and Peoples' Rights, which had been drafted with great difficulty. As late as June 21 a working group of foreign ministers reported wide disagreement over the terms of the charter. Several nondemocratic nations with poor human rights records reportedly considered the document to be potentially embarrassing.

The gap between the charter's promise and practice in many African states is great. Furthermore, the Organization of African Unity, under its charter of May 25, 1963, lacks the authority or the means to intervene even in a limited way in the affairs of its member states. All OAU resolutions are strictly advisory. Past attempts to strengthen the organization so that it could protect the political, civil, and human rights of African citizens and the democratic order of African states foundered on the fear that the OAU would splinter. The weakness of the OAU as an organization rests largely on the underlying weakness of democracy in its member states, which in turn undermines the promise of fundamental human rights embodied in the charter.

Preamble

The African States members of the Organization of African Unity, parties to the present convention entitled "African Charter on Human and Peoples' Rights,"

Recalling Decision 115-XVI of the Assembly of Heads of State and Government at its Sixteenth Ordinary Session held in Monrovia, Liberia, from 17 to 20 July 1979 on the preparation of "a preliminary draft of an African Charter on Human and Peoples' Rights providing *inter alia* for the establish-

ment of bodies to promote and protect human and peoples' rights";

Considering the Charter of the Organization of African Unity, which stipulates that "freedom, equality, justice and dignity are essential objectives for the achievement of the legitimate aspirations of the African peoples";

Reaffirming the pledge they solemnly made in Article 2 of the said Charter to eradicate all forms of colonialism from Africa, to coordinate and intensify their cooperation and efforts to achieve a better life for the peoples of Africa and to promote international cooperation having due regard to the Charter of the United Nations and the Universal Declaration of Human Rights;

Taking into consideration the virtues of their historical tradition and the values of African civilization which should inspire and characterize their reflection on the concept of human and peoples' rights;

Recognizing on the one hand, that fundamental human rights stem from the attributes of human beings, which justifies their international protection and on the other hand that the reality and respect of peoples' rights should necessarily guarantee human rights;

Considering that the enjoyment of rights and freedoms also implies the performance of duties on the part of everyone;

Convinced that it is henceforth essential to pay particular attention to the right to development and that civil and political rights cannot be dissociated from economic, social and cultural rights in their conception as well as universality and that the satisfaction of economic, social and cultural rights is a guarantee for the enjoyment of civil and political rights;

Conscious of their duty to achieve the total liberation of Africa, the peoples of which are still struggling for their dignity and genuine independence, and undertaking to eliminate colonialism, neocolonialism, apartheid, Zionism and to dismantle aggressive foreign military bases and all forms of discrimination, particularly those based on race, ethnic group, color, sex, language, religion or political opinions;

Reaffirming their adherence to the principles of human and peoples' rights and freedoms contained in the declarations, conventions and other instruments adopted by the Organization of African Unity, the Movement of Non-Aligned Countries and the United Nations;

Firmly convinced of their duty to promote and protect human and peoples' rights and freedoms taking into account the importance traditionally attached to these rights and freedoms in Africa;

Have agreed as follows:

Part I. Rights and Duties

Chapter 1. Human and Peoples' Rights

ARTICLE 1. The Member States of the Organization of African Unity, parties to the present Charter, shall recognize the rights, duties and freedoms enshrined in this Charter and shall undertake to adopt legislative or other measures to give effect to them.

ARTICLE 2. Every individual shall be entitled to the enjoyment of the rights and freedoms recognized and guaranteed in the present Charter without distinction of any kind such as race, ethnic group, color, sex, language, religion, political or any other opinion, national and social origin, fortune, birth or other status.

ARTICLE 3.
1. Every individual shall be equal before the law.
2. Every individual shall be entitled to equal protection of the law.

ARTICLE 4. Human beings are inviolable. Every human being shall be entitled to respect for his life and the integrity of his person. No one may be arbitrarily deprived of this right.

ARTICLE 5. Every individual shall have the right to respect for the dignity inherent in a human being and to the recognition of his legal status. All forms of exploitation and degradation of man, particularly slavery, slave trade, torture, cruel, inhuman or degrading punishment and treatment shall be prohibited.

ARTICLE 6. Every individual shall have the right to liberty and to the security of his person. No one may be deprived of his freedom except for reasons and conditions previously laid down by law. In particular, no one may be arbitrarily arrested or detained.

ARTICLE 7.
1. Every individual shall have the right to have his cause heard. This comprises:
a. the right to an appeal to competent national organs against acts violating his fundamental rights as recognized and guaranteed by conventions, laws, regulations and customs in force;
b. the right to be presumed innocent until proved guilty by a competent court or tribunal;
c. the right to defense, including the right to be defended by counsel of his choice;
d. the right to be tried within a reasonable time by an impartial court or tribunal.
2. No one may be condemned for an act or omission which did not constitute a legally punishable offense at the time it was committed. No penalty may be inflicted for an offense for which no provision was made at the time it was committed. Punishment is personal and can be imposed only on the offender.

ARTICLE 8. Freedom of conscience, the profession and free practice of religion shall be guaranteed. No one may, subject to law and order, be submitted to measures restricting the exercise of these freedoms.

ARTICLE 9.
1. Every individual shall have the right to receive information.
2. Every individual shall have the right to express and disseminate his opinions within the law.

ARTICLE 10.
1. Every individual shall have the right to free association provided that he abides by the law.

2. Subject to the obligation of solidarity provided for in Article 29 no one may be compelled to join an association.

ARTICLE 11. Every individual shall have the right to assemble freely with others. The exercise of this right shall be subject only to necessary restrictions provided for by law, in particular those enacted in the interest of national security, the safety, health, ethics and rights and freedoms of others.

ARTICLE 12.

1. Every individual shall have the right to freedom of movement and residence within the borders of a State provided he abides by the law.

2. Every individual shall have the right to leave any country including his own, and to return to his country. This right may only be subject to restrictions provided for by law for the protection of national security, law and order, public health or morality.

3. Every individual shall have the right, when persecuted, to seek and obtain asylum in other countries in accordance with the law of those countries and international conventions.

4. A non-national legally admitted in a territory of a State party to the present Charter may only be expelled from it by virtue of a decision taken in accordance with the law.

5. The mass expulsion of non-nationals shall be prohibited. Mass expulsion shall be that which is aimed at national, racial, ethnic or religious groups.

ARTICLE 13.

1. Every citizen shall have the right to participate freely in the government of his country, either directly or through freely chosen representatives in accordance with the provisions of the law.

2. Every citizen shall have the right of equal access to the public service of his country.

3. Every individual shall have the right of access to public property and services in strict equality of all persons before the law.

ARTICLE 14. The right to property shall be guaranteed. It may only be encroached upon in the interest of public need or in the general interest of the community and in accordance with the provisions of appropriate laws.

ARTICLE 15. Every individual shall have the right to work under equitable and satisfactory conditions, and shall receive equal pay for equal work.

ARTICLE 16.

1. Every individual shall have the right to enjoy the best attainable state of physical and mental health.

2. States parties to the present Charter shall take the necessary measures to protect the health of their people and to ensure that they receive medical attention when they are sick.

ARTICLE 17.

1. Every individual shall have the right to education.

2. Every individual may freely take part in the cultural life of his community.

3. The promotion and protection of morals and traditional values recognized by the community shall be the duty of the State.

ARTICLE 18.

1. The family shall be the natural unit and basis of society. It shall be protected by the State which shall take care of its physical and moral health.

2. The State shall have the duty to assist the family which is the custodian of morals and traditional values recognized by the community.

3. The State shall ensure the elimination of every discrimination against women and also ensure the protection of the rights of the woman and the child as stipulated in international declarations and conventions.

4. The aged and the disabled shall also have the right to special measures of protection in keeping with their physical or moral needs.

ARTICLE 19. All peoples shall be equal; they shall enjoy the same respect and shall have the same rights. Nothing shall justify the domination of a people by another.

ARTICLE 20.

1. All peoples shall have the right to existence. They shall have the unquestionable and inalienable right to self-determination. They shall freely determine their political status and shall pursue their economic and social development according to the policy they have freely chosen.

2. Colonized or oppressed peoples shall have the right to free themselves from the bonds of domination by resorting to any means recognized by the international community.

3. All peoples shall have the right to the assistance of the States parties to the present Charter in their liberation struggle against foreign domination, be it political, economic or cultural.

ARTICLE 21.

1. All peoples shall freely dispose of their wealth and natural resources. This right shall be exercised in the exclusive interest of the people. In no case shall a people be deprived of it.

2. In case of spoliation the dispossessed people shall have the right to the lawful recovery of its property as well as to an adequate compensation.

3. The free disposal of wealth and natural resources shall be exercised without prejudice to the obligation of promoting international economic cooperation based on mutual respect, equitable exchange and the principles of international law.

4. States parties to the present Charter shall individually and collectively exercise the right to free disposal of their wealth and natural resources with a view to strengthening African unity and solidarity.

5. States parties to the present Charter shall undertake to eliminate all forms of foreign economic exploitation particularly that practiced by international monopolies so as to enable their peoples fully to benefit from the advantages derived from their national resources.

ARTICLE 22.

1. All peoples shall have the right to their economic, social and cultural development with due regard to their freedom and identity and to the equal enjoyment of the common heritage of mankind.

2. States shall have the duty, individually or collectively, to ensure the exercise of the right to development.

ARTICLE 23.

1. All peoples shall have the right to national and international peace and security. The principles of solidarity and friendly relations implicitly affirmed by the Charter of the United Nations and reaffirmed by that of the Organization of African Unity shall govern relations between States.

2. For the purpose of strengthening peace, solidarity and friendly relations, States parties to the present Charter shall ensure that:

a. any individual enjoying the right of asylum under Article 12 of the present Charter shall not engage in subversive activities against his country of origin or any other State party to the present Charter;

b. their territories shall not be used as bases for subversive or terrorist activities against the people of any other State party to the present Charter.

ARTICLE 24. All peoples shall have the right to a general satisfactory environment favorable to their development.

ARTICLE 25. States parties to the present Charter shall have the duty to promote and ensure, through teaching, education and publication, respect for the rights and freedoms contained in the present Charter and to see to it that these freedoms and rights as well as corresponding obligations and duties are understood.

ARTICLE 26. States parties to the present Charter shall have the duty to guarantee the independence of the Courts and shall allow the establishment and improvement of appropriate national institutions entrusted with the promotion and protection of the rights and freedoms guaranteed by the present Charter.

Chapter 2. Duties

ARTICLE 27.

1. Every individual shall have duties towards his family and society, the State and other legally recognized communities and the international community.

2. The rights and freedoms of each individual shall be exercised with due regard to the rights of others, collective security, morality and common interest.

ARTICLE 28. Every individual shall have the duty to respect and consider his fellow beings without discrimination, and to maintain relations aimed at promoting, safeguarding and reinforcing mutual respect and tolerance.

ARTICLE 29. The individual shall also have the duty:

1. to preserve the harmonious development of the family and to work for the cohesion and respect of the family; to respect his parents at all times, to maintain them in case of need;

2. to serve his national community by placing his physical and intellectual abilities at its service;

3. not to compromise the security of the State whose national or resident he is;

4. to preserve and strengthen social and national solidarity, particularly when the latter is threatened;

5. to preserve and strengthen the national independence and the territorial integrity of his country and to contribute to its defense in accordance with the law;

6. to work to the best of his abilities and competence, and to pay taxes imposed by law in the interest of society;

7. to preserve and strengthen positive African cultural values in his relations with other members of society, in the spirit of tolerance, dialogue and consultation and, in general, to contribute to the promotion of the moral well-being of society;

8. to contribute to the best of his abilities, at all times and at all levels, to the promotion and achievement of African unity.

Part II. Safeguarding Measures

Chapter 1. Establishment and Organization of the African Commission on Human and Peoples' Rights

ARTICLE 30. An African Commission on Human and Peoples' Rights, hereinafter called "the Commission," shall be established within the Organization of African Unity to promote human and peoples' rights and ensure their protection in Africa.

ARTICLE 31.

1. The Commission shall consist of eleven members chosen from among African personalities of the highest reputation, known for their high morality, integrity, impartiality and competence in matters of human and peoples' rights; particular consideration being given to persons having legal experience.

2. The members of the Commission shall serve in their personal capacity.

ARTICLE 32. The Commission shall not include more than one national of the same State.

ARTICLE 33. The members of the Commission shall be elected by secret ballot by the Assembly of Heads of State and Government, from a list of persons nominated by the States parties to the present Charter.

ARTICLE 34. Each State party to the present Charter may not nominate more than two candidates. The candidates must have the nationality of one of the States parties to the present Charter. When two candidates are nominated by a State, one of them may not be a national of that State.

ARTICLE 35.

1. The Secretary General of the Organization of African Unity shall invite States parties to the present Charter at least four months before the elections to nominate candidates;

2. The Secretary General of the Organization of African Unity shall make an alphabetical list of the persons thus nominated and communicate it to the Heads of State and Government at least one month before the elections.

ARTICLE 36. The Members of the Commission shall be elected for a six-year period and shall be eligible for re-election. However, the term of office of four of the members elected at the first election shall terminate after two years and the term of office of three others, at the end of four years.

ARTICLE 37. Immediately after the first election, the Chairman of the Assembly of Heads of State and Government of the Organization of African Unity shall draw lots to decide the names of those members referred to in Article 36.

ARTICLE 38. After their election, the members of the Commission shall make a solemn declaration to discharge their duties impartially and faithfully.

ARTICLE 39.

1. In case of death or resignation of a member of the Commission, the Chairman of the Commission shall immediately inform the Secretary General of the Organization of African Unity, who shall declare the seat vacant from the date of death or from the date on which the resignation takes effect.

2. If, in the unanimous opinion of other members of the Commission, a member has stopped discharging his duties for any reason other than a temporary absence, the Chairman of the Commission shall inform the Secretary General of the Organization of African Unity, who shall then declare the seat vacant.

3. In each of the cases anticipated above, the Assembly of Heads of State and Government shall replace the member whose seat became vacant for the remaining period of his term unless the period is less than six months.

ARTICLE 40. Every member of the Commission shall be in office until the date his successor assumes office.

ARTICLE 41. The Secretary General of the Organization of African Unity shall appoint the Secretary of the Commission. He shall also provide the staff and services necessary for the effective discharge of the duties of the Commission. The Organization of African Unity shall bear the cost of the staff and services.

ARTICLE 42.

1. The Commission shall elect its Chairman and Vice Chairman for a two-year period. They shall be eligible for re-election.

2. The Commission shall lay down its rules of procedure.

3. Seven members shall form the quorum.

4. In the case of an equality of votes, the Chairman shall have a casting vote.

5. The Secretary General may attend the meetings of the Commission. He shall neither participate in deliberations nor shall he be entitled to vote. The Chairman of the Commission may, however, invite him to speak.

ARTICLE 43. In discharging their duties, members of the Commission shall enjoy diplomatic privileges and immunities provided for in the General Convention on the Privileges and Immunities of the Organization of African Unity.

ARTICLE 44. Provision shall be made for the emoluments and allowances of the members of the Commission in the regular budget of the Organization of African Unity.

Chapter 2. Mandate of the Commission

ARTICLE 45. The functions of the Commission shall be:

1. To promote human and peoples' rights and in particular:

a. to collect documents, undertake studies and research on African problems in the field of human and peoples' rights, organize seminars, symposia and conferences, disseminate information, encourage national and local institutions concerned with human and peoples' rights, and should the case arise, give its views or make recommendations to Governments;

b. to formulate and lay down principles and rules aimed at solving legal problems relating to human and peoples' rights and fundamental freedoms upon which African Governments may base their legislations;

c. to cooperate with other African and international institutions concerned with the promotion and protection of human and peoples' rights.

2. To ensure the protection of human and peoples' rights under conditions laid down by the present Charter.

3. To interpret all the provisions of the present Charter at the request of a State party, an institution of the OAU or an African organization recognized by the OAU.

4. To perform any other tasks which may be entrusted to it by the Assembly of Heads of State and Government.

Chapter 3. Procedure of the Commission

ARTICLE 46. The Commission may resort to any appropriate method of investigation; it may hear from the Secretary General of the Organization of African Unity or any other person capable of enlightening it.

I. Communications from States

ARTICLE 47. If a State party to the present Charter has good reasons to believe that another State party to this Charter has violated the provisions of the Charter, it may draw, by written communication, the attention of that State to the matter. This communication shall also be addressed to the Secretary General of the OAU and to the Chairman of the Commission. Within three months of the receipt of the communication, the State to which the communication is addressed shall give the inquiring State a written explanation or statement elucidating the matter. This should include as much relevant information as possible relating to the laws and rules of procedure applied and applicable and the redress already given or course of action available.

ARTICLE 48. If within three months from the date on which the original communication is received by the State to which it is addressed, the issue is not settled to the satisfaction of the two States involved through bilateral negotiation or by any other peaceful procedure, either State shall have the right to submit the matter to the Commission through the Chairman and shall notify the other State involved.

ARTICLE 49. Notwithstanding the provisions of Article 47, if a State party to the present Charter considers that another State party has violated the provisions of the Charter, it may refer the matter directly to the Commission by addressing a communication to the Chairman, to the Secretary General of the Organization of African Unity and the State concerned.

ARTICLE 50. The Commission can only deal with a matter submitted to it after making sure that all local remedies, if they exist, have been exhausted, unless it is obvious to the Commission that the procedure of achieving these remedies would be unduly prolonged.

ARTICLE 51.

1. The Commission may ask the States concerned to provide it with all relevant information.

2. When the Commission is considering the matter, the States concerned may be represented before it and submit written or oral representations.

ARTICLE 52. After having obtained from the States concerned and from other sources all the information it deems necessary and after having tried all appropriate means to reach an amicable solution based on respect for human and peoples' rights, the Commission shall prepare, within a reasonable period of time from the notification referred to in Article 48, a report stating the facts and its findings. This report shall be sent to the States concerned and communicated to the Assembly of Heads of State and Government.

ARTICLE 53. While transmitting its report, the Commission may make to the Assembly of Heads of State and Government such recommendations as it deems useful.

ARTICLE 54. The Commission shall submit to each Ordinary Session of the Assembly of Heads of State and Government a report on its activities.

II. Other Communications

ARTICLE 55.

1. Before each Session, the Secretary of the Commission shall make a list of the communications other than those of States parties to the present Charter and transmit them to the members of the Commission, who shall indicate which communications should be considered by the Commission.

2. A communication shall be considered by the Commission if a simple majority of its members so decide.

ARTICLE 56. Communications relating to human and peoples' rights referred to in Article 55 received by the Commission shall be considered if they:

1. indicate their authors even if the latter request anonymity;

2. are compatible with the Charter of the Organization of African Unity or with the present Charter;

3. are not written in disparaging or insulting language directed against the State concerned and its institutions or the Organization of African Unity;

4. are not based exclusively on news disseminated through the mass media;

5. are sent after exhausting local remedies, if any, unless it is obvious that this procedure is unduly prolonged;

6. are submitted within a reasonable period from the time local remedies are exhausted or from the date the Commission is seized of the matter; and

7. do not deal with cases which have been settled by the States involved in accordance with the principles of the Charter of the United Nations or the Charter of the Organization of African Unity, or the provisions of the present Charter.

ARTICLE 57. Prior to any substantive consideration, all communications shall be brought to the knowledge of the State concerned by the Chairman of the Commission.

ARTICLE 58.

1. When it appears after deliberations of the Commission that one or more communications apparently relate to special cases which reveal the existence of a series of serious or massive violations of human and peoples' rights, the Commission shall draw the attention of the Assembly of Heads of State and Government to these special cases.

2. The Assembly of Heads of State and Government may then request the Commission to undertake an in-depth study of these cases and make a factual report, accompanied by its finding and recommendations.

3. A case of emergency duly noticed by the Commission shall be submitted by the latter to the Chairman of the Assembly of Heads of State and Government who may request an in-depth study.

ARTICLE 59.

1. All measures taken within the provisions of the present Charter shall remain confidential until such a time as the Assembly of Heads of State and Government shall otherwise decide.

2. However, the report shall be published by the Chairman of the Commission upon the decision of the Assembly of Heads of State and Government.

3. The report on the activities of the Commission shall be published by its Chairman after it has been considered by the Assembly of Heads of State and Government.

Chapter 4. Applicable Principles

ARTICLE 60. The Commission shall draw inspiration from international law on human and peoples' rights, particularly from the provisions of various African instruments on human and peoples' rights, the Charter of the United Nations, the Charter of the Organization of African Unity, the Universal Declaration of Human Rights, other instruments adopted by the United Nations and by African countries in the field of human and peoples' rights as well as from the provisions of various instruments adopted within the specialized agencies of the United Nations of which the parties to the present Charter are members.

ARTICLE 61. The Commission shall also take into consideration, as subsidiary measures to determine the principles of law, other general or special international conventions, laying down rules expressly recognized by member states of the Organization of African Unity, African practices consistent with international norms on human and peoples' rights, customs generally accepted as law, general principles of law recognized by African states as well as legal precedents and doctrine.

ARTICLE 62. Each State party shall undertake to submit every two years, from the date the present Charter comes into force, a report on the legislative or other measures taken with a view to giving effect to the rights and freedoms recognized and guaranteed by the present Charter.

ARTICLE 63.

1. The present Charter shall be open to signature, ratification or adherence of the member States of the Organization of African Unity.

2. The instruments of ratification or adherence to the present Charter shall be deposited with the Secretary General of the Organization of African Unity.

3. The present Charter shall come into force three months after the reception by the Secretary General of the instruments of ratification or adherence of a simple majority of the member States of the Organization of African Unity.

Part III. General Provisions

ARTICLE 64.

1. After the coming into force of the present Charter, members of the Commission shall be elected in accordance with the relevant Articles of the present Charter.

2. The Secretary General of the Organization of African Unity shall convene the first meeting of the Commission at the Headquarters of the Organization within three months of the constitution of the Commission. Thereafter, the Commission shall be convened by its Chairman whenever necessary but at least once a year.

ARTICLE 65. For each of the States that will ratify or adhere to the present Charter after its coming into force, the Charter shall take effect three months after the date of the deposit by that State of its instruments of ratification or adherence.

ARTICLE 66. Special protocols or agreements may, if necessary, supplement the provisions of the present Charter.

ARTICLE 67. The Secretary General of the Organization of African Unity shall inform member States of the Organization of the deposit of each instrument of ratification or adherence.

ARTICLE 68. The present Charter may be amended if a State party makes a written request to that effect to the Secretary General of the Organization of African Unity. The Assembly of Heads of State and Government may only consider the draft amendment after all the States parties have been duly informed of it and the Commission has given its opinion on it at the request of the sponsoring State. The amendment shall be approved by a simple majority of the States parties. It shall come into force for each State which has accepted it in accordance with its constitutional procedure three months after the Secretary General has received notice of the acceptance.

INDEX

A

Abacha, Sani, 141, 142
Abbud, Ibrahim, 172
Abdallah bin Hussein, 107
Abiola, Moshood, 141
Aborigines, 42, 43, 45, 123
Acheampong, Ignatius Kutu, 78
Addis Ababa Accords (1972), 172, 173
Adebo, Simeon, 26
Afghanistan, 147
African Association of Public Administration
    and Management, 26
African National Congress of South Africa
    (ANC), 24, 159–160, 161–162
African Political Systems (Fortes, Evans-
    Pritchard), 183
"Africanization," 14
Aguiyi-Ironsi, Johnson, 139
Akayev, Askar, 36, 116, 117–118
Akintola, S. L., 138
Akuffo, Frederick, 78
Aligned nations, 9
Aliyev, Heydar, 57
All-African People's Conference (1958), 23, 24
Amin, Idi, 199
Amir Kabir, 89
Amnesty International, 67
Anand Panyarachun, 181, 182
ANC. *See* African National Congress of South
    Africa
Anglo-Burmese wars, 51
Ankrah, Joseph, 78
Anticolonialism, 185
Anticommunism, 68
Anyang' Nyong'o, Peter, 188
Apartheid, 17, 19, 159, 160–163, 184, 205
April Fifth Movement, 64
Aquino, Corazon, 148, 149
Arab-Israeli wars, 107, 108, 127. *See also* Six-Day
    War
Arabs, 99, 114, 121, 132, 196
Assassinations. *See* Terrorism, riots, and
    violence
Atatürk, Kemal, 192, 194
Aung San Suu Kyi, 53
Autochthony, 22, 25
Awolowo, Obafemi, 25, 137, 138, 139–140, 186
Ayub Khan, Mohammad, 145, 147
al-Azhari, Ismail, 172
Azikiwe, Nnamdi, 25, 137, 138, 139, 140, 185, 186

B

Babangida, Ibrahim, 140–141
Balewa, Abubakar Tafawa, 15, 138
Banda, Hastings Kamusu, 18
Bandaranaike, Sirimavo, 167
Bandaranaike, S. W. R. D., 167
Bangladesh, 143
al-Bashir, Umar Hassan Ahmad, 173

Bayar, Celal, 194, 195
Begin, Menachem, 98
Belgium, 68
Bello, Ahmadu, 137, 186
Ben Ali, Zine el-Abidine, 191–192
Ben Bella, Ahmed, 28
Ben-Gurion, David, 96
Benjedid, Chadli, 27, 28, 29
Bentham, Jeremy, 44
Berlin Conference (1884–1885), 14–15, 66
Berlin Wall, 18
Bhumibol Adulyadej, 179, 180, 181, 182
Bhutto, Benazir, 146
Bhutto, Zulfikar Ali, 145–146
Biko, Stephen, 161
Bill of rights
    Armenia, 32
    Iran, 90
    Philippines, 148
Biwott, Nicholas, 112
Biya, Paul, 13, 18
Blyden, Edward Wilmot, 22, 184
Boer War (1902), 158
Bongo, Omar, 13, 18
Botha, Pieter W., 161
Boudiaf, Muhammad, 29
Boumedienne, Houari, 28
Bourguiba, Habib, 189–191
Bratton, Michael, 188
British South Africa Company, 205
Buddhists
    Asia, Southeast, 37, 40
    Burma, 51
    India, 80
    Japan, 100, 105
    Sri Lanka, 166
Buhari, Muhammadu, 140
Bureaucracy, 105
Burmese Way to Socialism, 53
Busia, Kofi, 78

C

Cabral, Luis, 10
Cairo Conference (1943), 175
Carpot, François, 152
Central African Federation, 202
Chamoun, Camille, 120
Chang Myon (John M. Chang), 163–164
Chaovalit Yongchaiyut, 182
Chatchai Choonhavan, 180, 181
Chen Jiongming, 62
Chen Ziming, 64
Chiang Ching-kuo, 177
Chiang Kai-shek (Jiang Jieshi), 62, 177
Chiluba, Frederick, 19, 202, 203, 204
Chissano, Joaquim, 9
Christians
    Algeria, 27–28
    Asia, Southeast, 40

Burma, 51
Congo, Democratic Republic of the, 66
India, 80
Indonesia, 86, 87
Iran, 90
Lebanon, 119, 120, 121–122, 129
Nigeria, 136, 141
Philippines, 148
Senegal, 152
Sri Lanka, 167
Uganda, 199
Chun Doo Hwan, 71, 164, 166
Chyngyshev, Tursunbek, 117
Çiller, Tansu, 193, 195
Citizenship, 20, 128, 147
Civil disobedience and passive resistance, 81, 82,
    159, 161, 185
Civil rights and liberties. *See also* Human rights
    Botswana, 48
    Ghana, 78–79
    Iran, 91
    Malaysia, 125
    political parties and, 69–70
    Singapore, 156
    Thailand, 181
Civil war
    Afghanistan, 36
    Angola, 7, 11, 134
    Asia, Central, 36
    Asia, Southeast, 40
    Indonesia, 85, 87
    Lebanon, 119, 120, 121, 122
    Nigeria, 136, 139
    Somalia, 6
    Sudan, 17, 174
    Tajikistan, 117–118
    Uganda, 199–200
    Zimbabwe, 206
Cixi (Empress Dowager), 58
Coalitions and coalition making, 97, 107, 108, 138,
    153, 172, 173
Cold war
    Africa and, 17, 21, 67–68, 186
    decolonization, 186–187
    dominant party democracies in Asia, 70
    Middle East and, 127, 130
    Philippines, 150
    Soviet Union, 194
    Turkey, 194
    United States, 18
Colonies
    background, 14–18, 184
    Belgian, 14, 23, 66, 186
    Dutch, 85, 158, 166
    Egyptian, 171
    German, 133
    Italian, 5
    Japanese, 163
    Russian, 89

South African, 133–134
Spanish, 23, 37, 131, 148
Colonies, British. *See also* Great Britain
    African, 5, 12, 14, 15, 22, 23, 25–26, 48, 77,
        185–186
    Asian, 37, 39, 40, 51
    Australia and New Zealand, 42–43
    decolonization, 186, 205–206
    Egypt, 73
    India, 80, 143
    Iran, 89
    Iraq, 92
    Kenya, 110, 184
    Malaysia, 123
    Middle East, 127
    Namibia, 133
    Nigeria, 136, 138, 186
    South Africa, 157, 158, 159, 184
    Sri Lanka, 166
    Sudan, 171
    Uganda, 198
    Zambia (Rhodesia), 202–203
    Zimbabwe (Southern Rhodesia), 205–206
Colonies, French. *See also* France
    African, 6, 13, 14, 15, 18, 22, 25–26, 27–28, 184
    Asian, 37, 40
    decolonization, 186
    India, 80
    Middle East, 127
    Morocco, 131
    Senegal, 152
    Tunisia, 189
Colonies, Portuguese
    African, 7, 9, 10, 12, 14, 23, 184
    anticolonialism, 185
    Asian, 37
    decolonization, 186
    Sri Lanka, 166
Colonization
    anticolonialism, 185
    decolonization, 24, 25–26, 66–67, 185–187, 205
    democratic responses to, 22–26
    models of European colonial rule, 184
    nationalism and, 22
Communism and communist parties. *See also*
        Marxism-Leninism
    Armenia, 32
    Asia, Central, 36
    Asia, Southeast, 41
    Burma, 52
    Caucasus, 57
    China, 61, 62–63
    Indonesia, 87
    Japan, 105
    Kyrgyzstan, 36, 116–117
    South Africa, 159, 161
    Sudan, 171, 172, 173
    Tunisia, 191
Communitarianism, 156–157
Confucianism, 58, 100, 156, 163, 165
Constitutions
    Africa, 3, 5, 6, 10, 13, 17, 183
    Algeria, 28, 29, 30
    Asia, Central, 36
    Asia, Southeast, 41
    Australia, 43
    Botswana, 48
    Burma, 51, 52, 53
    Caucasus, 56–57
    China, 60, 61
    Congo, Democratic Republic of the, 67

Egypt, 73, 74
Indonesia, 86, 87
Iran, 89–91
Iraq, 94
Israel, 95, 96
Japan, 101, 102
Jordan, 128
Kenya, 112
Kuwait, 113
Kyrgyzstan, 117
Lebanon, 119–121
Morocco, 131, 132
Namibia, 134–135
New Zealand, 45–46
Nigeria, 137–138, 139, 142, 187
Pakistan, 144, 145, 147
Senegal, 153–154
South Africa, 161, 162, 163, 187–188
South Korea, 164
Sri Lanka, 167, 168
Taiwan, 175, 176, 177, 178–179
Thailand, 179, 182
Tunisia, 189
Turkey, 193, 194
Uganda, 199, 200
Zambia, 203
Zimbabwe, 206
Corruption and fraud
    Africa, 16, 18–19, 20, 188
    Armenia, 32
    Indonesia, 85
    Japan, 71, 72, 103–104, 106–107
    Kenya, 112
    Kyrgyzstan, 117, 118
    Nigeria, 136, 139, 140, 142
    Pakistan, 144, 146
    Philippines, 149, 150
    Senegal, 152
    South Africa, 162
    South Korea, 71, 166
    Turkey, 194
    Zimbabwe, 206–207
Costa, Manuel Pinto da, 9
Coups d'état. *See also* Military and militarism
    Africa, 3–4, 5–6, 10, 12, 13–14
    Algeria, 27, 28, 29
    Asia, Southeast, 40
    Burma, 51, 53–54
    Caucasus, 57
    China, 58
    Congo, Democratic Republic of the, 67
    Egypt, 74
    Ghana, 77, 78
    Indonesia, 87
    Iran, 90
    Iraq, 93
    Kenya, 112
    Middle East, 127
    Nigeria, 136, 139, 140
    Philippines, 150
    Senegal, 153
    South Korea, 164, 165
    Soviet Union, 117
    Sudan, 172, 173
    Thailand, 180–181, 182
    Tunisia, 191
    Turkey, 193, 194, 195
    Zambia, 203
Creating Political Order (Zolberg), 186–187
Cuba and Angola, 7
Cults of personality, 66, 67, 93–94

Cultural issues
    African, 16
    Algeria, 27–28
    Asia, Central, 34
    Asia, Southeast, 37
    Australia, 47
    Congo, Democratic Republic of the, 66
    dominant party democracies in Asia, 70–71
    Egypt, 73
    Israel, 98–99
    Middle East, 126–127
    New Zealand, 47
    Philippines, 148
    Singapore, 156–157
    South Africa, 187–188
    Zimbabwe, 188
Cultural Revolution, Great Proletarian, 63

D
al-Dahab, Abd al-Rahman Siwar, 173
Debeers, 50
de Klerk, Frederik W., 17–18, 157, 161, 162
Decolonization. *See* Colonization
Demirel, Süleyman, 195
Democratic South Africa? A (Horowitz), 187
Democracy
    African democratic theory, 183–189
    consolidation of, 204
    consociational model, 120, 121, 122, 129
    dominant party democracies in Asia, 69–72,
        124
    European, 185
    evolution of African democratic institutions,
        185–186
    and Islam, 126–130
    as a precondition for aid, 9, 18
    semidemocracies, 179
    Western democratic thought, 59
Democracy, by country. *See also* Historical back-
        ground, by country
    Australia, 43–45
    Botswana, 48–50, 187
    China, 58
    Gambia, 187
    Israel, 96–98, 99
    Japan, 100, 103–107
    Jordan, 108
    Kenya, 110
    Lebanon, 119, 121–122, 129
    Malaysia, 123–124, 125
    Mauritania, 187
    New Zealand, 45–46
    Nigeria, 138–140
    Pakistan, 143
    Senegal, 152
    Singapore, 155–157
    South Africa, 157, 160
    Sri Lanka, 166–170
    Tunisia, 188
    Turkey, 196–197
Democratization
    African decolonization and, 25–26
    economic factors in, 11, 21, 24, 30, 33, 37, 39, 40,
        188, 202
    failure of, 12–17, 24, 26, 36, 37, 62, 87, 108,
        120–121, 136, 142, 145
    historical background, 184–185
    international pressures, 18–19, 21, 36, 129, 163
Democratization, by country. *See also* Historical
        background, by country
    African independence movements, 22–26

Algeria, 28–33
Armenia, 31–33
Asia, Central, 34–37
Asia, Southeast, 40–42
Botswana, 48–50
Burma, 51
Caucasus, 57
China, 61–65
Congo, Democratic Republic of the, 68
Egypt, 73–76
India, 80, 82–85
Indonesia, 87–88
Iran, 91–92
Israel, 99
Japan, 70–71, 101–103
Jordan, 109
Kenya, 112–113
Kuwait, 113–115, 129
Kyrgyzstan, 116–118
Lebanon, 119–122
Middle East, 128–130
Namibia, 134–135
Nigeria, 136, 137–139, 141–142
Pakistan, 143–147
Philippines, 148–151
Saudi Arabia, 114
Senegal, 152–154
Singapore, 70
South Africa, 161–163
South Korea, 70, 163, 164–166
Taiwan, 70, 175–179
Thailand, 180–182
Turkey, 192–196
Uganda, 198–201
Zambia, 202–204
Zimbabwe, 205–207
Deng Xiaoping, 64
Dewey, John, 61
Dia, Mamadou, 153
Diagne, Blaise, 152
Diaspora, 32–33, 55, 98, 128
Dictatorships, 187
Diet, 101, 102
Diop, Mahjmout, 153
Diouf, Abdou, 153–154
Dklakama, Afonso, 9
dos Santos, José Eduardo, 8
Douglas, Roger, 46
Du Bois, W. E. B., 185

E
East India Company (British), 80, 155
EC. See European Community
Ecevit, Bülent, 194, 195
Economic issues
    capitalism, 88, 125, 138, 150
    democracy and, 11, 16–17, 19, 21, 33, 37, 39, 40,
        188, 202
    dominant party democracies in Asia and,
        71–72
    freedom ratings and, 39
    international influences, 14
    personal wealth, 16, 72, 138
Economic issues, by country
    Algeria, 28–29
    Asia, Central, 34
    Asia, Southeast, 37–38, 40–41
    Australia, 45
    Botswana, 50
    Congo, Democratic Republic of the, 67
    Egypt, 75, 130

Ghana, 79
Indonesia, 88
Iran, 89–90
Iraq, 94
Jordan, 108, 109
Kenya, 111, 112
Kuwait, 113–114
Kyrgyzstan, 116, 117, 118
Malaysia, 124, 125
Middle East, 129–130
Morocco, 131, 132
Namibia, 135
New Zealand, 45
Nigeria, 136, 138, 141–142
Pakistan, 143
Philippines, 149, 150, 151
Senegal, 154
Singapore, 155, 156–157
South Africa, 161, 163
South Korea, 164, 165
Sri Lanka, 168
Sudan, 171, 172
Taiwan, 176
Thailand, 179, 180, 182
Turkey, 195
Zambia, 203, 204
Zimbabwe, 206
Education
    Indonesia, 86
    Iran, 89
    Japan, 102
    Pakistan, 147
    Singapore, 156
    South Korea, 164
    Sri Lanka, 168
    Thailand, 182
    Zambia, 204
Elchibey, Abulfaz, 57
Elections. See also Voting
    Algeria, 28, 29
    Asia, Southeast, 41
    Australia, 44–45
    Botswana, 48
    China, 60
    Ghana, 79
    India, 82
    Indonesia, 87, 88
    Iraq, 93
    Japan, 103
    Jordan, 109
    Kuwait, 113–114, 115
    Kyrgyzstan, 117
    Lebanon, 122
    Malaysia, 125
    Namibia, 133–135
    New Zealand, 46
    Nigeria, 139–140, 141
    Pakistan, 145–146
    South Africa, 161, 162
    South Korea, 165
    Sri Lanka, 166, 168
    Sudan, 172–173
    Syria, 127
    Taiwan, 176, 177, 178
    Thailand, 181, 182
    Tunisia, 189, 190, 191
    Turkey, 193, 194
    Uganda, 199
    Zimbabwe, 205, 206, 207
Emigration and immigration
    Armenia, 32–33

Australia, 44
India, 84
Kuwait, 128
Kyrgyzstan, 116
Malaysia, 123
Middle East, 128
Zimbabwe, 205
Emperors. See Monarchies
Enahoro, Anthony, 185
Erbakan, Necmettin, 195
Ethics and morality, 72, 161
Ethnic, racial, and minority issues
    African colonialism and, 14–15
    Asian civil wars, 40
    consociational democracy and, 120, 129
    democratization and, 20
Ethnic, racial, and minority issues, by
        country
    Africa, 24
    Australia and New Zealand, 43, 45
    Botswana, 48–49, 50
    Burma, 51
    Caucasus, 55, 56
    Congo, Democratic Republic of the, 66, 67,
        68
    Ghana, 77
    India, 80, 83
    Indonesia, 85, 87
    Iran, 91
    Kenya, 113
    Malaysia, 123, 124–125
    Namibia, 133
    Nigeria, 17, 136–137, 138, 139, 141, 142, 187
    Pakistan, 143, 147
    Singapore, 155
    South Africa, 157, 158–163
    Sri Lanka, 166–167, 168
    Sudan, 170
    Tajikistan, 35
    Uganda, 198–199
    United States, 71
    Zimbabwe, 205, 206
"Ethnic cleansing," 56
European Community (EC), 45, 196
European Union (EU), 131, 196
Evans-Pritchard, E. E., 183
Evren, Kenan, 195

F
Faisal ibn Hussein (King Faisal I of Iraq), 92
Fang Lizhi, 65
Fascism and neofascism, 57, 62, 70
Federalism and federations
    Australia, 42, 43–44, 45
    China, 61–62
    French Africa, 25
    India, 83
    Indonesia, 85
    Malaysia, 123
    Nigeria, 17, 25, 137–138, 139, 141, 142
    role in ethnically divided societies, 20
Fortes, Meyer, 183
France. See also Colonies, French
    Africa during the cold war, 17
    Algeria, 28
    Congo, Democratic Republic of the, 68
    Djibouti, 6
    Lebanon and Syria, 119
    post-cold war pressures by, 18
    Senegal, 153
Freedom House, 18, 38–39

Japan, 101, 102, 103, 104
Jordan, 108, 109
Kenya, 110
Kuwait, 113, 114, 115
Lebanon, 119
Malaysia, 123
Morocco, 132
Namibia, 135
New Zealand, 45–46
Sri Lanka, 168
Turkey, 193
Uganda, 200
Zimbabwe, 206
Pass laws, 133
Paternalism and patrimony, 23, 115, 155, 158–159, 179
Pearl Harbor, 102
Peres, Shimon, 97
Perry, Matthew, 100
Persian Gulf War (1990–1991), 94, 115, 127, 129, 195
PLO. See Palestine Liberation Organization
Pol Pot, 40
Political parties and political movements
    democratization and, 25
    dominant party democracies, 69–72, 105, 110, 112, 149, 156, 187
    ethnic coalitions, 17
    tutelage by, 69–70
    Westminster system, 44, 45, 110, 155, 157, 159
Political parties and movements, by country
    Africa, 3, 4, 5–6, 7–13, 15–16, 20–21, 23, 24, 28
    Armenia, 31–32
    Asia, Central, 34–37
    Asia, Southeast, 41
    Australia, 44
    Botswana, 49
    Burma, 52, 53
    Caucasus, 55–56, 57
    China, 59–61, 70
    Congo, Democratic Republic of the, 66
    Egypt, 74–75, 76
    Ghana, 78
    India, 70, 82, 84
    Indonesia, 87–88
    Iran, 91
    Iraq, 93, 94
    Israel, 96–98
    Japan, 70–71, 101–102, 103–105
    Jordan, 109
    Kenya, 110–111, 112–113
    Kuwait, 113
    Kyrgyzstan, 116–117
    Lebanon, 120–121
    Middle East, 127–128
    Morocco, 132
    Namibia, 133
    New Zealand, 46–47
    Nigeria, 137, 138–140
    Philippines, 148–149
    Senegal, 152–153
    Singapore, 155–156
    South Africa, 162
    South Korea, 165
    Sri Lanka, 167–169
    Sudan, 171–172, 173
    Taiwan, 175, 177–178
    Turkey, 192–193, 194–196
    Uganda, 198, 199, 200
    Zambia, 202–204
Popular Struggles for Democracy in Africa (Anyang' Nyong'o), 188

Population
    Armenia, 30
    Asia, Central, 34
    Australia, 42–43
    Botswana, 48
    India, 80
    Indonesia, 85
    Kyrgyzstan, 116
    Nigeria, 136
    Senegal, 152
    Singapore, 155
    South Africa, 157, 160, 161
    Taiwan, 175
Portugal. See Colonies, Portuguese
Power
    colonial, 22
    competition and sharing in Africa, 17, 20
    Pacific Rim, 45
    personalized, 51–52, 53
    presidential, 20
Prem Tinsulanond, 180
Premadasa, Ranasinghe, 169, 170
Press. See Media and press
Pulatov, Abdurakhim, 35

Q
Qu Yuan, 58
Qureshi, Moeen, 146

R
Rabin, Yitzhak, 97
Raffles, Stamford, 155
Rahman, Mujibur, 143, 145
Rahman, Tunku Abdul, 123
Ramgoolam, Seewoosagur, 25
Ramos, Fidel, 150–151
Rawlings, Jerry, 13, 18, 77, 78–79
"Red Terror Campaign" (Ethiopia), 4
Refugees, 68, 147, 169, 170. See also Emigration and immigration
Religion and religious organizations, 19, 196. See also individual religions
Rhee, Syngman, 163
Rhodes, Cecil, 202, 205
Riots. See Terrorism, riots, and violence
Roh Tae Woo, 71, 165, 166
Rubia, Charles, 112
Russia and Russian Federation. See also Soviet Union
    Armenians in, 31
    Asia, Central and, 37
    Caucasus and, 55, 57
    Chechnya, 57

S
Sadat, Anwar, 74, 75
Samurai, 100
Saro-Wiwa, Kenule, 142
Savimbi, Jonas, 8–9
Selassie, Haile, 3, 5
Senanayake, D. S., 167
Senanayake, Dudley, 167
Senghor, Léopold Sédar, 15, 25, 152, 153–154
Shakhanov, Mukhtar, 36–37
Shamir, Yitzhak, 98
Sharif, Mian Mohammad Nawaz, 146
Shehu Shagari, Alhaji, 139–140, 141
Shevardnadze, Eduard, 57
Shintoism, 102
Shonekan, Ernest, 141

Siad Barre, Mohamed, 5–6, 17
Sidi Mohammed (Crown Prince of Morocco), 132
Sihanouk, Norodom, 40
Sikhism, 80
Singapore, 123
Sino-Japanese War (1894–1895), 58, 62
Six-Day War (1967), 97, 108–109, 120. See also Arab-Israeli wars
Sklar, Richard, 187
Slave trade, 183–184
Smith, Ian, 205–206
Sobukwe, Robert, 160
Socialism
    Africa, 15–16, 25
    India, 82
    Japan, 103, 104
    Middle East, 126
    Senegal, 153
Solikh, Muhammad, 35
Song Jiaoren, 60
Soviet Union. See also Russia
    Africa during the cold war, 17
    Algeria, 28
    Armenia and, 31, 33
    Asia, Central and, 34, 35, 36
    Caucasus and, 55–56
    collapse of, 9, 56
    Egypt and, 74
    nuclear testing, 35
    successor states, 116
    Turkey, 194
Soweto (South Africa), 161
Ssemogerere, Paul, 199
Statism, 14–15, 16
Students, 53, 61, 62, 64–65
Suchinda Kraprayoon, 180, 181, 182
Sudanese People's Liberation Movement, 172, 173
Suharto, 41, 86, 87–88
Sukarno, 85, 86, 87
Suleimenov, Olzhas, 35, 36–37
al-Sulh, Riyad, 119
Sun Yat-sen (Sun Zhangshan), 60, 61–62, 70, 176, 177
Sunthorn Kongsompond, 180

T
Ta'if Accords, 121–122
Takeshita, Noboru, 104
Tambo, Oliver, 159
Tamil Liberation Tigers, 169, 170
Tanaka, Kakuei, 104
Ter-Petrossian, Levon, 32
Terrorism, riots, and violence
    Algeria, 27, 29, 30
    Armenia, 31
    Asia, Central, 36
    Asia, Southeast, 40
    Burma, 53
    Caucasus, 56, 57
    China, 63
    Congo, Democratic Republic of the, 68
    Egypt, 76
    Europe, 62
    India, 83, 84
    Iran, 90, 128
    Jordan, 109, 128
    Kenya, 111, 112, 113
    Kuwait, 115, 128
    Kyrgyzstan, 116

Algeria, 28–33
Armenia, 31–33
Asia, Central, 34–37
Asia, Southeast, 40–42
Botswana, 48–50
Burma, 51
Caucasus, 57
China, 61–65
Congo, Democratic Republic of the, 68
Egypt, 73–76
India, 80, 82–85
Indonesia, 87–88
Iran, 91–92
Israel, 99
Japan, 70–71, 101–103
Jordan, 109
Kenya, 112–113
Kuwait, 113–115, 129
Kyrgyzstan, 116–118
Lebanon, 119–122
Middle East, 128–130
Namibia, 134–135
Nigeria, 136, 137–139, 141–142
Pakistan, 143–147
Philippines, 148–151
Saudi Arabia, 114
Senegal, 152–154
Singapore, 70
South Africa, 161–163
South Korea, 70, 163, 164–166
Taiwan, 70, 175–179
Thailand, 180–182
Turkey, 192–196
Uganda, 198–201
Zambia, 202–204
Zimbabwe, 205–207
Deng Xiaoping, 64
Dewey, John, 61
Dia, Mamadou, 153
Diagne, Blaise, 152
Diaspora, 32–33, 55, 98, 128
Dictatorships, 187
Diet, 101, 102
Diop, Mahjmout, 153
Diouf, Abdou, 153–154
Dklakama, Afonso, 9
dos Santos, José Eduardo, 8
Douglas, Roger, 46
Du Bois, W. E. B., 185

E
East India Company (British), 80, 155
EC. See European Community
Ecevit, Bülent, 194, 195
Economic issues
    capitalism, 88, 125, 138, 150
    democracy and, 11, 16–17, 19, 21, 33, 37, 39, 40,
        188, 202
    dominant party democracies in Asia and,
        71–72
    freedom ratings and, 39
    international influences, 14
    personal wealth, 16, 72, 138
Economic issues, by country
    Algeria, 28–29
    Asia, Central, 34
    Asia, Southeast, 37–38, 40–41
    Australia, 45
    Botswana, 50
    Congo, Democratic Republic of the, 67
    Egypt, 75, 130

Ghana, 79
Indonesia, 88
Iran, 89–90
Iraq, 94
Jordan, 108, 109
Kenya, 111, 112
Kuwait, 113–114
Kyrgyzstan, 116, 117, 118
Malaysia, 124, 125
Middle East, 129–130
Morocco, 131, 132
Namibia, 135
New Zealand, 45
Nigeria, 136, 138, 141–142
Pakistan, 143
Philippines, 149, 150, 151
Senegal, 154
Singapore, 155, 156–157
South Africa, 161, 163
South Korea, 164, 165
Sri Lanka, 168
Sudan, 171, 172
Taiwan, 176
Thailand, 179, 180, 182
Turkey, 195
Zambia, 203, 204
Zimbabwe, 206
Education
    Indonesia, 86
    Iran, 89
    Japan, 102
    Pakistan, 147
    Singapore, 156
    South Korea, 164
    Sri Lanka, 168
    Thailand, 182
    Zambia, 204
Elchibey, Abulfaz, 57
Elections. See also Voting
    Algeria, 28, 29
    Asia, Southeast, 41
    Australia, 44–45
    Botswana, 48
    China, 60
    Ghana, 79
    India, 82
    Indonesia, 87, 88
    Iraq, 93
    Japan, 103
    Jordan, 109
    Kuwait, 113–114, 115
    Kyrgyzstan, 117
    Lebanon, 122
    Malaysia, 125
    Namibia, 133–135
    New Zealand, 46
    Nigeria, 139–140, 141
    Pakistan, 145–146
    South Africa, 161, 162
    South Korea, 165
    Sri Lanka, 166, 168
    Sudan, 172–173
    Syria, 127
    Taiwan, 176, 177, 178
    Thailand, 181, 182
    Tunisia, 189, 190, 191
    Turkey, 193, 194
    Uganda, 199
    Zimbabwe, 205, 206, 207
Emigration and immigration
    Armenia, 32–33

Australia, 44
India, 84
Kuwait, 128
Kyrgyzstan, 116
Malaysia, 123
Middle East, 128
Zimbabwe, 205
Emperors. See Monarchies
Enahoro, Anthony, 185
Erbakan, Necmettin, 195
Ethics and morality, 72, 161
Ethnic, racial, and minority issues
    African colonialism and, 14–15
    Asian civil wars, 40
    consociational democracy and, 120, 129
    democratization and, 20
Ethnic, racial, and minority issues, by
        country
    Africa, 24
    Australia and New Zealand, 43, 45
    Botswana, 48–49, 50
    Burma, 51
    Caucasus, 55, 56
    Congo, Democratic Republic of the, 66, 67,
        68
    Ghana, 77
    India, 80, 83
    Indonesia, 85, 87
    Iran, 91
    Kenya, 113
    Malaysia, 123, 124–125
    Namibia, 133
    Nigeria, 17, 136–137, 138, 139, 141, 142, 187
    Pakistan, 143, 147
    Singapore, 155
    South Africa, 157, 158–163
    Sri Lanka, 166–167, 168
    Sudan, 170
    Tajikistan, 35
    Uganda, 198–199
    United States, 71
    Zimbabwe, 205, 206
"Ethnic cleansing," 56
European Community (EC), 45, 196
European Union (EU), 131, 196
Evans-Pritchard, E. E., 183
Evren, Kenan, 195

F
Faisal ibn Hussein (King Faisal I of Iraq), 92
Fang Lizhi, 65
Fascism and neofascism, 57, 62, 70
Federalism and federations
    Australia, 42, 43–44, 45
    China, 61–62
    French Africa, 25
    India, 83
    Indonesia, 85
    Malaysia, 123
    Nigeria, 17, 25, 137–138, 139, 141, 142
    role in ethnically divided societies, 20
Fortes, Meyer, 183
France. See also Colonies, French
    Africa during the cold war, 17
    Algeria, 28
    Congo, Democratic Republic of the, 68
    Djibouti, 6
    Lebanon and Syria, 119
    post-cold war pressures by, 18
    Senegal, 153
Freedom House, 18, 38–39

G

Gamsakhurdia, Zviad, 57
Gandhi, Indira, 80, 82–83, 84, 169
Gandhi, Mohandas K., 81
Gandhi, Rajiv, 169
Gang of Four, 64
Garang, John, 173
Gbedema, Komla, 78
German Development Agency, 130
Ghanouchi, Rachid, 190
Ghulam Mohammad, 144
Goh Chok Tong, 155
Gorbachev, Mikhail, 36, 56, 65, 116
Gowon, Yakubu, 139
Great Britain. *See also* Colonies, British
  Africa during the cold war, 17
  Australia and, 45
  Georgia and, 56
  Jordan, 107
  Kuwait, 113
  New Zealand and, 45
  Palestine and, 95, 107
  phases of decolonization, 26
  post-cold war pressures by, 18
Gürsel, Cemal, 194

H

Haile-Mariam, Mengistu, 4
Hammadi, Saadoun, 94
Harambee, 111–112
Hashemite Kingdom, 107–108
Hashimoto, Ryutaro, 107
Hassan II (King of Morocco), 130–132
Hassan Gouled Apitdon, 6
Hata, Tsutomu, 107
Hatta, Mohammad, 86
Herzl, Theodor, 95
Hilu, Charles, 120
Hindus, 80, 84, 166
Historical background, by country. *See also* Democratization
  Africa, 3–22
  Algeria, 27–28
  Armenia, 30–31
  Asia, Central, 34
  Asia, Southeast, 37–40
  Caucasus, 55–57
  China, 58–61
  Congo, Democratic Republic of the, 66–68
  Egypt, 73–74
  Ghana, 77–78, 183
  India, 80–82
  Indonesia, 86–87
  Iran, 89–91
  Iraq, 92–94
  Israel, 95–96
  Japan, 100–102
  Kenya, 110
  Kuwait, 113
  Lebanon, 119
  Morocco, 131
  Namibia, 133
  New Zealand, 45–46
  Nigeria, 136–137, 183
  Pakistan, 143
  Philippines, 148
  Senegal, 152–153, 184
  Sierra Leone, 184
  Singapore, 155
  South Africa, 158–161, 184
  South Korea, 163–164
  Sri Lanka, 166
  Sudan, 171, 183
  Thailand, 179
  Tunisia, 189
  Turkey, 192
  Uganda, 198–199
  Zambia, 202
  Zimbabwe, 205
Ho Chi Minh, 40
Hong Kong, 45
Horowitz, David, 187
Horton, James Africanus, 184
Hosokawa, Morihiro, 107
Houphouët-Boigny, Félix, 25
Hu Shi, 61, 62
Hu Yaobang, 64, 65
Human rights. *See also* Civil rights and liberties
  Armenia, 32
  Asia, Central, 36
  Congo, Democratic Republic of the, 67
  Egypt, 75, 76
  Kuwait, 115
  political parties and, 69–70
  Sudan, 173–174
  Uganda, 199, 200
Hundred Flowers Movement, 63
Huntington, Samuel, 188
Hussein bin Talal (King Hussein of Jordan), 108, 109
Hussein, Saddam, 93
Hussein, Uday, 94

I

Idiagbon, Tunde, 140
Imanyara, Gitobu, 112
IMF. *See* International Monetary Fund
Immigration. *See* Emigration and immigration
Individualism, 156–157
Indochina Wars (First, Second, Third), 40, 41
Indo-Sri Lanka Accord (1987), 169
Inönü, Ismet, 192–193, 194, 195
Intellectuals
  African, 19, 22, 24–25, 112
  Arab, 114
  Chinese, 61, 63, 64–65, 72
  South African, 159, 160
  South Korean, 164
  Taiwanese, 176
Interest groups, 49
International Covenant on Civil and Political Rights, 32
International Monetary Fund (IMF), 129, 140
Iraq-Iran War (1980–1988), 94, 127
Ishaq Khan, Ghulam, 146
Iskandarov, Akbarsho, 36
Islam. *See also* Muslims
  Asia, Central, 35, 36
  democracy and, 126–130, 147
  fundamentalism, 27, 29, 30, 75, 124, 132, 190–192
  Indonesia, 86, 87–88
  Iran, 91, 114, 126, 127
  al-Jihad group, 75
  Middle East, 126
  moudjahidines, 28
  Pakistan, 143, 146–147
  shari'a, 173
  Shi'ites, 92, 119, 122
  Sudan, 171, 173
  Tunisia, 190–192
  Turkey, 192, 195
Islamic Conference Organizations, 130
Islamic Development Bank, 130
Islamic Salvation Front, 29
Italy and Eritrea, 5

J

Japan and Burma, 52
Jawara, Dawda K., 12, 25
Jayewardene, J. R., 168, 169, 170
Jinnah, Mohammed Ali, 143
Judiciary
  Egypt, 76
  Iran, 91
  Israel, 97
  Japan, 103
  Namibia, 133, 135
  Oman, 128
  Zimbabwe, 206
Junblat, Kamal, 121

K

Kabila, Laurent, 68
al-Kadir, Abd, 28
Kafi, Ali, 29
K'ang Ning-hsiang, 178
Kang Youwei, 58
Kano, Mallam Aminu, 137, 139
Karimov, Islam, 35
Kariuki, J. M., 111
Kashmir, 143
Kassem, 'Abd al-Karim, 93, 113
Kaunda, Kenneth, 15, 18, 187, 202, 203, 204
Kenyatta, Jomo, 15, 110, 111, 185
Kerekou, Mathieu, 17, 18
Khalid, Malek Meraj, 146
Al Khalifa, 'Isa ibn Salman, 128
Khalil, Abdallah, 172
Khama, Seretse, 15, 25, 49
Khan, Liaquat Ali, 143
al-Khatim, Khalifa, 172
Khomeini, Ayatollah Ruhollah, 127
al-Khuri, Bishara, 119, 120
Kibaki, Mwai, 111
Kim Dae Jung, 164, 165
Kim Young Sam, 71, 165, 166
Kings. *See* Monarchies
Kinship alliances, 183, 188
Kiwanuka, Benedicto, 199
Knesset, 96
Korean War, 102, 163
Koudonazarov, Davla, 35
Kulov, Feliks, 116
Kumaratunga, Chandrika Bandaranaike, 170
Kurds, 196
Kwangju uprising (1980), 164

L

Land Acts of 1913 (South Africa), 158
League of Nations, 61, 92, 95, 133
Lee Kuan Yew, 71, 155, 156
Lee Teng-hui, 177, 178
Leghari, Sardar Farooq Ahmad Khan, 146
Leopold II, 66
Li Yizhe, 64
Liang Qichao, 58–59, 60, 61
Limann, Hilla, 78
Lin Biao, 63, 64
Liu Binyan, 65
Local government, 166, 199
Lumumba, Patrice, 68

Luthuli, Albert, 159
Lutwa, Tito Okello, 200

M
MacArthur, Douglas, 102
Mahathir bin Mohamad, 72, 124, 125
al-Mahdi, Sadiq, 173
Makhkamov, Khakhor, 35
Malek, Redha, 29
Mandela, Nelson, 15, 17–18, 24, 159, 162, 163, 207
Mao Zedong, 63, 64
Maori, 43, 45, 46
Marcos, Ferdinand, 148–149
Marxism-Leninism. *See also* Communism and
        communist parties
    Africa, 4, 7, 8, 9, 12, 16, 24–25
    Asia, 40
    Botswana, 49
    Kenya, 112
    one-party systems in Asia, 69
    Senegal, 154
    Sri Lanka, 168
Masaliyev, Absamat, 36, 116
Masire, Quett, 49
Mathai, Wangari, 113
Matiba, Kenneth, 112
Mau Mau rebellion, 110, 185
May Fourth Movement, 61
Mboya, Tom, 23
Media and press
    Botswana, 50
    Burma, 52, 53
    controls on, 36
    Egypt, 73, 76
    India, 82
    Indonesia, 88
    Iran, 90, 91, 92
    Iraq, 93, 94
    Japan, 106
    Kuwait, 114
    Kyrgyzstan, 117, 118
    Malaysia, 125
    Namibia, 135
    Nigeria, 136, 138, 140, 142
    South Africa, 160
    South Korea, 165
    Sri Lanka, 168
    Taiwan, 177, 178–179
    Thailand, 181
    Tunisia, 191
    Turkey, 194
Meiji Restoration, 101
Menderes, Adnan, 193, 194, 195
Menzies, Robert, 44
Mesopotamia, 92
Middle East Watch, 115
Military and militarism. *See also* Coups d'état
    Burma, 52–53
    Indonesia, 86–87
    Iraq, 92
    Japan, 102
    Nigeria, 136, 139, 140–142
    Pakistan, 143, 145, 147
    Sudan, 172, 173, 174
    Taiwan, 175–176, 177, 178–179
    Turkey, 193, 196–197
Minority issues. *See* Ethnic, racial, and minority
        issues
Mitterand, François, 18
Miyazawa, Kiichi, 103, 104
Mobutu Sese Seko, 66

Mohammed V (King of Morocco), 131
Moi, Daniel arap, 13, 17, 18, 110, 111–113
Monarchies
    Burma, 51
    Egypt, 73–74
    Ethiopia, 3
    Iran, 90–91
    Iraq, 92–93
    Japan, 100, 102
    Jordan, 107–108
    Kuwait, 112–115
    Middle East, 126, 128
    Morocco, 130–131
    Thailand, 179
Mondlane, Eduardo, 9
Money politics, 104
Monteiro, António, 10
Mossadegh, Mohammad, 90
Mphalele, Ezekiel, 24
Mubarak, Hosni, 75
Mugabe, Robert, 15, 206–207
Muhammad, Murtala, 139
Muite, Paul, 112
Murayama, Tomiichi, 107
Museveni, Yoweri Kaguta, 199, 200
Muslims. *See also* Islam
    Algeria, 27
    Asia, Central, 34
    Eritrea, 5
    Ghana, 78
    India and Pakistan, 81–82, 83–84
    Indonesia, 86, 87
    Iraq, 92
    Jordan, 107
    Kuwait, 113
    Lebanon, 119, 120–121, 122, 129
    Malaysia, 124–125
    Nigeria, 22, 136, 139, 141
    Pakistan, 143
    Philippines, 148, 151
    Senegal, 152–153
    Sri Lanka, 167
Muyongo, Mishake, 135
Muzorewa, Abel, 206
Myanmar, 51

N
Nabiyev, Rakhman, 35
Napoleon III, 152
Nasser, Gamal Abdel, 74, 108, 126
National Endowment for Democracy (U.S.), 19
Nationalism
    definition, 30
    political parties and, 25, 70
    religious, 84–85, 119
Nationalism, by country
    Africa, 4–5, 7, 21, 22–24, 25–26, 202–203
    Arab, 92, 114, 122, 126
    Armenia, 30–31
    Asia, Central, 34–36
    Caucasus, 56, 57
    China, 61, 62, 63
    Ghana, 77
    India, 80–82, 84
    Indonesia, 86–87
    Iran, 90
    Kenya, 111
    Pakistan, 143
    pan-African, 185
    South Africa, 159, 160–161
    Taiwan, 177–178

Naude, Byers, 19
Nazarbayev, Nursultan, 36
Nazimuddin, Khwaja, 144
Ne Win, 40, 52, 53
Nehru, Jawaharlal, 82, 84, 145
Netanyahu, Binyamin, 97
Ngubane, Jordan, 23
Niyazov, Sapamurad, 36
Njonjo, Charles, 111
Njoya, Timothy, 19
Nkomo, Joshua, 206
Nkrumah, Kwame, 13, 15–16, 23, 24–25, 77, 78, 185,
        186
Nonaligned nations, 7, 28
Nonviolence, Pan-African Movement, 23–24
Nujoma, Sam, 135
al-Numeiri, Jaafar Muhammed, 17, 172–173
Nyerere, Julius, 15–16, 24, 25, 187, 203

O
Obasanjo, Olusegun, 139
Obote, Milton, 15, 199, 200
October Revolution of 1964 (Sudan), 172
Odinga, Oginga, 113
Oil
    Algeria, 29, 30
    Angola, 7
    Asia, Southeast, 38, 39
    Indonesia, 88
    Kuwait, 113
    Middle East, 127
    Nigeria, 17, 139, 140, 142
    Sri Lanka, 168
Ojike, Mbonu, 185
Ojukwu, Odumwegwu, 139
Okullu, Henry, 19
Organization of African Unity, 21, 24
Oslo Accords, 129–130
Otunbayeva, Roza, 117
Ouko, Robert, 112
Overseas Development Administration, 130
Owusu, Victor, 78
Özal, Turgut, 194, 195, 196

P
PAFMECA. *See* Pan-African Freedom Movement
        of East and Central Africa
PAFMECSA. *See* Pan-African Freedom Move-
        ment of Eastern, Central, and Southern
        Africa
Pahlavi, Mohammad Reza, 127
Palestine Liberation Organization (PLO), 97, 109
Palestinians and Palestine, 99, 108, 109, 120–121,
        127, 128, 129–130
Pan-African Conference of 1900, 185
Pan-African Freedom Movement of East and
        Central Africa (PAFMECA), 24
Pan-African Freedom Movement of Eastern,
        Central, and Southern Africa (PAFMEC-
        SA), 24
Pan-Africanism, 185
Panturkism, 196
Paris Peace Conference (1946–1947), 5
Park Chung Hee, 164
Parliaments and parliamentary governments
    Asia, Central, 37
    Australia, 44–45
    Botswana, 48
    Burma, 52
    India, 80
    Israel, 95, 96

Japan, 101, 102, 103, 104
Jordan, 108, 109
Kenya, 110
Kuwait, 113, 114, 115
Lebanon, 119
Malaysia, 123
Morocco, 132
Namibia, 135
New Zealand, 45–46
Sri Lanka, 168
Turkey, 193
Uganda, 200
Zimbabwe, 206
Pass laws, 133
Paternalism and patrimony, 23, 115, 155, 158–159, 179
Pearl Harbor, 102
Peres, Shimon, 97
Perry, Matthew, 100
Persian Gulf War (1990–1991), 94, 115, 127, 129, 195
PLO. *See* Palestine Liberation Organization
Pol Pot, 40
Political parties and political movements
    democratization and, 25
    dominant party democracies, 69–72, 105, 110, 112, 149, 156, 187
    ethnic coalitions, 17
    tutelage by, 69–70
    Westminster system, 44, 45, 110, 155, 157, 159
Political parties and movements, by country
    Africa, 3, 4, 5–6, 7–13, 15–16, 20–21, 23, 24, 28
    Armenia, 31–32
    Asia, Central, 34–37
    Asia, Southeast, 41
    Australia, 44
    Botswana, 49
    Burma, 52, 53
    Caucasus, 55–56, 57
    China, 59–61, 70
    Congo, Democratic Republic of the, 66
    Egypt, 74–75, 76
    Ghana, 78
    India, 70, 82, 84
    Indonesia, 87–88
    Iran, 91
    Iraq, 93, 94
    Israel, 96–98
    Japan, 70–71, 101–102, 103–105
    Jordan, 109
    Kenya, 110–111, 112–113
    Kuwait, 113
    Kyrgyzstan, 116–117
    Lebanon, 120–121
    Middle East, 127–128
    Morocco, 132
    Namibia, 133
    New Zealand, 46–47
    Nigeria, 137, 138–140
    Philippines, 148–149
    Senegal, 152–153
    Singapore, 155–156
    South Africa, 162
    South Korea, 165
    Sri Lanka, 167–169
    Sudan, 171–172, 173
    Taiwan, 175, 177–178
    Turkey, 192–193, 194–196
    Uganda, 198, 199, 200
    Zambia, 202–204
Popular Struggles for Democracy in Africa (Anyang' Nyong'o), 188

Population
    Armenia, 30
    Asia, Central, 34
    Australia, 42–43
    Botswana, 48
    India, 80
    Indonesia, 85
    Kyrgyzstan, 116
    Nigeria, 136
    Senegal, 152
    Singapore, 155
    South Africa, 157, 160, 161
    Taiwan, 175
Portugal. *See* Colonies, Portuguese
Power
    colonial, 22
    competition and sharing in Africa, 17, 20
    Pacific Rim, 45
    personalized, 51–52, 53
    presidential, 20
Prem Tinsulanond, 180
Premadasa, Ranasinghe, 169, 170
Press. *See* Media and press
Pulatov, Abdurakhim, 35

Q
Qu Yuan, 58
Qureshi, Moeen, 146

R
Rabin, Yitzhak, 97
Raffles, Stamford, 155
Rahman, Mujibur, 143, 145
Rahman, Tunku Abdul, 123
Ramgoolam, Seewoosagur, 25
Ramos, Fidel, 150–151
Rawlings, Jerry, 13, 18, 77, 78–79
"Red Terror Campaign" (Ethiopia), 4
Refugees, 68, 147, 169, 170. *See also* Emigration and immigration
Religion and religious organizations, 19, 196. *See also* individual religions
Rhee, Syngman, 163
Rhodes, Cecil, 202, 205
Riots. *See* Terrorism, riots, and violence
Roh Tae Woo, 71, 165, 166
Rubia, Charles, 112
Russia and Russian Federation. *See also* Soviet Union
    Armenians in, 31
    Asia, Central and, 37
    Caucasus and, 55, 57
    Chechnya, 57

S
Sadat, Anwar, 74, 75
Samurai, 100
Saro-Wiwa, Kenule, 142
Savimbi, Jonas, 8–9
Selassie, Haile, 3, 5
Senanayake, D. S., 167
Senanayake, Dudley, 167
Senghor, Léopold Sédar, 15, 25, 152, 153–154
Shakhanov, Mukhtar, 36–37
Shamir, Yitzhak, 98
Sharif, Mian Mohammad Nawaz, 146
Shehu Shagari, Alhaji, 139–140, 141
Shevardnadze, Eduard, 57
Shintoism, 102
Shonekan, Ernest, 141

Siad Barre, Mohamed, 5–6, 17
Sidi Mohammed (Crown Prince of Morocco), 132
Sihanouk, Norodom, 40
Sikhism, 80
Singapore, 123
Sino-Japanese War (1894–1895), 58, 62
Six-Day War (1967), 97, 108–109, 120. *See also* Arab-Israeli wars
Sklar, Richard, 187
Slave trade, 183–184
Smith, Ian, 205–206
Sobukwe, Robert, 160
Socialism
    Africa, 15–16, 25
    India, 82
    Japan, 103, 104
    Middle East, 126
    Senegal, 153
Solikh, Muhammad, 35
Song Jiaoren, 60
Soviet Union. *See also* Russia
    Africa during the cold war, 17
    Algeria and, 28
    Armenia and, 31, 33
    Asia, Central and, 34, 35, 36
    Caucasus and, 55–56
    collapse of, 9, 56
    Egypt and, 74
    nuclear testing, 35
    successor states, 116
    Turkey, 194
Soweto (South Africa), 161
Ssemogerere, Paul, 199
Statism, 14–15, 16
Students, 53, 61, 62, 64–65
Suchinda Kraprayoon, 180, 181, 182
Sudanese People's Liberation Movement, 172, 173
Suharto, 41, 86, 87–88
Sukarno, 85, 86, 87
Suleimenov, Olzhas, 35, 36–37
al-Sulh, Riyad, 119
Sun Yat-sen (Sun Zhangshan), 60, 61–62, 70, 176, 177
Sunthorn Kongsompond, 180

T
Ta'if Accords, 121–122
Takeshita, Noboru, 104
Tambo, Oliver, 159
Tamil Liberation Tigers, 169, 170
Tanaka, Kakuei, 104
Ter-Petrossian, Levon, 32
Terrorism, riots, and violence
    Algeria, 27, 29, 30
    Armenia, 31
    Asia, Central, 36
    Asia, Southeast, 40
    Burma, 53
    Caucasus, 56, 57
    China, 63
    Congo, Democratic Republic of the, 68
    Egypt, 76
    Europe, 62
    India, 83, 84
    Iran, 90, 128
    Jordan, 109, 128
    Kenya, 111, 112, 113
    Kuwait, 115, 128
    Kyrgyzstan, 116

Malaysia, 123
Middle East, 128
Mozambique, 9
Namibia, 133
Nigeria, 138, 139
Pakistan, 143
Senegal, 153, 154
South Africa, 161, 162
South Korea, 164, 165
Sri Lanka, 167, 168, 169–170
Thailand, 181
Tunisia, 190, 191
Turkey, 193, 194, 196
Uganda, 198, 199–200
Zambia, 203
Zimbabwe, 206–207
Third Wave, The (Huntington), 188
Three People's Principles, 60, 62, 70
Tiananmen Square, 64, 72
Tofa, Bashir, 141
Touré, Ahmed Sékou, 15–16, 25, 186, 187
Trade, 14, 21, 80
Trade unions, 19, 50, 102, 153, 203
Treaty of Brest-Litovsk, 55
Treaty of Lausanne, 192
Treaty of Waitangi, 45
Trovoada, Miguel Anjos da Cunha, 10
Truman Doctrine, 194
Turgunaliyev, Topchubek, 117
Türkeş, Alpaslan, 196
Turkey and Armenia, 31
Tutu, Desmond, 19

U
U Nu, 52
Unions. *See* Trade unions

United Arab Republic, 74
United East Indies Company, 85
United Nations
    Angola, 8
    Eritrea, 5
    Israel, 96
    Middle East, 127
    Namibia, 134
    People's Republic of China, 177
    Somalia, 6
    South Korea, 163
    Zimbabwe, 206
United States
    Algeria, 28
    Africa, 17, 18, 68
    Japan, 102–103
    New Zealand, 47
    Saudi Arabia, 114
    Somalia, 6
    Vietnam, 40
Universal Declaration of Human Rights, 24

V
Verwoerd, Hendrik, 160
Vieira, João, 10
Viet Minh (Vietnamese Independence League),
    40
Violence. *See* Terrorism, riots, and violence
Voting. *See also* Elections
    compulsory, 44
    in Senegal, 152
    in South Korea, 165
    by women, 45, 46, 49–50, 82
    in Zambia, 204
    in Zimbabwe, 206

W
Wade, Abdoulaye, 153, 154
Wamalwa, William Ndala, 26
Wang Juntao, 64
Wang Ruowang, 65
Warlordism, 60–62
Wei Jing-sheng, 64
West New Guinea, 85–86
Westminster system, 44, 45, 110
Wilson, Woodrow, 61
Women
    elected to office, 94, 132, 167, 195
    literacy, 51
    political rights, 109
    right to vote, 45, 46, 49–50, 75, 91, 102
World Bank, 130
World War I, 55, 61, 82, 92, 119, 127
World War II, 45, 46, 52, 55, 93, 100, 102, 152, 155,
    163, 194

Y
Yahya Khan, Agha Mohammad, 145
Yan Jiaqi, 64
Yilmaz, Mesut, 195
Yuan Shikai, 60, 61

Z
Zenawe, Meles, 5
Zeroual, Liamine, 29
Zhao Ziyang, 64
Zheksheyev, Zhypar, 116
Zhou Enlai, 64
Zia ul-Haq, Mohammad, 146, 147
Zionism, 96
Zolberg, Aristide, 186–187